The Editor

J. PAUL HUNTER is Barbara E. and Richard J. Franke Professor of English Language and Literature at the University of Chicago, where he has taught since 1987. He is the author of *The Reluctant Pilgrim: Defoe's Emblematic Method and Quest for Form in* Robinson Crusoe; *Occasional Form: Henry Fielding and the Chains of Circumstance;* and *Before Novels: The Cultural Contexts of Eighteenth-Century English Fiction.* He is editor of *The Norton Introduction to Poetry* and co-editor of *The Norton Introduction to Literature* and *New Worlds of Literature.*

W. W. NORTON & COMPANY, INC.
Also Publishes

THE NORTON ANTHOLOGY OF AFRICAN AMERICAN LITERATURE
edited by Henry Louis Gates Jr. and Nellie Y. McKay et al.

THE NORTON ANTHOLOGY OF AMERICAN LITERATURE
edited by Nina Baym et al.

THE NORTON ANTHOLOGY OF CONTEMPORARY FICTION
edited by R. V. Cassill and Joyce Carol Oates

THE NORTON ANTHOLOGY OF ENGLISH LITERATURE
edited by M. H. Abrams and Stephen Greenblatt et al.

THE NORTON ANTHOLOGY OF LITERATURE BY WOMEN
edited by Sandra M. Gilbert and Susan Gubar

THE NORTON ANTHOLOGY OF MODERN POETRY
edited by Richard Ellmann and Robert O'Clair

THE NORTON ANTHOLOGY OF POETRY
edited by Margaret Ferguson, Mary Jo Salter, and Jon Stallworthy

THE NORTON ANTHOLOGY OF SHORT FICTION
edited by R. V. Cassill and Richard Bausch

THE NORTON ANTHOLOGY OF THEORY AND CRITICISM
edited by Vincent B. Leitch et al.

THE NORTON ANTHOLOGY OF WORLD LITERATURE
edited by Sarah Lawall et al.

THE NORTON FACSIMILE OF THE FIRST FOLIO OF SHAKESPEARE
prepared by Charlton Hinman

THE NORTON INTRODUCTION TO LITERATURE
edited by Alison Booth, J. Paul Hunter, and Kelly J. Mays

THE NORTON INTRODUCTION TO THE SHORT NOVEL
edited by Jerome Beaty

THE NORTON READER
edited by Linda H. Peterson, John C. Brereton, and Joan E. Hartman

THE NORTON SAMPLER
edited by Thomas Cooley

THE NORTON SHAKESPEARE, BASED ON THE OXFORD EDITION
edited by Stephen Greenblatt et al.

For a complete list of Norton Critical Editions, visit us at
www.wwnorton.com/college/english/nce.welcome.htm

A NORTON CRITICAL EDITION

Mary Shelley

FRANKENSTEIN

THE 1818 TEXT

CONTEXTS

NINETEENTH-CENTURY RESPONSES

MODERN CRITICISM

Edited by

J. PAUL HUNTER

UNIVERSITY OF CHICAGO

W • W • NORTON & COMPANY • *New York* • *London*

The text of this book is composed in Electra with the display set in Bernhard
Modern. Composition by Pennset. Manufacturing by Courier.
Cover illustration: *Sea of Ice*, c. 1823–24, by Caspar David Friedrich. Hamburger
Kunsthalle. Reproduced by permission.

Library of Congress Cataloging-in-Publication Data
Mary Shelley, Frankenstein : contexts, nineteenth-century responses,
criticism / edited by J. Paul Hunter.
p.   cm. — (A Norton critical edition)
Includes bibliographical references (p.   ).
1. Shelley, Mary Wollstonecraft, 1797–1851. Frankenstein.
2. Women and literature — England — History — 19th century. 3. Horror
tales, English — History and criticism. 4. Monsters in literature.
I. Hunter, J. Paul, 1934–
PR5397.F73M36   1995
823'.7 — dc20   95-37928
ISBN 0-393-96458-2 (pbk.)

W. W. Norton & Company, Inc., 500 Fifth Avenue, New York, N.Y. 10110
W. W. Norton & Company Ltd., Castle House, 75/76 Wells Street,
London W1T 3QT

1 2 3 4 5 6 7 8 9 0

Contents

Modern Criticism

Preface

You've heard the name: you know his story. But you may well know it from films, TV, and conversation, and you may not know whether Frankenstein is the monster or his scientist-creator (it's the latter). And you may not be aware that the story comes from a nineteenth-century novel by a young woman — only eighteen when she conceived the story and began to write it, not yet twenty when she finished it — who created it for a kind of ghost-story contest. The story of how the book came to be written by Mary Shelley is almost as mysterious and convoluted as the story *Frankenstein* itself tells. It too is a story of beauty and terror, ambition and disappointment, intellectual reaching and fear of knowledge, love and hate.

Frankenstein the book came about almost by accident. Weary of the boredoms of everyday life in England and irritated by the torments of conventional family values there, the author (with her lover and infant son) embarked in the summer of 1816 on a trip to Switzerland. There, among a small group of young English writers and intellectuals, she participated in intense literary and philosophical discussions. On stormy June nights on the shores of Lake Leman (near Geneva, almost within the shadow of the Alps), the group began lengthy readings of ghost stories, and she was drawn into an agreement (later abandoned by most of the others) to write a story of the supernatural — something that would involve sublimity, terror, and the unknown. She had not deliberately set out to write a book (not, anyway, at this moment), and in the beginning she apparently had no particular idea for a plot, only an intention of inventing a scary story. But other stories were read and told (there was then a great vogue of ghost stories, and a lot of published material was available), and the group talked about contemporary science and current theories of the origins of life, matters that were to become prominent in the narrative Mary Shelley ultimately wrote. The immediate occasion of the writing thus involved both serious intellectual issues and a simpler desire to entertain and tell a compelling story.

Even though she was still a teenager, Mary Shelley brought to the occasion a background of grim experience, vivid fears, and powerful ambition. Her own mother had died in the aftermath of giving her life, and she grew up in a chaotic family that included a half-sister, a stepmother, a stepbrother, and a stepsister, in addition to her brilliant but difficult father. At sixteen, accompanied by her stepsister, she fled to Europe with a married man whose wife was pregnant (the man she was living with as she began *Frankenstein*), and within months gave birth (prematurely) to a child who died within days. Her second child was born less than a year later and was five months old when she began *Frankenstein* (though he too would die, shortly after the book was published). For the young Mary, life and love were often associated with disappointment and tragedy, and birth and death sometimes seemed intertwined. But there were also powerful positives in her life. She was observant, highly intelligent, and extremely well read: according to her journal for the years in which she wrote *Frankenstein*, she read nearly a hundred books a year (in several languages), many of them long and difficult volumes in philosophy and history. She was sensitive, caring, and capable of giving and inspiring intense love, and (although not personally aggressive, perhaps even shy) she associated easily with the prominent and famous. She had famous parents — both of them writers and radical social reformers — and she was living with a man who, although only twenty-three years old himself, was already becoming as famous a writer as they were — the poet Percy Bysshe Shelley. Her name when she began to write *Frankenstein* was still Mary Wollstonecraft Godwin; six months later, she married him.

Mary Shelley's parents were William Godwin, whose reputation was based mainly on the social theories he espoused in *An Enquiry into Political Justice* but who was almost equally famous as a novelist, and Mary Wollstonecraft, whose feminist ideas (championed in works like *A Vindication of the Rights of Woman*) were either celebrated or hated by almost everyone in England or France and who had died, from complications of childbirth, less than two weeks after Mary was born. At the time she began writing *Frankenstein*, Mary had been living with Percy Shelley for two years; they married halfway through the year that she spent writing the novel (from June 1816 to May 1817), just weeks after his wife's suicide and two months after the suicide of Mary's half-sister. Her mind was full of powerful (and conflicting) hopes and anxieties; and she often saw in traditional opposites — birth and death, pleasure and pain, masculinity and femininity, power and fear, writing and silence, innovation and tradition, competitiveness and compliance, ambition and suppression — things that overlapped and resisted easy borders and definitions. And, like the structure of the novel's text — with its main plot of monster creation carefully distanced by being embedded in layers of telling by several tellers — the story of how Frankenstein's story took shape is textually as well as psychologically complex, its large cinemascopic and dreamlike imaginings often signaled by small life particulars.

Mary and Percy chose as the site of their wedding a church in Bread Street, London, where John Milton had been born two centuries earlier. They had been reading Milton's *Paradise Lost* together that spring—he often reading aloud to her—and although in spirit and emphasis *Frankenstein* may seem a long way from Milton, its epigraph and some of its most important assumptions and values derive from the Miltonic moral and mythological universe. The "creature"—the "hideous Progeny" of Victor Frankenstein (and of Mary)—learns some of his most basic social and philosophical lessons from Milton, and so does Mary Shelley. Like her parents and lover, Mary distrusted the past, but she also found it irrepressible and often prophetic. But the past (including texts like *Paradise Lost*) did not always teach Mary the same things her teachers tried to teach. Readers who know well the writings of William Godwin, Mary Wollstonecraft, and Percy Shelley often notice how different *Frankenstein* is in spirit from their work, how much less trustful Mary is of creativity, the imagination, intellectual ambition, and writing itself. Her feelings toward her parents and lover—all three of them important mentors to her, and powerful intimidating presences—were decidedly mixed: her admiration of each was strong, but so was resistance and suspicion (not always conscious or articulated) of their lives, their stories, their values, their books.

If the thoughts and feelings of *Frankenstein* grow out of Mary's complex emotions and a consciousness swirling with the themes of creation and destruction and with fears of knowledge and monstrosity, the immediate occasion of the writing suggests other anxieties and conflicts, especially ones involving fears of creativity and intellectual contestation. Here was an explicit competition—with established writers and proven intellects—to create an original and striking story and to produce a powerful emotional effect, and suddenly the modest and self-effacing Mary strained to conceive and establish her personal, social, and (above all) intellectual place in this high-powered group—to claim and justify her heritage at the same time that she demonstrated her intellectual "worthiness" of the man she was about to marry and her ability to compete with the best and most popular of contemporary writers. It was at once competition and no competition. That Percy Shelley edited, "corrected," and marketed her manuscript (and perhaps wrote himself into it in ways beyond his own intention) only made it more firmly hers, confirming her personal ambitions, accomplishment, and declaration of independence. Knowledgeable readers can readily find in *Frankenstein* traces of the radical ideas of her father, mother, and husband, but they will also find subtle (and some not-so-subtle) correctives she offered to their more strident views. They can also see Mary fully asserting herself among contemporary poets, storytellers, and competitors, predicting fearful outcomes from Promethean ambitions, yet daring herself to imagine the unimagined.

In the very making of the novel, one can see something of the desire that allowed Mary Shelley to harvest her genetic, literary, and cultural heritage (and in a sense to challenge her husband), though exactly what it was in her temperament that enabled her to distance herself from her several influences and mentors is harder to sort out exactly. At the time the novel began to be conceived, Mary and Percy were spending much of their time with Lord Byron, then the most popular poet in England and already a legendary figure (though Percy Shelley's fame as a poet and personality was rising too). It was, by Mary's account (see pp. 169–73) "a wet, ungenial summer," and ghost stories seemed congenial company on long nights. One June night, someone (perhaps Byron) proposed that they each write ghost stories in a kind of competition with those they had been reading—and with each other: the competitors were Byron, Percy, a bright and ambitious but bizarre man named Polidori (Byron's traveling companion and personal physician), possibly Mary's stepsister Claire Clairmont (though we have no evidence of her even beginning to write a story), and Mary herself. Percy apparently lost interest quickly and Byron not long after, though a fragment of what he wrote later became attached to one of his poems, *Mazeppa*. Polidori perhaps conceived at first a strange, Gothic tale that Mary found ludicrous (though his own account differs from Mary's [see p. 182 and pp. 169–73]), but then (typically) piggybacked on a Byron idea and published a vampire story under Byron's name. The only important result was *Frankenstein*, published anonymously but with broad hints that it might be by Percy Shelley or Byron; early reviewers *assumed* it was written by a man. It was hard for nineteenth-century critics (and many later ones through the mid-twentieth century) to believe that the young Mary was *that* good. And literary critics for a long time credited the accomplishment essentially to Percy's influence and help; "Mary undoubtedly received more than she gave," the *Dictionary of National Biography* (1897) says patronizingly: "Nothing but an absolute magnetising of her brain by [Percy] Shelley's can account for her having risen so far above her usual self as in 'Frankenstein'" (52:29). Percy Shelley did (with Mary's blessing) edit and "revise" the text, and twentieth-century scholarship has continued to debate just exactly what Percy is responsible for, and whether he improved or injured Mary's work. Mary Shelley, then, was the clear winner of the "contest," but her rewards (in the Shelley/Byron group and in the contexts of Romanticism's rigid sense of personal reputations generally) were not all that great.

Experience, psychological complexity, friendly influence, competitive instincts, fear of success—all these played their part in the origins of this remarkable story. There is an eerie appropriateness in the fact that the story has been taken over by a host of adapters, retellers, and revisionists and that Mary Shelley has seldom gotten full credit for her originality and creativity—that instead of being regarded as the clear winner of the competition, she has remained in the shadow of what

she created, even (until recently) in the shadow of her own creators
and conjugal reviser. Still, it is her story, and in coming to grips with
it yourself as a reader, it is especially appropriate (more than with most
texts) to think of it both through other people's critical perceptions and
through the personal experience and contextual history of the remarkable young woman who both resisted writing it and flaunted it before
her nearest and dearest.

If your acquaintance with the Frankenstein story comes from film
versions, the book may surprise you, for there is far more to it than the
scientist-creates-monster myth that popular culture has turned into one
of modernity's best known and most powerful stories. In recent years
Frankenstein has become one of the most popular texts for literature
courses, and Mary Shelley has come to be known as a major writer and
something of a culture hero, one of the major "Romantics." It was not
always so. For most of her life, Mary Shelley lived (apparently con-
tentedly) in the shadow of her famous parents and ultimately more
famous husband, and most of the century and a half since her death
in 1851 she has continued to be eclipsed by them. *Frankenstein* made
something of a splash on its first appearance, and it was reprinted twice
in her lifetime (in 1823 and 1831, the latter edition heavily revised).
Her later novels (six published in her lifetime, another not until 1959)
were respectfully but not enthusiastically received, and until the last
quarter of the twentieth century, Mary Shelley was mainly known (even
to historical students of literature) as Percy Bysshe Shelley's wife,
widow, and editor. *Frankenstein* remained known to readers (it has
never been out of print), but it had little reputation as "literature" —
increasingly less in the twentieth century than in the nineteenth, when
its oddity had given it a certain prominence. Mary's later works were
typically advertised as "by the author of *Frankenstein*"; the identity was
that of the author of a lucky piece of pop art, a one-book writer, a
cultural freak.

Feminist criticism and scholarship (in the wake of several popular
films) has firmly changed that over the past two decades, and now her
work — not just *Frankenstein* but her other writings as well — is not only
appreciated "in its own right," but often regarded as more sophisticated
in outlook and more accomplished in craft than anything of Percy's.
Contemporary criticism is almost unanimous now in regarding *Frankenstein* as not only canonical, after years of academic neglect, but
paradigm-breaking and exemplary: it is required reading for anyone
who wants to understand the nineteenth century or the making of the
modern consciousness. The critical essays at the back of this volume
both trace the early reception and reputation of the book and suggest
the wide range of textual and cultural interpretations that have made
it into a powerful text, nearly a mastertext, for the turn of the twenty-
first century.

The text printed here is that of the 1818 first edition, published in London in three volumes by Lackington, Hughes, Harding, Mavor, and Jones. Only glaring typographical errors have been corrected; otherwise the text reproduced here is that read by *Frankenstein*'s first readers, except that explanatory notes have been provided with the needs of modern students in mind. Until recently, the tradition has been to use the third-edition text of 1831, which Mary Shelley revised carefully — but from a later perspective when she was considerably older and more detached from the original conception. Scholarship now strongly prefers the first edition; for the issues involved, see the essays by M. K. Joseph and Anne Mellor on pp. 157–66.

In preparing this edition, I have been blessed over time with help and guidance from many colleagues and correspondents. I wish especially to acknowledge the generous sharing of work and knowledge by Sylvia Bowerbank, Marilyn Butler, James Chandler, Morris Eaves, Sandra Gilbert, Susan Gubar, Jerrold Hogle, Margaret Homans, Larry Lipking, Bette London, Maureen McLane, Anne Mellor, and James Rieger. Many people at W. W. Norton have provided counsel, support, and gentle prodding: I thank John Benedict, Barry Wade, Julia Reidhead, Donald Lamm, Alan Cameron, Carol Hollar-Zwick, Kate Lovelady, Marian Johnson, and (especially) Carol Bemis. I have also been fortunate to have had research assistants who did much valuable textual, bibliographical, and historical digging: Jayne Greenstein, Willard White, Marianne Eismann, Erica Zeinfeld, and (especially) Will Pritchard, who provided most of the notes and was more counsel and collaborator than assistant.

21 July 1995

The Text of
FRANKENSTEIN

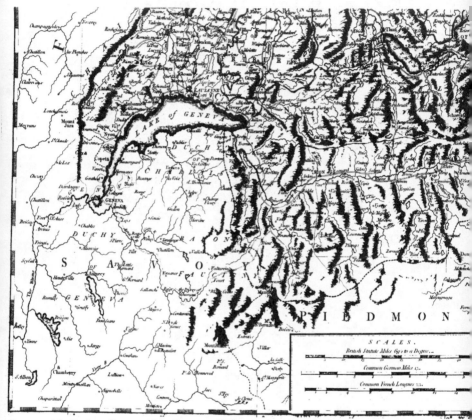

Geneva and Its Environs. Courtesy of the University of North Carolina, Chapel Hill, Library.

FRANKENSTEIN;

OR,

THE MODERN PROMETHEUS.[1]

IN THREE VOLUMES.

> Did I request thee, Maker, from my clay
> To mould me man ?   Did I solicit thee
> From darkness to promote me ?——
>   PARADISE LOST.[2]

VOL. I.

London:

PRINTED FOR

LACKINGTON, HUGHES, HARDING, MAVOR, & JONES,
FINSBURY SQUARE.

1818.

Courtesy of the Newberry Library.
1. In Greek mythology, the Titan Prometheus created humankind out of mud and water and then stole fire from the gods to give his creation; as punishment, Zeus chained him to a rock where an eagle pecked out his liver. In *Prometheus Unbound* (1820), a poetic drama by Percy Bysshe Shelley, Prometheus is eventually released from captivity.
2. By John Milton (1608–1674). These lines are from book X,743–45 and are spoken by Adam after the Fall. This epigraph appeared on the title page for each volume.

TO

WILLIAM GODWIN,[3]

AUTHOR OF POLITICAL JUSTICE, CALEB WILLIAMS, &c.

THESE VOLUMES

Are respectfully inscribed

BY

THE AUTHOR.

3. English philosopher and author (1756–1836), husband of Mary Wollstonecraft and father of Mary Shelley; *Enquiry Concerning Political Justice* (1793) was a work of political philosophy, popular in radical circles; *The Adventures of Caleb Williams* (1794) was a novel.

Preface[1]

The event on which this fiction is founded has been supposed, by Dr. Darwin, and some of the physiological writers of Germany,[2] as not of impossible occurrence. I shall not be supposed as according the remotest degree of serious faith to such an imagination; yet, in assuming it as the basis of a work of fancy, I have not considered myself as merely weaving a series of supernatural terrors. The event on which the interest of the story depends is exempt from the disadvantages of a mere tale of spectres or enchantment. It was recommended by the novelty of the situations which it developes; and, however impossible as a physical fact, affords a point of view to the imagination for the delineating of human passions more comprehensive and commanding than any which the ordinary relations of existing events can yield.

I have thus endeavoured to preserve the truth of the elementary principles of human nature, while I have not scrupled to innovate upon their combinations. The *Iliad*, the tragic poetry of Greece — Shakespeare, in the *Tempest* and *Midsummer Night's Dream*, — and most especially Milton, in *Paradise Lost*, conform to this rule; and the most humble novelist, who seeks to confer or receive amusement from his labours, may, without presumption, apply to prose fiction a licence, or rather a rule, from the adoption of which so many exquisite combinations of human feeling have resulted in the highest specimens of poetry.

The circumstance on which my story rests was suggested in casual conversation.[3] It was commenced, partly as a source of amusement, and partly as an expedient for exercising any untried resources of mind. Other motives were mingled with these, as the work proceeded. I am by no means indifferent to the manner in which whatever moral tendencies exist in the sentiments or characters it contains shall affect the reader; yet my chief concern in this respect has been limited to the avoiding the enervating effects of the novels of the present day,[4] and to

---

1. Written by Percy Bysshe Shelley; see the 1831 introduction (pp. 169–73, below) for Mary Shelley's account of the genesis of *Frankenstein*.
2. The German physiologists included Blumenbach, Rudolphi, and Tiedemann. Erasmus Darwin (1731–1802), English scientist and poet, proposed early theories of evolution (later developed by his grandson Charles). See the 1831 introduction for Mary Shelley's account of his search for "the principle of life."
3. With Byron and Percy Shelley.
4. Novel-reading was often viewed as both the cause and the result of idleness.

the exhibition of the amiableness of domestic affection, and the excellence of universal virtue. The opinions which naturally spring from the character and situation of the hero are by no means to be conceived as existing always in my own conviction; nor is any inference justly to be drawn from the following pages as prejudicing any philosophical doctrine of whatever kind.

It is a subject also of additional interest to the author, that this story was begun in the majestic region where the scene is principally laid, and in society which cannot cease to be regretted. I passed the summer of 1816 in the environs of Geneva. The season was cold and rainy, and in the evenings we crowded around a blazing wood fire, and occasionally amused ourselves with some German stories of ghosts, which happened to fall into our hands. These tales excited in us a playful desire of imitation. Two other friends (a tale from the pen of one of whom would be far more acceptable to the public than any thing I can ever hope to produce) and myself agreed to write each a story, founded on some supernatural occurrence.

The weather, however, suddenly became serene; and my two friends left me on a journey among the Alps, and lost, in the magnificent scenes which they present, all memory of their ghostly visions. The following tale is the only one which has been completed.

Volume I

Letter I.

To Mrs. Saville, England.

St. Petersburgh,[1] Dec. 11th, 17—.

You will rejoice to hear that no disaster has accompanied the commencement of an enterprise which you have regarded with such evil forebodings. I arrived here yesterday; and my first task is to assure my dear sister of my welfare, and increasing confidence in the success of my undertaking.

I am already far north of London; and as I walk in the streets of Petersburgh, I feel a cold northern breeze play upon my cheeks, which braces my nerves, and fills me with delight. Do you understand this feeling? This breeze, which has travelled from the regions towards which I am advancing, gives me a foretaste of those icy climes. Inspirited by this wind of promise, my day dreams become more fervent and vivid. I try in vain to be persuaded that the pole is the seat of frost and desolation; it ever presents itself to my imagination as the region of beauty and delight. There, Margaret, the sun is for ever visible; its broad disk just skirting the horizon, and diffusing a perpetual splendour. There—for with your leave, my sister, I will put some trust in preceding navigators—there snow and frost are banished; and, sailing over a calm sea, we may be wafted to a land surpassing in wonders and in beauty every region hitherto discovered on the habitable globe. Its productions and features may be without example, as the phænomena of the heavenly bodies undoubtedly are in those undiscovered solitudes. What may not be expected in a country of eternal light? I may there discover the wondrous power which attracts the needle; and may regulate a thousand celestial observations, that require only this voyage to render their seeming eccentricities consistent for ever. I shall satiate my ardent curiosity with the sight of a part of the world never before visited, and may tread a land never before imprinted by the foot of man. These are my enticements, and they are sufficient to conquer all fear of danger or death, and to induce me to commence this laborious voyage with

---

1. Russian city at the head of the Gulf of Finland.

the joy a child feels when he embarks in a little boat with his holiday mates, on an expedition of discovery up his native river. But, supposing all these conjectures to be false, you cannot contest the inestimable benefit which I shall confer on all mankind to the last generation, by discovering a passage near the pole to those countries, to reach which at present so many months are requisite; or by ascertaining the secret of the magnet, which, if at all possible, can only be effected by an undertaking such as mine.

These reflections have dispelled the agitation with which I began my letter, and I feel my heart glow with an enthusiasm[2] which elevates me to heaven; for nothing contributes so much to tranquillize the mind as a steady purpose, — a point on which the soul may fix its intellectual eye. This expedition has been the favourite dream of my early years. I have read with ardour the accounts of the various voyages which have been made in the prospect of arriving at the North Pacific Ocean through the seas which surround the pole. You may remember, that a history of all the voyages made for purposes of discovery composed the whole of our good uncle Thomas's library. My education was neglected, yet I was passionately fond of reading. These volumes were my study day and night, and my familiarity with them increased that regret which I had felt, as a child, on learning that my father's dying injunction had forbidden my uncle to allow me to embark in a sea-faring life.

These visions faded when I perused, for the first time, those poets whose effusions entranced my soul, and lifted it to heaven. I also became a poet, and for one year lived in a Paradise of my own creation; I imagined that I also might obtain a niche in the temple where the names of Homer and Shakespeare are consecrated. You are well acquainted with my failure, and how heavily I bore the disappointment. But just at that time I inherited the fortune of my cousin, and my thoughts were turned into the channel of their earlier bent.

Six years have passed since I resolved on my present undertaking. I can, even now, remember the hour from which I dedicated myself to this great enterprise. I commenced by inuring my body to hardship. I accompanied the whale-fishers on several expeditions to the North Sea; I voluntarily endured cold, famine, thirst, and want of sleep; I often worked harder than the common sailors during the day, and devoted my nights to the study of mathematics, the theory of medicine, and those branches of physical science from which a naval adventurer might derive the greatest practical advantage. Twice I actually hired myself as an undermate in a Greenland whaler, and acquitted myself to admiration. I must own I felt a little proud, when my captain offered me the second dignity in the vessel, and entreated me to remain with the greatest earnestness; so valuable did he consider my services.

---

2. Supernatural inspiration; poetic or prophetic frenzy.

And now, dear Margaret, do I not deserve to accomplish some great purpose. My life might have been passed in ease and luxury; but I preferred glory to every enticement that wealth placed in my path. Oh, that some encouraging voice would answer in the affirmative! My courage and my resolution is firm; but my hopes fluctuate, and my spirits are often depressed. I am about to proceed on a long and difficult voyage; the emergencies of which will demand all my fortitude: I am required not only to raise the spirits of others, but sometimes to sustain my own, when their's are failing.

This is the most favourable period for travelling in Russia. They fly quickly over the snow in their sledges; the motion is pleasant, and, in my opinion, far more agreeable than that of an English stage-coach. The cold is not excessive, if you are wrapt in furs, a dress which I have already adopted; for there is a great difference between walking the deck and remaining seated motionless for hours, when no exercise prevents the blood from actually freezing in your veins. I have no ambition to lose my life on the post-road between St. Petersburgh and Archangel.[3]

I shall depart for the latter town in a fortnight or three weeks; and my intention is to hire a ship there, which can easily be done by paying the insurance for the owner, and to engage as many sailors as I think necessary among those who are accustomed to the whale-fishing. I do not intend to sail until the month of June: and when shall I return? Ah, dear sister, how can I answer this question? If I succeed, many, many months, perhaps years, will pass before you and I may meet. If I fail, you will see me again soon, or never.

Farewell, my dear, excellent, Margaret. Heaven shower down blessings on you, and save me, that I may again and again testify my gratitude for all your love and kindness.

Your affectionate brother,
R. WALTON.

Letter II.

To Mrs. Saville, England.

Archangel, 28th March, 17 — .

How slowly the time passes here, encompassed as I am by frost and snow; yet a second step is taken towards my enterprise. I have hired a vessel, and am occupied in collecting my sailors; those whom I have already engaged appear to be men on whom I can depend, and are certainly possessed of dauntless courage.

---

3. A port on the northeast coast of Russia. *Post-road*: a road on which the mails were carried, a main road.

But I have one want which I have never yet been able to satisfy; and the absence of the object of which I now feel as a most severe evil. I have no friend, Margaret: when I am glowing with the enthusiasm of success, there will be none to participate my joy; if I am assailed by disappointment, no one will endeavour to sustain me in dejection. I shall commit my thoughts to paper, it is true; but that is a poor medium for the communication of feeling. I desire the company of a man who could sympathize[1] with me; whose eyes would reply to mine. You may deem me romantic,[2] my dear sister, but I bitterly feel the want of a friend. I have no one near me, gentle yet courageous, possessed of a cultivated as well as of a capacious mind, whose tastes are like my own, to approve or amend my plans. How would such a friend repair the faults of your poor brother! I am too ardent in execution, and too impatient of difficulties. But it is a still greater evil to me that I am self-educated: for the first fourteen years of my life I ran wild on a common, and read nothing but our uncle Thomas's books of voyages. At that age I became acquainted with the celebrated poets of our own country, but it was only when it had ceased to be in my power to derive its most important benefits from such a conviction, that I perceived the necessity of becoming acquainted with more languages than that of my native country. Now I am twenty-eight, and am in reality more illiterate than many school-boys of fifteen. It is true that I have thought more, and that my day dreams are more extended and magnificent; but they want (as the painters call it) keeping;[3] and I greatly need a friend who would have sense[4] enough not to despise me as romantic, and affection enough for me to endeavour to regulate my mind.

Well, these are useless complaints; I shall certainly find no friend on the wide ocean, nor even here in Archangel, among merchants and seamen. Yet some feelings, unallied to the dross of human nature,[5] beat even in these rugged bosoms. My lieutenant, for instance, is a man of wonderful courage and enterprise; he is madly desirous of glory. He is an Englishman, and in the midst of national and professional prejudices, unsoftened by cultivation, retains some of the noblest endowments of humanity. I first became acquainted with him on board a whale vessel: finding that he was unemployed in this city, I easily engaged him to assist in my enterprise.

The master is a person of an excellent disposition, and is remarkable in the ship for his gentleness, and the mildness of his discipline. He is,

---

1. Feel correspondingly. Here and elsewhere, Walton employs the vocabulary of "sentiment" popularized by such novels as *The Man of Feeling* (1771) by Henry Mackenzie (1745–1831) and *A Sentimental Journey* (1768) by Laurence Sterne (1713–1768) and parodied in *Sense and Sensibility* (1811) by Jane Austen (1775–1817).
2. Like a character in a romance; also, readily influenced by the imagination.
3. I.e., they lack the proper relation between near and distant objects (as in a picture).
4. Feeling.
5. I.e., not belonging to the worse part of human nature.

indeed, of so amiable a nature, that he will not hunt (a favourite, and almost the only amusement here), because he cannot endure to spill blood. He is, moreover, heroically generous. Some years ago he loved a young Russian lady, of moderate fortune; and having amassed a considerable sum in prize-money, the father of the girl consented to the match. He saw his mistress once before the destined ceremony; but she was bathed in tears, and, throwing herself at his feet, entreated him to spare her, confessing at the same time that she loved another, but that he was poor, and that her father would never consent to the union. My generous friend reassured the suppliant, and on being informed of the name of her lover instantly abandoned his pursuit. He had already bought a farm with his money, on which he had designed to pass the remainder of his life; but he bestowed the whole on his rival, together with the remains of his prize-money to purchase stock,[6] and then himself solicited the young woman's father to consent to her marriage with her lover. But the old man decidedly refused, thinking himself bound in honour to my friend; who, when he found the father inexorable, quitted his country, nor returned until he heard that his former mistress was married according to her inclinations. "What a noble fellow!" you will exclaim. He is so; but then he has passed all his life on board a vessel, and has scarcely an idea beyond the rope and the shroud.

But do not suppose that, because I complain a little, or because I can conceive a consolation for my toils which I may never know, that I am wavering in my resolutions. Those are as fixed as fate; and my voyage is only now delayed until the weather shall permit my embarkation. The winter has been dreadfully severe; but the spring promises well, and it is considered as a remarkably early season; so that, perhaps, I may sail sooner than I expected. I shall do nothing rashly; you know me sufficiently to confide in my prudence and considerateness whenever the safety of others is committed to my care.

I cannot describe to you my sensations on the near prospect of my undertaking. It is impossible to communicate to you a conception of the trembling sensation, half pleasurable and half fearful, with which I am preparing to depart. I am going to unexplored regions, to "the land of mist and snow;"[7] but I shall kill no albatross, therefore do not be alarmed for my safety.

Shall I meet you again, after having traversed immense seas, and returned by the most southern cape of Africa or America? I dare not expect such success, yet I cannot bear to look on the reverse of the picture. Continue to write to me by every opportunity: I may receive your letters (though the chance is very doubtful) on some occasions

6. Livestock.
7. Line 403 of "The Rime of the Ancient Mariner" (1798) by Samuel Taylor Coleridge (1772–1834); the mariner, by killing an albatross, brings a curse upon himself and his ship.

when I need them most to support my spirits. I love you very tenderly. Remember me with affection, should you never hear from me again.

Your affectionate brother,

ROBERT WALTON.

Letter III.

To Mrs. Saville, England.

July 7th, 17 — .

MY DEAR SISTER,

I write a few lines in haste, to say that I am safe, and well advanced on my voyage. This letter will reach England by a merchant-man now on its homeward voyage from Archangel; more fortunate than I, who may not see my native land, perhaps, for many years. I am, however, in good spirits: my men are bold, and apparently firm of purpose; nor do the floating sheets of ice that continually pass us, indicating the dangers of the region towards which we are advancing, appear to dismay them. We have already reached a very high latitude; but it is the height of summer, and although not so warm as in England, the southern gales, which blow us speedily towards those shores which I so ardently desire to attain, breathe a degree of renovating warmth which I had not expected.

No incidents have hitherto befallen us, that would make a figure[1] in a letter. One or two stiff gales, and the breaking of a mast, are accidents which experienced navigators scarcely remember to record; and I shall be well content, if nothing worse happen to us during our voyage.

Adieu, my dear Margaret. Be assured, that for my own sake, as well as your's, I will not rashly encounter danger. I will be cool, persevering, and prudent.

Remember me to all my English friends.

Most affectionately yours,

R. W.

Letter IV.

To Mrs. Saville, England.

August 5th, 17 — .

So strange an accident has happened to us, that I cannot forbear recording it, although it is very probable that you will see me before these papers can come into your possession.

Last Monday (July 31st), we were nearly surrounded by ice, which closed in the ship on all sides, scarcely leaving her the sea room in

---

1. Seem important.

which she floated. Our situation was somewhat dangerous, especially as we were compassed round by a very thick fog. We accordingly lay to, hoping that some change would take place in the atmosphere and weather.

About two o'clock the mist cleared away, and we beheld, stretched out in every direction, vast and irregular plains of ice, which seemed to have no end. Some of my comrades groaned, and my own mind began to grow watchful with anxious thoughts, when a strange sight suddenly attracted our attention, and diverted our solicitude from our own situation. We perceived a low carriage, fixed on a sledge and drawn by dogs, pass on towards the north, at the distance of half a mile: a being which had the shape of a man, but apparently of gigantic stature, sat in the sledge, and guided the dogs. We watched the rapid progress of the traveller with our telescopes, until he was lost among the distant inequalities[1] of the ice.

This appearance excited our unqualified wonder.[2] We were, as we believed, many hundred miles from any land; but this apparition seemed to denote that it was not, in reality, so distant as we had supposed. Shut in, however, by ice, it was impossible to follow his track, which we had observed with the greatest attention.

About two hours after this occurrence, we heard the ground sea;[3] and before night the ice broke, and freed our ship. We, however, lay to until the morning, fearing to encounter in the dark those large loose masses which float about after the breaking up of the ice. I profited of this time to rest for a few hours.

In the morning, however, as soon as it was light, I went upon deck, and found all the sailors busy on one side of the vessel, apparently talking to some one in the sea. It was, in fact, a sledge, like that we had seen before, which had drifted towards us in the night, on a large fragment of ice. Only one dog remained alive; but there was a human being within it, whom the sailors were persuading to enter the vessel. He was not, as the other traveller seemed to be, a savage inhabitant of some undiscovered island, but an European. When I appeared on deck, the master said, "Here is our captain, and he will not allow you to perish on the open sea."

On perceiving me, the stranger addressed me in English, although with a foreign accent. "Before I come on board your vessel," said he, "will you have the kindness to inform me whither you are bound?"

You may conceive my astonishment on hearing such a question addressed to me from a man on the brink of destruction, and to whom I

---

1. Irregularities; risings and fallings.
2. "Astonishment mingled with perplexity or bewildered curiosity" (*Oxford English Dictionary* [*OED*]).
3. Ground swell, deep undulation of the sea.

should have supposed that my vessel would have been a resource which he would not have exchanged for the most precious wealth the earth can afford. I replied, however, that we were on a voyage of discovery towards the northern pole.

Upon hearing this he appeared satisfied, and consented to come on board. Good God! Margaret, if you had seen the man who thus capitulated[4] for his safety, your surprise would have been boundless. His limbs were nearly frozen, and his body dreadfully emaciated by fatigue and suffering. I never saw a man in so wretched a condition. We attempted to carry him into the cabin; but as soon as he had quitted the fresh air, he fainted. We accordingly brought him back to the deck, and restored him to animation by rubbing him with brandy, and forcing him to swallow a small quantity. As soon as he shewed signs of life, we wrapped him up in blankets, and placed him near the chimney of the kitchen-stove. By slow degrees he recovered, and ate a little soup, which restored him wonderfully.

Two days passed in this manner before he was able to speak; and I often feared that his sufferings had deprived him of understanding. When he had in some measure recovered, I removed him to my own cabin, and attended on him as much as my duty would permit. I never saw a more interesting creature: his eyes have generally an expression of wildness, and even madness; but there are moments when, if any one performs an act of kindness towards him, or does him any the most trifling service, his whole countenance is lighted up, as it were, with a beam of benevolence and sweetness that I never saw equalled. But he is generally melancholy and despairing; and sometimes he gnashes his teeth, as if impatient of[5] the weight of woes that oppresses him.

When my guest was a little recovered, I had great trouble to keep off the men, who wished to ask him a thousand questions; but I would not allow him to be tormented by their idle curiosity, in a state of body and mind whose restoration evidently depended upon entire repose. Once, however, the lieutenant asked, Why he had come so far upon the ice in so strange a vehicle?

His countenance instantly assumed an aspect of the deepest gloom; and he replied, "To seek one who fled from me."

"And did the man whom you pursued travel in the same fashion?"

"Yes."

"Then I fancy we have seen him; for, the day before we picked you up, we saw some dogs drawing a sledge, with a man in it, across the ice."

This aroused the stranger's attention; and he asked a multitude of

4. Bargained.
5. Unable to endure.

questions concerning the route which the dæmon,[6] as he called him, had pursued. Soon after, when he was alone with me, he said, "I have, doubtless, excited your curiosity, as well as that of these good people; but you are too considerate to make inquiries."

"Certainly; it would indeed be very impertinent and inhuman in me to trouble you with any inquisitiveness of mine."

"And yet you rescued me from a strange and perilous situation; you have benevolently restored me to life."

Soon after this he inquired, if I thought that the breaking up of the ice had destroyed the other sledge? I replied, that I could not answer with any degree of certainty; for the ice had not broken until near midnight, and the traveller might have arrived at a place of safety before that time; but of this I could not judge.

From this time the stranger seemed very eager to be upon deck, to watch for the sledge which had before appeared; but I have persuaded him to remain in the cabin, for he is far too weak to sustain the rawness of the atmosphere. But I have promised that some one should watch for him, and give him instant notice if any new object should appear in sight.

Such is my journal of what relates to this strange occurrence up to the present day. The stranger has gradually improved in health, but is very silent, and appears uneasy when any one except myself enters his cabin. Yet his manners are so conciliating and gentle, that the sailors are all interested in him, although they have had very little communication with him. For my own part, I begin to love him as a brother; and his constant and deep grief fills me with sympathy and compassion. He must have been a noble creature in his better days, being even now in wreck so attractive and amiable.

I said in one of my letters, my dear Margaret, that I should find no friend on the wide ocean; yet I have found a man who, before his spirit had been broken by misery, I should have been happy to have possessed as the brother of my heart.

I shall continue my journal concerning the stranger at intervals, should I have any fresh incidents to record.

August 13th, 17—.

My affection for my guest increases every day. He excites at once my admiration[7] and my pity to an astonishing degree. How can I see so noble a creature destroyed by misery without feeling the most poignant grief? He is so gentle, yet so wise; his mind is so cultivated; and when

6. The OED distinguishes *daemon* (an inferior divinity) from *demon* (an evil spirit), but Mary Shelley does not appear to be making this distinction.
7. Wonder (or approval).

he speaks, although his words are culled with the choicest art, yet they flow with rapidity and unparalleled eloquence.

He is now much recovered from his illness, and is continually on the deck, apparently watching for the sledge that preceded his own. Yet, although unhappy, he is not so utterly occupied by his own misery, but that he interests himself deeply in the employments of others. He has asked me many questions concerning my design; and I have related my little history frankly to him. He appeared pleased with the confidence, and suggested several alterations in my plan, which I shall find exceedingly useful. There is no pedantry in his manner; but all he does appears to spring solely from the interest he instinctively takes in the welfare of those who surround him. He is often overcome by gloom, and then he sits by himself, and tries to over-come all that is sullen or unsocial in his humour.[8] These paroxysms pass from him like a cloud from before the sun, though his dejec-tion never leaves him. I have endeavoured to win his confidence; and I trust that I have succeeded. One day I mentioned to him the desire I had always felt of finding a friend who might sympathize with me, and direct me by his counsel. I said, I did not belong to that class of men who are offended by advice. "I am self-educated, and perhaps I hardly rely sufficiently upon my own powers.[9] I wish therefore that my companion should be wiser and more experienced than myself, to con-firm and support me; nor have I believed it impossible to find a true friend."

"I agree with you," replied the stranger, "in believing that friendship is not only a desirable, but a possible acquisition. I once had a friend, the most noble of human creatures, and am entitled, therefore, to judge respecting friendship. You have hope, and the world before you, and have no cause for despair. But I—I have lost every thing, and cannot begin life anew."

As he said this, his countenance became expressive of a calm settled grief, that touched me to the heart. But he was silent, and presently retired to his cabin.

Even broken in spirit as he is, no one can feel more deeply than he does the beauties of nature. The starry sky, the sea and every sight afforded by these wonderful regions, seems still to have the power of elevating his soul from earth. Such a man has a double existence: he may suffer misery, and be overwhelmed by disappointments; yet when he has retired into himself, he will be like a celestial spirit, that has a halo around him, within whose circle no grief or folly ventures.

Will you laugh at the enthusiasm I express concerning this divine wanderer? If you do, you must have certainly lost that simplicity which

8. Temperament, constitution.
9. I.e., I rely on my own powers, which are perhaps hardly sufficient.

was once your characteristic charm. Yet, if you will, smile at the warmth of my expressions, while I find every day new causes for repeating them.

August 19th, 17—.

Yesterday the stranger said to me, "You may easily perceive, Captain Walton, that I have suffered great and unparalleled misfortunes. I had determined, once, that the memory of these evils should die with me; but you have won me to alter my determination. You seek for knowledge and wisdom, as I once did; and I ardently hope that the gratification of your wishes may not be a serpent to sting you, as mine has been. I do not know that the relation of my misfortunes will be useful to you, yet, if you are inclined, listen to my tale. I believe that the strange incidents connected with it will afford a view of nature, which may enlarge your faculties and understanding. You will hear of powers and occurrences, such as you have been accustomed to believe impossible: but I do not doubt that my tale conveys in its series internal evidence of the truth of the events of which it is composed."

You may easily conceive that I was much gratified by the offered communication; yet I could not endure that he should renew his grief by a recital of his misfortunes. I felt the greatest eagerness to hear the promised narrative, partly from curiosity, and partly from a strong desire to ameliorate his fate, if it were in my power. I expressed these feelings in my answer.

"I thank you," he replied, "for your sympathy, but it is useless; my fate is nearly fulfilled. I wait but for one event, and then I shall repose in peace. I understand your feeling," continued he, perceiving that I wished to interrupt him; "but you are mistaken, my friend, if thus you will allow me to name you; nothing can alter my destiny: listen to my history, and you will perceive how irrevocably it is determined."

He then told me, that he would commence his narrative the next day when I should be at leisure. This promise drew from me the warmest thanks. I have resolved every night, when I am not engaged, to record, as nearly as possible in his own words, what he has related during the day. If I should be engaged, I will at least make notes. This manuscript will doubtless afford you the greatest pleasure: but to me, who know him, and who hear it from his own lips, with what interest and sympathy shall I read it in some future day!

Chapter I.

I am by birth a Genevese; and my family is one of the most distinguished of that republic. My ancestors had been for many years coun-

sellors and syndics;[1] and my father had filled several public situations
with honour and reputation. He was respected by all who knew him
for his integrity and indefatigable attention to public business. He
passed his younger days perpetually occupied by the affairs of his country; and it was not until the decline of life that he thought of marrying,
and bestowing on the state sons who might carry his virtues and his
name down to posterity.

As the circumstances of his marriage illustrate his character, I cannot
refrain from relating them. One of his most intimate friends was a
merchant, who, from a flourishing state, fell, through numerous mis-
chances, into poverty. This man, whose name was Beaufort, was of a
proud and unbending disposition, and could not bear to live in poverty
and oblivion in the same country where he had formerly been distinguished for his rank and magnificence. Having paid his debts, therefore,
in the most honourable manner, he retreated with his daughter to the
town of Lucerne, where he lived unknown and in wretchedness. My
father loved Beaufort with the truest friendship, and was deeply grieved
by his retreat in these unfortunate circumstances. He grieved also for
the loss of his society, and resolved to seek him out and endeavour
to persuade him to begin the world again through his credit and
assistance.

Beaufort had taken effectual measures to conceal himself; and it was
ten months before my father discovered his abode. Overjoyed at this
discovery, he hastened to the house, which was situated in a mean
street, near the Reuss. But when he entered, misery and despair alone
welcomed him. Beaufort had saved but a very small sum of money
from the wreck of his fortunes; but it was sufficient to provide him with
sustenance for some months, and in the mean time he hoped to procure some respectable employment in a merchant's house. The interval
was consequently spent in inaction; his grief only became more deep
and rankling, when he had leisure for reflection; and at length it took
so fast hold of his mind, that at the end of three months he lay on a
bed of sickness, incapable of any exertion.

His daughter attended him with the greatest tenderness; but she saw
with despair that their little fund was rapidly decreasing, and that there
was no other prospect of support. But Caroline Beaufort possessed a
mind of an uncommon mould; and her courage rose to support her in
her adversity. She procured plain work; she plaited straw; and by various
means contrived to earn a pittance scarcely sufficient to support life.

Several months passed in this manner. Her father grew worse; her
time was more entirely occupied in attending him; her means of sub-
sistence decreased; and in the tenth month her father died in her arms,
leaving her an orphan and a beggar. This last blow overcame her; and

1. Geneva, as a republic, had no monarch but was governed by a legislature; there were four
   syndics (chief magistrates).

she knelt by Beaufort's coffin, weeping bitterly, when my father entered the chamber. He came like a protecting spirit to the poor girl, who committed herself to his care, and after the interment of his friend he conducted her to Geneva, and placed her under the protection of a relation. Two years after this event Caroline became his wife.

When my father became a husband and a parent, he found his time so occupied by the duties of his new situation, that he relinquished many of his public employments, and devoted himself to the education of his children. Of these I was the eldest, and the destined successor to all his labours and utility. No creature could have more tender parents than mine. My improvement and health were their constant care, especially as I remained for several years their only child. But before I continue my narrative, I must record an incident which took place when I was four years of age.

My father had a sister, whom he tenderly loved, and who had married early in life an Italian gentleman. Soon after her marriage, she had accompanied her husband into her[2] native country, and for some years my father had very little communication with her. About the time I mentioned she died; and a few months afterwards he received a letter from her husband, acquainting him with his intention of marrying an Italian lady, and requesting my father to take charge of the infant Elizabeth, the only child of his deceased sister. "It is my wish," he said, "that you should consider her as your own daughter, and educate her thus. Her mother's fortune is secured[3] to her, the documents of which I will commit to your keeping. Reflect upon this proposition; and decide whether you would prefer educating your niece yourself to her being brought up by a stepmother."

My father did not hesitate, and immediately went to Italy that he might accompany the little Elizabeth to her future home. I have often heard my mother say, that she was at that time the most beautiful child she had ever seen, and shewed signs even then of a gentle and affectionate disposition. These indications, and a desire to bind as closely as possible the ties of domestic love, determined my mother to consider Elizabeth as my future wife; a design which she never found reason to repent.

From this time Elizabeth Lavenza became my playfellow, and, as we grew older, my friend. She was docile and good tempered, yet gay and playful as a summer insect. Although she was lively and animated, her feelings were strong and deep, and her disposition uncommonly affectionate. No one could better enjoy liberty, yet no one could submit with more grace than she did to constraint and caprice. Her imagination was luxuriant, yet her capability of application was great. Her person was the image of her mind; her hazel eyes, although as lively as a

2. A slip for "his."
3. Guaranteed.

bird's, possessed an attractive softness. Her figure was light and airy; and, though capable of enduring great fatigue, she appeared the most fragile creature in the world. While I admired her understanding and fancy, I loved to tend on her, as I should on a favourite animal; and I never saw so much grace both of person and mind united to so little pretension.

Every one adored Elizabeth. If the servants had any request to make, it was always through her intercession. We were strangers to any species of disunion and dispute; for although there was a great dissimilitude in our characters, there was an harmony in that very dissimilitude. I was more calm and philosophical than my companion; yet my temper was not so yielding. My application was of longer endurance; but it was not so severe whilst it endured. I delighted in investigating the facts relative to the actual world; she busied herself in following the aërial creations of the poets. The world was to me a secret, which I desired to discover; to her it was a vacancy; which she sought to people with imaginations of her own.

My brothers were considerably younger than myself; but I had a friend in one of my schoolfellows, who compensated for this deficiency. Henry Clerval was the son of a merchant of Geneva, an intimate friend of my father. He was a boy of singular talent and fancy. I remember, when he was nine years old, he wrote a fairy tale, which was the delight and amazement of all his companions. His favourite study consisted in books of chivalry and romance; and when very young, I can remember, that we used to act plays composed by him out of these favourite books, the principal characters of which were Orlando, Robin Hood, Amadis, and St. George.[4]

No youth could have passed more happily than mine. My parents were indulgent, and my companions amiable. Our studies were never forced; and by some means we always had an end placed in view, which excited us to ardour in the prosecution of them. It was by this method, and not by emulation, that we were urged to application. Elizabeth was not incited to apply herself to drawing, that her companions might not outstrip her; but through the desire of pleasing her aunt, by the representation of some favourite scene done by her own hand. We learned Latin and English, that we might read the writings in those languages; and so far from study being made odious to us through punishment, we loved application, and our amusements would have been the labours of other children. Perhaps we did not read so many books, or learn languages so quickly, as those who are disciplined according to the ordinary methods; but what we learned was impressed the more deeply on our memories.

4. Robin Hood and St. George are legendary English heroes. *Orlando Furioso* (1532) is a romance epic by Lodovico Ariosto (1474–1535). *Amadis de Gaul* is a Spanish or Portuguese romance of the late 1400s (Robert Southey produced an English version in 1803).

In this description of our domestic circle I include Henry Clerval; for he was constantly with us. He went to school with me, and generally passed the afternoon at our house; for being an only child, and destitute of companions at home, his father was well pleased that he should find associates at our house; and we were never completely happy when Clerval was absent.

I feel pleasure in dwelling on the recollections of childhood, before misfortune had tainted my mind, and changed its bright visions of extensive usefulness into gloomy and narrow reflections upon self. But, in drawing the picture of my early days, I must not omit to record those events which led, by insensible steps to my after tale of misery: for when I would account to myself for the birth of that passion, which afterwards ruled my destiny, I find it arise, like a mountain river, from ignoble and almost forgotten sources; but, swelling as it proceeded, it became the torrent which, in its course, has swept away all my hopes and joys.

Natural philosophy is the genius[5] that has regulated my fate; I desire therefore, in this narration, to state those facts which led to my predilection for that science. When I was thirteen years of age, we all went on a party of pleasure to the baths near Thonon: the inclemency of the weather obliged us to remain a day confined to the inn. In this house I chanced to find a volume of the works of Cornelius Agrippa.[6] I opened it with apathy; the theory which he attempts to demonstrate, and the wonderful facts which he relates, soon changed this feeling into enthusiasm. A new light seemed to dawn upon my mind; and, bounding with joy, I communicated my discovery to my father. I cannot help remarking here the many opportunities instructors possess of directing the attention of their pupils to useful knowledge, which they utterly neglect. My father looked carelessly at the title-page of my book, and said, "Ah! Cornelius Agrippa! My dear Victor, do not waste your time upon this; it is sad trash."

If, instead of this remark, my father had taken the pains to explain to me, that the principles of Agrippa had been entirely exploded, and that a modern system of science had been introduced, which possessed much greater powers than the ancient, because the powers of the latter were chimerical,[7] while those of the former were real and practical; under such circumstances, I should certainly have thrown Agrippa aside, and, with my imagination warmed as it was, should probably have applied myself to the more rational theory of chemistry which has resulted from modern discoveries. It is even possible, that the train of my ideas would never have received the fatal impulse that led to my ruin. But the cursory glance my father had taken of my volume by no

---

5. Attendant spirit or demon. *Natural philosophy*: the study of nature (i.e., science).
6. Heinrich Cornelius Agrippa (1486–1535), German physician, author of *De Occulta Philosophia* (1531), and reputed magician.
7. Imaginary, fanciful.

means assured me that he was acquainted with its contents; and I continued to read with the greatest avidity.

When I returned home, my first care was to procure the whole works of this author, and afterwards of Paracelsus and Albertus Magnus.[8] I read and studied the wild fancies of these writers with delight; they appeared to me treasures known to few beside myself; and although I often wished to communicate these secret stores of knowledge to my father, yet his indefinite censure of my favourite Agrippa[9] always withheld me. I disclosed my discoveries to Elizabeth, therefore, under a promise of strict secrecy; but she did not interest herself in the subject, and I was left by her to pursue my studies alone.

It may appear very strange, that a disciple of Albertus Magnus should arise in the eighteenth century; but our family was not scientifical, and I had not attended any of the lectures given at the schools of Geneva. My dreams were therefore undisturbed by reality; and I entered with the greatest diligence into the search of the philosopher's stone and the elixir of life.[1] But the latter obtained my most undivided attention: wealth was an inferior object; but what glory would attend the discovery, if I could banish disease from the human frame, and render man invulnerable to any but a violent death!

Nor were these my only visions. The raising of ghosts or devils was a promise liberally accorded by my favourite authors, the fulfilment of which I most eagerly sought; and if my incantations were always unsuccessful, I attributed the failure rather to my own inexperience and mistake, than to a want of skill or fidelity in my instructors.

The natural phænomena that take place every day before our eyes did not escape my examinations. Distillation, and the wonderful effects of steam, processes of which my favourite authors were utterly ignorant, excited my astonishment; but my utmost wonder was engaged by some experiments on an airpump,[2] which I saw employed by a gentleman whom we were in the habit of visiting.

The ignorance of the early philosophers on these and several other points served to decrease their credit with me: but I could not entirely throw them aside, before some other system should occupy their place in my mind.

When I was about fifteen years old, we had retired to our house near Belrive, when we witnessed a most violent and terrible thunder-storm. It advanced from behind the mountains of Jura; and the thunder burst

8. German philosopher, theologian, and scientist (called "doctor universalis") (c. 1200–1280), who wrote on the natural sciences. *Paracelsus*: Theophrastus Bombastus von Hohenheim (c. 1490–1541), Swiss physician; author of works on chemistry, medicine, and alchemy.
9. More than Paracelsus or Albertus Magnus, Agrippa was concerned with the occult and the supernatural.
1. Medieval alchemists sought the philosopher's stone, which would change other metals to gold or silver, and the elixir of life, which would prolong life indefinitely.
2. A machine that creates a vacuum.

at once with frightful loudness from various quarters of the heavens. I remained, while the storm lasted, watching its progress with curiosity and delight. As I stood at the door, on a sudden I beheld a stream of fire issue from an old and beautiful oak, which stood about twenty yards from our house; and so soon as the dazzling light vanished, the oak had disappeared, and nothing remained but a blasted stump. When we visited it the next morning, we found the tree shattered in a singular manner. It was not splintered by the shock, but entirely reduced to thin ribbands of wood. I never beheld any thing so utterly destroyed.

The catastrophe of this tree excited my extreme astonishment; and I eagerly inquired of my father the nature and origin of thunder and lightning. He replied, "Electricity;" describing at the same time the various effects of that power. He constructed a small electrical machine, and exhibited a few experiments; he made also a kite, with a wire and string, which drew down that fluid from the clouds.[3]

This last stroke completed the overthrow of Cornelius Agrippa, Albertus Magnus, and Paracelsus, who had so long reigned the lords of my imagination. But by some fatality I did not feel inclined to commence the study of any modern system; and this disinclination was influenced by the following circumstance.

My father expressed a wish that I should attend a course of lectures upon natural philosophy, to which I cheerfully consented. Some accident prevented my attending these lectures until the course was nearly finished. The lecture, being therefore one of the last, was entirely incomprehensible to me. The professor discoursed with the greatest fluency of potassium and boron, of sulphates and oxyds, terms to which I could affix no idea; and I became disgusted with the science of natural philosophy, although I still read Pliny and Buffon[4] with delight, authors, in my estimation, of nearly equal interest and utility.

My occupations at this age were principally the mathematics, and most of the branches of study appertaining to that science. I was busily employed in learning languages; Latin was already familiar to me, and I began to read some of the easiest Greek authors without the help of a lexicon. I also perfectly understood English and German. This is the list of my accomplishments at the age of seventeen and you may conceive that my hours were fully employed in acquiring and maintaining a knowledge of this various literature.

Another task also devolved upon me, when I became the instructor of my brothers. Ernest was six years younger than myself, and was my principal pupil. He had been afflicted with ill health from his infancy, through which Elizabeth and I had been his constant nurses: his dis-

---

3. An allusion to Benjamin Franklin's famous experiment (see his *Experiments and Observations on Electricity* [1751]).
4. Georges Louis Leclerc, comte de Buffon (1707–1788), author of the 44-volume *Histoire Naturelle* (pub. 1749–1804). Pliny the Elder (c. 23–79), Roman author of *Historiae Naturalis* (called by the *Encyclopedia Britannica* "a storehouse of ancient errors").

position was gentle, but he was incapable of any severe application. William, the youngest of our family, was yet an infant, and the most beautiful little fellow in the world, his lively blue eyes, dimpled cheeks, and endearing manners, inspired the tenderest affection.

Such was our domestic circle, from which care and pain seemed for ever banished. My father directed our studies, and my mother partook of our enjoyments. Neither of us possessed the slightest pre-eminence over the other; the voice of command was never heard amongst us; but mutual affection engaged us all to comply with and obey the slightest desire of each other.

Chapter II.

When I had attained the age of seventeen, my parents resolved that I should become a student at the university of Ingolstadt.[1] I had hitherto attended the schools of Geneva; but my father thought it necessary, for the completion of my education, that I should be made acquainted with other customs than those of my native country. My departure was therefore fixed at an early date; but, before the day resolved upon could arrive, the first misfortune of my life occurred — an omen, as it were, of my future misery.

Elizabeth had caught the scarlet fever; but her illness was not severe, and she quickly recovered. During her confinement, many arguments had been urged to persuade my mother to refrain from attending upon her. She had, at first, yielded to our entreaties; but when she heard that her favourite was recovering, she could no longer debar herself from her society, and entered her chamber long before the danger of infection was past. The consequences of this imprudence were fatal. On the third day my mother sickened; her fever was very malignant, and the looks of her attendants prognosticated the worst event. On her death-bed the fortitude and benignity of this admirable woman did not desert her. She joined the hands of Elizabeth and myself: "My children," she said, "my firmest hopes of future happiness were placed on the prospect of your union. This expectation will now be the consolation of your father. Elizabeth, my love, you must supply my place to your younger cousins. Alas! I regret that I am taken from you; and, happy and beloved as I have been, is it not hard to quit you all? But these are not thoughts befitting me; I will endeavour to resign myself

---

1. Founded in 1472, the university in this Bavarian town was important to the Counter-reformation and, later, was the birthplace of the Illuminati. This secret society of rational freethinkers, holding deistic and republican beliefs, was founded at Ingolstadt in 1776 by Professor Adam Weishaupt. The sect was outlawed in 1785, and the university was moved to Landshut in 1800 and then to Munich in 1826.

cheerfully to death, and will indulge a hope of meeting you in another world."

She died calmly; and her countenance expressed affection even in death. I need not describe the feelings of those whose dearest ties are rent by that most irreparable evil, the void that presents itself to the soul, and the despair that is exhibited on the countenance. It is so long before the mind can persuade itself that she, whom we saw every day, and whose very existence appeared a part of our own, can have departed for ever — that the brightness of a beloved eye can have been extinguished, and the sound of a voice so familiar, and dear to the ear, can be hushed, never more to be heard. These are the reflections of the first days; but when the lapse of time proves the reality of the evil, then the actual bitterness of grief commences. Yet from whom has not that rude hand rent away some dear connexion; and why should I describe a sorrow which all have felt, and must feel? The time at length arrives, when grief is rather an indulgence than a necessity; and the smile that plays upon the lips, although it may be deemed a sacrilege, is not banished. My mother was dead, but we had still duties which we ought to perform; we must continue our course with the rest, and learn to think ourselves fortunate, whilst one remains whom the spoiler has not seized.

My journey to Ingolstadt, which had been deferred by these events, was now again determined upon. I obtained from my father a respite of some weeks. This period was spent sadly; my mother's death, and my speedy departure, depressed our spirits; but Elizabeth endeavoured to renew the spirit of cheerfulness in our little society. Since the death of her aunt, her mind had acquired new firmness and vigour. She determined to fulfil her duties with the greatest exactness; and she felt that that most imperious[2] duty, of rendering her uncle and cousins happy, had devolved upon her. She consoled me, amused her uncle, instructed my brothers, and I never beheld her so enchanting as at this time, when she was continually endeavouring to contribute to the happiness of others, entirely forgetful of herself.

The day of my departure at length arrived. I had taken leave of all my friends, excepting Clerval, who spent the last evening with us. He bitterly lamented that he was unable to accompany me: but his father could not be persuaded to part with him, intending that he should become a partner with him in business, in compliance with his favourite theory, that learning was superfluous in the commerce of ordinary life. Henry had a refined mind; he had no desire to be idle, and was well pleased to become his father's partner, but he believed that a man might be a very good trader, and yet possess a cultivated understanding.

2. Urgent.

We sat late, listening to his complaints, and making many little arrangements for the future. The next morning early I departed. Tears gushed from the eyes of Elizabeth; they proceeded partly from sorrow at my departure, and partly because she reflected that the same journey was to have taken place three months before, when a mother's blessing would have accompanied me.

I threw myself into the chaise that was to convey me away, and indulged in the most melancholy reflections. I, who had ever been surrounded by amiable companions, continually engaged in endeavouring to bestow mutual pleasure, I was now alone. In the university, whither I was going, I must form my own friends, and be my own protector. My life had hitherto been remarkably secluded and domestic; and this had given me invincible repugnance to new countenances. I loved my brothers, Elizabeth, and Clerval, these were "old familiar faces;"[3] but I believed myself totally unfitted for the company of strangers. Such were my reflections as I commenced my journey; but as I proceeded, my spirits and hopes rose. I ardently desired the acquisition of knowledge. I had often, when at home, thought it hard to remain during my youth cooped up in one place, and had longed to enter the world, and take my station among other human beings. Now my desires were complied with, and it would, indeed, have been folly to repent.

I had sufficient leisure for these and many other reflections during my journey to Ingolstadt, which was long and fatiguing. At length the high white steeple of the town met my eyes. I alighted, and was conducted to my solitary apartment, to spend the evening as I pleased.

The next morning I delivered my letters of introduction, and paid a visit to some of the principal professors, and among others to M. Krempe, professor of natural philosophy. He received me with politeness, and asked me several questions concerning my progress in the different branches of science appertaining to natural philosophy. I mentioned, it is true, with fear and trembling, the only authors I had ever read upon those subjects. The professor stared: "Have you," he said, "really spent your time in studying such nonsense?"

I replied in the affirmative. "Every minute," continued M. Krempe with warmth, "every instant that you have wasted on those books is utterly and entirely lost. You have burdened your memory with exploded systems, and useless names. Good God! in what desert land have you lived, where no one was kind enough to inform you that these fancies, which you have so greedily imbibed, are a thousand years old, and as musty as they are ancient? I little expected in this enlightened and scientific age to find a disciple of Albertus Magnus and Paracelsus. My dear Sir, you must begin your studies entirely anew."

So saying, he stept aside, and wrote down a list of several books

3. The title of a 1798 poem by the English writer Charles Lamb (1775–1834).

treating of natural philosophy, which he desired me to procure, and dismissed me, after mentioning that in the beginning of the following week he intended to commence a course of lectures upon natural philosophy in its general relations, and that M. Waldman, a fellow-professor, would lecture upon chemistry the alternate days that he missed.

I returned home, not disappointed, for I had long considered those authors useless whom the professor had so strongly reprobated; but I did not feel much inclined to study the books which I procured at his recommendation. M. Krempe was a little squat man, with a gruff voice and repulsive countenance; the teacher, therefore, did not prepossess me in favour of his doctrine. Besides, I had a contempt for the uses of modern natural philosophy. It was very different, when the masters of the science sought immortality and power; such views, although futile, were grand: but now the scene was changed. The ambition of the inquirer seemed to limit itself to the annihilation of those visions on which my interest in science was chiefly founded. I was required to exchange chimeras of boundless grandeur for realities of little worth.

Such were my reflections during the first two or three days spent almost in solitude. But as the ensuing week commenced, I thought of the information which M. Krempe had given me concerning the lectures. And although I could not consent to go and hear that little conceited fellow deliver sentences[4] out of a pulpit, I recollected what he had said of M. Waldman, whom I had never seen, as he had hitherto been out of town.

Partly from curiosity, and partly, from idleness, I went into the lecturing room, which M. Waldman entered shortly after. This professor was very unlike his colleague. He appeared about fifty years of age, but with an aspect expressive of the greatest benevolence; a few gray hairs covered his temples, but those at the back of his head were nearly black. His person was short, but remarkably erect; and his voice the sweetest I had ever heard. He began his lecture by a recapitulation of the history of chemistry and the various improvements made by different men of learning, pronouncing with fervour the names of the most distinguished discoverers. He then took a cursory view of the present state of the science, and explained many of its elementary terms. After having made a few preparatory experiments, he concluded with a panegyric upon modern chemistry, the terms of which I shall never forget: —

"The ancient teachers of this science," said he, "promised impossibilities, and performed nothing. The modern masters promise very little; they know that metals cannot be transmuted, and that the elixir of life is a chimera. But these philosophers, whose hands seem only made to dabble in dirt, and their eyes to pour over the microscope or crucible,

4. Pronouncements.

have indeed performed miracles. They penetrate into the recesses of nature, and shew how she works in her hiding places. They ascent into the heavens; they have discovered how the blood circulates, and the nature of the air we breathe.[5] They have acquired new and almost unlimited powers; they can command the thunders of heaven, mimic the earthquake, and even mock the invisible world with its own shadows."

I departed highly pleased with the professor and his lecture, and paid him a visit the same evening. His manners in private were even more mild and attractive than in public; for there was a certain dignity in his mien during his lecture, which in his own house was replaced by the greatest affability and kindness. He heard with attention my little narration concerning my studies, and smiled at the names of Cornelius Agrippa and Paracelsus, but without the contempt that M. Krempe had exhibited. He said, that "these were men to whose indefatigable zeal modern philosophers were indebted for most of the foundations of their knowledge. They had left to us, as an easier task, to give new names, and arrange in connected classifications, the facts which they in a great degree had been the instruments of bringing to light. The labours of men of genius, however erroneously directed, scarcely ever fail in ultimately turning to the solid advantage of mankind." I listened to his statement, which was delivered without any presumption or affectation; and then added, that his lecture had removed my prejudices against modern chemists; and I, at the same time, requested his advice concerning the books I ought to procure.

"I am happy," said M. Waldman, "to have gained a disciple; and if your application equals your ability, I have no doubt of your success. Chemistry is that branch of natural philosophy in which the greatest improvements have been and may be made; it is on that account that I have made it my peculiar[6] study; but at the same time I have not neglected the other branches of science.[7] A man would make but a very sorry chemist, if he attended to that department of human knowledge alone. If your wish is to become really a man of science, and not merely a petty experimentalist, I should advise you to apply to every branch of natural philosophy, including mathematics."

He then took me into his laboratory, and explained to me the uses of his various machines; instructing me as to what I ought to procure, and promising me the use of his own, when I should have advanced far enough in the science not to derange their mechanism. He also gave me the list of books which I had requested; and I took my leave.

Thus ended a day memorable to me; it decided my future destiny.

---

5. William Harvey (1578–1657) discovered the circulation of the blood in 1628. Robert Boyle (1627–1691) performed a series of experiments on the properties of air. His *The Sceptical Chymist* (1661) attacked the scientific theories of Aristotle and Paracelsus.
6. Personal, particular.
7. Science was at the time a more general term meaning learning and knowledge.

Chapter III.

From this day natural philosophy, and particularly chemistry, in the most comprehensive sense of the term, became nearly my sole occupation. I read with ardour those works, so full of genius and discrimination, which modern inquirers have written on these subjects. I attended the lectures, and cultivated the acquaintance, of the men of science of the university; and I found even in M. Krempe a great deal of sound sense and real information, combined, it is true, with a repulsive physiognomy and manners, but not on that account the less valuable. In M. Waldman I found a true friend. His gentleness was never tinged by dogmatism; and his instructions were given with an air of frankness and good nature, that banished every idea of pedantry. It was, perhaps, the amiable character of this man that inclined me more to that branch of natural philosophy which he professed, than an intrinsic love for the science itself. But this state of mind had place only in the first steps towards knowledge: the more fully I entered into the science, the more exclusively I pursued it for its own sake. That application, which at first had been a matter of duty and resolution, now became so ardent and eager, that the stars often disappeared in the light of morning whilst I was yet engaged in my laboratory.

As I applied so closely,[1] it may be easily conceived that I improved rapidly. My ardour was indeed the astonishment of the students; and my proficiency, that of the masters. Professor Krempe often asked me, with a sly smile, how Cornelius Agrippa went on? whilst M. Waldman expressed the most heartfelt exultation in my progress. Two years passed in this manner, during which I paid no visit to Geneva, but was engaged, heart and soul, in the pursuit of some discoveries, which I hoped to make. None but those who have experienced them can conceive of the enticements of science. In other studies you go as far as others have gone before you, and there is nothing more to know; but in a scientific pursuit there is continual food for discovery and wonder. A mind of moderate capacity, which closely pursues one study, must infallibly arrive at great proficiency in that study; and I, who continually sought the attainment of one object of pursuit, and was solely wrapt up in this, improved so rapidly, that, at the end of two years, I made some discoveries in the improvement of some chemical instruments, which procured me great esteem and admiration at the university. When I had arrived at this point, and had become as well acquainted with the theory and practice of natural philosophy as depended on the lessons of any of the professors at Ingolstadt, my residence there being no longer conducive to my improvements, I thought of returning to my friends and my native town, when an incident happened that protracted my stay.

1. Worked with such devotion.

One of the phænonema which had peculiarly attracted my attention was the structure of the human frame, and, indeed, any animal endued with life. Whence, I often asked myself, did the principle[2] of life proceed? It was a bold question, and one which has ever been considered as a mystery; yet with how many things are we upon the brink of becoming acquainted, if cowardice or carelessness did not restrain our inquiries. I revolved these circumstances in my mind, and determined thenceforth to apply myself more particularly to those branches of natural philosophy which relate to physiology.[3] Unless I had been animated by an almost supernatural enthusiasm, my application to this study would have been irksome, and almost intolerable. To examine the causes of life, we must first have recourse to death. I became acquainted with the science of anatomy: but this was not sufficient; I must also observe the natural decay and corruption of the human body. In my education my father had taken the greatest precautions that my mind should be impressed with no supernatural horrors. I do not ever remember to have trembled at a tale of superstition, or to have feared the apparition of a spirit. Darkness had no effect upon my fancy; and a church-yard was to me merely the receptacle of bodies deprived of life, which, from being the seat of beauty and strength, had become food for the worm. Now I was led to examine the cause and progress of this decay, and forced to spend days and nights in vaults and charnel houses.[4] My attention was fixed upon every object the most insupportable to the delicacy of the human feelings. I saw how the fine form of man was degraded and wasted; I beheld the corruption of death succeed to the blooming cheek of life; I saw how the worm inherited the wonders of the eye and brain. I paused, examining and analysing all the minutiæ of causation, as exemplified in the change from life to death, and death to life, until from the midst of this darkness a sudden light broke in upon me — a light so brilliant and wondrous, yet so simple, that while I became dizzy with the immensity of the prospect which it illustrated, I was surprised that among so many men of genius, who had directed their inquiries towards the same science, that I alone should be reserved to discover so astonishing a secret.

Remember, I am not recording the vision of a madman. The sun does not more certainly shine in the heavens, than that which I now affirm is true. Some miracle might have produced it, yet the stages of the discovery were distinct and probable. After days and nights of incredible labour and fatigue, I succeeded in discovering the cause of generation and life; nay, more, I became myself capable of bestowing animation upon lifeless matter.

The astonishment which I had at first experienced on this discovery

2. Origin, source.
3. The science of living things.
4. Houses for dead bodies.

soon gave place to delight and rapture. After so much time spent in painful labour, to arrive at once at the summit of my desires, was the most gratifying consummation of my toils. But this discovery was so great and overwhelming, that all the steps by which I had been progressively led to it were obliterated, and I beheld only the result. What had been the study and desire of the wisest men since the creation of the world, was now within my grasp. Not that, like a magic scene, it all opened upon me at once: the information I had obtained was of a nature rather to direct my endeavours so soon as I should point them towards the object of my search, than to exhibit that object already accomplished. I was like the Arabian who had been buried with the dead, and found a passage to life aided only by one glimmering, and seemingly ineffectual, light.[5]

I see by your eagerness, and the wonder and hope which your eyes express, my friend, that you expect to be informed of the secret with which I am acquainted; that cannot be: listen patiently until the end of my story, and you will easily perceive why I am reserved upon that subject. I will not lead you on, unguarded and ardent as I then was, to your destruction and infallible misery. Learn from me, if not by my precepts, at least by my example, how dangerous is the acquirement of knowledge, and how much happier that man is who believes his native town to be the world, than he who aspires to become greater than his nature will allow.

When I found so astonishing a power placed within my hands, I hesitated a long time concerning the manner in which I should employ it. Although I possessed the capacity of bestowing animation, yet to prepare a frame for the reception of it, with all its intricacies of fibres, muscles, and veins, still remained a work of inconceivable difficulty and labour. I doubted at first whether I should attempt the creation of a being like myself or one of simpler organization; but my imagination was too much exalted by my first success to permit me to doubt of my ability to give life to an animal as complex and wonderful as man. The materials at present within my command hardly appeared adequate to so arduous an undertaking; but I doubted not that I should ultimately succeed. I prepared myself for a multitude of reverses; my operations might be incessantly baffled, and at last my work be imperfect: yet, when I considered the improvement which every day takes place in science and mechanics, I was encouraged to hope my present attempts would at least lay the foundations of future success. Nor could I consider the magnitude and complexity of my plan as any argument of its impracticability. It was with these feelings that I began the creation of a human being. As the minuteness of the parts formed a great hin-

5. Sinbad is buried alive with the corpse of his wife; he perceives and follows a distant light, which turns out to be a small passage through which he escapes (see "Sinbad's Fourth Voyage," *One Thousand Nights and One Night*).

drance to my speed, I resolved, contrary to my first intention, to make the being of a gigantic stature; that is to say, about eight feet in height, and proportionably large. After having formed this determination, and having spent some months in successfully collecting and arranging my materials, I began.

No one can conceive the variety of feelings which bore me onwards, like a hurricane, in the first enthusiasm of success. Life and death appeared to me ideal bounds,[6] which I should first break through, and pour a torrent of light into our dark world. A new species would bless me as its creator and source; many happy and excellent natures would owe their being to me. No father could claim the gratitude of his child so completely as I should deserve their's. Pursuing these reflections, I thought, that if I could bestow animation upon lifeless matter, I might in process of time (although I now found it impossible) renew life where death had apparently devoted the body to corruption.

These thoughts supported my spirits, while I pursued my undertaking with unremitting ardour. My cheek had grown pale with study, and my person had become emaciated with confinement. Sometimes, on the very brink of certainty, I failed; yet still I clung to the hope which the next day or the next hour might realize. One secret which I alone possessed was the hope to which I had dedicated myself, and the moon gazed on my midnight labours, while, with unrelaxed and breathless eagerness, I pursued nature to her hiding places. Who shall conceive the horrors of my secret toil, as I dabbled among the unhallowed damps of the grave, or tortured the living animal to animate the lifeless clay? My limbs now tremble, and my eyes swim with the remembrance; but then a resistless, and almost frantic impulse, urged me forward; I seemed to have lost all soul or sensation but for this one pursuit. It was indeed but a passing trance, that only made me feel with renewed acuteness so soon as, the unnatural stimulus ceasing to operate, I had returned to my old habits. I collected bones from charnel houses; and disturbed, with profane fingers, the tremendous secrets of the human frame. In a solitary chamber, or rather cell, at the top of the house, and separated from all the other apartments by a gallery and staircase, I kept my workshop of filthy creation; my eyeballs were starting from their sockets in attending to the details of my employment. The dissecting room and the slaughter-house furnished many of my materials; and often did my human nature turn with loathing from my occupation, whilst, still urged on by an eagerness which perpetually increased, I brought my work near to a conclusion.

The summer months passed while I was thus engaged, heart and soul, in one pursuit. It was a most beautiful season; never did the fields bestow a more plentiful harvest, or the vines yield a more luxuriant

6. Imaginary boundaries.

vintage: but my eyes were insensible to the charms of nature. And the same feelings which made me neglect the scenes around me caused me also to forget those friends who were so many miles absent, and whom I had not seen for so long a time. I knew my silence disquieted them; and I well remembered the words of my father: "I know that while you are pleased with yourself, you will think of us with affection, and we shall hear regularly from you. You must pardon me, if I regard any interruption in your correspondence as a proof that your other duties are equally neglected."

I knew well therefore what would be my father's feelings; but I could not tear my thoughts from my employment, loathsome in itself, but which had taken an irresistible hold of my imagination. I wished, as it were, to procrastinate all that related to my feelings of affection until the great object, which swallowed up every habit of my nature, should be completed.

I then thought that my father would be unjust if he ascribed my neglect to vice, or faultiness on my part; but I am now convinced that he was justified in conceiving that I should not be altogether free from blame. A human being in perfection ought always to preserve a calm and peaceful mind, and never to allow passion or a transitory desire to disturb his tranquillity. I do not think that the pursuit of knowledge is an exception to this rule. If the study to which you apply yourself has a tendency to weaken your affections, and to destroy your taste for those simple pleasures in which no alloy can possibly mix, then that study is certainly unlawful, that is to say, not befitting the human mind. If this rule were always observed; if no man allowed any pursuit whatsoever to interfere with the tranquillity of his domestic affections, Greece had not been enslaved; Cæsar would have spared his country; America would have been discovered more gradually; and the empires of Mexico and Peru had not been destroyed.

But I forget that I am moralizing in the most interesting part of my tale; and your looks remind me to proceed.

My father made no reproach in his letters; and only took notice of my silence by inquiring into my occupations more particularly than before. Winter, spring, and summer, passed away during my labours; but I did not watch the blossom or the expanding leaves—sights which before always yielded me supreme delight, so deeply was I engrossed in my occupation. The leaves of that year had withered before my work drew near to a close; and now every day shewed me more plainly how well I had succeeded. But my enthusiasm was checked by my anxiety, and I appeared rather like one doomed by slavery to toil in the mines, or any other unwholesome trade, than an artist occupied by his favourite employment. Every night I was oppressed by a slow fever, and I became nervous to a most painful degree; a disease that I regretted the more because I had hitherto enjoyed most excellent health, and had always boasted of the firmness of my nerves. But I believed that exercise and amusement would soon drive away such symptoms; and I promised myself both of these, when my creation should be complete.

Chapter IV.

It was on a dreary night of November, that I beheld the accomplishment of my toils. With an anxiety that almost amounted to agony, I collected the instruments of life around me, that I might infuse a spark of being into the lifeless thing that lay at my feet. It was already one in the morning; the rain pattered dismally against the panes, and my candle was nearly burnt out, when, by the glimmer of the half-extinguished light, I saw the dull yellow eye of the creature open; it breathed hard, and a convulsive motion agitated its limbs.

How can I describe my emotions at this catastrophe, or how delineate the wretch whom with such infinite pains and care I had endeavoured to form? His limbs were in proportion, and I had selected his features as beautiful. Beautiful! — Great God! His yellow skin scarcely covered the work of muscles and arteries beneath; his hair was of a lustrous black, and flowing; his teeth of a pearly whiteness; but these luxuriances only formed a more horrid contrast with his watery eyes, that seemed almost of the same colour as the dun white sockets in which they were set, his shrivelled complexion, and straight black lips.

The different accidents of life are not so changeable as the feelings of human nature. I had worked hard for nearly two years, for the sole purpose of infusing life into an inanimate body. For this I had deprived myself of rest and health. I had desired it with an ardour that far exceeded moderation; but now that I had finished, the beauty of the dream vanished, and breathless horror and disgust filled my heart. Unable to endure the aspect of the being I had created, I rushed out of the room, and continued a long time traversing my bed-chamber, unable to compose my mind to sleep. At length lassitude succeeded to the tumult I had before endured; and I threw myself on the bed in my clothes, endeavouring to seek a few moments of forgetfulness. But it was in vain: I slept indeed, but I was disturbed by the wildest dreams. I thought I saw Elizabeth, in the bloom of health, walking in the streets of Ingolstadt. Delighted and surprised, I embraced her; but as I imprinted the first kiss on her lips, they became livid with the hue of death; her features appeared to change, and I thought that I held the corpse of my dead mother in my arms; a shroud enveloped her form, and I saw the grave-worms crawling in the folds of the flannel. I started from my sleep with horror; a cold dew covered my forehead, my teeth chattered, and every limb became convulsed; when, by the dim and yellow light of the moon, as it forced its way through the window-shutters, I beheld the wretch—the miserable monster whom I had created. He held up the curtain of the bed; and his eyes, if eyes they may be called, were fixed on me. His jaws opened, and he muttered some inarticulate sounds, while a grin wrinkled his cheeks. He might have spoken, but I did not hear; one hand was stretched out, seemingly to detain me, but I escaped, and rushed down stairs. I took refuge in the court-yard belonging to the house which I inhabited; where I remained during the rest of the night, walking up and down in the greatest agitation, listening attentively, catching and fearing each sound as if it were to announce the approach of the demoniacal corpse to which I had so miserably given life.

Oh! no mortal could support the horror of that countenance. A mummy again endued with animation could not be so hideous as that wretch. I had gazed on him while unfinished; he was ugly then; but when those muscles and joints were rendered capable of motion, it became a thing such as even Dante[1] could not have conceived.

I passed the night wretchedly. Sometimes my pulse beat so quickly and hardly, that I felt the palpitation of every artery; at others, I nearly sank to the ground through languor and extreme weakness. Mingled with this horror, I felt the bitterness of disappointment: dreams that had been my food and pleasant rest for so long a space, were now become a hell to me; and the change was so rapid, the overthrow so complete!

Morning, dismal and wet, at length dawned, and discovered to my sleepless and aching eyes the church of Ingolstadt, its white steeple and clock, which indicated the sixth hour. The porter opened the gates of the court, which had that night been my asylum, and I issued into the streets, pacing them with quick steps, as if I sought to avoid the wretch whom I feared every turning of the street would present to my view. I did not dare return to the apartment which I inhabited, but felt impelled to hurry on, although wetted by the rain, which poured from a black and comfortless sky.

I continued walking in this manner for some time, endeavouring, by bodily exercise, to ease the load that weighed upon my mind. I traversed the streets, without any clear conception of where I was, or what I was doing. My heart palpitated in the sickness of fear; and I hurried on with irregular steps, not daring to look about me:

> Like one who, on a lonely road,
>   Doth walk in fear and dread,
>   And, having once turn'd round, walks on,

---

1. Dante Alighieri (1265–1321), Italian poet; *The Inferno,* the first book of his *Divine Comedy,* is a guided tour of Hell.

And turns no more his head;
Because he knows a frightful fiend
Doth close behind him tread.[2]

Continuing thus, I came at length opposite to the inn at which the various diligences[3] and carriages usually stopped. Here I paused, I knew not why; but I remained some minutes with my eyes fixed on a coach that was coming towards me from the other end of the street. As it drew nearer, I observed that it was the Swiss diligence: it stopped just where I was standing; and, on the door being opened, I perceived Henry Clerval, who, on seeing me, instantly sprung out. "My dear Frankenstein," exclaimed he, "how glad I am to see you! how fortunate that you should be here at the very moment of my alighting!"

Nothing could equal my delight on seeing Clerval; his presence brought back to my thoughts my father, Elizabeth, and all those scenes of home so dear to my recollection. I grasped his hand, and in a moment forgot my horror and misfortune; I felt suddenly, and for the first time during many months calm and serene joy. I welcomed my friend, therefore, in the most cordial manner, and we walked towards my college. Clerval continued talking for some time about our mutual friends, and his own good fortune in being permitted to come to Ingolstadt. "You may easily believe," said he, "how great was the difficulty to persuade my father that it was not absolutely necessary for a merchant not to understand any thing except book-keeping; and, indeed, I believe I left him incredulous to the last, for his constant answer to my unwearied entreaties was the same as that of the Dutch schoolmaster in the Vicar of Wakefield: 'I have ten thousand florins a year without Greek, I eat heartily without Greek.'[4] But his affection for me at length overcame his dislike of learning, and he has permitted me to undertake a voyage of discovery to the land of knowledge."

"It gives me the greatest delight to see you; but tell me how you left my father, brothers, and Elizabeth."

"Very well, and very happy, only a little uneasy that they hear from you so seldom. By the bye, I mean to lecture you a little upon their account myself. — But, my dear Frankenstein," continued he, stopping short, and gazing full in my face, "I did not before remark how very ill you appear; so thin and pale; you look as if you had been watching for several nights."

"You have guessed right; I have lately been so deeply engaged in one occupation, that I have not allowed myself sufficient rest, as you see: but I hope, I sincerely hope, that all these employments are now at an end, and that I am at length free."

I trembled excessively; I could not endure to think of, and far less to

2. Coleridge's "Ancient Mariner" [Mary Shelley's note], lines 446–51. See n. 7, p. 11, above.
3. Public stagecoaches.
4. From chapter 20 of *The Vicar of Wakefield* (1766), a novel by Oliver Goldsmith (1730–1774).

allude to the occurrences of the preceding night. I walked with a quick pace, and we soon arrived at my college. I then reflected, and the thought made me shiver, that the creature whom I had left in my apartment might still be there, alive, and walking about. I dreaded to behold this monster; but I feared still more that Henry should see him. Entreating him therefore to remain a few minutes at the bottom of the stairs, I darted up towards my own room. My hand was already on the lock of the door before I recollected myself. I then paused; and a cold shivering came over me. I threw the door forcibly open, as children are accustomed to do when they expect a spectre to stand in waiting for them on the other side; but nothing appeared. I stepped fearfully in: the apartment was empty; and my bedroom was also freed from its hideous guest. I could hardly believe that so great a good-fortune could have befallen me; but when I became assured that my enemy had indeed fled, I clapped my hands for joy, and ran down to Clerval.

We ascended into my room, and the servant presently brought breakfast; but I was unable to contain myself. It was not joy only that possessed me; I felt my flesh tingle with excess of sensitiveness, and my pulse beat rapidly. I was unable to remain for a single instant in the same place; I jumped over the chairs, clapped my hands, and laughed aloud. Clerval at first attributed my unusual spirits to joy on his arrival; but when he observed me more attentively, he saw a wildness in my eyes for which he could not account; and my loud, unrestrained, heartless laughter, frightened and astonished him.

"My dear Victor," cried he, "what, for God's sake, is the matter? Do not laugh in that manner. How ill you are! What is the cause of all this?"

"Do not ask me," cried I, putting my hands before my eyes, for I thought I saw the dreaded spectre glide into the room; "*he* can tell. — Oh, save me! save me!" I imagined that the monster seized me; I struggled furiously, and fell down in a fit.

Poor Clerval! what must have been his feelings? A meeting, which he anticipated with such joy, so strangely turned to bitterness. But I was not the witness of his grief; for I was lifeless, and did not recover my senses for a long, long time.

This was the commencement of a nervous fever, which confined me for several months. During all that time Henry was my only nurse. I afterwards learned that, knowing my father's advanced age, and unfitness for so long a journey, and how wretched my sickness would make Elizabeth, he spared them this grief by concealing the extent of my disorder. He knew that I could not have a more kind and attentive nurse than himself; and, firm in the hope he felt of my recovery, he did not doubt that, instead of doing harm, he performed the kindest action that he could towards them.

But I was in reality very ill; and surely nothing but the unbounded and unremitting attentions of my friend could have restored me to life. The form of the monster on whom I had bestowed existence was for ever before my eyes, and I raved incessantly concerning him. Doubtless my words surprised Henry: he at first believed them to be the wanderings of my disturbed imagination; but the pertinacity with which I continually recurred to the same subject persuaded him that my disorder indeed owed its origin to some uncommon and terrible event.

By very slow degrees, and with frequent relapses, that alarmed and grieved my friend, I recovered. I remember the first time I became capable of observing outward objects with any kind of pleasure, I perceived that the fallen leaves had disappeared, and that the young buds were shooting forth from the trees that shaded my window. It was a divine spring; and the season contributed greatly to my convalescence. I felt also sentiments of joy and affection revive in my bosom; my gloom disappeared, and in a short time I became as cheerful as before I was attacked by the fatal passion.

"Dearest Clerval," exclaimed I, "how kind, how very good you are to me. This whole winter, instead of being spent in study, as you promised yourself, has been consumed in my sick room. How shall I ever repay you? I feel the greatest remorse for the disappointment of which I have been the occasion; but you will forgive me."

"You will repay me entirely, if you do not discompose yourself, but get well as fast as you can; and since you appear in such good spirits, I may speak to you on one subject, may I not?"

I trembled. One subject! what could it be? Could he allude to an object on whom I dared not even think?

"Compose yourself," said Clerval, who observed my change of colour, "I will not mention it, if it agitates you; but your father and cousin would be very happy if they received a letter from you in your own hand-writing. They hardly know how ill you have been, and are uneasy at your long silence."

"Is that all? my dear Henry. How could you suppose that my first thought would not fly towards those dear, dear friends whom I love, and who are so deserving of my love?"

"If this is your present temper, my friend, you will perhaps be glad to see a letter that has been lying here some days for you: it is from your cousin, I believe."

Chapter V.

Clerval then put the following letter into my hands.

"To V. Frankenstein.

"MY DEAR COUSIN,

"I cannot describe to you the uneasiness we have all felt concerning your health. We cannot help imagining that your friend Clerval conceals the extent of your disorder: for it is now several months since we have seen your hand-writing; and all this time you have been obliged to dictate your letters to Henry. Surely, Victor, you must have been exceedingly ill; and this makes us all very wretched, as much so nearly as after the death of your dear mother. My uncle was almost persuaded that you were indeed dangerously ill, and could hardly be restrained from undertaking a journey to Ingolstadt. Clerval always writes that you are getting better; I eagerly hope that you will confirm this intelligence soon in your own hand-writing; for indeed, indeed, Victor, we are all very miserable on this account. Relieve us from this fear, and we shall be the happiest creatures in the world. Your father's health is now so vigorous, that he appears ten years younger since last winter. Ernest also is so much improved, that you would hardly know him: he is now nearly sixteen, and has lost that sickly appearance which he had some years ago; he is grown quite robust and active.

"My uncle and I conversed a long time last night about what profession Ernest should follow. His constant illness when young has deprived him of the habits of application; and now that he enjoys good health, he is continually in the open air, climbing the hills, or rowing on the lake. I therefore proposed that he should be a farmer; which you know, Cousin, is a favourite scheme of mine. A farmer's is a very healthy happy life; and the least hurtful, or rather the most beneficial profession of any. My uncle had an idea of his being educated as an advocate, that through his interest he might become a judge. But, besides that he is not at all fitted for such an occupation, it is certainly more creditable to cultivate the earth for the sustenance of man, than to be the confidant, and sometimes the accomplice, of his vices; which is the profession of a lawyer. I said, that the employments of a prosperous farmer, if they were not a more honourable, they were at least a happier species of occupation than that of a judge, whose misfortune it was always to meddle with the dark side of human nature. My uncle smiled, and said, that I ought to be an advocate myself, which put an end to the conversation on that subject.

"And now I must tell you a little story that will please, and perhaps amuse you. Do you not remember Justine Moritz? Probably you do not; I will relate her history, therefore, in a few words. Madame Moritz, her mother, was a widow with four children, of whom Justine was the third. This girl had always been the favourite of her father; but, through a strange perversity, her mother could not endure her, and, after the death of M. Moritz, treated her very ill. My aunt observed this; and, when Justine was twelve years of age, prevailed on her mother to allow her to live at her house. The republican institutions of our country have produced simpler and happier manners than those which prevail in the great monarchies that surround it. Hence there is less distinction between the several classes of its inhabitants; and the lower orders being neither so poor nor so despised, their manners are more refined and moral. A servant in Geneva does not mean the same thing as a servant in France and England. Justine, thus received in our family, learned the duties of a servant; a condition which, in our fortunate country, does not include the idea of ignorance, and a sacrifice of the dignity of a human being.

"After what I have said, I dare say you well remember the heroine of my little tale: for Justine was a great favourite of your's; and I recollect you once remarked, that if you were in an ill humour, one glance from Justine could dissipate it, for the same reason that Ariosto gives concerning the beauty of Angelica — she looked so frank-hearted and happy.[1] My aunt conceived a great attachment for her, by which she was induced to give her an education superior to that which she had at first intended. This benefit was fully repaid; Justine was the most grateful little creature in the world: I do not mean that she made any professions,[2] I never heard one pass her lips; but you could see by her eyes that she almost adored her protectress. Although her disposition was gay, and in many respects inconsiderate, yet she paid the greatest attention to every gesture of my aunt. She thought her the model of all excellence, and endeavoured to imitate her phraseology and manners, so that even now she often reminds me of her.

"When my dearest aunt died, every one was too much occupied in their own grief to notice poor Justine, who had attended her during her illness with the most anxious affection. Poor Justine was very ill; but other trials were reserved for her.

"One by one, her brothers and sister died; and her mother, with the exception of her neglected daughter, was left childless. The conscience of the woman was troubled; she began to think that the deaths of her favourites was a judgment from heaven to chastise her partiality. She was a Roman Catholic; and I believe her confessor confirmed the idea which she had conceived. Accordingly, a few months after your departure for Ingoldstadt, Justine

1. Angelica is the heroine of *Orlando Furioso* (see n. 4, p. 20, above).
2. Declarations, avowals.

was called home by her repentant mother. Poor girl! she wept when she quitted our house: she was much altered since the death of my aunt; grief had given softness and a winning mildness to her manners, which had before been remarkable for vivacity. Nor was her residence at her mother's house of a nature to restore her gaiety. The poor woman was very vacillating in her repentance. She sometimes begged Justine to forgive her unkindness, but much oftener accused her of having caused the deaths of her brothers and sister. Perpetual fretting at length threw Madame Moritz into a decline, which at first increased her irritability, but she is now at peace for ever. She died on the first approach of cold weather, at the beginning of this last winter. Justine has returned to us; and I assure you I love her tenderly. She is very clever and gentle, and extremely pretty; as I mentioned before, her mien and her expressions continually remind me of my dear aunt.

"I must say also a few words to you, my dear cousin, of little darling William. I wish you could see him; he is very tall of his age, with sweet laughing blue eyes, dark eye-lashes, and curling hair. When he smiles, two little dimples appear on each cheek, which are rosy with health. He has already had one or two little *wives*, but Louisa Biron is his favourite, a pretty little girl of five years of age.

"Now, dear Victor, I dare say you wish to be indulged in a little gossip concerning the good people of Geneva. The pretty Miss Mansfield has already received the congratulatory visits on her approaching marriage with a young Englishman, John Melbourne, Esq. Her ugly sister, Manon, married M. Duvillard, the rich banker, last autumn. Your favourite schoolfellow, Louis Manoir, has suffered several misfortunes since the departure of Clerval from Geneva. But he has already recovered his spirits, and is reported to be on the point of marrying a very lively pretty Frenchwoman, Madame Tavernier. She is a widow, and much older than Manoir; but she is very much admired, and a favourite with every body.

"I have written myself into good spirits, dear cousin; yet I cannot conclude without again anxiously inquiring concerning your health. Dear Victor, if you are not very ill, write yourself, and make your father and all of us happy; or — I cannot bear to think of the other side of the question; my tears already flow. Adieu, my dearest cousin.

"ELIZABETH LAVENZA.

"Geneva, March 18th, 17 — ."

"Dear, dear Elizabeth!" I exclaimed when I had read her letter, "I will write instantly, and relieve them from the anxiety they must feel."

I wrote, and this exertion greatly fatigued me; but my convalescence had commenced, and proceeded regularly. In another fortnight I was able to leave my chamber.

One of my first duties on my recovery was to introduce Clerval to the several professors of the university. In doing this, I underwent a kind of rough usage, ill befitting the wounds that my mind had sustained. Ever since the fatal night, the end of my labours, and the beginning of my misfortunes, I had conceived a violent antipathy even to the name of natural philosophy. When I was otherwise quite restored to health, the sight of a chemical instrument would renew all the agony of my nervous symptoms. Henry saw this, and had removed all my apparatus from my view. He had also changed my apartment; for he perceived that I had acquired a dislike for the room which had previously been my laboratory. But these cares of Clerval were made of no avail when I visited the professors. M. Waldman inflicted torture when he praised, with kindness and warmth, the astonishing progress I had made in the sciences. He soon perceived that I disliked the subject; but, not guessing the real cause, he attributed my feelings to modesty, and changed the subject from my improvement to the science itself, with a desire, as I evidently saw, of drawing me out. What could I do? He meant to please, and he tormented me. I felt as if he had placed carefully, one by one, in my view those instruments which were to be afterwards used in putting me to a slow and cruel death. I writhed under his words, yet dared not exhibit the pain I felt. Clerval, whose eyes and feelings were always quick in discerning the sensations of others, declined the subject, alleging, in excuse, his total ignorance; and the conversation took a more general turn. I thanked my friend from my heart, but I did not speak. I saw plainly that he was surprised, but he never attempted to draw my secret from me; and although I loved him with a mixture of affection and reverence that knew no bounds, yet I could never persuade myself to confide to him that event which was so often present to my recollection, but which I feared the detail to another would only impress more deeply.

M. Krempe was not equally docile; and in my condition at that time, of almost insupportable sensitiveness, his harsh blunt encomiums gave me even more pain than the benevolent approbation of M. Waldman. "D—n the fellow!" cried he; "why, M. Clerval, I assure you he has outstript us all. Aye, stare if you please; but it is nevertheless true. A youngster who, but a few years ago, believed Cornelius Agrippa as firmly as the gospel, has now set himself at the head of the university; and if he is not soon pulled down,[3] we shall all be out of countenance. — Aye, aye," continued he, observing my face expressive of suffering, "M. Frankenstein is modest; an excellent quality in a

3. Deposed, dethroned.

young man. Young men should be diffident of themselves, you know, M. Clerval; I was myself when young: but that wears out in a very short time."

M. Krempe had now commenced an eulogy on himself, which happily turned the conversation from a subject that was so annoying to me.

Clerval was no natural philosopher. His imagination was too vivid for the minutiæ of science. Languages were his principal study; and he sought, by acquiring their elements, to open a field for self-instruction on his return to Geneva. Persian, Arabic, and Hebrew, gained his attention, after he had made himself perfectly master of Greek and Latin. For my own part, idleness had ever been irksome to me; and now that I wished to fly from reflection, and hated my former studies, I felt great relief in being the fellow-pupil with my friend, and found not only instruction but consolation in the works of the orientalists. Their melancholy is soothing, and their joy elevating to a degree I never experienced in studying the authors of any other country. When you read their writings, life appears to consist in a warm sun and garden of roses, — in the smiles and frowns of a fair enemy, and the fire that consumes your own heart. How different from the manly and heroical poetry of Greece and Rome.

Summer passed away in these occupations, and my return to Geneva was fixed for the latter end of autumn; but being delayed by several accidents, winter and snow arrived, the roads were deemed impassable, and my journey was retarded until the ensuing spring. I felt this delay very bitterly; for I longed to see my native town, and my beloved friends. My return had only been delayed so long from an unwillingness to leave Clerval in a strange place, before he had become acquainted with any of its inhabitants. The winter, however, was spent cheerfully; and although the spring was uncommonly late, when it came, its beauty compensated for its dilatoriness.

The month of May had already commenced, and I expected the letter daily which was to fix the date of my departure, when Henry proposed a pedestrian tour in the environs of Ingoldstadt that I might bid a personal farewell to the country I had so long inhabited. I acceded with pleasure to this proposition: I was fond of exercise, and Clerval had always been my favourite companion in the rambles of this nature that I had taken among the scenes of my native country.

We passed a fortnight in these perambulations: my health and spirits had long been restored, and they gained additional strength from the salubrious air I breathed, the natural incidents of our progress, and the conversation of my friend. Study had before secluded me from the intercourse of my fellow-creatures, and rendered me unsocial; but Clerval called forth the better feelings of my heart; he again taught me to love the aspect of nature, and the cheerful faces of children. Excellent friend! how sincerely did you love me, and endeavour to elevate my mind, until it was on a level with your own. A selfish pursuit had cramped and narrowed me, until your gentleness and affection warmed and opened my senses; I became the same happy creature who, a few years ago, loving and beloved by all, had no sorrow or care. When happy, inanimate nature had the power of bestowing on me the most delightful sensations. A serene sky and verdant fields filled me with ecstacy. The present season was indeed divine; the flowers of spring bloomed in the hedges, while those of summer were already in bud: I was undisturbed by thoughts which during the preceding year had pressed upon me, notwithstanding my endeavours to throw them off, with an invincible burden.

Henry rejoiced in my gaiety, and sincerely sympathized in my feelings: he exerted himself to amuse me, while he expressed the sensations that filled his soul. The resources of his mind on this occasion were truly astonishing: his conversation was full of imagination; and very often, in imitation of the Persian and Arabic writers, he invented tales of wonderful fancy and passion. At other times he repeated my favourite poems, or drew me out into arguments, which he supported with great ingenuity.

We returned to our college on a Sunday afternoon: the peasants were dancing, and every one we met appeared gay and happy. My own spirits were high, and I bounded along with feelings of unbridled joy and hilarity.

Chapter VI.

On my return, I found the following letter from my father: —

"*To* V. FRANKENSTEIN

"MY DEAR VICTOR,

"You have probably waited impatiently for a letter to fix the date of your return to us; and I was at first tempted to write only a few lines, merely mentioning the day on which I should expect you. But that would be a cruel kindness, and I dare not do it. What would be your surprise, my son, when you expected a happy and gay welcome, to behold, on the contrary, tears and wretchedness? And how, Victor, can I relate our misfortune? Absence cannot have rendered you callous to our joys and griefs; and how shall I inflict pain on an absent child? I wish to prepare you for the woeful news, but I know it is impossible; even now your eye skims over the page, to seek the words which are to convey to you the horrible tidings.

"William is dead! — that sweet child, whose smiles delighted and warmed my heart, who was so gentle, yet so gay! Victor, he is murdered!

"I will not attempt to console you; but will simply relate the circumstances of the transaction.

"Last Thursday (May 7th) I, my niece, and your two brothers, went to walk in Plainpalais. The evening was warm and serene, and we prolonged our walk farther than usual. It was already dusk before we thought of returning; and then we discovered that William and Ernest, who had gone on before, were not to be found. We accordingly rested on a seat until they should return. Presently Ernest came, and inquired if we had seen his brother: he said, that they had been playing together, that William had run away to hide himself, and that he vainly sought for him, and afterwards waited for him a long time, but that he did not return.

"This account rather alarmed us, and we continued to search for him until night fell, when Elizabeth conjectured that he might have returned to the house. He was not there. We returned again, with torches; for I could not rest, when I thought that my sweet boy had lost himself, and was exposed to all the damps and dews of night: Elizabeth also suffered extreme anguish. About five in the morning I discovered my lovely boy, whom the night before I had seen blooming and active in health, stretched on the grass livid and motionless: the print of the murderer's finger was on his neck.

"He was conveyed home, and the anguish that was visible in my countenance betrayed the secret to Elizabeth. She was very earnest to see the corpse. At first I attempted to prevent her; but she persisted, and entering the room where it lay, hastily examined the neck of the victim, and clasping her hands exclaimed, 'O God! I have murdered my darling infant!'

"She fainted, and was restored with extreme difficulty. When she again lived, it was only to weep and sigh. She told me, that that same evening William had teazed her to let him wear a very valuable miniature that she possessed of your mother. This picture is gone, and was doubtless the temptation which urged the murderer to the deed. We have no trace of him at present, although our exertions to discover him are unremitted; but they will not restore my beloved William.

"Come, dearest Victor; you alone can console Elizabeth. She weeps continually, and accuses herself unjustly as the cause of his death; her words pierce my heart. We are all unhappy; but will not that be an additional motive for you, my son, to return and be our comforter? Your dear mother! Alas, Victor! I now say, Thank God she did not live to witness the cruel, miserable death of her youngest darling!

"Come, Victor; not brooding thoughts of vengeance against the assassin, but with feelings of peace and gentleness, that will heal, instead of festering the wounds of our minds. Enter the house of mourning, my friend, but with kindness and affection for those who love you, and not with hatred for your enemies.

"Your affectionate and afflicted father,

"ALPHONSE FRANKENSTEIN.

"Geneva, May 12th, 17 — ."

Clerval, who had watched my countenance as I read this letter, was surprised to observe the despair that succeeded to the joy I at first expressed on receiving news from my friends. I threw the letter on the table, and covered my face with my hands.

"My dear Frankenstein," exclaimed Henry, when he perceived me weep with bitterness, "are you always to be unhappy? My dear friend, what has happened?"

I motioned to him to take up the letter, while I walked up and down the room in the extremest agitation. Tears also gushed from the eyes of Clerval, as he read the account of my misfortune.

"I can offer you no consolation, my friend," said he; "your disaster is irreparable. What do you intend to do?"

"To go instantly to Geneva: come with me, Henry, to order the horses."

During our walk, Clerval endeavoured to raise my spirits. He did not do this by common topics of consolation, but by exhibiting the truest sympathy. "Poor William!" said he, "that dear child; he now sleeps with his angel mother. His friends mourn and weep, but he is at rest: he does not now feel the murderer's grasp; a sod covers his gentle form, and he knows no pain. He can no longer be a fit subject for pity; the survivors are the greatest sufferers, and for them time is the only consolation. Those maxims of the Stoics,[1] that death was no evil, and that the mind of man ought to be superior to despair on the eternal absence of a beloved object, ought not to be urged. Even Cato[2] wept over the dead body of his brother."

Clerval spoke thus as we hurried through the streets; the words impressed themselves on my mind, and I remembered them afterwards in solitude. But now, as soon as the horses arrived, I hurried into a cabriole,[3] and bade farewell to my friend.

My journey was very melancholy. At first I wished to hurry on, for I longed to console and sympathize with my loved and sorrowing friends; but when I drew near my native town, I slackened my progress. I could hardly sustain the multitude of feelings that crowded into my mind. I passed through scenes familiar to my youth, but which I had not seen

1. A philosophical sect in ancient Greece and Rome that emphasized reason and patient endurance.
2. Antagonist of Caesar and notable Stoic (95–46 B.C.).
3. A two-wheeled, horse-drawn carriage.

for nearly six years. How altered every thing might be during that time? One sudden and desolating change had taken place; but a thousand little circumstances might have by degrees worked other alterations, which, although they were done more tranquilly, might not be the less decisive. Fear overcame me; I dared not advance, dreading a thousand nameless evils that made me tremble, although I was unable to define them.

I remained two days at Lausanne, in this painful state of mind. I contemplated the lake: the waters were placid; all around was calm, and the snowy mountains, "the palaces of nature,"[4] were not changed. By degrees the calm and heavenly scene restored me, and I continued my journey towards Geneva.

The road ran by the side of the lake, which became narrower as I approached my native town. I discovered more distinctly the black sides of Jura, and the bright summit of Mont Blanc.[5] I wept like a child: "Dear mountains! my own beautiful lake! how do you welcome your wanderer? Your summits are clear; the sky and lake are blue and placid. Is this to prognosticate peace, or to mock at my unhappiness?"

I fear, my friend, that I shall render myself tedious by dwelling on these preliminary circumstances; but they were days of comparative happiness, and I think of them with pleasure. My country, my beloved country! who but a native can tell the delight I took in again beholding thy streams, thy mountains, and, more than all, thy lovely lake.

Yet, as I drew nearer home, grief and fear again overcame me. Night also closed around; and when I could hardly see the dark mountains, I felt still more gloomily. The picture appeared a vast and dim scene of evil, and I foresaw obscurely that I was destined to become the most wretched of human beings. Alas! I prophesied truly, and failed only in one single circumstance, that in all the misery I imagined and dreaded, I did not conceive the hundredth part of the anguish I was destined to endure.

It was completely dark when I arrived in the environs of Geneva; the gates of the town were already shut; and I was obliged to pass the night at Secheron, a village half a league to the east of the city. The sky was serene; and, as I was unable to rest, I resolved to visit the spot where my poor William had been murdered. As I could not pass through the town, I was obliged to cross the lake in a boat to arrive at Plainpalais. During this short voyage I saw the lightnings playing on the summit of Mont Blanc in the most beautiful figures. The storm appeared to approach rapidly; and, on landing, I ascended a low hill, that I might observe its progress. It advanced; the heavens were clouded, and I soon

---

4. From canto III of Byron's *Childe Harold's Pilgrimage* (1816): "Above me are the Alps, / The palaces of Nature, whose vast walls / Have pinnacled in clouds their snowy scalps, / And throned Eternity in icy halls / Of cold sublimity" (lxii. 590–94).
5. Percy Shelley wrote "Mont Blanc" (subtitled "Lines written in the vale of Chamouni") in 1816. See p. 175, below.

felt the rain coming slowly in large drops, but its violence quickly increased.

I quitted my seat, and walked on, although the darkness and storm increased every minute, and the thunder burst with a terrific crash over my head. It was echoed from Salêve, the Juras, and the Alps of Savoy; vivid flashes of lightning dazzled my eyes, illuminating the lake, making it appear like a vast sheet of fire; then for an instant every thing seemed of a pitchy darkness, until the eye recovered itself from the preceding flash. The storm, as is often the case in Switzerland, appeared at once in various parts of the heavens. The most violent storm hung exactly north of the town, over that part of the lake which lies between the promontory of Belrive and the village of Copêt. Another storm enlightened Jura with faint flashes; and another darkened and sometimes disclosed the Môle, a peaked mountain to the east of the lake.

While I watched the storm, so beautiful yet terrific,[6] I wandered on with a hasty step. This noble war in the sky elevated my spirits; I clasped my hands and exclaimed aloud, "William, dear angel! this is thy funeral, this thy dirge!" As I said these words, I perceived in the gloom a figure which stole from behind a clump of trees near me; I stood fixed, gazing intently: I could not be mistaken. A flash of lightning illuminated the object, and discovered its shape plainly to me; its gigantic stature, and the deformity of its aspect, more hideous than belongs to humanity, instantly informed me that it was the wretch, the filthy dæmon to whom I had given life. What did he there? Could he be (I shuddered at the conception) the murderer of my brother? No sooner did that idea cross my imagination, than I became convinced of its truth; my teeth chattered, and I was forced to lean against a tree for support. The figure passed me quickly, and I lost it in the gloom. Nothing in human shape could have destroyed that fair child. He was the murderer! I could not doubt it. The mere presence of the idea was an irresistible proof of the fact. I thought of pursuing the devil; but it would have been in vain, for another flash discovered him to me hanging among the rocks of the nearly perpendicular ascent of Mont Salêve, a hill that bounds Plainpalais on the south. He soon reached the summit, and disappeared.

I remained motionless. The thunder ceased; but the rain still continued, and the scene was enveloped in an impenetrable darkness. I revolved in my mind the events which I had until now sought to forget: the whole train of my progress towards the creation; the appearance of the work of my own hands alive at my bed side, its departure. Two years had now nearly elapsed since the night on which he first received life; and was this his first crime? Alas! I had turned loose into the world

6. Terrifying.

a depraved wretch, whose delight was in carnage and misery; had he not murdered my brother?

No one can conceive the anguish I suffered during the remainder of the night, which I spent, cold and wet, in the open air. But I did not feel the inconvenience of the weather; my imagination was busy in scenes of evil and despair. I considered the being whom I had cast among mankind, and endowed with the will and power to effect purposes of horror, such as the deed which he had now done, nearly in the light of my own vampire,[7] my own spirit let loose from the grave, and forced to destroy all that was dear to me.

Day dawned; and I directed my steps towards the town. The gates were open; and I hastened to my father's house. My first thought was to discover what I knew of the murderer, and cause instant pursuit to be made. But I paused when I reflected on the story that I had to tell. A being whom I myself had formed, and endued with life, had met me at midnight among the precipices of an inaccessible mountain. I remembered also the nervous fever with which I had been seized just at the time that I dated my creation, and which would give an air of delirium to a tale otherwise so utterly improbable. I well knew that if any other had communicated such a relation to me, I should have looked upon it as the ravings of insanity. Besides, the strange nature of the animal would elude all pursuit, even if I were so far credited as to persuade my relatives to commence it. Besides, of what use would be pursuit? Who could arrest a creature capable of scaling the overhanging sides of Mont Salêve? These reflections determined me, and I resolved to remain silent.

It was about five in the morning when I entered my father's house. I told the servants not to disturb the family, and went into the library to attend their usual hour of rising.

Six years had elapsed, passed as a dream but for one indelible trace, and I stood in the same place where I had last embraced my father before my departure for Ingolstadt. Beloved and respectable parent! He still remained to me. I gazed on the picture of my mother, which stood over the mantlepiece. It was an historical subject, painted at my father's desire, and represented Caroline Beaufort in an agony of despair, kneeling by the coffin of her dead father. Her garb was rustic, and her cheek pale; but there was an air of dignity and beauty, that hardly permitted the sentiment of pity. Below this picture was a miniature of William; and my tears flowed when I looked upon it. While I was thus engaged, Ernest entered; he had heard me arrive, and hastened to welcome me. He expressed a sorrowful delight to see me: "Welcome, my dearest Victor," said he. "Ah! I wish you had come

7. A reanimated corpse.

three months ago, and then you would have found us all joyous and delighted. But we are now unhappy; and, I am afraid, tears instead of smiles will be your welcome. Our father looks so sorrowful: this dreadful event seems to have revived in his mind his grief on the death of Mamma. Poor Elizabeth also is quite inconsolable." Ernest began to weep as he said these words.

"Do not," said I, "welcome me thus; try to be more calm, that I may not be absolutely miserable the moment I enter my father's house after so long an absence. But, tell me, how does my father support his misfortunes? and how is my poor Elizabeth?"

"She indeed requires consolation; she accused herself of having caused the death of my brother, and that made her very wretched. But since the murderer has been discovered——"

"The murderer discovered! Good God! how can that be? who could attempt to pursue him? It is impossible; one might as well try to overtake the winds, or confine a mountain-stream with a straw."

"I do not know what you mean; but we were all very unhappy when she was discovered. No one would believe it at first; and even now Elizabeth will not be convinced, notwithstanding all the evidence. Indeed, who would credit that Justine Moritz, who was so amiable, and fond of all the family, could all at once become so extremely wicked?"

"Justine Moritz! Poor, poor girl, is she the accused? But it is wrongfully; every one knows that; no one believes it, surely, Ernest?"

"No one did at first; but several circumstances came out, that have almost forced conviction upon us: and her own behaviour has been so confused, as to add to the evidence of facts a weight that, I fear, leaves no hope for doubt. But she will be tried to-day, and you will then hear all."

He related that, the morning on which the murder of poor William had been discovered, Justine had been taken ill, and confined to her bed; and, after several days, one of the servants, happening to examine the apparel she had worn on the night of the murder, had discovered in her pocket the picture of my mother, which had been judged to be the temptation of the murderer. The servant instantly shewed it to one of the others, who, without saying a word to any of the family, went to a magistrate; and, upon their deposition, Justine was apprehended. On being charged with the fact, the poor girl confirmed the suspicion in a great measure, by her extreme confusion of manner.

This was a strange tale, but it did not shake my faith; and I replied earnestly, "You are all mistaken; I know the murderer. Justine, poor, good Justine, is innocent."

At that instant my father entered. I saw unhappiness deeply impressed on his countenance, but he endeavoured to welcome me cheerfully; and, after we had exchanged our mournful greeting, would have introduced some other topic than that of our disaster, had not Ernest exclaimed, "Good God, Papa! Victor says that he knows who was the murderer of poor William."

"We do also, unfortunately," replied my father; "for indeed I had rather have been for ever ignorant than have discovered so much depravity and ingratitude in one I valued so highly."

"My dear father, you are mistaken; Justine is innocent."

"If she is, God forbid that she should suffer as guilty. She is to be tried to-day, and I hope, I sincerely hope, that she will be acquitted."

This speech calmed me. I was firmly convinced in my own mind that Justine, and indeed every human being, was guiltless of this murder. I had no fear, therefore, that any circumstantial evidence could be brought forward strong enough to convict her; and, in this assurance, I calmed myself, expecting the trial with eagerness, but without prognosticating an evil result.

We were soon joined by Elizabeth. Time had made great alterations in her form since I had last beheld her. Six years before she had been a pretty, good-humoured girl, whom every one loved and caressed. She was now a woman in stature and expression of countenance, which was uncommonly lovely. An open and capacious forehead gave indications of a good understanding, joined to great frankness of disposition. Her eyes were hazel, and expressive of mildness, now through recent affliction allied to sadness. Her hair was of a rich dark auburn, her complexion fair, and her figure slight and graceful. She welcomed me with the greatest affection. "Your arrival, my dear cousin," said she, "fills me with hope. You perhaps will find some means to justify my poor guiltless Justine. Alas! who is safe, if she be convicted of crime? I rely on her innocence as certainly as I do upon my own. Our misfortune is doubly hard to us; we have not only lost that lovely darling boy, but this poor girl, whom I sincerely love, is to be torn away by even a worse fate. If she is condemned, I never shall know joy more. But she will not, I am sure she will not; and then I shall be happy again, even after the sad death of my little William."

"She is innocent, my Elizabeth," said I, "and that shall be proved; fear nothing, but let your spirits be cheered by the assurance of her acquittal."

"How kind you are! every one else believes in her guilt, and that made me wretched; for I knew that it was impossible: and to see every one else prejudiced in so deadly a manner, rendered me hopeless and despairing." She wept.

"Sweet niece," said my father, "dry your tears. If she is, as you believe, innocent, rely on the justice of our judges, and the activity with which I shall prevent the slightest shadow of partiality."

Chapter VII.

We passed a few sad hours, until eleven o'clock, when the trial was to commence. My father and the rest of the family being obliged to attend as witnesses, I accompanied them to the court. During the whole of this wretched mockery of justice, I suffered living torture. It was to be decided, whether the result of my curiosity and lawless devices would cause the death of two of my fellow-beings: one a smiling babe, full of innocence and joy; the other far more dreadfully murdered, with every aggravation of infamy that could make the murder memorable in horror. Justine also was a girl of merit, and possessed qualities which promised to render her life happy: now all was to be obliterated in an ignominious grave; and I the cause! A thousand times rather would I have confessed myself guilty of the crime ascribed to Justine; but I was absent when it was committed, and such a declaration would have been considered as the ravings of a madman, and would not have exculpated her who suffered through me.

The appearance of Justine was calm. She was dressed in mourning; and her countenance, always engaging, was rendered, by the solemnity of her feelings, exquisitely beautiful. Yet she appeared confident in innocence, and did not tremble, although gazed on and execrated by thousands; for all the kindness which her beauty might otherwise have excited, was obliterated in the minds of the spectators by the imagination of the enormity she was supposed to have committed. She was tranquil, yet her tranquillity was evidently constrained; and as her confusion had before been adduced as a proof of her guilt, she worked up her mind to an appearance of courage. When she entered the court, she threw her eyes round it, and quickly discovered where we were seated. A tear seemed to dim her eye when she saw us; but she quickly recovered herself, and a look of sorrowful affection seemed to attest her utter guiltlessness.

The trial began; and after the advocate against her had stated the charge, several witnesses were called. Several strange facts combined against her, which might have staggered any one who had not such proof of her innocence as I had. She had been out the whole of the night on which the murder had been committed, and towards morning had been perceived by a market-woman not far from the spot where the body of the murdered child had been afterwards found. The woman asked her what she did there; but she looked very strangely, and only returned a confused and unintelligible answer. She returned to the house about eight o'clock; and when one inquired where she had passed the night, she replied, that she had been looking for the child, and demanded earnestly, if any thing had been heard concerning him. When shewn the body, she fell into violent hysterics, and kept her bed for several days. The picture was then produced, which the servant had found in her pocket; and when Elizabeth, in a faltering voice, proved that it was the same which, an hour before the child had been missed, she had placed round his neck, a murmur of horror and indignation filled the court.

Justine was called on for her defence. As the trial had proceeded, her countenance had altered. Surprise, horror, and misery, were strongly expressed. Sometimes she struggled with her tears; but when she was desired to plead, she collected her powers, and spoke in an audible although variable voice: —

"God knows," she said, "how entirely I am innocent. But I do not pretend that my protestations should acquit me: I rest my innocence on a plain and simple explanation of the facts which have been adduced against me; and I hope the character I have always borne will incline my judges to a favourable interpretation, where any circumstance appears doubtful or suspicious."

She then related that, by the permission of Elizabeth, she had passed the evening of the night on which the murder had been committed, at the house of an aunt at Chêne, a village situated at about a league from Geneva. On her return, at about nine o'clock, she met a man, who asked her if she had seen any thing of the child who was lost. She was alarmed by this account, and passed several hours in looking for him, when the gates of Geneva were shut, and she was forced to remain several hours of the night in a barn belonging to a cottage, being unwilling to call up the inhabitants, to whom she was well known. Unable to rest or sleep, she quitted her asylum early, that she might again endeavour to find my brother. If she had gone near the spot where his body lay, it was without her knowledge. That she had been bewildered when questioned by the market-woman, was not surprising, since she had passed a sleepless night, and the fate of poor William was yet uncertain. Concerning the picture she could give no account.

"I know," continued the unhappy victim, "how heavily and fatally this one circumstance weighs against me, but I have no power of explaining it; and when I have expressed my utter ignorance, I am only left to conjecture concerning the probabilities by which it might have been placed in my pocket. But here also I am checked. I believe that I have no enemy on earth, and none surely would have been so wicked as to destroy me wantonly. Did the murderer place it there? I know of no opportunity afforded him for so doing; or if I had, why should he have stolen the jewel, to part with it again so soon?

"I commit my cause to the justice of my judges, yet I see no room for hope. I beg permission to have a few witnesses examined concerning my character; and if their testimony shall not overweigh my supposed guilt, I must be condemned, although I would pledge my salvation on my innocence."

Several witnesses were called, who had known her for many years, and they spoke well of her; but fear, and hatred of the crime of which they supposed her guilty, rendered them timorous, and unwilling to come forward. Elizabeth saw even this last resource, her excellent dispositions and irreproachable conduct, about to fail the accused, when, although violently agitated, she desired permission to address the court.

"I am," said she, "the cousin of the unhappy child who was murdered, or rather his sister, for I was educated by and have lived with his parents ever since and even long before his birth. It may therefore be judged indecent in me to come forward on this occasion; but when I see a fellow-creature about to perish through the cowardice of her pretended friends, I wish to be allowed to speak, that I may say what I know of her character. I am well acquainted with the accused. I have lived in the same house with her, at one time for five, and at another for nearly two years. During all that period she appeared to me the most amiable and benevolent of human creatures. She nursed Madame Frankenstein, my aunt, in her last illness with the greatest affection and care; and afterwards attended her own mother during a tedious[1] illness, in a manner that excited the admiration of all who knew her. After which she again lived in my uncle's house, where she was beloved by all the family. She was warmly attached to the child who is now dead, and acted towards him like a most affectionate mother. For my own part, I do not hesitate to say, that, notwithstanding all the evidence produced against her, I believe and rely on her perfect innocence. She had no temptation for such an action: as to the bauble on which the chief proof rests, if she had earnestly desired it, I should have willingly given it to her; so much do I esteem and value her."

Excellent Elizabeth! A murmur of approbation was heard; but it was excited by her generous interference, and not in favour of poor Justine, on whom the public indignation was turned with renewed violence, charging her with the blackest ingratitude. She herself wept as Elizabeth spoke, but she did not answer. My own agitation and anguish was extreme during the whole trial. I believed in her innocence; I knew it. Could the dæmon, who had (I did not for a minute doubt) murdered my brother, also in his hellish sport have betrayed the innocent to death and ignominy. I could not sustain the horror of my situation; and when I perceived that the popular voice, and the countenances of the judges, had already condemned my unhappy victim, I rushed out of the court in agony. The tortures of the accused did not equal mine; she was sustained by innocence, but the fangs of remorse tore my bosom, and would not forego their hold.

I passed a night of unmingled wretchedness. In the morning I went

1. Wearisome.

to the court; my lips and throat were parched. I dared not ask the fatal question; but I was known, and the officer guessed the cause of my visit. The ballots[2] had been thrown; they were all black, and Justine was condemned.

I cannot pretend to describe what I then felt. I had before experienced sensations of horror; and I have endeavoured to bestow upon them adequate expressions, but words cannot convey an idea of the heart-sickening despair that I then endured. The person to whom I addressed myself added, that Justine had already confessed her guilt. "That evidence," he observed, "was hardly required in so glaring a case, but I am glad of it; and, indeed, none of our judges like to condemn a criminal upon circumstantial evidence, be it ever so decisive."

When I returned home, Elizabeth eagerly demanded the result.

"My cousin," replied I, "it is decided as you may have expected; all judges had rather that ten innocent should suffer, than that one guilty should escape. But she has confessed."

This was a dire blow to poor Elizabeth, who had relied with firmness upon Justine's innocence. "Alas!" said she, "how shall I ever again believe in human benevolence? Justine, whom I loved and esteemed as my sister, how could she put on those smiles of innocence only to betray; her mild eyes seemed incapable of any severity or ill-humour, and yet she has committed a murder."

Soon after we heard that the poor victim had expressed a wish to see my cousin. My father wished her not to go; but said, that he left it to her own judgment and feelings to decide. "Yes," said Elizabeth, "I will go, although she is guilty; and you, Victor, shall accompany me: I cannot go alone." The idea of this visit was torture to me, yet I could not refuse.

We entered the gloomy prison-chamber, and beheld Justine sitting on some straw at the further end; her hands were manacled, and her head rested on her knees. She rose on seeing us enter; and when we were left alone with her, she threw herself at the feet of Elizabeth, weeping bitterly. My cousin wept also.

"Oh, Justine!" said she, "why did you rob me of my last consolation. I relied on your innocence; and although I was then very wretched, I was not so miserable as I am now."

"And do you also believe that I am so very, very wicked? Do you also join with my enemies to crush me?" Her voice was suffocated with sobs.

"Rise, my poor girl," said Elizabeth, "why do you kneel, if you are innocent? I am not one of your enemies; I believed you guiltless, notwithstanding every evidence, until I heard that you had yourself de-

2. Small balls used for secret voting.

clared your guilt. That report, you say, is false; and be assured, dear Justine, that nothing can shake my confidence in you for a moment, but your own confession."

"I did confess; but I confessed a lie. I confessed, that I might obtain absolution; but now that falsehood lies heavier at my heart than all my other sins. The God of heaven forgive me! Ever since I was condemned, my confessor has besieged me; he threatened and menaced, until I almost began to think that I was the monster that he said I was. He threatened excommunication and hell fire in my last moments, if I continued obdurate. Dear lady, I had none to support me; all looked on me as a wretch doomed to ignominy and perdition. What could I do? In an evil hour I subscribed to a lie; and now only am I truly miserable."

She paused, weeping, and then continued — "I thought with horror, my sweet lady, that you should believe your Justine, whom your blessed aunt had so highly honoured, and whom you loved, was a creature capable of a crime which none but the devil himself could have perpetrated. Dear William! dearest blessed child! I soon shall see you again in heaven, where we shall all be happy; and that consoles me, going as I am to suffer ignominy and death."

"Oh, Justine! forgive me for having for one moment distrusted you. Why did you confess? But do not mourn, my dear girl; I will every where proclaim your innocence, and force belief. Yet you must die; you, my playfellow, my companion, my more than sister. I never can survive so horrible a misfortune."

"Dear, sweet Elizabeth, do not weep. You ought to raise me with thoughts of a better life, and elevate me from the petty cares of this world of injustice and strife. Do not you, excellent friend, drive me to despair."

"I will try to comfort you; but this, I fear, is an evil too deep and poignant to admit of consolation, for there is no hope. Yet heaven bless thee, my dearest Justine, with resignation, and a confidence elevated beyond this world. Oh! how I hate its shews and mockeries! when one creature is murdered, another is immediately deprived of life in a slow torturing manner; then the executioners, their hands yet reeking with the blood of innocence, believe that they have done a great deed. They call this *retribution*. Hateful name! When that word is pronounced, I know greater and more horrid punishments are going to be inflicted than the gloomiest tyrant has ever invented to satiate his utmost revenge. Yet this is not consolation for you, my Justine, unless indeed that you may glory in escaping from so miserable a den. Alas! I would I were in peace with my aunt and my lovely William, escaped from a world which is hateful to me, and the visages of men which I abhor."

Justine smiled languidly. "This, dear lady, is despair, and not resignation. I must not learn the lesson that you would teach me. Talk of something else, something that will bring peace, and not increase of misery."

During this conversation I had retired to a corner of the prison-room, where I could conceal the horrid anguish that possessed me. Despair! Who dared talk of that? The poor victim, who on the morrow was to pass the dreary boundary between life and death, felt not as I did, such deep and bitter agony. I gnashed my teeth, and ground them together, uttering a groan that came from my inmost soul. Justine started. When she saw who it was, she approached me, and said, "Dear Sir, you are very kind to visit me; you, I hope, do not believe that I am guilty."

I could not answer. "No, Justine," said Elizabeth; "he is more convinced of your innocence than I was; for even when he heard that you had confessed, he did not credit it."

"I truly thank him. In these last moments I feel the sincerest gratitude towards those who think of me with kindness. How sweet is the affection of others to such a wretch as I am! It removes more than half my misfortune; and I feel as if I could die in peace, now that my innocence is acknowledged by you, dear lady, and your cousin."

Thus the poor sufferer tried to comfort others and herself. She indeed gained the resignation she desired. But I, the true murderer, felt the never-dying worm alive in my bosom, which allowed of no hope or consolation. Elizabeth also wept, and was unhappy; but her's also was the misery of innocence, which, like a cloud that passes over the fair moon, for a while hides, but cannot tarnish its brightness. Anguish and despair had penetrated into the core of my heart; I bore a hell within me, which nothing could extinguish. We staid several hours with Justine; and it was with great difficulty that Elizabeth could tear herself away. "I wish," cried she, "that I were to die with you; I cannot live in this world of misery."

Justine assumed an air of cheerfulness, while she with difficulty repressed her bitter tears. She embraced Elizabeth, and said, in a voice of half-suppressed emotion, "Farewell, sweet lady, dearest Elizabeth, my beloved and only friend; may heaven in its bounty bless and preserve you; may this be the last misfortune that you will ever suffer. Live, and be happy, and make others so."

As we returned, Elizabeth said, "You know not, my dear Victor, how much I am relieved, now that I trust in the innocence of this unfortunate girl. I never could again have known peace, if I had been deceived in my reliance on her. For the moment that I did believe her guilty, I felt an anguish that I could not have long sustained. Now my heart is lightened. The innocent suffers; but she whom I thought amiable and good has not betrayed the trust I reposed in her, and I am consoled.

Amiable cousin! such were your thoughts, mild and gentle as your own dear eyes and voice. But I—I was a wretch, and none ever conceived of the misery that I then endured.

END OF VOL. I.

Volume II

Chapter I.

Nothing is more painful to the human mind, than, after the feelings have been worked up by a quick succession of events, the dead calmness of inaction and certainty which follows, and deprives the soul both of hope and fear. Justine died; she rested; and I was alive. The blood flowed freely in my veins, but a weight of despair and remorse pressed on my heart, which nothing could remove. Sleep fled from my eyes; I wandered like an evil spirit, for I had committed deeds of mischief beyond description horrible, and more, much more, (I persuaded myself) was yet behind. Yet my heart overflowed with kindness, and the love of virtue. I had begun life with benevolent intentions, and thirsted for the moment when I should put them in practice, and make myself useful to my fellow-beings. Now all was blasted:[1] instead of that serenity of conscience, which allowed me to look back upon the past with self-satisfaction, and from thence to gather promise of new hopes, I was seized by remorse and the sense of guilt, which hurried me away to a hell of intense tortures, such as no language can describe.

This state of mind preyed upon my health, which had entirely recovered from the first shock it had sustained. I shunned the face of man; all sound of joy or complacency was torture to me; solitude was my only consolation — deep, dark, death-like solitude.

My father observed with pain the alteration perceptible in my disposition and habits, and endeavoured to reason with me on the folly of giving way to immoderate grief. "Do you think, Victor," said he, "that I do not suffer also? No one could love a child more than I loved your brother;" (tears came into his eyes as he spoke); "but is it not a duty to the survivors, that we should refrain from augmenting their unhappiness by an appearance of immoderate grief? It is also a duty owed to yourself; for excessive sorrow prevents improvement or enjoyment, or even the discharge of daily usefulness, without which no man is fit for society."

This advice, although good, was totally inapplicable to my case; I

---

1. Literally, blown or breathed on by a malignant force, blighted; more generally, cursed or damned.

should have been the first to hide my grief, and console my friends, if remorse had not mingled its bitterness with my other sensations. Now I could only answer my father with a look of despair, and endeavour to hide myself from his view.

About this time we retired to our house at Belrive. This change was particularly agreeable to me. The shutting of the gates regularly at ten o'clock, and the impossibility of remaining on the lake after that hour, had rendered our residence within the walls of Geneva very irksome to me. I was now free. Often, after the rest of the family had retired for the night, I took the boat, and passed many hours upon the water. Sometimes, with my sails set, I was carried by the wind; and sometimes, after rowing into the middle of the lake, I left the boat to pursue its own course, and gave way to my own miserable reflections. I was often tempted, when all was at peace around me, and I the only unquiet thing that wandered restless in a scene so beautiful and heavenly, if I except[2] some bat, or the frogs, whose harsh and interrupted croaking was heard only when I approached the shore — often, I say, I was tempted to plunge into the silent lake, that the waters might close over me and my calamities for ever. But I was restrained, when I thought of the heroic and suffering Elizabeth, whom I tenderly loved, and whose existence was bound up in mine. I thought also of my father, and surviving brother: should I by my base desertion leave them exposed and unprotected to the malice of the fiend whom I had let loose among them?

At these moments I wept bitterly, and wished that peace would revisit my mind only that I might afford them consolation and happiness. But that could not be. Remorse extinguished every hope. I had been the author of unalterable evils; and I lived in daily fear, lest the monster whom I had created should perpetrate some new wickedness. I had an obscure feeling that all was not over, and that he would still commit some signal[3] crime, which by its enormity should almost efface the recollection of the past. There was always scope for fear, so long as any thing I loved remained behind. My abhorrence of this fiend cannot be conceived. When I thought of him, I gnashed my teeth, my eyes became inflamed, and I ardently wished to extinguish that life which I had so thoughtlessly bestowed. When I reflected on his crimes and malice, my hatred and revenge burst all bounds of moderation. I would have made a pilgrimage to the highest peak of the Andes, could I, when there, have precipitated him to their base. I wished to see him again, that I might wreak the utmost extent of anger on his head, and avenge the deaths of William and Justine.

Our house was the house of mourning. My father's health was deeply shaken by the horror of the recent events. Elizabeth was sad and de-

2. Leave out, exclude.
3. Remarkable, notable.

sponding; she no longer took delight in her ordinary occupations; all pleasure seemed to her sacrilege toward the dead; eternal woe and tears she then thought was the just tribute she should pay to innocence so blasted and destroyed. She was no longer that happy creature, who in earlier youth wandered with me on the banks of the lake, and talked with ecstacy of our future prospects. She had become grave, and often conversed of the inconstancy of fortune, and the instability of human life.

"When I reflect, my dear cousin," said she, "on the miserable death of Justine Moritz, I no longer see the world and its works as they before appeared to me. Before, I looked upon the accounts of vice and injustice, that I read in books or heard from others, as tales of ancient days, or imaginary evils; at least they were remote, and more familiar to reason than to the imagination; but now misery has come home, and men appear to me as monsters thirsting for each other's blood. Yet I am certainly unjust. Every body believed that poor girl to be guilty; and if she could have committed the crime for which she suffered, assuredly she would have been the most depraved of human creatures. For the sake of a few jewels, to have murdered the son of her benefactor and friend, a child whom she had nursed from its birth, and appeared to love as if it had been her own! I could not consent to the death of any human being; but certainly I should have thought such a creature unfit to remain in the society of men. Yet she was innocent. I know, I feel she was innocent; you are of the same opinion, and that confirms me. Alas! Victor, when falsehood can look so like the truth, who can look so like the truth, who can assure themselves of certain happiness? I feel as if I were walking on the edge of a precipice, towards which thousands are crowding, and endeavouring to plunge me into the abyss. William and Justine were assassinated, and the murderer escapes; he walks about the world free, and perhaps respected. But even if I were condemned to suffer on the scaffold for the same crimes, I would not change places with such a wretch."

I listened to this discourse with the extremest agony. I, not in deed, but in effect, was the true murderer. Elizabeth read my anguish in my countenance, and kindly taking my hand said, "My dearest cousin, you must calm yourself. These events have affected me, God knows how deeply; but I am not so wretched as you are. There is an expression of despair, and sometimes of revenge, in your countenance, that makes me tremble. Be calm, my dear Victor; I would sacrifice my life to your peace. We surely shall be happy: quiet in our native country, and not mingling in the world, what can disturb our tranquillity?"

She shed tears as she said this, distrusting the very solace that she gave; but at the same time she smiled, that she might chase away the fiend that lurked in my heart. My father, who saw in the unhappiness that was painted in my face only an exaggeration of that sorrow which

I might naturally feel, thought that an amusement suited to my taste would be the best means of restoring to me my wonted serenity. It was from this cause that he had removed to the country; and, induced by the same motive, he now proposed that we should all make an excursion to the valley of Chamounix. I had been there before, but Elizabeth and Ernest never had; and both had often expressed an earnest desire to see the scenery of this place, which had been described to them as so wonderful and sublime.[4] Accordingly we departed from Geneva on this tour about the middle of the month of August, nearly two months after the death of Justine.

The weather was uncommonly fine; and if mine had been a sorrow to be chased away by any fleeting circumstance, this excursion would certainly have had the effect intended by my father. As it was, I was somewhat interested in the scene; it sometimes lulled, although it could not extinguish my grief. During the first day we travelled in a carriage. In the morning we had seen the mountains at a distance, towards which we gradually advanced. We perceived that the valley through which we wound, and which was formed by the river Arve, whose course we followed, closed in upon us by degrees; and when the sun had set, we beheld immense mountains and precipices overhanging us on every side, and heard the sound of the river raging among rocks, and the dashing of waterfalls around.

The next day we pursued our journey upon mules; and as we ascended still higher, the valley assumed a more magnificent and astonishing character. Ruined castles hanging on the precipices of piny mountains; the impetuous Arve, and cottages every here and there peeping forth from among the trees, formed a scene of singular beauty. But it was augmented and rendered sublime by the mighty Alps, whose white and shining pyramids and domes towered above all, as belonging to another earth, the habitations of another race of beings.

We passed the bridge of Pelissier, where the ravine, which the river forms, opened before us, and we began to ascend the mountain that overhangs it. Soon after we entered the valley of Chamounix. This valley is more wonderful and sublime, but not so beautiful and picturesque[5] as that of Servox, through which we had just passed. The high and snowy mountains were its immediate boundaries; but we saw no more ruined castles and fertile fields. Immense glaciers approached the road; we heard the rumbling thunder of the falling avelânche, and marked the smoke of its passage. Mont Blanc, the supreme and mag-

4. "Affecting the mind with a sense of overwhelming grandeur or irresistible power; calculated to inspire awe, deep reverence, or lofty emotion, by reason of its beauty, vastness or grandeur" (OED).
5. "Possessing pleasing and interesting qualities of form and colour (but not implying the highest beauty or sublimity)" (OED).

nificent Mont Blanc, raised itself from the surrounding *aiguilles*, and its tremendous *dome*[6] overlooked the valley.

During this journey, I sometimes joined Elizabeth, and exerted myself to point out to her the various beauties of the scene. I often suffered my mule to lag behind, and indulged in the misery of reflection. At other times I spurred on the animal before my companions, that I might forget them, the world, and, more than all, myself. When at a distance, I alighted, and threw myself on the grass, weighed down by horror and despair. At eight in the evening I arrived at Chamounix. My father and Elizabeth were very much fatigued; Ernest, who accompanied us, was delighted, and in high spirits: the only circumstance that detracted from his pleasure was the south wind, and the rain it seemed to promise for the next day.

We retired early to our apartments, but not to sleep; at least I did not. I remained many hours at the window, watching the pallid lightning that played above Mont Blanc, and listening to the rushing of the Arve, which ran below my window.

Chapter II.

The next day, contrary to the prognostications of our guides, was fine, although clouded. We visited the source of the Arveiron, and rode about the valley until evening. These sublime and magnificent scenes afforded me the greatest consolation that I was capable of receiving. They elevated me from all littleness of feeling; and although they did not remove my grief, they subdued and tranquillized it. In some degree, also, they diverted my mind from the thoughts over which it had brooded for the last month. I returned in the evening, fatigued, but less unhappy, and conversed with my family with more cheerfulness than had been my custom for some time. My father was pleased, and Elizabeth overjoyed. "My dear cousin," said she, "you see what happiness you diffuse when you are happy; do not relapse again!"

The following morning the rain poured down in torrents, and thick mists hid the summits of the mountains. I rose early, but felt unusually melancholy. The rain depressed me; my old feelings recurred, and I was miserable. I knew how disappointed my father would be at this sudden change, and I wished to avoid him until I had recovered myself so far as to be enabled to conceal those feelings that overpowered me. I knew that they would remain that day at the inn; and as I had ever inured myself to rain, moisture, and cold, I resolved to go alone to the summit of Montanvert. I remembered the effect that the view of the

6. Convex, rounded summit; Mont Blanc's is capped with ice. *Aiguilles*: slender, sharply pointed peaks.

tremendous and ever-moving glacier had produced upon my mind when I first saw it. It had then filled me with a sublime ecstacy that gave wings to the soul, and allowed it to soar from the obscure world to light and joy. The sight of the awful[1] and majestic in nature had indeed always the effect of solemnizing my mind, and causing me to forget the passing cares of life. I determined to go alone, for I was well acquainted with the path, and the presence of another would destroy the solitary grandeur of the scene.

The ascent is precipitous, but the path is cut into continual and short windings, which enable you to surmount the perpendicularity of the mountain. It is a scene terrifically desolate. In a thousand spots the traces of the winter avalanche may be perceived, where trees lie broken and strewed on the ground; some entirely destroyed, others bent, leaning upon the jutting rocks of the mountain, or transversely upon other trees. The path, as you ascend higher, is intersected by ravines of snow, down which stones continually roll from above; one of them is particularly dangerous, as the slightest sound, such as even speaking in a loud voice, produces a concussion[2] of air sufficient to draw destruction upon the head of the speaker. The pines are not tall or luxuriant, but they are sombre, and add an air of severity to the scene. I looked on the valley beneath; vast mists were rising from the rivers which ran through it, and curling in thick wreaths around the opposite mountains, whose summits were hid in the uniform clouds, while rain poured from the dark sky, and added to the melancholy impression I received from the objects around me. Alas! why does man boast of sensibilities superior to those apparent in the brute; it only renders them more necessary[3] beings. If our impulses were confined to hunger, thirst, and desire, we might be nearly free; but now we are moved by every wind that blows, and a chance word or scene that that word may convey to us.

> We rest; a dream has power to poison sleep.
>   We rise; one wand'ring thought pollutes the day.
> We feel, conceive, or reason; laugh, or weep,
>   Embrace fond woe, or cast our cares away;
> It is the same: for, be it joy or sorrow,
>   The path of its departure still is free.
> Man's yesterday may ne'er be like his morrow;
>   Naught may endure but mutability![4]

It was nearly noon when I arrived at the top of the ascent. For some time I sat upon the rock that overlooks the sea of ice. A mist covered both that and the surrounding mountains. Presently a breeze dissipated

1. Awe-inspiring.
2. Agitation, violent shaking.
3. Dependent, lacking volition.
4. These lines are the second half of Percy Shelley's "On Mutability" (1816).

the cloud, and I descended upon the glacier. The surface is very uneven, rising like the waves of a troubled sea, descending low, and interspersed by rifts that sink deep. The field of ice is almost a league in width, but I spent nearly two hours in crossing it. The opposite mountain is a bare perpendicular rock. From the side where I now stood Montanvert was exactly opposite, at the distance of a league; and above it rose Mont Blanc, in awful majesty. I remained in a recess of the rock, gazing on this wonderful and stupendous scene. The sea, or rather the vast river of ice, wound among its dependent mountains, whose aërial summits hung over its recesses. Their icy and glittering peaks shone in the sunlight over the clouds. My heart, which was before sorrowful, now swelled with something like joy; I exclaimed — "Wandering spirits, if indeed ye wander, and do not rest in your narrow beds, allow me this faint happiness, or take me, as your companion, away from the joys of life."

As I said this, I suddenly beheld the figure of a man, at some distance, advancing towards me with superhuman speed. He bounded over the crevices in the ice, among which I had walked with caution; his stature also, as he approached, seemed to exceed that of man. I was troubled: a mist came over my eyes, and I felt a faintness seize me; but I was quickly restored by the cold gale of the mountains. I perceived, as the shape came nearer, (sight tremendous and abhorred!) that it was the wretch whom I had created. I trembled with rage and horror, resolving to wait his approach, and then close with him in mortal combat. He approached; his countenance bespoke bitter anguish, combined with disdain and malignity, while its unearthly ugliness rendered it almost too horrible for human eyes. But I scarcely observed this; anger and hatred had at first deprived me of utterance, and I recovered only to overwhelm him with words expressive of furious detestation and contempt.

"Devil!" I exclaimed, "do you dare approach me? and do not you fear the fierce vengeance of my arm wreaked on your miserable head? Begone, vile insect! or rather stay, that I may trample you to dust! and, oh, that I could, with the extinction of your miserable existence, restore those victims whom you have so diabolically murdered!"

"I expected this reception," said the dæmon. "All men hate the wretched; how then must I be hated, who am miserable beyond all living things! Yet you, my creator, detest and spurn me, thy creature, to whom thou art bound by ties only dissoluble by the annihilation of one of us. You purpose to kill me. How dare you sport thus with life? Do your duty towards me, and I will do mine towards you and the rest of mankind. If you will comply with my conditions, I will leave them and you at peace; but if you refuse, I will glut the maw of death, until it be satiated with the blood of your remaining friends."

"Abhorred monster! fiend that thou art! the tortures of hell are too mild a vengeance for thy crimes. Wretched devil! you reproach me with your creation; come on then, that I may extinguish the spark which I so negligently bestowed."

My rage was without bounds; I sprang on him, impelled by all the feelings which can arm one being against the existence of another.

He easily eluded me, and said,

"Be calm! I entreat you to hear me, before you give vent to your hatred on my devoted head. Have I not suffered enough, that you seek to increase my misery? Life, although it may only be an accumulation of anguish, is dear to me, and I will defend it. Remember, thou hast made me more powerful than thyself; my height is superior to thine; my joints more supple. But I will not be tempted to set myself in opposition to thee. I am thy creature,[5] and I will be even mild and docile to my natural lord and king, if thou wilt also perform thy part, the which thou owest me. Oh, Frankenstein, be not equitable to every other, and trample upon me alone, to whom thy justice, and even thy clemency and affection, is most due. Remember, that I am thy creature: I ought to be thy Adam; but I am rather the fallen angel, whom thou drivest from joy for no misdeed. Every where I see bliss, from which I alone am irrevocably excluded. I was benevolent and good; misery made me a fiend. Make me happy, and I shall again be virtuous."

"Begone! I will not hear you. There can be no community between you and me; we are enemies. Begone, or let us try our strength in a fight, in which one must fall."

"How can I move thee? Will no entreaties cause thee to turn a favourable eye upon thy creature, who implores thy goodness and compassion. Believe me, Frankenstein: I was benevolent; my soul glowed with love and humanity: but am I not alone, miserably alone? You, my creator, abhor me; what hope can I gather from your fellow-creatures, who owe me nothing? they spurn and hate me. The desert mountains and dreary glaciers are my refuge. I have wandered here many days; the caves of ice, which I only do not fear, are a dwelling to me, and the only one which man does not grudge. These bleak skies I hail, for they are kinder to me than your fellow-beings. If the multitude of mankind knew of my existence, they would do as you do, and arm themselves for my destruction. Shall I not then hate them who abhor me? I will keep no terms with my enemies. I am miserable, and they shall share my wretchedness. Yet it is in your power to recompense me, and deliver them from an evil which it only remains for you to make so great, that not only you and your family, but thousands of others, shall be swallowed up in the whirlwinds of its rage. Let your compassion be moved, and do not disdain me. Listen to my tale: when you have heard

5. Creation.

that, abandon or commiserate me, as you shall judge that I deserve. But hear me. The guilty are allowed, by human laws, bloody as they may be, to speak in their own defence before they are condemned. Listen to me, Frankenstein. You accuse me of murder; and yet you would, with a satisfied conscience, destroy your own creature. Oh, praise the eternal justice of man! Yet I ask you not to spare me: listen to me; and then, if you can, and if you will, destroy the work of your hands."

"Why do you call to my remembrance circumstances of which I shudder to reflect, that I have been the miserable origin and author? Cursed be the day, abhorred devil, in which you first saw light! Cursed (although I curse myself) be the hands that formed you! You have made me wretched beyond expression. You have left me no power to consider whether I am just to you, or not. Begone! relieve me from the sight of your detested form."

"Thus I relieve thee, my creator," he said, and placed his hated hands before my eyes, which I flung from me with violence; "thus I take from thee a sight which you abhor. Still thou canst listen to me, and grant me thy compassion. By the virtues that I once possessed, I demand this from you. Hear my tale; it is long and strange, and the temperature of this place is not fitting to your fine[6] sensations; come to the hut upon the mountain. The sun is yet high in the heavens; before it descends to hide itself behind yon snowy precipices, and illuminate another world, you will have heard my story, and can decide. On you it rests, whether I quit for ever the neighbourhood of man, and lead a harmless life, or become the scourge of your fellow-creatures, and the author of your own speedy ruin."

As he said this, he led the way across the ice: I followed. My heart was full, and I did not answer him; but, as I proceeded, I weighed the various arguments that he had used, and determined at least to listen to his tale. I was partly urged by curiosity, and compassion confirmed my resolution. I had hitherto supposed him to be the murderer of my brother, and I eagerly sought a confirmation or denial of this opinion. For the first time, also, I felt what the duties of a creator towards his creature were, and that I ought to render him happy before I complained of his wickedness. These motives urged me to comply with his demand. We crossed the ice, therefore, and ascended the opposite rock. The air was cold, and the rain again began to descend: we entered the hut, the fiend with an air of exultation, I with a heavy heart, and depressed spirits. But I consented to listen; and, seating myself by the fire which my odious companion had lighted, he thus began his tale.

6. Delicate.

Chapter III.

"It is with considerable difficulty that I remember the original æra of my being: all the events of that period appear confused and indistinct. A strange multiplicity of sensations seized me, and I saw, felt, heard, and smelt, at the same time; and it was, indeed, a long time before I learned to distinguish between the operations of my various senses. By degrees, I remember, a stronger light pressed upon my nerves, so that I was obliged to shut my eyes. Darkness then came over me, and troubled me; but hardly had I felt this, when, by opening my eyes, as I now suppose, the light poured in upon me again. I walked, and, I believe, descended; but I presently found a great alteration in my sensations. Before, dark and opaque bodies had surrounded me, impervious to my touch or sight; but I now found that I could wander on at liberty, with no obstacles which I could not either surmount or avoid. The light became more and more oppressive to me; and, the heat wearying me as I walked, I sought a place where I could receive shade. This was the forest near Ingolstadt; and here I lay by the side of a brook resting from my fatigue, until I felt tormented by hunger and thirst. This roused me from my nearly dormant state, and I ate some berries which I found hanging on the trees, or lying on the ground. I slaked my thirst at the brook; and then lying down, was overcome by sleep.

"It was dark when I awoke; I felt cold also, and half-frightened as it were instinctively, finding myself so desolate. Before I had quitted your apartment, on a sensation of cold, I had covered myself with some clothes; but these were insufficient to secure me from the dews of night. I was a poor, helpless, miserable wretch; I knew, and could distinguish, nothing; but, feeling pain invade me on all sides, I sat down and wept.

"Soon a gentle light stole over the heavens, and gave me a sensation of pleasure. I started up, and beheld a radiant form rise from among the trees. I gazed with a kind of wonder. It moved slowly, but it enlightened my path; and I again went out in search of berries. I was still cold, when under one of the trees I found a huge cloak, with which I covered myself, and sat down upon the ground. No distinct ideas occupied my mind; all was confused. I felt light, and hunger, and thirst, and darkness; innumerable sounds rung in my ears, and on all sides various scents saluted[1] me: the only object that I could distinguish was the bright moon, and I fixed my eyes on that with pleasure.

"Several changes of day and night passed, and the orb of night had greatly lessened when I began to distinguish my sensations from each other. I gradually saw plainly the clear stream that supplied me with drink, and the trees that shaded me with their foliage. I was delighted when I first discovered that a pleasant sound, which often saluted my

---

1. Greeted.

ears, procceded from the throats of the little winged animals who had often intercepted the light from my eyes. I began also to observe, with greater accuracy, the forms that surrounded me, and to perceive the boundaries of the radiant roof of light which canopied me. Somctimes I tried to imitate the pleasant songs of the birds, but was unable. Sometimes I wished to express my sensations in my own mode, but the uncouth and inarticulate sounds which broke from me frightened me into silence again.

"The moon had disappeared from the night, and again, with a lessened form, shewed itself, while I still remained in the forest. My sensations had, by this time, become distinct, and my mind received cvcry day additional ideas. My eyes became accustomed to the light, and to perceive objects in their right forms; I distinguished the insect from the herb, and, by degrees, one herb from another. I found that the sparrow uttered none but harsh notes, whilst those of the blackbird and thrush were sweet and enticing.

"One day, when I was oppressed by cold, I found a fire which had been left by some wandering beggars, and was overcome with delight at the warmth I experienced from it. In my joy I thrust my hand into the live embers, but quickly drew it out again with a cry of pain. How strange, I thought, that the same cause should produce such opposite effects! I examined the materials of the fire, and to my joy found it to be composed of wood. I quickly collected some branches; but they were wet, and would not burn. I was pained at this, and sat still watching the operation of the fire. The wet wood which I had placed ncar the heat dried, and itself became inflamed. I reflected on this; and, by touching the various branches, I discovered the cause, and busied myself in collecting a great quantity of wood, that I might dry it, and have a plentiful supply of fire. When night came on, and brought sleep with it, I was in the greatest fear lest my fire should be extinguished. I covcred it carefully with dry wood and leaves, and placed wet branches upon it; and then, spreading my cloak, I lay on the ground, and sunk into sleep.

"It was morning when I awoke, and my first care was to visit the fire. I uncovered it, and a gentle breezc quickly fanned it into a flame. I observed this also, and contrived a fan of branches, which roused the embers when they were nearly extinguished. When night came again, I found, with pleasure, that the fire gave light as well as heat; and that the discovery of this element was useful to me in my food; for I found some of the offals that the travellers had left had been roasted, and tasted much more savoury than the berries I gathered from the trees. I tried, therefore, to dress my food in the same manner, placing it on the live embers. I found that the berries were spoiled by this operation, and the nuts and roots much improved.

"Food, however, became scarce; and I often spent the whole day searching in vain for a few acorns to assuage the pangs of hunger. When I found this, I resolved to quit the place that I had hitherto inhabited, to seek for one where the few wants I experienced would be more easily satisfied. In this emigration, I exceedingly lamented the loss of the fire which I had obtained through accident, and knew not how to re-produce it. I gave several hours to the serious consideration of this difficulty; but I was obliged to relinquish all attempt to supply it; and, wrapping myself up in my cloak, I struck across the wood towards the setting sun. I passed three days in these rambles, and at length discov-ered the open country. A great fall of snow had taken place the night before, and the fields were of one uniform white; the appearance was disconsolate, and I found my feet chilled by the cold damp substance that covered the ground.

"It was about seven in the morning, and I longed to obtain food and shelter; at length I perceived a small hut, on a rising ground, which had doubtless been built for the convenience of some shepherd. This was a new sight to me; and I examined the structure with great curiosity. Finding the door open, I entered. An old man sat in it, near a fire, over which he was preparing his breakfast. He turned on hearing a noise; and, perceiving me, shrieked loudly, and, quitting the hut, ran across the fields with a speed of which his debilitated form hardly ap-peared capable. His appearance, different from any I had ever before seen, and his flight, somewhat surprised me. But I was enchanted by the appearance of the hut: here the snow and rain could not penetrate; the ground was dry; and it presented to me then as exquisite and divine a retreat as Pandæmonium appeared to the dæmons of hell after their sufferings in the lake of fire.[2] I greedily devoured the remnants of the shepherd's breakfast, which consisted of bread, cheese, milk, and wine; the latter, however, I did not like. [Then] overcome by fatigue, I lay down among some straw, and fell asleep.

"It was noon when I awoke; and, allured by the warmth of the sun, which shone brightly on the white ground, I determined to recom-mence my travels; and, depositing the remains of the peasant's breakfast in a wallet[3] I found, I proceeded across the fields for several hours, until at sunset I arrived at a village. How miraculous did this appear! the huts, the neater cottages, and stately houses, engaged my admiration by turns. The vegetables in the gardens, the milk and cheese that I saw placed at the windows of some of the cottages, allured my appetite. One of the best of these I entered; but I had hardly placed my foot within the door, before the children shrieked, and one of the women fainted. The whole village was roused; some fled, some attacked me, until, grievously bruised by stones and many other kinds of missile[4]

---

2. See *Paradise Lost* I.670ff.
3. A beggar's bag.
4. Thrown.

weapons, I escaped to the open country, and fearfully took refuge in a low hovel, quite bare, and making a wretched appearance after the palaces I had beheld in the village. This hovel, however, joined a cottage of a neat and pleasant appearance; but, after my late dearly-bought experience, I dared not enter it. My place of refuge was constructed of wood, but so low, that I could with difficulty sit upright in it. No wood, however, was placed on the earth, which formed the floor, but it was dry; and although the wind entered it by innumerable chinks, I found it an agreeable asylum from the snow and rain.

"Here then I retreated, and lay down, happy to have found a shelter, however miserable, from the inclemency of the season, and still more from the barbarity of man.

"As soon as morning dawned, I crept from my kennel, that I might view the adjacent cottage, and discover if I could remain in the habitation I had found. It was situated against the back of the cottage, and surrounded on the sides which were exposed by a pig-stye and a clear pool of water. One part was open, and by that I had crept in; but now I covered every crevice by which I might be perceived with stones and wood, yet in such a manner that I might move them on occasion to pass out: all the light I enjoyed came through the stye, and that was sufficient for me.

"Having thus arranged my dwelling, and carpeted it with clean straw, I retired; for I saw the figure of a man at a distance, and I remembered too well my treatment the night before, to trust myself in his power. I had first, however, provided for my sustenance for that day, by a loaf of coarse bread, which I purloined, and a cup with which I could drink, more conveniently than from my hand, of the pure water which flowed by my retreat. The floor was a little raised, so that it was kept perfectly dry, and by its vicinity to the chimney of the cottage it was tolerably warm.

"Being thus provided, I resolved to reside in this hovel, until something should occur which might alter my determination. It was indeed a paradise, compared to the bleak forest, my former residence, the rain-dropping branches, and dank earth. I ate my breakfast with pleasure, and was about to remove a plank to procure myself a little water, when I heard a step, and, looking through a small chink, I beheld a young creature, with a pail on her head, passing before my hovel. The girl was young and of gentle[5] demeanour, unlike what I have since found cottagers and farm-house servants to be. Yet she was meanly dressed, a coarse blue petticoat and a linen jacket being her only garb; her fair hair was plaited, but not adorned; she looked patient, yet sad. I lost sight of her; and in about a quarter of an hour she returned, bearing the pail, which was now partly filled with milk. As she walked along,

5. Well-born, or having the character appropriate to one who is well-born.

seemingly incommoded by the burden, a young man met her, whose countenance expressed a deeper despondence. Uttering a few sounds with an air of melancholy, he took the pail from her head, and bore it to the cottage himself. She followed, and they disappeared. Presently I saw the young man again, with some tools in his hand, cross the field behind the cottage; and the girl was also busied, sometimes in the house, and sometimes in the yard.

"On examining my dwelling, I found that one of the windows of the cottage had formerly occupied a part of it, but the panes had been filled up with wood. In one of these was a small and almost imperceptible chink, through which the eye could just penetrate. Through this crevice, a small room was visible, white-washed and clean, but very bare of furniture. In one corner, near a small fire, sat an old man, leaning his head on his hands in a disconsolate attitude. The young girl was occupied in arranging the cottage; but presently she took something out of a drawer, which employed her hands, and she sat down beside the old man, who, taking up an instrument, began to play, and to produce sounds, sweeter than the voice of the thrush or the nightingale. It was a lovely sight, even to me, poor wretch! who had never beheld aught[6] beautiful before. The silver hair and benevolent countenance of the aged cottager, won my reverence; while the gentle manners of the girl enticed my love. He played a sweet mournful air, which I perceived drew tears from the eyes of his amiable companion, of which the old man took no notice, until she sobbed audibly; he then pronounced a few sounds, and the fair creature, leaving her work, knelt at his feet. He raised her, and smiled with such kindness and affection, that I felt sensations of a peculiar and overpowering nature: they were a mixture of pain and pleasure, such as I had never before experienced, either from hunger or cold, warmth or food; and I withdrew from the window, unable to bear these emotions.

"Soon after this the young man returned, bearing on his shoulders a load of wood. The girl met him at the door, helped to relieve him of his burden, and, taking some of the fuel into the cottage, placed it on the fire; then she and the youth went apart into a nook of the cottage, and he shewed her a large loaf and a piece of cheese. She seemed pleased; and went into the garden for some roots and plants, which she placed in water, and then upon the fire. She afterwards continued her work, whilst the young man went into the garden, and appeared busily employed in digging and pulling up roots. After he had been employed thus about an hour, the young woman joined him, and they entered the cottage together.

"The old man had, in the mean time, been pensive; but, on the appearance of his companions, he assumed a more cheerful air, and

6. Anything.

they sat down to eat. The meal was quickly dispatched. The young woman was again occupied in arranging the cottage; the old man walked before the cottage in the sun for a few minutes, leaning on the arm of the youth. Nothing could exceed in beauty the contrast between these two excellent creatures. One was old, with silver hairs and a countenance beaming with benevolence and love: the younger was slight and graceful in his figure, and his features were moulded with the finest symmetry; yet his eyes and attitude expressed the utmost sadness and despondency. The old man returned to the cottage; and the youth, with tools different from those he had used in the morning, directed his steps across the fields.

"Night quickly shut in; but, to my extreme wonder, I found that the cottagers had a means of prolonging light, by the use of tapers, and was delighted to find, that the setting of the sun did not put an end to the pleasure I experienced in watching my human neighbours. In the evening, the young girl and her companion were employed in various occupations which I did not understand; and the old man again took up the instrument, which produced the divine sounds that had enchanted me in the morning. So soon as he had finished, the youth began, not to play, but to utter sounds that were monotonous, and neither resembling the harmony of the old man's instrument or the songs of the birds; I since found that he read aloud, but at that time I knew nothing of the science of words or letters.

"The family, after having been thus occupied for a short time, extinguished their lights, and retired, as I conjectured, to rest.

Chapter IV.

"I lay on my straw, but I could not sleep. I thought of the occurrences of the day. What chiefly struck me was the gentle manners of these people; and I longed to join them, but dared not. I remembered too well the treatment I had suffered the night before from the barbarous villagers, and resolved, whatever course of conduct I might hereafter think it right to pursue, that for the present I would remain quietly in my hovel, watching, and endeavouring to discover the motives which influenced their actions.

"The cottagers arose the next morning before the sun. The young woman arranged the cottage, and prepared the food; and the youth departed after the first meal.

"This day was passed in the same routine as that which preceded it. The young man was constantly employed out of doors, and the girl in various laborious occupations within. The old man, whom I soon perceived to be blind, employed his leisure hours on his instrument, or in contemplation. Nothing could exceed the love and respect which the younger cottagers exhibited towards their venerable companion. They performed towards him every little office of affection and duty with gentleness; and he rewarded them by his benevolent smiles.

"They were not entirely happy. The young man and his companion often went apart, and appeared to weep. I saw no cause for their unhappiness; but I was deeply affected by it. If such lovely creatures were miserable, it was less strange that I, an imperfect and solitary being, should be wretched. Yet why were these gentle beings unhappy? They possessed a delightful house (for such it was in my eyes), and every luxury; they had a fire to warm them when chill, and delicious viands when hungry; they were dressed in excellent clothes; and, still more, they enjoyed one another's company and speech, interchanging each day looks of affection and kindness. What did their tears imply? Did they really express pain? I was at first unable to solve these questions; but perpetual attention, and time, explained to me many appearances which were at first enigmatic.

"A considerable period elapsed before I discovered one of the causes of the uneasiness of this amiable family; it was poverty: and they suffered that evil in a very distressing degree. Their nourishment consisted entirely of the vegetables of their garden, and the milk of one cow, who gave very little during the winter, when its masters could scarcely procure food to support it. They often, I believe, suffered the pangs of hunger very poignantly, especially the two younger cottagers; for several times they placed food before the old man, when they reserved none for themselves.

"This trait of kindness moved me sensibly. I had been accustomed, during the night, to steal a part of their store for my own consumption; but when I found that in doing this I inflicted pain on the cottagers, I abstained, and satisfied myself with berries, nuts, and roots, which I gathered from a neighbouring wood.

"I discovered also another means through which I was enabled to assist their labours. I found that the youth spent a great part of each day in collecting wood for the family fire; and, during the night, I often took his tools, the use of which I quickly discovered, and brought home firing sufficient for the consumption of several days.

"I remember, the first time that I did this, the young woman, when she opened the door in the morning, appeared greatly astonished on seeing a great pile of wood on the outside. She uttered some words in a loud voice, and the youth joined her, who also expressed surprise. I observed, with pleasure, that he did not go to the forest that day, but spent it in repairing the cottage, and cultivating the garden.

"By degrees I made a discovery of still greater moment. I found that these people possessed a method of communicating their experience and feelings to one another by articulate sounds. I perceived that the

words they spoke sometimes produced pleasure or pain, smiles or sadness, in the minds and countenances of the hearers. This was indeed
a godlike science, and I ardently desired to become acquainted with it.
But I was baffled in every attempt I made for this purpose. Their pro-
nunciation was quick; and the words they uttered, not having any apparent connexion with visible objects, I was unable to discover any clue
by which I could unravel the mystery of their reference. By great application, however, and after having remained during the space of several revolutions of the moon in my hovel, I discovered the names that
were given to some of the most familiar objects of discourse: I learned
and applied the words *fire*, *milk*, *bread*, and *wood*. I learned also the
names of the cottagers themselves. The youth and his companion had
each of them several names, but the old man had only one, which was
father. The girl was called *sister*, or *Agatha*; and the youth *Felix*, *brother*,
or *son*. I cannot describe the delight I felt when I learned the ideas
appropriated to each of these sounds, and was able to pronounce them.
I distinguished several other words, without being able as yet to understand or apply them; such as *good*, *dearest*, *unhappy*.

"I spent the winter in this manner. The gentle manners and beauty
of the cottagers greatly endeared them to me: when they were unhappy,
I felt depressed; when they rejoiced, I sympathized in their joys. I saw
few human beings beside them; and if any other happened to enter the
cottage, their harsh manners and rude gait only enhanced to me the
superior accomplishments of my friends. The old man, I could perceive, often endeavoured to encourage his children, as sometimes I
found that he called them, to cast off their melancholy. He would talk
in a cheerful accent, with an expression of goodness that bestowed
pleasure even upon me. Agatha listened with respect, her eyes sometimes filled with tears, which she endeavoured to wipe away unperceived; but I generally found that her countenance and tone were more
cheerful after having listened to the exhortations of her father. It was
not thus with Felix. He was always the saddest of the groupe; and, even
to my unpractised senses, he appeared to have suffered more deeply
than his friends. But if his countenance was more sorrowful, his voice
was more cheerful than that of his sister, especially when he addressed
the old man.

"I could mention innumerable instances, which, although slight,
marked the dispositions of these amiable cottagers. In the midst of poverty and want, Felix carried with pleasure to his sister the first little
white flower that peeped out from beneath the snowy ground. Early in
the morning before she had risen, he cleared away the snow that obstructed her path to the milk-house, drew water from the well, and
brought the wood from the outhouse, where, to his perpetual astonishment, he found his store always replenished by an invisible hand. In
the day, I believe, he worked sometimes for a neighbouring farmer,

because he often went forth, and did not return until dinner, yet brought no wood with him. At other times he worked in the garden; but, as there was little to do in the frosty season, he read to the old man and Agatha.

"This reading had puzzled me extremely at first; but, by degrees, I discovered that he uttered many of the same sounds when he read as when he talked. I conjectured, therefore, that he found on the paper signs for speech which he understood, and I ardently longed to comprehend these also; but how was that possible, when I did not even understand the sounds for which they stood as signs? I improved, however, sensibly in this science, but not sufficiently to follow up any kind of conversation, although I applied my whole mind to the endeavour: for I easily perceived that, although I eagerly longed to discover myself to the cottagers, I ought not to make the attempt until I had first become master of their language; which knowledge might enable me to make them overlook the deformity of my figure; for with this also the contrast perpetually presented to my eyes had made me acquainted.

"I had admired the perfect forms of my cottagers — their grace, beauty, and delicate complexions: but how was I terrified, when I viewed myself in a transparent pool! At first I started back, unable to believe that it was indeed I who was reflected in the mirror; and when I became fully convinced that I was in reality the monster that I am, I was filled with the bitterest sensations of despondence and mortification. Alas! I did not yet entirely know the fatal effects of this miserable deformity.

"As the sun became warmer, and the light of day longer, the snow vanished, and I beheld the bare trees and the black earth. From this time Felix was more employed; and the heart-moving indications of impending famine disappeared. Their food, as I afterwards found, was coarse, but it was wholesome; and they procured a sufficiency of it. Several new kinds of plants sprung up in the garden, which they dressed; and these signs of comfort increased daily as the season advanced.

"The old man, leaning on his son, walked each day at noon, when it did not rain, as I found it was called when the heavens poured forth its waters. This frequently took place; but a high wind quickly dried the earth, and the season became far more pleasant than it had been.

"My mode of life in my hovel was uniform. During the morning I attended the motions of the cottagers; and when they were dispersed in various occupations, I slept: the remainder of the day was spent in observing my friends. When they had retired to rest, if there was any moon, or the night was star-light, I went into the woods, and collected my own food and fuel for the cottage. When I returned, as often as it was necessary, I cleared their path from the snow, and performed those offices that I had seen done by Felix. I afterwards found that these labours, performed by an invisible hand, greatly astonished them; and once or twice I heard them, on these occasions, utter the words *good spirit, wonderful*; but I did not then understand the signification of these terms.

"My thoughts now became more active, and I longed to discover the motives and feelings of these lovely creatures; I was inquisitive to know why Felix appeared so miserable, and Agatha so sad. I thought (foolish wretch!) that it might be in my power to restore happiness to these deserving people. When I slept, or was absent, the forms of the venerable blind father, the gentle Agatha, and the excellent Felix, flitted before me. I looked upon them as superior beings, who would be the arbiters of my future destiny. I formed in my imagination a thousand pictures of presenting myself to them, and their reception of me. I imagined that they would be disgusted, until, by my gentle demeanour and conciliating words, I should first win their favour, and afterwards their love.

"These thoughts exhilarated me, and led me to apply with fresh ardour to the acquiring the art of language. My organs were indeed harsh, but supple; and although my voice was very unlike the soft music of their tones, yet I pronounced such words as I understood with tolerable ease. It was as the ass and the lap-dog; yet surely the gentle ass, whose intentions were affectionate, although his manners were rude, deserved better treatment than blows and execration.

"The pleasant showers and genial warmth of spring greatly altered the aspect of the earth. Men, who before this change seemed to have been hid in caves, dispersed themselves, and were employed in various arts of cultivation. The birds sang in more cheerful notes, and the leaves began to bud forth on the trees. Happy, happy earth! fit habitation for gods, which, so short a time before, was bleak, damp, and unwholesome. My spirits were elevated by the enchanting appearance of nature; the past was blotted from my memory, the present was tranquil, and the future gilded by bright rays of hope, and anticipations of joy.

Chapter V.

"I now hasten to the more moving part of my story. I shall relate events that impressed me with feelings which, from what I was, have made me what I am.

"Spring advanced rapidly; the weather became fine, and the skies cloudless. It surprised me, that what before was desert and gloomy should now bloom with the most beautiful flowers and verdure. My senses were gratified and refreshed by a thousand scents of delight, and a thousand sights of beauty.

"It was on one of these days, when my cottagers periodically rested from labour — the old man played on his guitar, and the children listened to him — I observed that the countenance of Felix was melancholy beyond expression: he sighed frequently; and once his father paused in his music, and I conjectured by his manner that he inquired the cause of his son's sorrow. Felix replied in a cheerful accent, and the old man was recommencing his music, when some one tapped at the door.

"It was a lady on horseback, accompanied by a countryman as a guide. The lady was dressed in a dark suit, and covered with a thick black veil. Agatha asked a question; to which the stranger only replied by pronouncing, in a sweet accent, the name of Felix. Her voice was musical, but unlike that of either of my friends. On hearing this word, Felix came up hastily to the lady; who, when she saw him, threw up her veil, and I beheld a countenance of angelic beauty and expression. Her hair of a shining raven black, and curiously braided; her eyes were dark, but gentle, although animated; her features of a regular proportion, and her complexion wondrously fair, each cheek tinged with a lovely pink.

"Felix seemed ravished with delight when he saw her, every trait of sorrow vanished from his face, and it instantly expressed a degree of ecstatic joy, of which I could hardly have believed it capable; his eyes sparkled, as his cheek flushed with pleasure; and at that moment I thought him as beautiful as the stranger. She appeared affected by different feelings; wiping a few tears from her lovely eyes, she held out her hand to Felix, who kissed it rapturously, and called her, as well as I could distinguish, his sweet Arabian. She did not appear to understand him, but smiled. He assisted her to dismount, and, dismissing her guide, conducted her into the cottage. Some conversation took place between him and his father; and the young stranger knelt at the old man's feet, and would have kissed his hand, but he raised her, and embraced her affectionately.

"I soon perceived, that although the stranger uttered articulate sounds, and appeared to have a language of her own, she was neither understood by, or herself understood, the cottagers. They made many signs which I did not comprehend; but I saw that her presence diffused gladness through the cottage, dispelling their sorrow as the sun dissipates the morning mists. Felix seemed peculiarly happy, and with smiles of delight welcomed his Arabian. Agatha, the ever-gentle Agatha, kissed the hands of the lovely stranger; and, pointing to her brother, made signs which appeared to me to mean that he had been sorrowful until she came. Some hours passed thus, while they, by their countenances, expressed joy, the cause of which I did not comprehend. Presently I found, by the frequent recurrence of one sound which the stranger repeated after them, that she was endeavouring to learn their language; and the idea instantly occurred to me, that I should make use of the same instructions to the same end. The stranger learned about twenty words at the first lesson, most of them indeed were those which I had before understood, but I profited by the others.

"As night came on, Agatha and the Arabian retired early. When they separated, Felix kissed the hand of the stranger, and said, 'Good night, sweet Safie.' He sat up much longer, conversing with his father; and, by the frequent repetition of her name, I conjectured that their lovely guest was the subject of their conversation. I ardently desired to understand them, and bent every faculty towards that purpose, but found it utterly impossible.

"The next morning Felix went out to his work; and, after the usual occupations of Agatha were finished, the Arabian sat at the feet of the old man, and, taking his guitar, played some airs so entrancingly beautiful, that they at once drew tears of sorrow and delight from my eyes. She sang, and her voice flowed in a rich cadence, swelling or dying away, like a nightingale of the woods.

"When she had finished, she gave the guitar to Agatha, who at first declined it. She played a simple air, and her voice accompanied it in sweet accents, but unlike the wondrous strain of the stranger. The old man appeared enraptured, and said some words, which Agatha endeavoured to explain to Safie, and by which he appeared to wish to express that she bestowed on him the greatest delight by her music."

"The days now passed as peaceably as before, with the sole alteration, that joy had taken place of sadness in the countenances of my friends. Safie was always gay and happy; she and I improved rapidly in the knowledge of language, so that in two months I began to comprehend most of the words uttered by my protectors."

"In the meanwhile also the black ground was covered with herbage, and the green banks interspersed with innumerable flowers, sweet to the scent and the eyes, stars of pale radiance among the moonlight woods; the sun became warmer, the nights clear and balmy; and my nocturnal rambles were an extreme pleasure to me, although they were considerably shortened by the late setting and early rising of the sun; for I never ventured abroad during daylight, fearful of meeting with the same treatment as I had formerly endured in the first village which I entered."

"My days were spent in close attention, that I might more speedily master the language; and I may boast that I improved more rapidly than the Arabian, who understood very little, and conversed in broken accents, whilst I comprehended and could imitate almost every word that was spoken.

"While I improved in speech, I also learned the science of letters, as it was taught to the stranger; and this opened before me a wide field for wonder and delight."

"The book from which Felix instructed Safie was Volney's *Ruins of*

Empires.[1] I should not have understood the purport of this book, had not Felix, in reading it, given very minute explanations. He had chosen this work, he said, because the declamatory style was framed in imitation of the eastern authors. Through this work I obtained a cursory knowledge of history, and a view of the several empires at present existing in the world; it gave me an insight into the manners, governments, and religions of the different nations of the earth. I heard of the slothful Asiatics; of the stupendous genius and mental activity of the Grecians; of the wars and wonderful virtue of the early Romans—of their subsequent degeneration—of the decline of that mighty empire; of chivalry, christianity, and kings. I heard of the discovery of the American hemisphere, and wept with Safie over the hapless fate of its original inhabitants.

"These wonderful narrations inspired me with strange feelings. Was man, indeed, at once so powerful, so virtuous, and magnificent, yet so vicious and base? He appeared at one time a mere scion of the evil principle, and at another as all that can be conceived of noble and godlike. To be a great and virtuous man appeared the highest honour that can befall a sensitive being; to be base and vicious, as many on record have been, appeared the lowest degradation, a condition more abject than that of the blind mole or harmless worm. For a long time I could not conceive how one man could go forth to murder his fellow, or even why there were laws and governments; but when I heard details of vice and bloodshed, my wonder ceased, and I turned away with disgust and loathing.

"Every conversation of the cottagers now opened new wonders to me. While I listened to the instructions which Felix bestowed upon the Arabian, the strange system of human society was explained to me. I heard of the division of property, of immense wealth and squalid poverty; of rank, descent, and noble blood.

"The words induced me to turn towards myself. I learned that the possessions most esteemed by your fellow-creatures were, high and unsullied descent[2] united with riches. A man might be respected with only one of these acquisitions; but without either he was considered, except in very rare instances, as a vagabond and a slave, doomed to waste his powers for the profit of the chosen few. And what was I? Of my creation and creator I was absolutely ignorant; but I knew that I possessed no money, no friends, no kind of property. I was, besides, endowed with a figure hideously deformed and loathsome; I was not even of the same nature as man. I was more agile than they, and could subsist upon coarser diet; I bore the extremes of heat and cold with less injury to my frame; my stature far exceeded their's. When I looked

---

1. *Les Ruines, ou Meditations sur les Revolutions des Empires* (1791), by Constantin François Chasseboeuf, comte de Volney (1757–1820).
2. Lineage, ancestry.

around, I saw and heard of none like me. Was I then a monster, a blot upon the earth, from which all men fled, and whom all men disowned?

"I cannot describe to you the agony that these reflections inflicted upon me; I tried to dispel them, but sorrow only increased with knowledge. Oh, that I had for ever remained in my native wood, nor known or felt beyond the sensations of hunger, thirst, and heat!

"Of what a strange nature is knowledge! It clings to the mind, when it has once seized on it, like a lichen on the rock. I wished sometimes to shake off all thought and feeling; but I learned that there was but one means to overcome the sensation of pain, and that was death — a state which I feared yet did not understand. I admired virtue and good feelings, and loved the gentle manners and amiable qualities of my cottagers; but I was shut out from intercourse with them, except through means which I obtained by stealth, when I was unseen and unknown, and which rather increased than satisfied the desire I had of becoming one among my fellows. The gentle words of Agatha, and the animated smiles of the charming Arabian, were not for me. The mild exhortations of the old man, and the lively conversation of the loved Felix, were not for me. Miserable, unhappy wretch!

"Other lessons were impressed upon me even more deeply. I heard of the difference of sexes; of the birth and growth of children; how the father doated on the smiles of the infant, and the lively sallies of the older child; how all the life and cares of the mother were wrapt up in the precious charge; how the mind of youth expanded and gained knowledge; of brother, sister, and all the various relationships which bind one human being to another in mutual bonds.

"But where were my friends and relations? No father had watched my infant days, no mother had blessed me with smiles and caresses; or if they had, all my past life was now a blot, a blind vacancy in which I distinguished nothing. From my earliest remembrance I had been as I then was in height and proportion. I had never yet seen a being resembling me, or who claimed any intercourse with me. What was I? The question again recurred, to be answered only with groans.

"I will soon explain to what these feelings tended; but allow me now to return to the cottagers, whose story excited in me such various feelings of indignation, delight, and wonder, but which all terminated in additional love and reverence for my protectors (for so I loved, in an innocent, half painful self-deceit, to call them).

Chapter VI.

"Some time elapsed before I learned the history of my friends. It was one which could not fail to impress itself deeply on my mind, unfolding as it did a number of circumstances each interesting and wonderful to one so utterly inexperienced as I was.

"The name of the old man was De Lacey. He was descended from a good family in France, where he had lived for many years in affluence, respected by his superiors, and beloved by his equals. His son was bred in the service of his country; and Agatha had ranked with ladies of the highest distinction. A few months before my arrival, they had lived in a large and luxurious city, called Paris, surrounded by friends, and possessed of every enjoyment which virtue, refinement of intellect, or taste, accompanied by a moderate fortune, could afford.

"The father of Safie had been the cause of their ruin. He was a Turkish merchant, and had inhabited Paris for many years, when, for some reason which I could not learn, he became obnoxious to the government. He was seized and cast into prison the very day that Safie arrived from Constantinople to join him. He was tried, and condemned to death. The injustice of his sentence was very flagrant; all Paris was indignant; and it was judged that his religion and wealth, rather than the crime alleged against him, had been the cause of his condemnation.

"Felix had been present at the trial; his horror and indignation were uncontrollable, when he heard the decision of the court. He made, at that moment, a solemn vow to deliver him, and then looked around for the means. After many fruitless attempts to gain admittance to the prison, he found a strongly grated window in an unguarded part of the building, which lighted the dungeon of the unfortunate Mahometan; who, loaded with chains, waited in despair the execution of the barbarous sentence. Felix visited the grate at night, and made known to the prisoner his intentions in his favour. The Turk, amazed and delighted, endeavoured to kindle the zeal of his deliverer by promises of reward and wealth. Felix rejected his offers with contempt; yet when he saw the lovely Safie, who was allowed to visit her father, and who, by her gestures, expressed her lively gratitude, the youth could not help owning to his own mind, that the captive possessed a treasure which would fully reward his toil and hazard.

"The Turk quickly perceived the impression that his daughter had made on the heart of Felix, and endeavoured to secure him more entirely in his interests by the promise of her hand in marriage, so soon as he should be conveyed to a place of safety. Felix was too delicate[1] to accept this offer; yet he looked forward to the probability of that event as to the consummation of his happiness.

"During the ensuing days, while the preparations were going forward for the escape of the merchant, the zeal of Felix was warmed by several letters that he received from this lovely girl, who found means to express her thoughts in the language of her lover by the aid of an old man, a

1. Sensitive to what is proper.

servant of her father's, who understood French. She thanked him in the most ardent terms for his intended services towards her father; and at the same time she gently deplored her own fate.

"I have copies of these letters; for I found means, during my residence in the hovel, to procure the implements of writing; and the letters were often in the hands of Felix or Agatha. Before I depart, I will give them to you, they will prove the truth of my tale; but at present, as the sun is already far declined, I shall only have time to repeat the substance of them to you.

"Safie related, that her mother was a Christian Arab, seized and made a slave by the Turks; recommended by her beauty, she had won the heart of the father of Safie, who married her. The young girl spoke in high and enthusiastic terms of her mother, who, born in freedom spurned the bondage to which she was now reduced. She instructed her daughter in the tenets of her religion, and taught her to aspire to higher powers of intellect, and an independence of spirit, forbidden to the female followers of Mahomet. This lady died; but her lessons were indelibly impressed on the mind of Safie, who sickened at the prospect of again returning to Asia, and the being immured within the walls of a haram, allowed only to occupy herself with puerile amusements, ill suited to the temper of her soul, now accustomed to grand ideas and a noble emulation for virtue. The prospect of marrying a Christian, and remaining in a country where women were allowed to take a rank in society, was enchanting to her.

"The day for the execution of the Turk was fixed; but, on the night previous to it, he had quitted prison, and before morning was distant many leagues from Paris. Felix had procured passports in the name of his father, sister, and himself. He had previously communicated his plan to the former, who aided the deceit by quitting his house, under the pretence of a journey, and concealed himself, with his daughter, in an obscure part of Paris.

"Felix conducted the fugitives through France to Lyons, and across Mont Cenis to Leghorn, where the merchant had decided to wait a favourable opportunity of passing into some part of the Turkish dominions.

"Safie resolved to remain with her father until the moment of his departure, before which time the Turk renewed his promise that she should be united to his deliverer; and Felix remained with them in expectation of that event; and in the mean time he enjoyed the society of the Arabian, who exhibited towards him the simplest and tenderest affection. They conversed with one another through the means of an interpreter, and sometimes with the interpretation of looks; and Safie sang to him the divine airs of her native country.

"The Turk allowed this intimacy to take place, and encouraged the hopes of the youthful lovers, while in his heart he had formed far other plans. He loathed the idea that his daughter should be united to a Christian; but he feared the resentment of Felix if he should appear lukewarm; for he knew that he was still in the power of his deliverer, if he should choose to betray him to the Italian state which they inhabited. He revolved a thousand plans by which he should be enabled to prolong the deceit until it might be no longer necessary, and secretly to take his daughter with him when he departed. His plans were greatly facilitated by the news which arrived from Paris.

"The government of France were greatly enraged at the escape of their victim, and spared no pains to detect and punish his deliverer. The plot of Felix was quickly discovered, and De Lacey and Agatha were thrown into prison. The news reached Felix, and roused him from his dream of pleasure. His blind and aged father, and his gentle sister, lay in a noisome dungeon, while he enjoyed the free air, and the society of her whom he loved. This idea was torture to him. He quickly arranged with the Turk, that if the latter should find a favourable opportunity for escape before Felix could return to Italy, Safie should remain as a boarder at a convent at Leghorn; and then, quitting the lovely Arabian, he hastened to Paris, and delivered himself up to the vengeance of the law, hoping to free De Lacey and Agatha by this proceeding.

"He did not succeed. They remained confined for five months before the trial took place; the result of which deprived them of their fortune, and condemned them to a perpetual exile from their native country.

"They found a miserable asylum in the cottage in Germany, where I discovered them. Felix soon learned that the treacherous Turk, for whom he and his family endured such unheard-of oppression, on discovering that his deliverer was thus reduced to poverty and impotence, became a traitor to good feeling and honour, and had quitted Italy with his daughter, insultingly sending Felix a pittance of money to aid him, as he said, in some plan of future maintenance.

"Such were the events that preyed on the heart of Felix, and rendered him, when I first saw him, the most miserable of his family. He could have endured poverty, and when this distress had been the meed of his virtue, he would have gloried in it: but the ingratitude of the Turk, and the loss of his beloved Safie, were misfortunes more bitter and irreparable. The arrival of the Arabian now infused new life into his soul.

"When the news reached Leghorn, that Felix was deprived of his wealth and rank, the merchant commanded his daughter to think no more of her lover, but to prepare to return with him to her native country. The generous nature of Safie was outraged by this command; she attempted to expostulate with her father, but he left her angrily, reiterating his tyrannical mandate.

"A few days after, the Turk entered his daughter's apartment, and told her hastily, that he had reason to believe that his residence at Leghorn had been divulged, and that he should speedily be delivered up to the French government; he had, consequently, hired a vessel to convey him to Constantinople, for which city he should sail in a few hours. He intended to leave his daughter under the care of a confidential servant, to follow at her leisure with the greater part of his property, which had not yet arrived at Leghorn.

"When alone, Safie resolved in her own mind the plan of conduct that it would become her to pursue in this emergency. A residence in Turkey was abhorrent to her; her religion and feelings were alike adverse to it. By some papers of her father's, which fell into her hands, she heard of the exile of her lover, and learnt the name of the spot where he then resided. She hesitated some time, but at length she formed her determination. Taking with her some jewels that belonged to her, and a small sum of money, she quitted Italy, with an attendant, a native of Leghorn, but who understood the common language of Turkey, and departed for Germany.

"She arrived in safety at a town about twenty leagues from the cottage of De Lacey, when her attendant fell dangerously ill. Safie nursed her with the most devoted affection; but the poor girl died, and the Arabian was left alone, unacquainted with the language of the country, and utterly ignorant of the customs of the world. She fell, however, into good hands. The Italian had mentioned the name of the spot for which they were bound; and, after her death, the woman of the house in which they had lived took care that Safie should arrive in safety at the cottage of her lover.

Chapter VII.

"Such was the history of my beloved cottagers. It impressed me deeply. I learned, from the views of social life which it developed, to admire their virtues, and to deprecate the vices of mankind.

As yet I looked upon crime as a distant evil; benevolence and generosity were ever present before me, inciting within me a desire to become an actor in the busy scene where so many admirable qualities were called forth and displayed. But, in giving an account of the progress of my intellect, I must not omit a circumstance which occurred in the beginning of the month of August of the same year.

"One night, during my accustomed visit to the neighbouring wood, where I collected my own food, and brought home firing for my protectors, I found on the ground a leathern portmanteau, containing several articles of dress and some books. I eagerly seized the prize, and returned with it to my hovel. Fortunately the books were written in the language the elements of which I had acquired at the cottage;[1] they consisted of *Paradise Lost*, a volume of *Plutarch's Lives*, and the *Sorrows of Werter*.[2] The possession of these treasures gave me extreme delight; I now continually studied and exercised my mind upon these histories, whilst my friends were employed in their ordinary occupations.

"I can hardly describe to you the effect of these books. They produced in me an infinity of new images and feelings, that sometimes raised me to ecstacy, but more frequently sunk me into the lowest dejection. In the *Sorrows of Werter*, besides the interest of its simple and affecting story, so many opinions are canvassed, and so many lights thrown upon what had hitherto been to me obscure subjects, that I found in it a never-ending source of speculation and astonishment. The gentle and domestic manners it described, combined with lofty sentiments and feelings, which had for their object something out of self,[3] accorded well with my experience among my protectors, and with the wants which were for ever alive in my own bosom. But I thought Werter himself a more divine being than I had ever beheld or imagined; his character contained no pretension, but it sunk deep. The disquisitions upon death and suicide were calculated to fill me with wonder. I did not pretend to enter into the merits of the case, yet I inclined towards the opinions of the hero, whose extinction I wept, without precisely understanding it.

"As I read, however, I applied much personally to my own feelings and condition. I found myself similar, yet at the same time strangely unlike the beings concerning whom I read, and to whose conversation I was a listener. I sympathized with, and partly understood them, but I was unformed in mind; I was dependent on none, and related to none. 'The path of my departure was free;'[4] and there was none to lament my annihilation. My person was hideous, and my stature gigantic: what did this mean? Who was I? What was I? Whence did I come? What was my destination? These questions continually recurred, but I was unable to solve them.

"The volume of *Plutarch's Lives* which I possessed, contained the histories of the first founders of the ancient republics. This book had a far different effect upon me from the *Sorrors of Werter*. I learned from Werter's imaginations despondency and gloom: but Plutarch taught me high thoughts; he elevated me above the wretched sphere of my own reflections, to admire and love the heroes of past ages. Many things I read surpassed my understanding and experience. I had a very confused

---

1. I.e., French.
2. *The Sorrows of Young Werther* (1774), by Johann Wolfgang von Goethe (1749–1832), is a novel about a sensitive young artist in love with a woman who is engaged to another. Plutarch (c. 46–119), Greek biographer, author of "parallel lives" of Greek and Roman heroes.
3. Other than self-interest.
4. From Percy Shelley's "On Mutability," quoted on p. 64, above.

knowledge of kingdoms, wide extents of country, mighty rivers, and boundless seas. But I was perfectly unacquainted with towns, and large assemblages of men. The cottage of my protectors had been the only school in which I had studied human nature; but this book developed new and mightier scenes of action. I read of men concerned in public affairs governing or massacring their species. I felt the greatest ardour for virtue rise within me, and abhorrence for vice, as far as I understood the signification of those terms, relative as they were, as I applied them, to pleasure and pain alone. Induced by these feelings, I was of course led to admire peaceable law-givers, Numa, Solon, and Lycurgus,[5] in preference to Romulus and Theseus.[6] The patriarchal[7] lives of my protectors caused these impressions to take a firm hold on my mind; perhaps, if my first introduction to humanity had been made by a young soldier, burning for glory and slaughter, I should have been imbued with different sensations.

"But *Paradise Lost* excited different and far deeper emotions. I read it, as I had read the other volumes which had fallen into my hands, as a true history. It moved every feeling of wonder and awe, that the picture of an omnipotent God warring with his creatures was capable of exciting. I often referred the several situations, as their similarity struck me, to my own. Like Adam, I was created apparently united by no link to any other being in existence; but his state was far different from mine in every other respect. He had come forth from the hands of God a perfect creature, happy and prosperous, guarded by the especial care of his Creator; he was allowed to converse with, and acquire knowledge from beings of a superior nature: but I was wretched, helpless, and alone. Many times I considered Satan as the fitter emblem of my condition; for often, like him, when I viewed the bliss of my protectors, the bitter gall of envy rose within me.

"Another circumstance strengthened and confirmed these feelings. Soon after my arrival in the hovel, I discovered some papers in the pocket of the dress which I had taken from your laboratory. At first I had neglected them; but now that I was able to decypher the characters in which they were written, I began to study them with diligence. It was your journal of the four months that preceded my creation. You minutely described in these papers every step you took in the progress of your work; this history was mingled with accounts of domestic occurrences. You, doubtless, recollect these papers. Here they are. Every thing is related in them which bears reference to my accursed origin; the whole detail of that series of disgusting circumstances which produced it is set in view; the minutest description of my odious and

---

5. Athenian statesman and reformer (c. 390–324 B.C.). Numa Pompilius (715–673 B.C.), second king of Rome. Solon (6th century B.C.), Athenian statesman and poet.
6. Legendary Athenian hero. Romulus, legendary founder (with Remus) of Rome.
7. Hierarchical, deferential.

loathsome person is given, in language which painted your own horrors, and rendered mine ineffaceable. I sickened as I read. 'Hateful day when I received life!' I exclaimed in agony. 'Cursed creator! Why did you form a monster so hideous that even you turned from me in disgust? God in pity made man beautiful and alluring, after his own image; but my form is a filthy type of your's, more horrid from its very resemblance. Satan had his companions, fellow-devils, to admire and encourage him; but I am solitary and detested.'

"These were the reflections of my hours of despondency and solitude; but when I contemplated the virtues of the cottagers, their amiable and benevolent dispositions, I persuaded myself that when they should become acquainted with my admiration of their virtues, they would compassionate me, and overlook my personal deformity. Could they turn from their door one, however monstrous, who solicited their compassion and friendship? I resolved, at least, not to despair, but in every way to fit myself for an interview with them which would decide my fate. I postponed this attempt for some months longer; for the importance attached to its success inspired me with a dread lest I should fail. Besides, I found that my understanding improved so much with every day's experience, that I was unwilling to commence this undertaking until a few more months should have added to my wisdom.

"Several changes, in the mean time, took place in the cottage. The presence of Safie diffused happiness among its inhabitants; and I also found that a greater degree of plenty reigned there. Felix and Agatha spent more time in amusement and conversation, and were assisted in their labours by servants. They did not appear rich, but they were contented and happy; their feelings were serene and peaceful, while mine became every day more tumultuous. Increase of knowledge only discovered to me more clearly what a wretched outcast I was. I cherished hope, it is true; but it vanished, when I beheld my person reflected in water, or my shadow in the moon-shine, even as that frail image and that inconstant shade.

"I endeavoured to crush these fears, and to fortify myself for the trial which in a few months I resolved to undergo; and sometimes I allowed my thoughts, unchecked by reason, to ramble in the fields of Paradise, and dared to fancy amiable and lovely creatures sympathizing with my feelings and cheering my gloom; their angelic countenances breathed smiles of consolation. But it was all a dream: no Eve soothed my sorrows, or shared my thoughts; I was alone. I remembered Adam's supplication to his Creator;[8] but where was mine? he had abandoned me, and, in the bitterness of my heart, I cursed him.

"Autumn passed thus. I saw, with surprise and grief, the leaves decay and fall, and nature again assume the barren and bleak appearance it

---

8. Adam asks God for a "human consort" in *Paradise Lost* VIII.357ff.; see also p. 3, above.

had worn when I first beheld the woods and the lovely moon. Yet I did not heed the bleakness of the weather; I was better fitted by my conformation[9] for the endurance of cold than heat. But my chief delights were the sight of the flowers, the birds, and all the gay apparel of summer; when those deserted me, I turned with more attention towards the cottagers. Their happiness was not decreased by the absence of summer. They loved, and sympathized with one another; and their joys, depending on each other, were not interrupted by the casualties that took place around them. The more I saw of them, the greater became my desire to claim their protection and kindness; my heart yearned to be known and loved by these amiable creatures: to see their sweet looks turned towards me with affection, was the utmost limit of my ambition. I dared not think that they would turn them from me with disdain and horror. The poor that stopped at their door were never driven away. I asked, it is true, for greater treasures than a little food or rest; I required kindness and sympathy; but I did not believe myself utterly unworthy of it.

"The winter advanced, and an entire revolution of the seasons had taken place since I awoke into life. My attention, at this time, was solely directed towards my plan of introducing myself into the cottage of my protectors. I revolved many projects; but that on which I finally fixed was, to enter the dwelling when the blind old man should be alone. I had sagacity enough to discover, that the unnatural hideousness of my person was the chief object of horror with those who had formerly beheld me. My voice, although harsh, had nothing terrible in it; I thought, therefore, that if, in the absence of his children, I could gain the good-will and mediation of the old De Lacy,[1] I might, by his means, be tolerated by my younger protectors.

"One day, when the sun shone on the red leaves that strewed the ground, and diffused cheerfulness, although it denied warmth, Safie, Agatha, and Felix, departed on a long country walk, and the old man, at his own desire, was left alone in the cottage. When his children had departed, he took up his guitar, and played several mournful, but sweet airs, more sweet and mournful than I had ever heard him play before. At first his countenance was illuminated with pleasure, but, as he continued, thoughtfulness and sadness succeeded; at length, laying aside the instrument, he sat absorbed in reflection.

"My heart beat quick; this was the hour and moment of trial, which would decide my hopes, or realize my fears. The servants were gone to a neighbouring fair. All was silent in and around the cottage: it was an excellent opportunity; yet, when I proceeded to execute my plan, my limbs failed me, and I sunk to the ground. Again I rose; and, exerting all the firmness of which I was master, removed the planks which I had

9. Constitution, design.
1. This name changes its spelling at this point in the 1818 edition.

placed before my hovel to conceal my retreat. The fresh air revived me, and, with renewed determination, I approached the door of their cottage.

"I knocked. 'Who is there?' said the old man — 'Come in.'

"I entered; 'Pardon this intrusion,' said I, 'I am a traveller in want of a little rest; you would greatly oblige me, if you would allow me to remain a few minutes before the fire.'

" 'Enter,' said De Lacy; 'and I will try in what manner I can relieve your wants; but, unfortunately, my children are from home, and, as I am blind, I am afraid I shall find it difficult to procure food for you.'

" 'Do not trouble yourself, my kind host, I have food; it is warmth and rest only that I need.'

"I sat down, and a silence ensued. I knew that every minute was precious to me, yet I remained irresolute in what manner to commence the interview; when the old man addressed me —

" 'By your language, stranger, I suppose you are my countryman; — are you French?'

" 'No; but I was educated by a French family, and understand that language only. I am now going to claim the protection of some friends, whom I sincerely love, and of whose favour I have some hopes.'

" 'Are these Germans?'

" 'No, they are French. But let us change the subject. I am an unfortunate and deserted creature; I look around, and I have no relation or friend upon earth. These amiable people to whom I go have never seen me, and know little of me. I am full of fears; for if I fail there, I am an outcast in the world for ever.'

" 'Do not despair. To be friendless is indeed to be unfortunate; but the hearts of men, when unprejudiced by any obvious self-interest, are full of brotherly love and charity. Rely, therefore, on your hopes; and if these friends are good and amiable, do not despair.'

" 'They are kind — they are the most excellent creatures in the world; but, unfortunately, they are prejudiced against me. I have good dispositions; my life has been hitherto harmless, and, in some degree, beneficial; but a fatal prejudice clouds their eyes, and where they ought to see a feeling and kind friend, they behold only a detestable monster.'

" 'That is indeed unfortunate; but if you are really blameless, cannot you undeceive them?'

" 'I am about to undertake that task; and it is on that account that I feel so many overwhelming terrors. I tenderly love these friends; I have, unknown to them, been for many months in the habits of daily kindness towards them; but they believe that I wish to injure them, and it is that prejudice which I wish to overcome.'

" 'Where do these friends reside?'

" 'Near this spot.'

"The old man paused, and then continued, 'If you will unreservedly confide to me the particulars of your tale, I perhaps may be of use in undeceiving them. I am blind, and cannot judge of your countenance, but there is something in your words which persuades me that you are sincere. I am poor, and an exile; but it will afford me true pleasure to be in any way serviceable to a human creature.'

" 'Excellent man! I thank you, and accept your generous offer. You raise me from the dust by this kindness; and I trust that, by your aid, I shall not be driven from the society and sympathy of your fellow-creatures.'

" 'Heaven forbid! even if you were really criminal; for that can only drive you to desperation, and not instigate you to virtue. I also am unfortunate; I and my family have been condemned, although innocent: judge, therefore, if I do not feel for your misfortunes.'

" 'How can I thank you, my best and only benefactor? from your lips first have I heard the voice of kindness directed towards me; I shall be for ever grateful; and your present humanity assures me of success with those friends whom I am on the point of meeting.'

" 'May I know the names and residence of those friends?'

"I paused. This, I thought, was the moment of decision, which was to rob me of, or bestow happiness on me for ever. I struggled vainly for firmness sufficient to answer him, but the effort destroyed all my remaining strength; I sank on the chair, and sobbed aloud. At that moment I heard the steps of my younger protectors. I had not a moment to lose; but, seizing the hand of the old man, I cried, 'Now is the time! — save and protect me! You and your family are the friends whom I seek. Do not you desert me in the hour of trial!'

" 'Great God!' exclaimed the old man, 'who are you?'

"At that instant the cottage door was opened, and Felix, Safie, and Agatha entered. Who can describe their horror and consternation on beholding me? Agatha fainted; and Safie, unable to attend to her friend, rushed out of the cottage. Felix darted forward, and with supernatural force tore me from his father, to whose knees I clung: in a transport of fury, he dashed me to the ground, and struck me violently with a stick. I could have torn him limb from limb, as the lion rends the antelope. But my heart sunk within me as with bitter sickness, and I refrained. I saw him on the point of repeating his blow, when, overcome by pain and anguish, I quitted the cottage, and in the general tumult escaped unperceived to my hovel.

Chapter VIII.

"Cursed, cursed creator! Why did I live? Why, in that instant, did I not extinguish the spark of existence which you had so wantonly bestowed?

I know not; despair had not yet taken possession of me; my feelings were those of rage and revenge. I could with pleasure have destroyed the cottage and its inhabitants, and have glutted myself with their shrieks and misery.

"When night came, I quitted my retreat, and wandered in the wood; and now, no longer restrained by the fear of discovery, I gave vent to my anguish in fearful howlings. I was like a wild beast that had broken the toils; destroying the objects that obstructed me, and ranging through the wood with a stag-like swiftness. Oh! what a miserable night I passed! the cold stars shone in mockery, and the bare trees waved their branches above me: now and then the sweet voice of a bird burst forth amidst the universal stillness. All, save I, were at rest or in enjoyment: I, like the arch fiend, bore a hell within me;[1] and, finding myself unsympathized with, wished to tear up the trees, spread havoc and destruction around me, and then to have sat down and enjoyed the ruin.

"But this was a luxury of sensation that could not endure; I became fatigued with excess of bodily exertion, and sank on the damp grass in the sick impotence of despair. There was none among the myriads of men that existed who would pity or assist me; and should I feel kindness towards my enemies? No: from that moment I declared everlasting war against the species, and, more than all, against him who had formed me, and sent me forth to this insupportable misery.

"The sun rose; I heard the voices of men, and knew that it was impossible to return to my retreat during that day. Accordingly I hid myself in some thick underwood, determining to devote the ensuing hours to reflection on my situation.

"The pleasant sunshine, and the pure air of day, restored me to some degree of tranquillity; and when I considered what had passed at the cottage, I could not help believing that I had been too hasty in my conclusions. I had certainly acted imprudently. It was apparent that my conversation had interested the father in my behalf, and I was a fool in having exposed my person to the horror of his children. I ought to have familiarized the old De Lacy to me, and by degrees have discovered myself to the rest of his family, when they should have been prepared for my approach. But I did not believe my errors to be irretrievable; and, after much consideration, I resolved to return to the cottage, seek the old man, and by my representations win him to my party.

"These thoughts calmed me, and in the afternoon I sank into a profound sleep; but the fever of my blood did not allow me to be visited by peaceful dreams. The horrible scene of the preceding day was for ever acting before my eyes; the females were flying, and the enraged

---

1. Cf. Satan in *Paradise Lost*: "Me miserable! which way shall I fly / Infinite wrath, and infinite despair? / Which way I fly is Hell; myself am Hell" (IV.73–75).

Felix tearing me from his father's feet. I awoke exhausted; and, finding that it was already night, I crept forth from my hiding-place, and went in search of food.

"When my hunger was appeased, I directed my steps towards the well-known path that conducted to the cottage. All there was at peace. I crept into my hovel, and remained in silent expectation of the accustomed hour when the family arose. That hour past, the sun mounted high in the heavens, but the cottagers did not appear. I trembled violently, apprehending some dreadful misfortune. The inside of the cottage was dark, and I heard no motion; I cannot describe the agony of this suspence.

"Presently two countrymen passed by; but, pausing near the cottage, they entered into conversation, using violent gesticulations; but I did not understand what they said, as they spoke the language of the country,[2] which differed from that of my protectors. Soon after, however, Felix approached with another man: I was surprised, as I knew that he had not quitted the cottage that morning, and waited anxiously to discover, from his discourse, the meaning of these unusual appearances.

" 'Do you consider,' said his companion to him, 'that you will be obliged to pay three months' rent, and to lose the produce of your garden? I do not wish to take any unfair advantage, and I beg therefore that you will take some days to consider of your determination.'

" 'It is utterly useless,' replied Felix, 'we can never again inhabit your cottage. The life of my father is in the greatest danger, owing to the dreadful circumstance that I have related. My wife and my sister will never recover their horror. I entreat you not to reason with me any more. Take possession of your tenement, and let me fly from this place.'

"Felix trembled violently as he said this. He and his companion entered the cottage, in which they remained for a few minutes, and then departed. I never saw any of the family of De Lacy more.

"I continued for the remainder of the day in my hovel in a state of utter and stupid despair. My protectors had departed, and had broken the only link that held me to the world. For the first time the feelings of revenge and hatred filled my bosom, and I did not strive to controul them; but, allowing myself to be borne away by the stream, I bent my mind towards injury and death. When I thought of my friends, of the mild voice of De Lacy, the gentle eyes of Agatha, and the exquisite beauty of the Arabian, these thoughts vanished, and a gush of tears somewhat soothed me. But again, when I reflected that they had spurned and deserted me, anger returned, a rage of anger; and, unable to injure any thing human, I turned my fury towards inanimate objects. As night advanced, I placed a variety of combustibles around the cottage; and, after having destroyed every vestige of cultivation in the gar-

2. I.e., German.

den, I waited with forced impatience until the moon had sunk to commence my operations.

"As the night advanced, a fierce wind arose from the woods, and quickly dispersed the clouds that had loitered in the heavens: the blast tore along like a mighty avelanche, and produced a kind of insanity in my spirits, that burst all bounds of reason and reflection. I lighted the dry branch of a tree, and danced with fury around the devoted cottage, my eyes still fixed on the western horizon, the edge of which the moon nearly touched. A part of its orb was at length hid, and I waved my brand; it sunk, and, with a loud scream, I fired the straw, and heath, and bushes, which I had collected. The wind fanned the fire, and the cottage was quickly enveloped by the flames, which clung to it, and licked it with their forked and destroying tongues.

"As soon as I was convinced that no assistance could save any part of the habitation, I quitted the scene, and sought for refuge in the woods.

"And now, with the world before me, whither should I bend my steps?[3] I resolved to fly far from the scene of my misfortunes; but to me, hated and despised, every country must be equally horrible. At length the thought of you crossed my mind. I learned from your papers that you were my father, my creator; and to whom could I apply with more fitness than to him who had given me life? Among the lessons that Felix had bestowed upon Safie geography had not been omitted: I had learned from these the relative situations of the different countries of the earth. You had mentioned Geneva as the name of your native town; and towards this place I resolved to proceed.

"But how was I to direct myself? I knew that I must travel in a south-westerly direction to reach my destination; but the sun was my only guide. I did not know the names of the towns that I was to pass through, nor could I ask information from a single human being; but I did not despair. From you only could I hope for succour, although towards you I felt no sentiment but that of hatred. Unfeeling, heartless creator! you had endowed me with perceptions and passions, and then cast me abroad an object for the scorn and horror of mankind. But on you only had I any claim for pity and redress, and from you I determined to seek that justice which I vainly attempted to gain from any other being that wore the human form.

"My travels were long, and the sufferings I endured intense. It was late in autumn when I quitted the district where I had so long resided. I travelled only at night, fearful of encountering the visage of a human being. Nature decayed around me, and the sun became heatless; rain and snow poured around me; mighty rivers were frozen; the surface of

---

3. Cf. the final lines of *Paradise Lost*: "The World was all before them, where to choose / Thir place of rest, and Providence thir guide: / They hand in hand with wand'ring steps and slow, / Through *Eden* took thir solitary way" (XII.646–69).

the earth was hard, and chill, and bare, and I found no shelter. Oh, earth! how often did I imprecate curses on the cause of my being! The mildness of my nature had fled, and all within me was turned to gall and bitterness. The nearer I approached to your habitation, the more deeply did I feel the spirit of revenge enkindled in my heart. Snow fell, and the waters were hardened, but I rested not. A few incidents now and then directed me, and I possessed a map of the country; but I often wandered wide from my path. The agony of my feelings allowed me no respite: no incident occurred from which my rage and misery could not extract its food; but a circumstance that happened when I arrived on the confines of Switzerland, when the sun had recovered its warmth, and the earth again began to look green, confirmed in an especial manner the bitterness and horror of my feelings.

"I generally rested during the day, and travelled only when I was secured by night from the view of man. One morning, however, finding that my path lay through a deep wood, I ventured to continue my journey after the sun had risen; the day, which was one of the first of spring, cheered even me by the loveliness of its sunshine and the balminess of the air. I felt emotions of gentleness and pleasure, that had long appeared dead, revive within me. Half surprised by the novelty of these sensations, I allowed myself to be borne away by them; and, forgetting my solitude and deformity, dared to be happy. Soft tears again bedewed my cheeks, and I even raised my humid eyes with thankfulness towards the blessed sun which bestowed such joy upon me.

"I continued to wind among the paths of the wood, until I came to its boundary, which was skirted by a deep and rapid river, into which many of the trees bent their branches, now budding with the fresh spring. Here I paused, not exactly knowing what path to pursue, when I heard the sound of voices, that induced me to conceal myself under the shade of a cypress. I was scarcely hid, when a young girl came running towards the spot where I was concealed, laughing as if she ran from some one in sport. She continued her course along the precipitous sides of the river, when suddenly her foot slipt; and she fell into the rapid stream. I rushed from my hiding place, and, with extreme labour from the force of the current, saved her, and dragged her to shore. She was senseless; and I endeavoured, by every means in my power, to restore animation, when I was suddenly interrupted by the approach of a rustic, who was probably the person from whom she had playfully fled. On seeing me, he darted towards me, and, tearing the girl from my arms, hastened towards the deeper parts of the wood. I followed speedily, I hardly knew why; but when the man saw me draw near, he aimed a gun, which he carried, at my body, and fired. I sunk to the ground, and my injurer, with increased swiftness, escaped into the wood.

"This was then the reward of my benevolence! I had saved a human being from destruction, and, as a recompence, I now writhed under the miserable pain of a wound, which shattered the flesh and bone. The feelings of kindness and gentleness, which I had entertained but a few moments before, gave place to hellish rage and gnashing of teeth. Inflamed by pain, I vowed eternal hatred and vengeance to all mankind. But the agony of my wound overcame me; my pulses paused, and I fainted.

"For some weeks I led a miserable life in the woods, endeavouring to cure the wound which I had received. The ball had entered my shoulder, and I knew not whether it had remained there or passed through; at any rate I had no means of extracting it. My sufferings were augmented also by the oppressive sense of the injustice and ingratitude of their infliction. My daily vows rose for revenge — a deep and deadly revenge, such as would alone compensate for the outrages and anguish I had endured.

"After some weeks my wound healed, and I continued my journey. The labours I endured were no longer to be alleviated by the bright sun or gentle breezes of spring; all joy was but a mockery, which insulted my desolate state, and made me feel more painfully that I was not made for the enjoyment of pleasure.

"But my toils now drew near a close; and, two months from this time, I reached the environs of Geneva.

"It was evening when I arrived, and I retired to a hiding-place among the fields that surround it, to meditate in what manner I should apply to you. I was oppressed by fatigue and hunger, and far too unhappy to enjoy the gentle breezes of evening, or the prospect of the sun setting behind the stupendous mountains of Jura.

"At this time a slight sleep relieved me from the pain of reflection, which was disturbed by the approach of a beautiful child, who came running into the recess I had chosen with all the sportiveness of infancy. Suddenly, as I gazed on him, an idea seized me, that this little creature was unprejudiced, and had lived too short a time to have imbibed a horror of deformity. If, therefore, I could seize him, and educate him as my companion and friend, I should not be so desolate in this peopled earth.

"Urged by this impulse, I seized on the boy as he passed, and drew him towards me. As soon as he beheld my form, he placed his hands before his eyes, and uttered a shrill scream: I drew his hand forcibly from his face, and said, 'Child, what is the meaning of this? I do not intend to hurt you; listen to me.'

"He struggled violently; 'Let me go,' he cried; 'monster! ugly wretch! you wish to eat me, and tear me to pieces — You are an ogre — Let me go, or I will tell my papa.'

" 'Boy, you will never see your father again; you must come with me.'

" 'Hideous monster! let me go; My papa is a Syndic—he is M. Frankenstein—he would punish you. You dare not keep me.'

" 'Frankenstein! you belong then to my enemy—to him towards whom I have sworn eternal revenge, you shall be my first victim.'

"The child still struggled, and loaded me with epithets which carried despair to my heart: I grasped his throat to silence him, and in a moment he lay dead at my feet.

"I gazed on my victim, and my heart swelled with exultation and hellish triumph: clapping my hands, I exclaimed, 'I, too, can create desolation; my enemy is not impregnable; this death will carry despair to him, and a thousand other miseries shall torment and destroy him.'

"As I fixed my eyes on the child, I saw something glittering on his breast. I took it; it was a portrait of a most lovely woman. In spite of my malignity, it softened and attracted me. For a few moments I gazed with delight on her dark eyes, fringed by deep lashes, and her lovely lips; but presently my rage returned: I remembered that I was for ever deprived of the delights that such beautiful creatures could bestow; and that she whose resemblance I contemplated would, in regarding me, have changed that air of divine benignity to one expressive of disgust and affright.

"Can you wonder that such thoughts transported me with rage? I only wonder that at that moment, instead of venting my sensations in exclamations and agony, I did not rush among mankind, and perish in the attempt to destroy them.

"While I was overcome by these feelings, I left the spot where I had committed the murder, and was seeking a more secluded hiding-place, when I perceived a woman passing near me. She was young, not indeed so beautiful as her whose portrait I held, but of an agreeable aspect, and blooming in the loveliness of youth and health. Here, I thought, is one of those whose smiles are bestowed on all but me; she shall not escape: thanks to the lessons of Felix, and the sanguinary[4] laws of man, I have learned how to work mischief. I approached her unperceived, and placed the portrait securely in one of the folds of her dress.

"For some days I haunted the spot where these scenes had taken place; sometimes wishing to see you, sometimes resolved to quit the world and its miseries for ever. At length I wandered towards these mountains, and have ranged through their immense recesses, consumed by a burning passion which you alone can gratify. We may not part until you have promised to comply with my requisition.[5] I am alone, and miserable; man will not associate with me; but one as deformed and horrible as myself would not deny herself to me. My companion must be of the same species, and have the same defects. This being you must create."

4. Bloodthirsty.
5. Demand or requirement.

Chapter IX.

The being finished speaking, and fixed his looks upon me in expectation of a reply. But I was bewildered, perplexed, and unable to arrange my ideas sufficiently to understand the full extent of his proposition. He continued—

"You must create a female for me, with whom I can live in the interchange of those sympathies necessary for my being. This you alone can do; and I demand it of you as a right which you must not refuse."

The latter part of his tale had kindled anew in me the anger that had died away while he narrated his peaceful life among the cottagers, and, as he said this, I could no longer suppress the rage that burned within me.

"I do refuse it," I replied; "and no torture shall ever extort a consent from me. You may render me the most miserable of men, but you shall never make me base in my own eyes. Shall I create another like yourself, whose joint wickedness might desolate the world. Begone! I have answered you; you may torture me, but I will never consent."

"You are in the wrong,' replied the fiend; "and, instead of threatening, I am content to reason with you. I am malicious because I am miserable; am I not shunned and hated by all mankind? You, my creator, would tear me to pieces, and triumph; remember that, and tell me why I should pity man more than he pities me? You would not call it murder, if you could precipitate me into one of those ice-rifts, and destroy my frame, the work of your own hands. Shall I respect man, when he contemns[1] me? Let him live with me in the interchange of kindness, and, instead of injury, I would bestow every benefit upon him with tears of gratitude at his acceptance. But that cannot be; the human senses are insurmountable barriers to our union. Yet mine shall not be the submission of abject slavery. I will revenge my injuries: if I cannot inspire love, I will cause fear; and chiefly towards you my arch-enemy, because my creator, do I swear inextinguishable hatred. Have a care: I will work at your destruction, nor finish until I desolate your heart, so that you curse the hour of your birth."

A fiendish rage animated him as he said this; his face was wrinkled into contortions too horrible for human eyes to behold; but presently he calmed himself, and proceeded—

"I intended to reason. This passion is detrimental to me; for you do not reflect that you are the cause of its excess. If any being felt emotions of benevolence towards me, I should return them an hundred and an hundred fold; for that one creature's sake, I would make peace with the whole kind! But I now indulge in dreams of bliss that cannot be realized. What I ask of you is reasonable and moderate; I demand a

---

1. Treats with contempt.

creature of another sex, but as hideous as myself: the gratification is small, but it is all that I can receive, and it shall content me. It is true, we shall be monsters, cut off from all the world; but on that account we shall be more attached to one another. Our lives will not be happy, but they will be harmless, and free from the misery I now feel. Oh! my creator, make me happy; let me feel gratitude towards you for one benefit! Let me see that I excite the sympathy of some existing thing; do not deny me my request!"

I was moved. I shuddered when I thought of the possible conse-quences of my consent; but I felt that there was some justice in his argument. His tale, and the feelings he now expressed, proved him to be a creature of fine sensations; and did I not, as his maker, owe him all the portion of happiness that it was in my power to bestow? He saw my change of feeling, and continued —

"If you consent, neither you nor any other human being shall ever see us again: I will go to the vast wilds of South America. My food is not that of man; I do not destroy the lamb and the kid, to glut my appetite; acorns and berries afford me sufficient nourishment. My com-panion will be of the same nature as myself, and will be content with the same fare. We shall make our bed of dried leaves; the sun will shine on us as on man, and will ripen our food. The picture I present to you is peaceful and human, and you must feel that you could deny it only in the wantonness of power and cruelty. Pitiless as you have been towards me, I now see compassion in your eyes; let me seize the favourable moment, and persuade you to promise what I so ardently desire."

"You propose," replied I, "to fly from the habitations of man, to dwell in those wilds where the beasts of the field will be your only compan-ions. How can you, who long for the love and sympathy of man, per-severe in this exile? You will return, and again seek their kindness, and you will meet with their detestation; your evil passions will be renewed, and you will then have a companion to aid you in the task of destruc-tion. This may not be; cease to argue the point, for I cannot consent."

"How inconstant are your feelings! but a moment ago you were moved by my representations, and why do you again harden yourself to my complaints? I swear to you, by the earth which I inhabit, and by you that made me, that, with the companion you bestow, I will quit the neighbourhood of man, and dwell, as it may chance, in the most savage of places. My evil passions will have fled, for I shall meet with sympathy; my life will flow quietly away, and, in my dying moments, I shall not curse my maker."

His words had a strange effect upon me. I compassionated him, and sometimes felt a wish to console him; but when I looked upon him, when I saw the filthy mass that moved and talked, my heart sickened, and my feelings were altered to those of horror and hatred. I tried to stifle these sensations; I thought, that as I could not sympathize with him, I had no right to withhold from him the small portion of happiness which was yet in my power to bestow.

"You swear," I said, "to be harmless; but have you not already shewn a degree of malice that should reasonably make me distrust you? May not even this be a feint that will increase your triumph by affording a wider scope for your revenge?"

"How is this? I thought I had moved your compassion, and yet you still refuse to bestow on me the only benefit that can soften my heart, and render me harmless. If I have no ties and no affections, hatred and vice must be my portion; the love of another will destroy the cause of my crimes, and I shall become a thing, of whose existence every one will be ignorant. My vices are the children of a forced solitude that I abhor; and my virtues will necessarily arise when I live in communion with an equal. I shall feel the affections of a sensitive being, and become linked to the chain of existence and events, from which I am now excluded."

I paused some time to reflect on all he had related, and the various arguments which he had employed. I thought of the promise of virtues which he had displayed on the opening of his existence, and the subsequent blight of all kindly feeling by the loathing and scorn which his protectors had manifested towards him. His power and threats were not omitted in my calculations: a creature who could exist in the ice caves of the glaciers, and hide himself from pursuit among the ridges of inaccessible precipices, was a being possessing faculties it would be vain to cope with. After a long pause of reflection, I concluded, that the justice due both to him and my fellow-creatures demanded of me that I should comply with his request. Turning to him, therefore, I said—

"I consent to your demand, on your solemn oath to quit Europe for ever, and every other place in the neighbourhood of man, as soon as I shall deliver into your hands a female who will accompany you in your exile."

"I swear," he cried, "by the sun, and by the blue sky of heaven, that if you grant my prayer, while they exist you shall never behold me again. Depart to your home, and commence your labours: I shall watch their progress with unutterable anxiety; and fear not but that when you are ready I shall appear."

Saying this, he suddenly quitted me, fearful, perhaps, of any change in my sentiments. I saw him descend the mountain with greater speed than the flight of an eagle, and quickly lost him among the undulations of the sea of ice.

His tale had occupied the whole day; and the sun was upon the verge of the horizon when he departed. I knew that I ought to hasten my descent towards the valley, as I should soon be encompassed in darkness; but my heart was heavy, and my steps slow. The labour of winding among the little paths of the mountains, and fixing my feet firmly as I advanced, perplexed me, occupied as I was by the emotions which the occurrences of the day had produced. Night was far advanced, when I came to the half-way resting-place, and seated myself beside the fountain. The stars shone at intervals, as the clouds passed from over them; the dark pines rose before me, and every here and there a broken tree lay on the ground: it was a scene of wonderful solemnity, and stirred strange thoughts within me. I wept bitterly; and, clasping my hands in agony, I exclaimed, "Oh! stars, and clouds, and winds, ye are all about to mock me: if ye really pity me, crush sensation and memory; let me become as nought; but if not, depart, depart and leave me in darkness."

These were wild and miserable thoughts; but I cannot describe to you how the eternal twinkling of the stars weighed upon me, and how I listened to every blast of wind, as if it were a dull ugly siroc[2] on its way to consume me.

Morning dawned before I arrived at the village of Chamounix; but my presence, so haggard and strange, hardly calmed the fears of my family, who had waited the whole night in anxious expectation of my return.

The following day we returned to Geneva. The intention of my father in coming had been to divert my mind, and to restore me to my lost tranquillity; but the medicine had been fatal. And, unable to account for the excess of misery I appeared to suffer, he hastened to return home, hoping the quiet and monotony of a domestic life would by degrees alleviate my sufferings from whatsoever cause they might spring.

For myself, I was passive in all their arrangements; and the gentle affection of my beloved Elizabeth was inadequate to draw me from the depth of my despair. The promise I had made to the dæmon weighed upon my mind, like Dante's iron cowl on the heads of the hellish hypocrites.[3] All pleasures of earth and sky passed before me like a dream, and that thought only had to me the reality of life. Can you wonder, that sometimes a kind of insanity possessed me, or that I saw continually about me a multitude of filthy animals inflicting on me incessant torture, that often extorted screams and bitter groans?

By degrees, however, these feelings became calmed. I entered again into the every-day scene of life, if not with interest, at least with some degree of tranquillity.

END OF VOL. II.

---

2. Sirocco; a hot and blighting wind that blows from North Africa across the Mediterranean.
3. In canto XXIII of Dante's *Inferno* (see p. 35, n. 1, above), the hypocrites wear monks' hoods that are dazzling on the outside but inside are lined with lead.

Volume III

Chapter I.

Day after day, week after week, passed away on my return to Geneva; and I could not collect the courage to recommence my work. I feared the vengeance of the disappointed fiend, yet I was unable to overcome my repugnance to the task which was enjoined me. I found that I could not compose a female without again devoting several months to profound study and laborious disquisition.[1] I had heard of some discoveries having been made by an English philosopher, the knowledge of which was material to my success, and I sometimes thought of obtaining my father's consent to visit England for this purpose; but I clung to every pretence of delay, and could not resolve to interrupt my returning tranquillity. My health, which had hitherto declined, was now much restored; and my spirits, when unchecked by the memory of my unhappy promise, rose proportionably. My father saw this change with pleasure, and he turned his thoughts towards the best method of eradicating the remains of my melancholy, which every now and then would return by fits, and with a devouring blackness overcast the approaching sunshine. At these moments I took refuge in the most perfect solitude. I passed whole days on the lake alone in a little boat, watching the clouds, and listening to the rippling of the waves, silent and listless. But the fresh air and bright sun seldom failed to restore me to some degree of composure; and, on my return, I met the salutations of my friends with a readier smile and a more cheerful heart.

It was after my return from one of these rambles that my father, calling me aside, thus addressed me: —

"I am happy to remark, my dear son, that you have resumed your former pleasures, and seem to be returning to yourself. And yet you are still unhappy, and still avoid our society. For some time I was lost in conjecture as to the cause of this; but yesterday an idea struck me, and if it is well founded, I conjure you to avow it. Reserve on such a point would be not only useless, but draw down treble misery on us all."

I trembled violently at this exordium,[2] and my father continued —

1. Investigation, research.
2. Beginning (of a discourse).

"I confess, my son, that I have always looked forward to your marriage with your cousin as the tie of our domestic comfort, and the stay of my declining years. You were attached to each other from your earliest infancy; you studied together, and appeared, in dispositions and tastes, entirely suited to one another. But so blind is the experience of man, that what I conceived to be the best assistants to my plan may have entirely destroyed it. You, perhaps, regard her as your sister, without any wish that she might become your wife. Nay, you may have met with another whom you may love; and, considering yourself as bound in honour to your cousin, this struggle may occasion the poignant misery which you appear to feel."

"My dear father, re-assure yourself. I love my cousin tenderly and sincerely. I never saw any woman who excited, as Elizabeth does, my warmest admiration and affection. My future hopes and prospects are entirely bound up in the expectation of our union."

"The expression of your sentiments on this subject, my dear Victor, gives me more pleasure than I have for some time experienced. If you feel thus, we shall assuredly be happy, however present events may cast a gloom over us. But it is this gloom, which appears to have taken so strong a hold of your mind, that I wish to dissipate. Tell me, therefore, whether you object to an immediate solemnization of the marriage. We have been unfortunate, and recent events have drawn us from that every-day tranquillity befitting my years and infirmities. You are younger; yet I do not suppose, possessed as you are of a competent fortune, that an early marriage would at all interfere with any future plans of honour and utility that you may have formed. Do not suppose, however, that I wish to dictate happiness to you, or that a delay on your part would cause me any serious uneasiness. Interpret my words with candour,[3] and answer me, I conjure you, with confidence and sincerity."

I listened to my father in silence, and remained for some time incapable of offering any reply. I revolved rapidly in my mind a multitude of thoughts, and endeavoured to arrive at some conclusion. Alas! to me the idea of an immediate union with my cousin was one of horror and dismay. I was bound by a solemn promise, which I had not yet fulfilled, and dared not break; or, if I did, what manifold miseries might not impend over me and my devoted family! Could I enter into a festival with this deadly weight yet hanging round my neck, and bowing me to the ground. I must perform my engagement,[4] and let the monster depart with his mate, before I allowed myself to enjoy the delight of an union from which I expected peace.

I remembered also the necessity imposed upon me of either journeying to England, or entering into a long correspondence with those philosophers of that country, whose knowledge and discoveries were of

3. Kindliness, favorable disposition.
4. Promise, obligation.

indispensable use to me in my present undertaking. The latter method of obtaining the desired intelligence was dilatory and unsatisfactory: besides, any variation was agreeable to me, and I was delighted with the idea of spending a year or two in change of scene and variety of occupation, in absence from my family; during which period some event might happen which would restore me to them in peace and happiness: my promise might be fulfilled, and the monster have departed; or some accident might occur to destroy him, and put an end to my slavery for ever.

These feelings dictated my answer to my father. I expressed a wish to visit England; but, concealing the true reasons of this request, I clothed my desires under the guise of wishing to travel and see the world before I sat down for life within the walls of my native town.

I urged my entreaty with earnestness, and my father was easily induced to comply; for a more indulgent and less dictatorial parent did not exist upon earth. Our plan was soon arranged. I should travel to Strasburgh, where Clerval would join me. Some short time would be spent in the towns of Holland, and our principal stay would be in England. We should return by France; and it was agreed that the tour should occupy the space of two years.

My father pleased himself with the reflection, that my union with Elizabeth should take place immediately on my return to Geneva. "These two years," said he, "will pass swiftly, and it will be the last delay that will oppose itself to your happiness. And, indeed, I earnestly desire that period to arrive, when we shall all be united, and neither hopes or fears arise to disturb our domestic calm."

"I am content," I replied, "with your arrangement. By that time we shall both have become wiser, and I hope happier, than we at present are." I sighed; but my father kindly forbore to question me further concerning the cause of my dejection. He hoped that new scenes, and the amusement of travelling, would restore my tranquillity.

I now made arrangements for my journey; but one feeling haunted me, which filled me with fear and agitation. During my absence I should leave my friends unconscious of the existence of their enemy, and unprotected from his attacks, exasperated as he might be by my departure. But he had promised to follow me wherever I might go; and would he not accompany me to England? This imagination was dreadful in itself, but soothing, inasmuch as it supposed the safety of my friends. I was agonized with the idea of the possibility that the reverse of this might happen. But through the whole period during which I was the slave of my creature, I allowed myself to be governed by the impulses of the moment; and my present sensations strongly intimated that the fiend would follow me, and exempt my family from the danger of his machinations.

It was in the latter end of August that I departed, to pass two years of exile. Elizabeth approved of the reasons of my departure, and only regretted that she had not the same opportunities of enlarging her experience, and cultivating her understanding. She wept, however, as she bade me farewell, and entreated me to return happy and tranquil. "We all," said she, "depend upon you; and if you are miserable, what must be our feelings?"

I threw myself into the carriage that was to convey me away, hardly knowing whither I was going, and careless of what was passing around. I remembered only, and it was with a bitter anguish that I reflected on it, to order that my chemical instruments should be packed to go with me: for I resolved to fulfil my promise while abroad, and return, if possible, a free man. Filled with dreary imaginations, I passed through many beautiful and majestic scenes; but my eyes were fixed and unobserving. I could only think of the bourne[5] of my travels, and the work which was to occupy me whilst they endured.

After some days spent in listless indolence, during which I traversed many leagues, I arrived at Strasburgh, where I waited two days for Clerval. He came. Alas, how great was the contrast between us! He was alive to every new scene; joyful when he saw the beauties of the setting sun, and more happy when he beheld it rise, and recommence a new day. He pointed out to me the shifting colours of the landscape, and the appearances of the sky. "This is what it is to live;" he cried, "now I enjoy existence! But you, my dear Frankenstein, wherefore are you desponding and sorrowful?" In truth, I was occupied by gloomy thoughts, and neither saw the descent of the evening star, nor the golden sun-rise reflected in the Rhine. — And you, my friend, would be far more amused with the journal of Clerval, who observed the scenery with an eye of feeling and delight, than to listen to my reflections. I, a miserable wretch, haunted by a curse that shut up every avenue to enjoyment.

We had agreed to descend the Rhine in a boat from Strasburgh to Rotterdam, whence we might take shipping for London. During this voyage, we passed by many willowy islands, and saw several beautiful towns. We staid a day at Manheim, and, on the fifth from our departure from Strasburgh, arrived at Mayence. The course of the Rhine below Mayence becomes much more picturesque. The river descends rapidly, and winds between hills, not high, but steep, and of beautiful forms. We saw many ruined castles standing on the edges of precipices, surrounded by black woods, high and inaccessible. This part of the Rhine, indeed, presents a singularly variegated landscape. In one spot you view rugged hills, ruined castles overlooking tremendous precipices, with the dark Rhine rushing beneath; and, on the sudden turn of a promontory,

5. Goal, destination.

flourishing vineyards, with green sloping banks, and a meandering river, and populous towns, occupy the scene.

We travelled at the time of the vintage, and heard the song of the labourers, as we glided down the stream. Even I, depressed in mind, and my spirits continually agitated by gloomy feelings, even I was pleased. I lay at the bottom of the boat, and, as I gazed on the cloudless blue sky, I seemed to drink in a tranquillity to which I had long been a stranger. And if these were my sensations, who can describe those of Henry? He felt as if he had been transported to Fairy-land, and enjoyed a happiness seldom tasted by man. "I have seen," he said, "the most beautiful scenes of my own country; I have visited the lakes of Lucerne and Uri, where the snowy mountains descend almost perpendicularly to the water, casting black and impenetrable shades, which would cause a gloomy and mournful appearance, were it not for the most verdant islands that relieve the eye by their gay appearance; I have seen this lake agitated by a tempest, when the wind tore up whirlwinds of water, and gave you an idea of what the water-spout must be on the great ocean, and the waves dash with fury the base of the mountain, where the priest and his mistress were overwhelmed by an avalanche, and where their dying voices are still said to be heard amid the pauses of the nightly wind; I have seen the mountains of La Valais, and the Pays de Vaud: but this country, Victor, pleases me more than all those wonders. The mountains of Switzerland are more majestic and strange; but there is a charm in the banks of this divine river, that I never before saw equalled. Look at that castle which overhangs you precipice; and that also on the island, almost concealed amongst the foliage of those lovely trees; and now that group of labourers coming from among their vines; and that village half-hid in the recess of the mountain. Oh, surely, the spirit that inhabits and guards this place has a soul more in harmony with man, than those who pile[6] the glacier, or retire to the inaccessible peaks of the mountains of our own country."

Clerval! beloved friend! even now it delights me to record your words, and to dwell on the praise of which you are so eminently deserving. He was a being formed in the "very poetry of nature."[7] His wild and enthusiastic imagination was chastened by the sensibility of his heart. His soul overflowed with ardent affections, and his friendship was of that devoted and wondrous nature that the worldly-minded teach us to look for only in the imagination. But even human sympathies were not sufficient to satisfy his eager mind. The scenery of external nature, which others regard only with admiration, he loved with ardour:

6. Drive piles into (in order to build upon).
7. Leigh Hunt's "Rimini" [Mary Shelley's note]. *The Story of Rimini* (1816), a narrative poem by Leigh Hunt (1784–1859) about Paolo and Francesca, famous lovers in Dante's *Inferno*.

———"The sounding cataract
Haunted *him* like a passion: the tall rock,
The mountain, and the deep and gloomy wood,
Their colours and their forms, were then to him
An appetite; a feeling, and a love,
That had no need of a remoter charm,
By thought supplied, or any interest
Unborrowed from the eye."[8]

And where does he now exist? Is this gentle and lovely being lost for
ever? Has this mind so replete with ideas, imaginations fanciful and
magnificent, which formed a world, whose existence depended on the
life of its creator; has this mind perished? Does it now only exist in my
memory? No, it is not thus; your form so divinely wrought, and beaming with beauty, has decayed, but your spirit still visits and consoles
your unhappy friend.

Pardon this gush of sorrow; these ineffectual words are but a slight
tribute to the unexampled worth of Henry, but they soothe my heart,
overflowing with the anguish which his remembrance creates. I will
proceed with my tale.

Beyond Cologne we descended to the plains of Holland; and we
resolved to post[9] the remainder of our way; for the wind was contrary,
and the stream of the river was too gentle to aid us.

Our journey here lost the interest arising from beautiful scenery; but
we arrived in a few days at Rotterdam, whence we proceeded by sea to
England. It was on a clear morning, in the latter days of December,
that I first saw the white cliffs of Britain. The banks of the Thames
presented a new scene; they were flat, but fertile, and almost every town
was marked by the remembrance of some story. We saw Tilbury Fort,
and remembered the Spanish armada; Gravesend, Woolwich, and
Greenwich, places which I had heard of even in my country.

At length we saw the numerous steeples of London, St. Paul's tow-
ering above all, and the Tower famed in English history.

Chapter II.

London was our present point of rest; we determined to remain several
months in this wonderful and celebrated city. Clerval desired the intercourse of[1] the men of genius and talent who flourished at this time;
but this was with me a secondary object; I was principally occupied

8. Wordsworth's "Tintern Abbey" [Mary Shelley's note]. Lines 76–83 of "Lines composed a few
   miles above Tintern Abbey" (1798), by William Wordsworth (1770–1850); Mary Shelley has
   changed "me" to "him."
9. Travel by horse.
1. Conversation with.

with the means of obtaining the information necessary for the completion of my promise, and quickly availed myself of the letters of introduction that I had brought with me, addressed to the most distinguished
natural philosophers.

If this journey had taken place during my days of study and happiness, it would have afforded me inexpressible pleasure. But a blight had
come over my existence, and I only visited these people for the sake of
the information they might give me on the subject in which my interest
was so terribly profound. Company was irksome to me; when alone, I
could fill my mind with the sights of heaven and earth; the voice of
Henry soothed me, and I could thus cheat myself into a transitory
peace. But busy uninteresting joyous faces brought back despair to my
heart. I saw an insurmountable barrier placed between me and my
fellow-men; this barrier was sealed with the blood of William and Justine; and to reflect on the events connected with those names filled my
soul with anguish.

But in Clerval I saw the image of my former self; he was inquisitive,
and anxious to gain experience and instruction. The difference of manners which he observed was to him an inexhaustible source of instruction and amusement. He was for ever busy; and the only check to his
enjoyments was my sorrowful and dejected mien. I tried to conceal this
as much as possible, that I might not debar him from the pleasures
natural to one who was entering on a new scene of life, undisturbed
by any care or bitter recollection. I often refused to accompany him,
alleging another engagement, that I might remain alone. I now also
began to collect the materials necessary for my new creation, and this
was to me like the torture of single drops of water continually falling
on the head. Every thought that was devoted to it was an extreme
anguish, and every word that I spoke in allusion to it caused my lips
to quiver, and my heart to palpitate.

After passing some months in London, we received a letter from a
person in Scotland, who had formerly been our visitor at Geneva. He
mentioned the beauties of his native country, and asked us if those
were not sufficient allurements to induce us to prolong our journey as
far north as Perth, where he resided. Clerval eagerly desired to accept
this invitation; and I, although I abhorred society, wished to view again
mountains and streams, and all the wondrous works with which Nature
adorns her chosen dwelling-places.

We had arrived in England at the beginning of October, and it was
now February. We accordingly determined to commence our journey
towards the north at the expiration of another month. In this expedition
we did not intend to follow the great road to Edinburgh, but to visit
Windsor, Oxford, Matlock, and the Cumberland lakes, resolving to arrive at the completion of this tour about the end of July. I packed my
chemical instruments, and the materials I had collected, resolving to

finish my labours in some obscure nook in the northern highlands of Scotland.

We quitted London on the 27th of March, and remained a few days at Windsor, rambling in its beautiful forest. This was a new scene to us mountaineers; the majestic oaks, the quantity of game, and the herds of stately deer, were all novelties to us.

From thence we proceeded to Oxford. As we entered this city, our minds were filled with the remembrance of the events that had been transacted here more than a century and a half before. It was here that Charles I. had collected his forces. This city had remained faithful to him, after the whole nation had forsaken his cause to join the standard of parliament and liberty. The memory of that unfortunate king, and his companions, the amiable Falkland, the insolent Gower, his queen, and son,[2] gave a peculiar interest to every part of the city, which they might be supposed to have inhabited. The spirit of elder days found a dwelling here, and we delighted to trace its footsteps. If these feelings had not found an imaginary gratification, the appearance of the city had yet in itself sufficient beauty to obtain our admiration. The colleges are ancient and picturesque; the streets are almost magnificent; and the lovely Isis,[3] which flows beside it through meadows of exquisite verdure, is spread forth into a placid expanse of waters, which reflects its majestic assemblage of towers, and spires, and domes, embosomed among aged trees.

I enjoyed this scene; and yet my enjoyment was embittered both by the memory of the past, and the anticipation of the future. I was formed for peaceful happiness. During my youthful days discontent never visited my mind; and if I was ever overcome by *ennui*,[4] the sight of what is beautiful in nature, or the study of what is excellent and sublime in the productions of man, could always interest my heart, and communicate elasticity to my spirits. But I am a blasted tree; the bolt has entered my soul; and I felt then that I should survive to exhibit, what I shall soon cease to be — a miserable spectacle of wrecked humanity, pitiable to others, and abhorrent to myself.

We passed a considerable period at Oxford, rambling among its environs, and endeavouring to identify every spot which might relate to the most animating epoch of English history. Our little voyages of discovery were often prolonged by the successive objects that presented themselves. We visited the tomb of the illustrious Hampden, and the

---

2. Henrietta Maria (1609–1669) and Charles (1630–1685), who became Charles II in 1660. *The amiable Falkland*: Lucius Cary, second Viscount Falkland (1610–1643), Royalist, killed in battle at Newberry. *The insolent Gower*: corrected to "Goring" in 1831; George Goring, Baron Goring (1608–1657), fought as a Royalist after twice switching sides.
3. The river Thames is known in Oxford as the Isis.
4. Weariness and dissatisfaction.

field on which that patriot fell.[5] For a moment my soul was elevated
from its debasing and miserable fears to contemplate the divine ideas
of liberty and self-sacrifice, of which these sights were the monuments
and the remembrancers. For an instant I dared to shake off my chains,
and look around me with a free and lofty spirit; but the iron had eaten
into my flesh, and I sank again, trembling and hopeless, into my miserable self.

We left Oxford with regret, and proceeded to Matlock, which was
our next place of rest. The country in the neighbourhood of this village
resembled, to a greater degree, the scenery of Switzerland; but every
thing is on a lower scale, and the green hills want the crown of distant
white Alps, which always attend on the piny mountains of my native
country. We visited the wondrous cave, and the little cabinets of natural
history, where the curiosities[6] are disposed in the same manner as in
the collections at Servox and Chamounix. The latter name made me
tremble, when pronounced by Henry; and I hastened to quit Matlock,
with which that terrible scene was thus associated.

From Derby still journeying northward, we passed two months in
Cumberland and Westmoreland.[7] I could now almost fancy myself
among the Swiss mountains. The little patches of snow which yet lin-
gered on the northern sides of the mountains, the lakes, and the dashing
of the rocky streams, were all familiar and dear sights to me. Here also
we made some acquaintances, who almost contrived to cheat me into
happiness. The delight of Clerval was proportionably greater than mine;
his mind expanded in the company of men of talent, and he found in
his own nature greater capacities and resources than he could have
imagined himself to have possessed while he associated with his infe-
riors. "I could pass my life here," said he to me; "and among these
mountains I should scarcely regret Switzerland and the Rhine."

But he found that a traveller's life is one that includes much pain
amidst its enjoyments. His feelings are for ever on the stretch;[8] and
when he begins to sink into repose, he finds himself obliged to quit
that on which he rests in pleasure for something new, which again
engages his attention, and which also he forsakes for other novelties.

We had scarcely visited the various lakes of Cumberland and Westmoreland, and conceived an affection for some of the inhabitants, when
the period of our appointment with our Scotch friend approached, and
we left them to travel on. For my own part I was not sorry. I had now
neglected my promise for some time, and I feared the effects of the
dæmon's disappointment. He might remain in Switzerland, and wreak

---

5. John Hampden (1594–1643), leader of the parliamentary opposition to Charles I, was killed
   on Chalgrove Field, near Oxford.
6. Rare or strange objects. *Cabinets:* rooms where works of art and natural wonders were
   displayed.
7. The Lake District, associated with the "Lake Poets" (Wordsworth, Coleridge, and Southey).
8. Tense.

his vengeance on my relatives. This idea pursued me, and tormented me at every moment from which I might otherwise have snatched repose and peace. I waited for my letters with feverish impatience: if they were delayed, I was miserable, and overcome by a thousand fears; and when they arrived, and I saw the superscription[9] of Elizabeth or my father, I hardly dared to read and ascertain my fate. Sometimes I thought that the fiend followed me, and might expedite my remissness by murdering my companion. When these thoughts possessed me, I would not quit Henry for a moment, but followed him as his shadow, to protect him from the fancied rage of his destroyer. I felt as if I had committed some great crime, the consciousness of which haunted me. I was guiltless, but I had indeed drawn down a horrible curse upon my head, as mortal as that of crime.

I visited Edinburgh with languid eyes and mind; and yet that city might have interested the most unfortunate being. Clerval did not like it so well as Oxford; for the antiquity of the latter city was more pleasing to him. But the beauty and regularity of the new town of Edinburgh, its romantic castle, and its environs, the most delightful in the world, Arthur's Seat, St. Bernard's Well, and the Pentland Hills, compensated him for the change, and filled him with cheerfulness and admiration. But I was impatient to arrive at the termination of my journey.

We left Edinburgh in a week, passing through Coupar, St. Andrews, and along the banks of the Tay, to Perth, where our friend expected us. But I was in no mood to laugh and talk with strangers, or enter into their feelings or plans with the good humour expected from a guest; and accordingly I told Clerval that I wished to make the tour of Scotland alone. "Do you," said I, "enjoy yourself, and let this be our rendezvous. I may be absent a month or two; but do not interfere with my motions, I entreat you: leave me to peace and solitude for a short time; and when I return, I hope it will be with a lighter heart, more congenial to your own temper."

Henry wished to dissuade me; but, seeing me bent on this plan, ceased to remonstrate. He entreated me to write often. "I had rather be with you," he said, "in your solitary rambles, than with these Scotch people, whom I do not know: hasten then, my dear friend, to return, that I may again feel myself somewhat at home, which I cannot do in your absence."

Having parted from my friend, I determined to visit some remote spot of Scotland, and finish my work in solitude. I did not doubt but that the monster followed me, and would discover himself to me when I should have finished, that he might receive his companion.

With this resolution I traversed the northern highlands, and fixed on one of the remotest of the Orkneys as the scene labours.[1] It was a place

9. The name or address at the head of a letter.
1. Corrected in 1831 to "scene of my labours." *Orkneys:* islands off the north coast of Scotland.

fitted for such a work, being hardly more than a rock, whose high sides were continually beaten upon by the waves. The soil was barren, scarcely affording pasture for a few miserable cows, and oatmeal for its inhabitants, which consisted of five persons, whose gaunt and scraggy limbs gave tokens of their miserable fare. Vegetables and bread, when they indulged in such luxuries, and even fresh water, was to be procured from the main land, which was about five miles distant.

On the whole island there were but three miserable huts, and one of these was vacant when I arrived. This I hired. It contained but two rooms, and these exhibited all the squalidness of the most miserable penury. The thatch had fallen in, the walls were unplastered, and the door was off its hinges. I ordered it to be repaired, bought some furniture, and took possession; an incident which would, doubtless, have occasioned some surprise, had not all the senses of the cottagers been benumbed by want and squalid poverty. As it was, I lived ungazed at and unmolested, hardly thanked for the pittance of food and clothes which I gave; so much does suffering blunt even the coarsest sensations of men.

In this retreat I devoted the morning to labour; but in the evening, when the weather permitted, I walked on the stony beach of the sea, to listen to the waves as they roared, and dashed at my feet. It was a monotonous, yet ever-changing scene. I thought of Switzerland; it was far different from this desolate and appalling landscape. Its hills are covered with vines, and its cottages are scattered thickly in the plains. Its fair lakes reflect a blue and gentle sky; and, when troubled by the winds, their tumult is but as the play of a lively infant, when compared to the roarings of the giant ocean.

In this manner I distributed my occupations when I first arrived; but, as I proceeded in my labour, it became every day more horrible and irksome to me. Sometimes I could not prevail on myself to enter my laboratory for several days; and at other times I toiled day and night in order to complete my work. It was indeed a filthy process in which I was engaged. During my first experiment, a kind of enthusiastic frenzy had blinded me to the horror of my employment; my mind was intently fixed on the sequel[2] of my labour, and my eyes were shut to the horror of my proceedings. But now I went to it in cold blood, and my heart often sickened at the work of my hands.

Thus situated, employed in the most detestable occupation, immersed in a solitude where nothing could for an instant call my attention from the actual scene in which I was engaged, my spirits became unequal;[3] I grew restless and nervous. Every moment I feared to meet my persecutor. Sometimes I sat with my eyes fixed on the ground, fearing to raise them lest they should encounter the object which I so

2. Results.
3. Unbalanced.

much dreaded to behold. I feared to wander from the sight of my fellow-creatures, lest when alone he should come to claim his companion.

In the mean time I worked on, and my labour was already considerably advanced. I looked towards its completion with a tremulous and eager hope, which I dared not trust myself to question, but which was intermixed with obscure forebodings of evil, that made my heart sicken in my bosom.

Chapter III.

I sat one evening in my laboratory; the sun had set, and the moon was just rising from the sea; I had not sufficient light for my employment, and I remained idle, in a pause of consideration of whether I should leave my labour for the night, or hasten its conclusion by an unremitting attention to it. As I sat, a train of reflection occurred to me, which led me to consider the effects of what I was now doing. Three years before I was engaged in the same manner, and had created a fiend whose unparalleled barbarity had desolated my heart, and filled it for ever with the bitterest remorse. I was now about to form another being, of whose dispositions I was alike ignorant; she might become ten thousand times more malignant than her mate, and delight, for its own sake, in murder and wretchedness. He had sworn to quit the neighbourhood of man, and hide himself in deserts; but she had not; and she, who in all probability was to become a thinking and reasoning animal, might refuse to comply with a compact made before her creation. They might even hate each other; the creature who already lived loathed his own deformity, and might he not conceive a greater abhorrence for it when it came before his eyes in the female form? She also might turn with disgust from him to the superior beauty of man; she might quit him, and he be again alone, exasperated by the fresh provocation of being deserted by one of his own species.

Even if they were to leave Europe, and inhabit the deserts of the new world, yet one of the first results of those sympathies for which the dæmon thirsted would be children, and a race of devils would be propagated upon the earth, who might make the very existence of the species of man a condition precarious and full of terror. Had I a right, for my own benefit, to inflict this curse upon everlasting generations? I had before been moved by the *sophisms*[1] of the being I had created; I had been struck senseless by his fiendish threats: but now, for the first time, the wickedness of my promise burst upon me; I shuddered to think that future ages might curse me as their pest, whose selfishness had not

1. Deceptive and misleading arguments.

hesitated to buy its own peace at the price perhaps of the existence of the whole human race.

I trembled, and my heart failed within me; when, on looking up, I saw, by the light of the moon, the dæmon at the casement. A ghastly grin wrinkled his lips as he gazed on me, where I sat fulfilling the task which he had allotted to me. Yes, he had followed me in my travels; he had loitered in forests, hid himself in caves, or taken refuge in wide and desert heaths; and he now came to mark my progress, and claim the fulfilment of my promise.

As I looked on him, his countenance expressed the utmost extent of malice and treachery. I thought with a sensation of madness on my promise of creating another like to him, and, trembling with passion, tore to pieces the thing on which I was engaged. The wretch saw me destroy the creature on whose future existence he depended for happiness, and, with a howl of devilish despair and revenge, withdrew.

I left the room, and, locking the door, made a solemn vow in my own heart never to resume my labours; and then, with trembling steps, I sought my own apartment. I was alone; none were near me to dissipate the gloom, and relieve me from the sickening oppression of the most terrible reveries.

Several hours past, and I remained near my window gazing on the sea; it was almost motionless, for the winds were hushed, and all nature reposed under the eye of the quiet moon. A few fishing vessels alone specked the water, and now and then the gentle breeze wafted the sound of voices, as the fishermen called to one another. I felt the silence, although I was hardly conscious of its extreme profundity, until my ear was suddenly arrested by the paddling of oars near the shore, and a person landed close to my house.

In a few minutes after, I heard the creaking of my door, as if some one endeavoured to open it softly. I trembled from head to foot; I felt a presentiment of who it was, and wished to rouse one of the peasants who dwelt in a cottage not far from mine; but I was overcome by the sensation of helplessness, so often felt in frightful dreams, when you in vain endeavour to fly from an impending danger, and was rooted to the spot.

Presently I heard the sound of footsteps along the passage; the door opened, and the wretch whom I dreaded appeared. Shutting the door, he approached me, and said, in a smothered voice —

"You have destroyed the work which you began; what is it that you intend? Do you dare to break your promise? I have endured toil and misery: I left Switzerland with you; I crept along the shores of the Rhine, among its willow islands, and over the summits of its hills. I have dwelt many months in the heaths of England, and among the deserts of Scotland. I have endured incalculable fatigue, and cold, and hunger; do you dare destroy my hopes?"

"Begone! I do break my promise; never will I create another like yourself, equal in deformity and wickedness."

"Slave, I before reasoned with you, but you have proved yourself unworthy of my condescension. Remember that I have power; you believe yourself miserable, but I can make you so wretched that the light of day will be hateful to you. You are my creator, but I am your master; — obey!"

"The hour of my weakness is past, and the period[2] of your power is arrived. Your threats cannot move me to do an act of wickedness; but they confirm me in a resolution of not creating you a companion in vice. Shall I, in cool blood, set loose upon the earth a dæmon, whose delight is in death and wretchedness. Begone! I am firm, and your words will only exasperate my rage."

The monster saw my determination in my face, and gnashed his teeth in the impotence of anger. "Shall each man," cried he, "find a wife for his bosom, and each beast have his mate, and I be alone? I had feelings of affection, and they were requited by detestation and scorn. Man, you may hate; but beware! Your hours will pass in dread and misery, and soon the bolt will fall which must ravish from you your happiness for ever. Are you to be happy, while I grovel in the intensity of my wretchedness? You can blast my other passions; but revenge remains — revenge, henceforth dearer than light or food! I may die; but first you, my tyrant and tormentor, shall curse the sun that gazes on your misery. Beware; for I am fearless, and therefore powerful. I will watch with the wiliness of a snake, that I may sting with its venom. Man, you shall repent of the injuries you inflict."

"Devil, cease; and do not poison the air with these sounds of malice. I have declared my resolution to you, and I am no coward to bend beneath words. Leave me; I am inexorable."

"It is well. I go; but remember, I shall be with you on your wedding-night."

I started forward, and exclaimed, "Villain! before you sign my death-warrant, be sure that you are yourself safe."

I would have seized him; but he eluded me, and quitted the house with precipitation: in a few moments I saw him in his boat, which shot across the waters with an arrowy swiftness, and was soon lost amidst the waves.

All was again silent; but his words rung in my ears. I burned with rage to pursue the murderer of my peace, and precipitate him into the ocean. I walked up and down my room hastily and perturbed, while my imagination conjured up a thousand images to torment and sting me. Why had I not followed him, and closed[3] with him in mortal strife? But I had suffered him to depart, and he had directed his course to-

2. Ending.
3. Fought hand-to-hand.

wards the main land. I shuddered to think who might be the next victim
sacrificed to his insatiate revenge. And then I thought again of his
words — "I will be with you on your wedding-night." That then was the
period fixed for the fulfilment of my destiny. In that hour I should die,
and at once satisfy and extinguish his malice. The prospect did not
move me to fear; yet when I thought of my beloved Elizabeth, — of her
tears and endless sorrow, when she should find her lover so barbarously
snatched from her, — tears, the first I had shed for many months,
streamed from my eyes, and I resolved not to fall before my enemy
without a bitter struggle.

The night passed away, and the sun rose from the ocean; my feelings
became calmer, if it may be called calmness, when the violence of rage
sinks into the depths of despair. I left the house, the horrid scene of
the last night's contention, and walked on the beach of the sea, which
I almost regarded as an insuperable barrier between me and my fellow-
creatures; nay, a wish that such should prove the fact stole across me.
I desired that I might pass my life on that barren rock, wearily it is true,
but uninterrupted by any sudden shock of misery. If I returned, it was
to be sacrificed, or to see those whom I most loved die under the grasp
of a dæmon whom I had myself created.

I walked about the isle like a restless spectre, separated from all it
loved, and miserable in the separation. When it became noon, and the
sun rose higher, I lay down on the grass, and was overpowered by a
deep sleep. I had been awake the whole of the preceding night, my
nerves were agitated, and my eyes inflamed by watching and misery.
The sleep into which I now sunk refreshed me; and when I awoke, I
again felt as if I belonged to a race of human beings like myself, and
I began to reflect upon what had passed with greater composure; yet
still the words of the fiend rung in my ears like a death-knell, they
appeared like a dream, yet distinct and oppressive as a reality.

The sun had far descended, and I still sat on the shore, satisfying my
appetite, which had become ravenous, with an oaten cake, when I saw
a fishing-boat land close to me, and one of the men brought me a
packet; it contained letters from Geneva, and one from Clerval, entreating me to join him. He said that nearly a year had elapsed since
we had quitted Switzerland, and France was yet unvisited. He entreated
me, therefore, to leave my solitary isle, and meet him at Perth, in a
week from that time, when we might arrange the plan of our future
proceedings. This letter in a degree recalled me to life, and I determined to quit my island at the expiration of two days.

Yet, before I departed, there was a task to perform, on which I shuddered to reflect: I must pack my chemical instruments; and for that
purpose I must enter the room which had been the scene of my odious
work, and I must handle those utensils, the sight of which was sickening
to me. The next morning, at day-break, I summoned sufficient courage,

and unlocked the door of my laboratory. The remains of the half-finished creature, whom I had destroyed, lay scattered on the floor, and I almost felt as if I had mangled the living flesh of a human being. I paused to collect myself, and then entered the chamber. With trembling hand I conveyed the instruments out of the room; but I reflected that I ought not to leave the relics of my work to excite the horror and suspicion of the peasants, and I accordingly put them into a basket, with a great quantity of stones, and laying them up, determined to throw them into the sea that very night; and in the mean time I sat upon the beach, employed in cleaning and arranging my chemical apparatus.

Nothing could be more complete than the alteration that had taken place in my feelings since the night of the appearance of the dæmon. I had before regarded my promise with a gloomy despair, as a thing that, with whatever consequences, must be fulfilled; but I now felt as if a film had been taken from before my eyes, and that I, for the first time, saw clearly. The idea of renewing my labours did not for one instant occur to me; the threat I had heard weighed on my thoughts, but I did not reflect that a voluntary act of mine could avert it. I had resolved in my own mind, that to create another like the fiend I had first made would be an act of the basest and most atrocious selfishness; and I banished from my mind every thought that could lead to a different conclusion.

Between two and three in the morning the moon rose; and I then, putting my basket aboard a little skiff, sailed out about four miles from the shore. The scene was perfectly solitary: a few boats were returning towards land, but I sailed away from them. I felt as if I was about the commission of a dreadful crime, and avoided with shuddering anxiety any encounter with my fellow-creatures. At one time the moon, which had before been clear, was suddenly overspread by a thick cloud, and I took advantage of the moment of darkness, and cast my basket into the sea; I listened to the gurgling sound as it sunk, and then sailed away from the spot. The sky became clouded; but the air was pure, although chilled by the north-east breeze that was then rising. But it refreshed me, and filled me with such agreeable sensations, that I resolved to prolong my stay on the water, and fixing the rudder in a direct position, stretched myself at the bottom of the boat. Clouds hid the moon, every thing was obscure, and I heard only the sound of the boat, as its keel cut through the waves; the murmur lulled me, and in a short time I slept soundly.

I do not know how long I remained in this situation, but when I awoke I found that the sun had already mounted considerably. The wind was high, and the waves continually threatened the safety of my little skiff. I found that the wind was north-east, and must have driven me far from the coast from which I had embarked. I endeavoured to change my course, but quickly found that if I again made the attempt the boat would be instantly filled with water. Thus situated, my only resource was to drive before the wind. I confess that I felt a few sensations of terror. I had no compass with me, and was so little acquainted with the geography of this part of the world that the sun was of little benefit to me. I might be driven into the wide Atlantic, and feel all the tortures of starvation, or be swallowed up in the immeasurable waters that roared and buffeted around me. I had already been out many hours, and felt the torment of a burning thirst,[4] a prelude to my other sufferings. I looked on the heavens, which were covered by clouds that flew before the wind only to be replaced by others: I looked upon the sea, it was to be my grave. "Fiend," I exclaimed, "your task is already fulfilled!" I thought of Elizabeth, of my father, and of Clerval; and sunk into a reverie, so despairing and frightful, that even now, when the scene is on the point of closing before me for ever, I shudder to reflect on it.

Some hours passed thus; but by degrees, as the sun declined towards the horizon, the wind died away into a gentle breeze, and the sea became free from breakers. But these gave place to a heavy swell; I felt sick, and hardly able to hold the rudder, when suddenly I saw a line of high land towards the south.

Almost spent, as I was, by fatigue, and the dreadful suspense I endured for several hours, this sudden certainty of life rushed like a flood of warm joy to my heart, and tears gushed from my eyes.

How mutable are our feelings, and how strange is that clinging love we have of life even in the excess of misery! I constructed another sail with a part of my dress, and eagerly steered my course towards the land. It had a wild and rocky appearance; but as I approached nearer, I easily perceived the traces of cultivation. I saw vessels near the shore, and found myself suddenly transported back to the neighbourhood of civilized man. I eagerly traced the windings of the land, and hailed a steeple which I at length saw issuing from behind a small promontory. As I was in a state of extreme debility, I resolved to sail directly towards the town as a place where I could most easily procure nourishment. Fortunately I had money with me. As I turned the promontory, I perceived a small neat town and a good harbour, which I entered, my heart bounding with joy at my unexpected escape.

As I was occupied in fixing the boat and arranging the sails, several people crowded towards the spot. They seemed very much surprised at my appearance; but, instead of offering me any assistance, whispered together with gestures that at any other time might have produced in me a slight sensation of alarm. As it was, I merely remarked that they

4. Cf. Coleridge's "Ancient Mariner," lines 115ff.

spoke English; and I therefore addressed them in that language: "My good friends," said I, "will you be so kind as to tell me the name of this town, and inform me where I am?"

"You will know that soon enough," replied a man with a gruff voice. "May be you are come to a place that will not prove much to your taste; but you will not be consulted as to your quarters, I promise you."

I was exceedingly surprised on receiving so rude an answer from a stranger; and I was also disconcerted on perceiving the frowning and angry countenances of his companions. "Why do you answer me so roughly?" I replied: "surely it is not the custom of Englishmen to receive strangers so inhospitably."

"I do not know," said the man, "what the custom of the English may be; but it is the custom of the Irish to hate villains."

While this strange dialogue continued, I perceived the crowd rapidly increase. Their faces expressed a mixture of curiosity and anger, which annoyed, and in some degree alarmed me. I inquired the way to the inn; but no one replied. I then moved forward, and a murmuring sound arose from the crowd as they followed and surrounded me; when an ill-looking man approaching, tapped me on the shoulder, and said, "Come, Sir, you must follow me to Mr. Kirwin's, to give an account of yourself."

"Who is Mr. Kirwin? Why am I to give an account of myself? Is not this a free country?"

"Aye, Sir, free enough for honest folks. Mr. Kirwin is a magistrate; and you are to give an account of the death of a gentleman who was found murdered here last night."

This answer startled me; but I presently recovered myself. I was innocent; that could easily be proved: accordingly I followed my conductor in silence, and was led to one of the best houses in the town. I was ready to sink from fatigue and hunger; but, being surrounded by a crowd, I thought it politic to rouse all my strength, that no physical debility might be construed into apprehension or conscious guilt. Little did I then expect the calamity that was in a few moments to overwhelm me, and extinguish in horror and despair all fear of ignominy or death.

I must pause here; for it requires all my fortitude to recall the memory of the frightful events which I am about to relate, in proper detail, to my recollection.

Chapter IV.

I was soon introduced into the presence of the magistrate, an old benevolent man, with calm and mild manners. He looked upon me, however, with some degree of severity; and then, turning towards my conductors, he asked who appeared as witnesses on this occasion.

About half a dozen men came forward; and one being selected by the magistrate, he deposed, that he had been out fishing the night before with his son and brother-in-law, Daniel Nugent, when, about ten o'clock, they observed a strong northerly blast rising, and they accordingly put in for port. It was a very dark night, as the moon had not yet risen; they did not land at the harbour, but, as they had been accustomed, at a creek about two miles below. He walked on first, carrying a part of the fishing tackle, and his companions followed him at some distance. As he was proceeding along the sands, he struck his foot against something, and fell all his length on the ground. His companions came up to assist him; and, by the light of their lantern, they found that he had fallen on the body of a man, who was to all appearance dead. Their first supposition was, that it was the corpse of some person who had been drowned, and was thrown on shore by the waves; but, upon examination, they found that the clothes were not wet, and even that the body was not then cold. They instantly carried it to the cottage of an old woman near the spot, and endeavoured, but in vain, to restore it to life. He appeared to be a handsome young man, about five and twenty years of age. He had apparently been strangled; for there was no sign of any violence, except the black mark of fingers on his neck.

The first part of this deposition did not in the least interest me; but when the mark of the fingers was mentioned, I remembered the murder of my brother, and felt myself extremely agitated; my limbs trembled, and a mist came over my eyes, which obliged me to lean on a chair for support. The magistrate observed me with a keen eye, and of course drew an unfavourable augury from my manner.

The son confirmed his father's account: but when Daniel Nugent was called, he swore positively that, just before the fall of his companion, he saw a boat, with a single man in it, at a short distance from the shore; and, as far as he could judge by the light of a few stars, it was the same boat in which I had just landed.

A woman deposed, that she lived near the beach, and was standing at the door of her cottage, waiting for the return of the fishermen, about an hour before she heard of the discovery of the body, when she saw a boat, with only only one man in it, push off from that part of the shore where the corpse was afterwards found.

Another woman confirmed the account of the fishermen having brought the body into her house; it was not cold. They put it into a bed, and rubbed it; and Daniel went to the town for an apothecary, but life was quite gone.

Several other men were examined concerning my landing; and they agreed, that, with the strong north wind that had arisen during the night, it was very probable that I had beaten about for many hours, and had been obliged to return nearly to the same spot from which I had departed. Besides, they observed that it appeared that I had brought the body from another place, and it was likely, that as I did not appear to know the shore, I might have put into the harbour ignorant of the distance of the town of ——from the place where I had deposited the corpse.

Mr. Kirwin, on hearing this evidence, desired that I should be taken into the room where the body lay for interment, that it might be observed what effect the sight of it would produce upon me. This idea was probably suggested by the extreme agitation I had exhibited when the mode of the murder had been described. I was accordingly conducted, by the magistrate and several other persons, to the inn. I could not help being struck by the strange coincidences that had taken place during this eventful night; but, knowing that I had been conversing with several persons in the island I had inhabited about the time that the body had been found, I was perfectly tranquil as to the consequences[1] of the affair.

I entered the room where the corpse lay, and was led up to the coffin. How can I describe my sensations on beholding it? I feel yet parched with horror, nor can I reflect on that terrible moment without shuddering and agony, that faintly reminds me of the anguish of the recognition. The trial, the presence of the magistrate and witnesses, passed like a dream from my memory, when I saw the lifeless form of Henry Clerval stretched before me. I gasped for breath; and, throwing myself on the body, I exclaimed, "Have my murderous machinations deprived you also, my dearest Henry, of life? Two I have already destroyed; other victims await their destiny: but you, Clerval, my friend, my benefactor" —

The human frame could no longer support the agonizing suffering that I endured, and I was carried out of the room in strong convulsions.

A fever succeeded to this. I lay for two months on the point of death: my ravings, as I afterwards heard, were frightful; I called myself the murderer of William, of Justine, and of Clerval. Sometimes I entreated my attendants to assist me in the destruction of the fiend by whom I was tormented; and, at others, I felt the fingers of the monster already grasping my neck, and screamed aloud with agony and terror. Fortunately, as I spoke my native language, Mr. Kirwin alone understood me; but my gestures and bitter cries were sufficient to affright the other witnesses.

Why did I not die? More miserable than man ever was before, why did I not sink into forgetfulness and rest? Death snatches away many blooming children, the only hopes of their doating parents: how many

1. Outcome.

brides and youthful lovers have been one day in the bloom of health and hope, and the next a prey for worms and the decay of the tomb! Of what materials was I made, that I could thus resist so many shocks, which, like the turning of the wheel, continually renewed the torture.

But I was doomed to live; and, in two months, found myself as awaking from a dream, in a prison, stretched on a wretched bed, surrounded by gaolers,[2] turnkeys, bolts, and all the miserable apparatus of a dungeon. It was morning, I remember, when I thus awoke to understanding: I had forgotten the particulars of what had happened, and only felt as if some great misfortune had suddenly overwhelmed me; but when I looked around, and saw the barred windows, and the squalidness of the room in which I was, all flashed across my memory, and I groaned bitterly.

This sound disturbed an old woman who was sleeping in a chair beside me. She was a hired nurse, the wife of one of the turnkeys, and her countenance expressed all those bad qualities which often characterize that class. The lines of her face were hard and rude, like that of persons accustomed to see without sympathizing in sights of misery. Her tone expressed her entire indifference; she addressed me in English, and the voice struck me as one that I had heard during my sufferings:

"Are you better now, Sir?" said she.

I replied in the same language, with a feeble voice, "I believe I am; but if it be all true, if indeed I did not dream, I am sorry that I am still alive to feel this misery and horror."

"For that matter," replied the old woman, "if you mean about the gentleman you murdered, I believe that it were better for you if you were dead, for I fancy it will go hard with you; but you will be hung when the next sessions[3] come on. However, that's none of my business, I am sent to nurse you, and get you well; I do my duty with a safe conscience, it were well if every body did the same."

I turned with loathing from the woman who could utter so unfeeling a speech to a person just saved, on the very edge of death; but I felt languid, and unable to reflect on all that had passed. The whole series of my life appeared to me as a dream; I sometimes doubted if indeed it were all true, for it never presented itself to my mind with the force of reality.

As the images that floated before me became more distinct, I grew feverish; a darkness pressed around me; no one was near me who soothed me with the gentle voice of love; no dear hand supported me. The physician came and prescribed medicines, and the old woman prepared them for me; but utter carelessness was visible in the first, and the expression of brutality was strongly marked in the visage of the

2. Jailers.
3. Judicial sittings.

second. Who could be interested in the fate of a murderer, but the hangman who would gain his fee?

These were my first reflections; but I soon learned that Mr. Kirwin had shewn me extreme kindness. He had caused the best room in the prison to be prepared for me (wretched indeed was the best); and it was he who had provided a physician and a nurse. It is true, he seldom came to see me; for, although he ardently desired to relieve the sufferings of every human creature, he did not wish to be present at the agonies and miserable ravings of a murderer. He came, therefore, sometimes to see that I was not neglected; but his visits were short, and at long intervals.

One day, when I was gradually recovering, I was seated in a chair, my eyes half open, and my cheeks livid like those in death, I was overcome by gloom and misery, and often reflected I had better seek death than remain miserably pent up only to be let loose in a world replete with wretchedness. At one time I considered whether I should not declare myself guilty, and suffer the penalty of the law, less innocent than poor Justine had been. Such were my thoughts, when the door of my apartment was opened, and Mr. Kirwin entered. His countenance expressed sympathy and compassion; he drew a chair close to mine, and addressed me in French—

"I fear that this place is very shocking to you; can I do any thing to make you more comfortable?"

"I thank you; but all that you mention is nothing to me: on the whole earth there is no comfort which I am capable of receiving."

"I know that the sympathy of a stranger can be but of little relief to one borne down as you are by so strange a misfortune. But you will, I hope, soon quit this melancholy abode; for, doubtless, evidence can easily be brought to free you from the criminal charge."

"That is my least concern: I am, by a course of strange events, become the most miserable of mortals. Persecuted and tortured as I am and have been, can death be any evil to me?"

"Nothing indeed could be more unfortunate and agonizing than the strange chances that have lately occurred. You were thrown, by some surprising accident, on this shore, renowned for its hospitality; seized immediately, and charged with murder. The first sight that was presented to your eyes was the body of your friend, murdered in so unaccountable a manner, and placed, as it were, by some fiend across your path."

As Mr. Kirwin said this, notwithstanding the agitation I endured on this retrospect of my sufferings, I also felt considerable surprise at the knowledge he seemed to possess concerning me. I suppose some astonishment was exhibited in my countenance; for Mr. Kirwin hastened to say—

"It was not until a day or two after your illness that I thought of examining your dress, that I might discover some trace by which I could send to your relations an account of your misfortune and illness. I found several letters, and, among others, one which I discovered from its commencement to be from your father. I instantly wrote to Geneva: nearly two months have elapsed since the departure of my letter. — But you are ill; even now you tremble: you are unfit for agitation of any kind."

"This suspense is a thousand times worse than the most horrible event: tell me what new scene of death has been acted, and whose murder I am now to lament."

"Your family is perfectly well," said Mr. Kirwin, with gentleness; "and some one, a friend, is come to visit you."

I know not by what chain of thought the idea presented itself, but it instantly darted into my mind that the murderer had come to mock at my misery, and taunt me with the death of Clerval, as a new incitement for me to comply with his hellish desires. I put my hand before my eyes, and cried out in agony—

"Oh! take him away! I cannot see him; for God's sake, do not let him enter!"

Mr. Kirwin regarded me with a troubled countenance. He could not help regarding my exclamation as a presumption of my guilt, and said, in rather a severe tone—

"I should have thought, young man, that the presence of your father would have been welcome, instead of inspiring such violent repugnance."

"My father!" cried I, while every feature and every muscle was relaxed from anguish to pleasure. "Is my father, indeed, come? How kind, how very kind. But where is he, why does he not hasten to me?"

My change of manner surprised and pleased the magistrate; perhaps he thought that my former exclamation was a momentary return of delirium, and now he instantly resumed his former benevolence. He rose, and quitted the room with my nurse, and in a moment my father entered it.

Nothing, at this moment, could have given me greater pleasure than the arrival of my father. I stretched out my hand to him, and cried—

"Are you then safe — and Elizabeth — and Ernest?"

My father calmed me with assurances of their welfare, and endeavoured, by dwelling on these subjects so interesting to my heart, to raise my desponding spirits; but he soon felt that a prison cannot be the abode of cheerfulness. "What a place is this that you inhabit, my son!" said he, looking mournfully at the barred windows, and wretched appearance of the room. "You travelled to seek happiness, but a fatality seems to pursue you. And poor Clerval—"

The name of my unfortunate and murdered friend was an agitation too great to be endured in my weak state; I shed tears.

"Alas! yes, my father," replied I; "some destiny of the most horrible kind hangs over me, and I must live to fulfil it, or surely I should have died on the coffin of Henry."

We were not allowed to converse for any length of time, for the precarious state of my health rendered every precaution necessary that could insure tranquillity. Mr. Kirwin came in, and insisted that my strength should not be exhausted by too much exertion. But the appearance of my father was to me like that of my good angel, and I gradually recovered my health.

As my sickness quitted me, I was absorbed by a gloomy and black melancholy, that nothing could dissipate. The image of Clerval was for ever before me, ghastly and murdered. More than once the agitation into which these reflections threw me made my friends dread a dangerous relapse. Alas! why did they preserve so miserable and detested a life? It was surely that I might fulfil my destiny, which is now drawing to a close. Soon, oh, very soon, will death extinguish these throbbings, and relieve me from the mighty weight of anguish that bears me to the dust; and, in executing the award of justice, I shall also sink to rest. Then the appearance of death was distant, although the wish was ever present to my thoughts; and I often sat for hours motionless and speechless, wishing for some mighty revolution that might bury me and my destroyer in its ruins.

The season of the assizes[4] approached. I had already been three months in prison; and although I was still weak, and in continual danger of a relapse, I was obliged to travel nearly a hundred miles to the county-town, where the court was held. Mr. Kirwin charged himself with every care of collecting witnesses, and arranging my defence. I was spared the disgrace of appearing publicly as a criminal, as the case was not brought before the court that decides on life and death. The grand jury rejected the bill, on its being proved that I was on the Orkney Islands at the hour the body of my friend was found, and a fortnight after my removal I was liberated from prison.

My father was enraptured on finding me freed from the vexations of a criminal charge, that I was again allowed to breathe the fresh atmosphere, and allowed to return to my native country. I did not participate in these feelings; for to me the walls of a dungeon or a palace were alike hateful. The cup of life was poisoned for ever; and although the sun shone upon me, as upon the happy and gay of heart, I saw around me nothing but a dense and frightful darkness, penetrated by no light but the glimmer of two eyes that glared upon me. Sometimes they were the expressive eyes of Henry, languishing in death, the dark orbs nearly covered by the lids, and the long black lashes that fringed them; sometimes it was the watery clouded eyes of the monster, as I first saw them in my chamber at Ingolstadt.

4. Court sessions held periodically.

My father tried to awaken in me the feelings of affection. He talked of Geneva, which I should soon visit — of Elizabeth, and Ernest; but these words only drew deep groans from me. Sometimes, indeed, I felt a wish for happiness; and thought, with melancholy delight, of my beloved cousin; or longed, with a devouring *maladie du pays*,[5] to see once more the blue lake and rapid Rhone, that had been so dear to me in early childhood: but my general state of feeling was a torpor, in which a prison was as welcome a residence as the divinest scene in nature; and these fits were seldom interrupted, but by paroxysms of anguish and despair. At these moments I often endeavoured to put an end to the existence I loathed; and it required unceasing attendance and vigilance to restrain me from committing some dreadful act of violence.

I remember, as I quitted the prison, I heard one of the men say, "He may be innocent of the murder, but he has certainly a bad conscience." These words struck me. A bad conscience! yes, surely I had one. William, Justine, and Clerval, had died through my infernal machinations; "And whose death," cried I, "is to finish the tragedy? Ah! my father, do not remain in this wretched country; take me where I may forget myself, my existence, and all the world."

My father easily acceded to my desire; and, after having taken leave of Mr. Kirwin, we hastened to Dublin. I felt as if I was relieved from a heavy weight, when the packet sailed with a fair wind from Ireland, and I had quitted for ever the country which had been to me the scene of so much misery.

It was midnight. My father slept in the cabin; and I lay on the deck, looking at the stars, and listening to the dashing of the waves. I hailed the darkness that shut Ireland from my sight, and my pulse beat with a feverish joy, when I reflected that I should soon see Geneva. The past appeared to me in the light of a frightful dream; yet the vessel in which I was, the wind that blew me from the detested shore of Ireland, and the sea which surrounded me, told me too forcibly that I was deceived by no vision, and that Clerval, my friend and dearest companion, had fallen a victim to me and the monster of my creation. I repassed, in my memory, my whole life; my quiet happiness while residing with my family in Geneva, the death of my mother, and my departure for Ingolstadt. I remembered shuddering at the mad enthusiasm that hurried me on to the creation of my hideous enemy, and I called to mind the night during which he first lived. I was unable to pursue the train of thought; a thousand feelings pressed upon me, and I wept bitterly.

Ever since my recovery from the fever I had been in the custom of taking every night a small quantity of laudanum;[6] for it was by means of this drug only that I was enabled to gain the rest necessary for the

5. Homesickness.
6. An opium preparation.

preservation of life. Oppressed by the recollection of my various misfortunes, I now took a double dose, and soon slept profoundly. But
sleep did not afford me respite from thought and misery; my dreams
presented a thousand objects that scared me. Towards morning I was
possessed by a kind of night-mare; I felt the fiend's grasp in my neck,
and could not free myself from it; groans and cries rung in my ears.
My father, who was watching over me, perceiving my restlessness,
awoke me, and pointed to the port of Holyhead,[7] which we were now
entering.

Chapter V.

We had resolved not to go to London, but to cross the country to
Portsmouth, and thence to embark for Havre.[1] I preferred this plan
principally because I dreaded to see again those places in which I had
enjoyed a few moments of tranquillity with my beloved Clerval. I
thought with horror of seeing again those persons whom we had been
accustomed to visit together, and who might make inquiries concerning
an event, the very remembrance of which made me again feel the pang
I endured when I gazed on his lifeless form in the inn at ———.

As for my father, his desires and exertions were bounded to the[2] again
seeing me restored to health and peace of mind. His tenderness and
attentions were unremitting; my grief and gloom was obstinate, but he
would not despair. Sometimes he thought that I felt deeply the degradation of being obliged to answer a charge of murder, and he endeavoured to prove to me the futility of pride.

"Alas! my father," said I, "how little do you know me. Human beings,
their feelings and passions, would indeed be degraded, if such a wretch
as I felt pride. Justine, poor unhappy Justine, was as innocent as I, and
she suffered the same charge; she died for it; and I am the cause of
this—I murdered her. William, Justine, and Henry—they all died by
my hands."

My father had often, during my imprisonment, heard me make the
same assertion; when I thus accused myself, he sometimes seemed to
desire an explanation, and at others he appeared to consider it as caused
by delirium, and that, during my illness, some idea of this kind had
presented itself to my imagination, the remembrance of which I preserved in my convalescence. I avoided explanation, and maintained a
continual silence concerning the wretch I had created. I had a feeling
that I should be supposed mad, and this for ever chained my tongue,

7. On the Isle of Anglesey, Wales.
1. Le Havre, in France.
2. I.e., limited to a wish of.

when I would have given the whole world to have confided the fatal secret.

Upon this occasion my father said, with an expression of unbounded wonder, "What do you mean, Victor? are you mad? My dear son, I entreat you never to make such an assertion again."

"I am not mad," I cried energetically; "the sun and the heavens, who have viewed my operations, can bear witness of my truth. I am the assassin of those most innocent victims; they died by my machinations. A thousand times would I have shed my own blood drop by drop, to have saved their lives but I could not, my father, indeed, could not sacrifice the whole human race."

The conclusion of this speech convinced my father that my ideas were deranged, and he instantly changed the subject of our conversation, and endeavoured to alter the course of my thoughts. He wished as much as possible to obliterate the memory of the scenes that had taken place in Ireland, and never alluded to them, or suffered me to speak of my misfortunes.

As time passed away I became more calm: misery had her dwelling in my heart, but I no longer talked in the same incoherent manner of my own crimes; sufficient for me was the consciousness of them. By the utmost self-violence, I curbed the imperious voice of wretchedness, which sometimes desired to declare itself to the whole world; and my manners were calmer and more composed than they had ever been since my journey to the sea of ice.

We arrived at Havre on the 8th of May, and instantly proceeded to Paris, where my father had some business which detained us a few weeks. In this city, I received the following letter from Elizabeth:—

"*To* Victor Frankenstein.

"my dearest friend,

"It gave me the greatest pleasure to receive a letter from my uncle dated at Paris; you are no longer at a formidable distance, and I may hope to see you in less than a fortnight. My poor cousin, how much you must have suffered! I expect to see you looking even more ill than when you quitted Geneva. This winter has been passed most miserably, tortured as I have been by anxious suspense; yet I hope to see peace in your countenance, and to find that your heart is not totally devoid of comfort and tranquillity.

"Yet I fear that the same feelings now exist that made you so miserable a year ago, even perhaps augmented by time. I would not disturb you at this period, when so many misfortunes weigh upon you; but a conversation that I had with my uncle previous to his departure renders some explanation necessary before we meet.

"Explanation! you may possibly say; what can Elizabeth have to explain? If you really say this, my questions are answered, and I have no more to do than to sign myself your affectionate cousin. But you are distant from me, and it is possible that you may dread, and yet be pleased with this explanation; and, in a probability of this being the case, I dare not any longer postpone writing what, during your absence, I have often wished to express to you, but have never had the courage to begin.

"You well know, Victor, that our union had been the favourite plan of your parents ever since our infancy. We were told this when young, and taught to look forward to it as an event that would certainly take place. We were affectionate playfellows during childhood, and, I believe, dear and valued friends to one another as we grew older. But as brother and sister often entertain a lively affection towards each other, without desiring a more intimate union, may not such also be our case? Tell me, dearest Victor. Answer me, I conjure[3] you, by our mutual happiness, with simple truth — Do you not love another?

"You have travelled; you have spent several years of your life at Ingolstadt; and I confess to you, my friend, that when I saw you last autumn so unhappy, flying to solitude, from the society of every creature, I could not help supposing that you might regret our connexion, and believe yourself bound in honour to fulfil the wishes of your parents, although they opposed themselves to your inclinations. But this is false reasoning. I confess to you, my cousin, that I love you, and that in my airy dreams of futurity you have been my constant friend and companion. But it is your happiness I desire as well as my own, when I declare to you, that our marriage would render me eternally miserable, unless it were the dictate of your own free choice. Even now I weep to think, that, borne down as you are by the cruelest misfortunes, you may stifle, by the word *honour*, all hope of that love and happiness which would alone restore you to yourself. I, who have so interested an affection for you, may increase your miseries ten-fold, by being an obstacle to your wishes. Ah, Victor, be assured that your cousin and playmate has too sincere a love for you not to be made miserable by this supposition. Be happy, my friend; and if you obey me in this one request, remain satisfied that nothing on earth will have the power to interrupt my tranquillity.

"Do not let this letter disturb you; do not answer it to-morrow, or the next day, or even until you come, if it will give you pain. My uncle will send me news of your health; and if I see but one smile on your lips when we meet, occasioned by this or any other exertion of mine, I shall need no other happiness.

"ELIZABETH LAVENZA

"Geneva, May 18th, 17—."

3. Constrain by oath.

This letter revived in my memory what I had before forgotten, the threat of the fiend—"*I will be with you on your wedding-night!*" Such was my sentence, and on that night would the dæmon employ every art to destroy me, and tear me from the glimpse of happiness which promised partly to console my sufferings. On that night he had determined to consummate[4] his crimes by my death. Well, be it so; a deadly struggle would then assuredly take place, in which if he was victorious, I should be at peace, and his power over me be at an end. If he were vanquished, I should be a free man. Alas! what freedom? such as the peasant enjoys when his family have been massacred before his eyes, his cottage burnt, his lands laid waste, and he is turned adrift, homeless, pennyless, and alone, but free. Such would be my liberty, except that in my Elizabeth I possessed a treasure; alas! balanced by those horrors of remorse and guilt, which would pursue me until death.

Sweet and beloved Elizabeth! I read and re-read her letter, and some softened feelings stole into my heart, and dared to whisper paradisaical dreams of love and joy; but the apple was already eaten, and the angel's arm bared to drive me from all hope. Yet I would die to make her happy. If the monster executed his threat, death was inevitable; yet, again, I considered whether my marriage would hasten my fate. My destruction might indeed arrive a few months sooner; but if my torturer should suspect that I postponed it, influenced by his menaces, he would surely find other, and perhaps more dreadful means of revenge. He had vowed *to be with me on my wedding-night*, yet he did not consider that threat as binding him to peace in the mean time; for, as if to shew me that he was not yet satiated with blood, he had murdered Clerval immediately after the enunciation of his threats. I resolved, therefore, that if my immediate union with my cousin would conduce either to her's or my father's happiness, my adversary's designs against my life should not retard it a single hour.

In this state of mind I wrote to Elizabeth. My letter was calm and affectionate. "I fear, my beloved girl," I said, "little happiness remains for us on earth; yet all that I may one day enjoy is concentered in you. Chase away your idle fears; to you alone do I consecrate my life, and my endeavours for contentment. I have one secret, Elizabeth, a dreadful one; when revealed to you, it will chill your frame with horror, and then, far from being surprised at my misery, you will only wonder that I survive what I have endured. I will confide this tale of misery and terror to you the day after our marriage shall take place; for, my sweet cousin, there must be perfect confidence between us. But until then, I conjure you, do not mention or allude to it. This I most earnestly entreat, and I know you will comply."

In about a week after the arrival of Elizabeth's letter, we returned to

---

4. Complete, perfect.

Geneva. My cousin welcomed me with warm affection; yet tears were in her eyes, as she beheld my emaciated frame and feverish cheeks. I saw a change in her also. She was thinner, and had lost much of that heavenly vivacity that had before charmed me; but her gentleness, and soft looks of compassion, made her a more fit companion for one blasted and miserable as I was.

The tranquillity which I now enjoyed did not endure. Memory brought madness with it; and when I thought on what had passed, a real insanity possessed me; sometimes I was furious, and burnt with rage, sometimes low and despondent. I neither spoke or looked, but sat motionless, bewildered by the multitude of miseries that overcame me.

Elizabeth alone had the power to draw me from these fits; her gentle voice would soothe me when transported by passion, and inspire me with human feelings when sunk in torpor. She wept with me, and for me. When reason returned, she would remonstrate, and endeavour to inspire me with resignation. Ah! it is well for the unfortunate to be resigned, but for the guilty there is no peace. The agonies of remorse poison the luxury there is otherwise sometimes found in indulging the excess of grief.

Soon after my arrival my father spoke of my immediate marriage with my cousin. I remained silent.

"Have you, then, some other attachment?"

"None on earth. I love Elizabeth, and look forward to our union with delight. Let the day therefore be fixed; and on it I will consecrate myself, in life or death, to the happiness of my cousin."

"My dear Victor, do not speak thus. Heavy misfortunes have befallen us; but let us only cling closer to what remains, and transfer our love for those whom we have lost to those who yet live. Our circle will be small, but bound close by the ties of affection and mutual misfortune. And when time shall have softened your despair, new and dear objects of care will be born to replace those of whom we have been so cruelly deprived."

Such were the lessons of my father. But to me the remembrance of the threat returned: nor can you wonder, that, omnipotent as the fiend had yet been in his deeds of blood, I should almost regard him as invincible; and that when he had pronounced the words, "*I shall be with you on your wedding-night,*" I should regard the threatened fate as unavoidable. But death was no evil to me, if the loss of Elizabeth were balanced with it; and I therefore, with a contented and even cheerful countenance, agreed with my father, that if my cousin would consent, the ceremony should take place in ten days, and thus put, as I imagined, the seal to my fate.

Great God! if for one instant I had thought what might be the hellish intention of my fiendish adversary, I would rather have banished myself for ever from my native country, and wandered a friendless outcast over the earth, than have consented to this miserable marriage. But, as if possessed of magic powers, the monster had blinded me to his real intentions; and when I thought that I prepared only my own death, I hastened that of a far dearer victim.

As the period fixed for our marriage drew nearer, whether from cowardice or a prophetic feeling, I felt my heart sink within me. But I concealed my feelings by an appearance of hilarity, that brought smiles and joy to the countenance of my father, but hardly deceived the ever-watchful and nicer[5] eye of Elizabeth. She looked forward to our union with placid contentment, not unmingled with a little fear, which past misfortunes had impressed, that what now appeared certain and tangible happiness, might soon dissipate into an airy dream, and leave no trace but deep and everlasting regret.

Preparations were made for the event; congratulatory visits were received; and all wore a smiling appearance. I shut up, as well as I could, in my own heart the anxiety that preyed there, and entered with seeming earnestness into the plans of my father, although they might only serve as the decorations of my tragedy. A house was purchased for us near Cologny, by which we should enjoy the pleasures of the country, and yet be so near Geneva as to see my father every day; who would still reside within the walls, for the benefit of Ernest, that he might follow his studies at the schools.

In the mean time I took every precaution to defend my person, in case the fiend should openly attack me. I carried pistols and a dagger constantly about me, and was ever on the watch to prevent artifice; and by these means gained a greater degree of tranquillity. Indeed, as the period approached, the threat appeared more as a delusion, not to be regarded as worthy to disturb my peace, while the happiness I hoped for in my marriage wore a greater appearance of certainty, as the day fixed for its solemnization drew nearer, and I heard it continually spoken of as an occurrence which no accident could possibly prevent.

Elizabeth seemed happy; my tranquil demeanour contributed greatly to calm her mind. But on the day that was to fulfil my wishes and my destiny, she was melancholy, and a presentiment of evil pervaded her; and perhaps also she thought of the dreadful secret, which I had promised to reveal to her the following day. My father was in the mean time overjoyed, and, in the bustle of preparation, only observed in the melancholy of his niece the diffidence of a bride.

After the ceremony was performed, a large party assembled at my father's; but it was agreed that Elizabeth and I should pass the afternoon and night at Evian, and return to Cologny the next morning. As the day was fair, and the wind favourable, we resolved to go by water.

Those were the last moments of my life during which I enjoyed the

5. More discriminating.

feeling of happiness. We passed rapidly along: the sun was hot, but we were sheltered from its rays by a kind of canopy, while we enjoyed the beauty of the scene, sometimes on one side of the lake, where we saw Mont Salêve, the pleasant banks of Montalêgre, and at a distance, surmounting all, the beautiful Mont Blânc, and the assemblage of snowy mountains that in vain endeavour to emulate her; sometimes coasting the opposite banks, we saw the mighty Jura opposing its dark side to the ambition that would quit its native country, and an almost insurmountable barrier to the invader who should wish to enslave it.

I took the hand of Elizabeth: "You are sorrowful, my love. Ah! if you knew what I have suffered, and what I may yet endure, you would endeavour to let me taste the quiet, and freedom from despair, that this one day at least permits me to enjoy."

"Be happy, my dear Victor," replied Elizabeth; "there is, I hope, nothing to distress you; and be assured that if a lively joy is not painted in my face, my heart is contented. Something whispers to me not to depend too much on the prospect that is opened before us; but I will not listen to such a sinister voice. Observe how fast we move along, and how the clouds which sometimes obscure, and sometimes rise above the dome of Mont Blânc, render this scene of beauty still more interesting. Look also at the innumerable fish that are swimming in the clear waters, where we can distinguish every pebble that lies at the bottom. What a divine day! how happy and serene all nature appears!"

Thus Elizabeth endeavoured to divert her thoughts and mine from all reflection upon melancholy subjects. But her temper was fluctuating; joy for a few instants shone in her eyes, but it continually gave place to distraction and reverie.

The sun sunk lower in the heavens; we passed the river Drance, and observed its path through the chasms of the higher, and the glens of the lower hills. The Alps here come closer to the lake, and we approached the amphitheatre of mountains which forms its eastern boundary. The spire of Evian shone under the woods that surrounded it, and the range of mountain above mountain by which it was overhung.

The wind, which had hitherto carried us along with amazing rapidity, sunk at sunset to a light breeze; the soft air just ruffled the water, and caused a pleasant motion among the trees as we approached the shore, from which it wafted the most delightful scent of flowers and hay. The sun sunk beneath the horizon as we landed; and as I touched the shore, I felt those cares and fears revive, which soon were to clasp me, and cling to me for ever.

Chapter VI.

It was eight o'clock when we landed; we walked for a short time on the shore, enjoying the transitory light, and then retired to the inn, and contemplated the lovely scene of waters, woods, and mountains, obscured in darkness, yet still displaying their black outlines.

The wind, which had fallen in the south, now rose with great violence in the west. The moon had reached her summit in the heavens, and was beginning to descend; the clouds swept across it swifter than the flight of the vulture, and dimmed her rays, while the lake reflected the scene of the busy heavens, rendered still busier by the restless waves that were beginning to rise. Suddenly a heavy storm of rain descended.

I had been calm during the day; but so soon as night obscured the shapes of objects, a thousand fears arose in my mind. I was anxious and watchful, while my right hand grasped a pistol which was hidden in my bosom; every sound terrified me; but I resolved that I would sell my life dearly, and not relax the impending conflict until my own life, or that of my adversary, were extinguished.

Elizabeth observed my agitation for some time in timid and fearful silence; at length she said, "What is it that agitates you, my dear Victor? What is it you fear?"

"Oh! peace, peace, my love," replied I, "this night, and all will be safe: but this night is dreadful, very dreadful."

I passed an hour in this state of mind, when suddenly I reflected how dreadful the combat which I momentarily expected would be to my wife, and I earnestly entreated her to retire, resolving not to join her until I had obtained some knowledge as to the situation of my enemy.

She left me, and I continued some time walking up and down the passages of the house, and inspecting every corner that might afford a retreat to my adversary. But I discovered no trace of him, and was beginning to conjecture that some fortunate chance had intervened to prevent the execution of his menaces; when suddenly I heard a shrill and dreadful scream. It came from the room into which Elizabeth had retired. As I heard it, the whole truth rushed into my mind, my arms dropped, the motion of every muscle and fibre was suspended; I could feel the blood trickling in my veins, and tingling in the extremities of my limbs. This state lasted but for an instant; the scream was repeated, and I rushed into the room.

Great God! why did I not then expire! Why am I here to relate the destruction of the best hope, and the purest creature of earth. She was there, lifeless and inanimate, thrown across the bed, her head hanging down, and her pale and distorted features half covered by her hair. Every where I turn I see the same figure — her bloodless arms and relaxed form flung by the murderer on its bridal bier. Could I behold this, and live? Alas! life is obstinate, and clings closest where it is most hated. For a moment only did I lose recollection; I fainted.

When I recovered, I found myself surrounded by the people of the inn; their countenances expressed a breathless terror: but the horror of others appeared only as a mockery, a shadow of the feelings that oppressed me. I escaped from them to the room where lay the body of Elizabeth, my love, my wife, so lately living, so dear, so worthy. She had been moved from the posture in which I had first beheld her; and now, as she lay, her head upon her arm, and a handkerchief thrown across her face and neck, I might have supposed her asleep. I rushed towards her, and embraced her with ardour; but the deathly languor and coldness of the limbs told me, that what I now held in my arms had ceased to be the Elizabeth whom I had loved and cherished. The murderous mark of the fiend's grasp was on her neck, and the breath had ceased to issue from her lips.

While I still hung over her in the agony of despair, I happened to look up. The windows of the room had before been darkened; and I felt a kind of panic on seeing the pale yellow light of the moon illuminate the chamber. The shutters had been thrown back; and, with a sensation of horror not to be described, I saw at the open window a figure the most hideous and abhorred. A grin was on the face of the monster; he seemed to jeer, as with his fiendish finger he pointed towards the corpse of my wife. I rushed towards the window, and drawing a pistol from my bosom, shot; but he eluded me, leaped from his station, and, running with the swiftness of lightning, plunged into the lake.

The report of the pistol brought a crowd into the room. I pointed to the spot where he had disappeared, and we followed the track with boats; nets were cast, but in vain. After passing several hours, we returned hopeless, most of my companions believing it to have been a form conjured by my fancy. After having landed, they proceeded to search the country, parties going in different directions among the woods and vines.

I did not accompany them; I was exhausted: a film covered my eyes, and my skin was parched with the heat of fever. In this state I lay on a bed, hardly conscious of what had happened; my eyes wandered round the room, as if to seek something that I had lost.

At length I remembered that my father would anxiously expect the return of Elizabeth and myself, and that I must return alone. This reflection brought tears into my eyes, and I wept for a long time; but my thoughts rambled to various subjects, reflecting on my misfortunes, and their cause. I was bewildered in a cloud of wonder and horror. The death of William, the execution of Justine, the murder of Clerval, and lastly of my wife; even at that moment I knew not that my only remaining friends were safe from the malignity of the fiend; my father even now might be writhing under his grasp, and Ernest might be dead at his feet. This idea made me shudder, and recalled me to action. I started up, and resolved to return to Geneva with all possible speed.

There were no horses to be procured, and I must return by the lake; but the wind was unfavourable, and the rain fell in torrents. However, it was hardly morning, and I might reasonably hope to arrive by night. I hired men to row, and took an oar myself, for I had always experienced relief from mental torment in bodily exercise. But the overflowing misery I now felt, and the excess of agitation that I endured, rendered me incapable of any exertion. I threw down the oar; and, leaning my head upon my hands, gave way to every gloomy idea that arose. If I looked up, I saw the scenes which were familiar to me in my happier time, and which I had contemplated but the day before in the company of her who was now but a shadow and a recollection. Tears streamed from my eyes. The rain had ceased for a moment, and I saw the fish play in the waters as they had done a few hours before; they had then been observed by Elizabeth. Nothing is so painful to the human mind as a great and sudden change. The sun might shine, or the clouds might lour;[1] but nothing could appear to me as it had done the day before. A fiend had snatched from me every hope of future happiness: no creature had ever been so miserable as I was; so frightful an event is single in the history of man.

But why should I dwell upon the incidents that followed this last overwhelming event. Mine has been a tale of horrors; I have reached their *acme*, and what I must now relate can but be tedious to you. Know that, one by one, my friends were snatched away; I was left desolate. My own strength is exhausted; and I must tell, in a few words, what remains of my hideous narration.

I arrived at Geneva. My father and Ernest yet lived; but the former sunk under the tidings that I bore. I see him now, excellent and venerable old man! his eyes wandered in vacancy, for they had lost their charm and their delight—his niece, his more than daughter, whom he doated on with all that affection which a man feels, who, in the decline of life, having few affections, clings more earnestly to those that remain. Cursed, cursed be the fiend that brought misery on his grey hairs, and doomed him to waste in wretchedness! He could not live under the horrors that were accumulated around him; an apoplectic fit was brought on, and in a few days he died in my arms.

What then became of me? I know not; I lost sensation, and chains and darkness were the only objects that pressed upon me. Sometimes, indeed, I dreamt that I wandered in flowery meadows and pleasant vales

1. Look dark or threatening.

with the friends of my youth; but awoke, and found myself in a dungeon. Melancholy followed, but by degrees I gained a clear conception of my miseries and situation, and was then released from my prison. For they had called me mad; and during many months, as I understood, a solitary cell had been my habitation.

But liberty had been a useless gift to me had I not, as I awakened to reason, at the same time awakened to revenge. As the memory of past misfortunes pressed upon me, I began to reflect on their cause — the monster whom I had created, the miserable dæmon whom I had sent abroad into the world for my destruction. I was possessed by a maddening rage when I thought of him, and desired and ardently prayed that I might have him within my grasp to wreak a great and signal revenge on his cursed head.

Nor did my hate long confine itself to useless wishes; I began to reflect on the best means of securing him; and for this purpose, about a month after my release, I repaired to a criminal judge in the town, and told him that I had an accusation to make; that I knew the destroyer of my family; and that I required him to exert his whole authority for the apprehension of the murderer.

The magistrate listened to me with attention and kindness: "Be assured, sir," said he, "no pains or exertions on my part shall be spared to discover the villain."

"I thank you," replied I; "listen, therefore, to the deposition that I have to make. It is indeed a tale so strange, that I should fear you would not credit it, were there not something in truth which, however wonderful, forces conviction. The story is too connected to be mistaken for a dream, and I have no motive for falsehood." My manner, as I thus addressed him, was impressive, but calm; I had formed in my own heart a resolution to pursue my destroyer to death; and this purpose quieted my agony, and provisionally reconciled me to life. I now related my history briefly, but with firmness and precision, marking the dates with accuracy, and never deviating into invective or exclamation.

The magistrate appeared at first perfectly incredulous, but as I continued he became more attentive and interested; I saw him sometimes shudder with horror, at others a lively surprise, unmingled with disbelief, was painted on his countenance.

When I had concluded my narration, I said, "This is the being whom I accuse, and for whose detection and punishment I call upon you to exert your whole power. It is your duty as a magistrate, and I believe and hope that your feelings as a man will not revolt from the execution of those functions on this occasion."

This address caused a considerable change in the physiognomy of my auditor. He had heard my story with that half kind of belief that is given to a tale of spirits and supernatural events; but when he was called upon to act officially in consequence, the whole tide of his incredulity returned. He, however, answered mildly, "I would willingly afford you every aid in your pursuit; but the creature of whom you speak appears to have powers which would put all my exertions to defiance. Who can follow an animal which can traverse the sea of ice, and inhabit caves and dens, where no man would venture to intrude? Besides, some months have elapsed since the commission of his crimes, and no one can conjecture to what place he has wandered, or what region he may now inhabit."

"I do not doubt that he hovers near the spot which I inhabit; and if he has indeed taken refuge in the Alps, he may be hunted like the chamois,[2] and destroyed as a beast of prey. But I perceive your thoughts: you do not credit my narrative, and do not intend to pursue my enemy with the punishment which is his desert."

As I spoke, rage sparkled in my eyes; the magistrate was intimidated; "You are mistaken," said he, "I will exert myself; and if it is in my power to seize the monster, be assured that he shall suffer punishment proportionate to his crimes. But I fear, from what you have yourself described to be his properties, that this will prove impracticable, and that, while every proper measure is pursued, you should endeavour to make up your mind to disappointment."

"That cannot be; but all that I can say will be of little avail. My revenge is of no moment[3] to you; yet, while I allow it to be a vice, I confess that it is the devouring and only passion of my soul. My rage is unspeakable, when I reflect that the murderer, whom I have turned loose upon society, still exists. You refuse my just demand: I have but one resource; and I devote myself, either in my life or death, to his destruction."

I trembled with excess of agitation as I said this; there was a phrenzy in my manner, and something, I doubt not, of that haughty fierceness, which the martyrs of old are said to have possessed. But to a Genevan magistrate, whose mind was occupied by far other ideas than those of devotion and heroism, this elevation of mind had much the appearance of madness. He endeavoured to soothe me as a nurse does a child, and reverted to[4] my tale as the effects of delirium.

"Man," I cried, "how ignorant art thou in thy pride of wisdom! Cease; you know not what it is you say."

I broke from the house angry and disturbed, and retired to meditate on some other mode of action.

2. An Alpine antelope.
3. Importance.
4. Looked back at.

Chapter VII.

My present situation was one in which all voluntary thought was swallowed up and lost. I was hurried away by fury; revenge alone endowed me with strength and composure; it modelled my feelings, and allowed me to be calculating and calm, at periods when otherwise delirium or death would have been my portion.

My first resolution was to quit Geneva for ever; my country, which, when I was happy and beloved, was dear to me, now, in my adversity, became hateful. I provided myself with a sum of money, together with a few jewels which had belonged to my mother, and departed.

And now my wanderings began, which are to cease but with life. I have traversed a vast portion of the earth, and have endured all the hardships which travellers, in deserts and barbarous countries, are wont to meet. How I have lived I hardly know; many times have I stretched my failing limbs upon the sandy plain, and prayed for death. But revenge kept me alive; I dared not die, and leave my adversary in being.

When I quitted Geneva, my first labour was to gain some clue by which I might trace the steps of my fiendish enemy. But my plan was unsettled; and I wandered many hours around the confines of the town, uncertain what path I should pursue. As night approached, I found myself at the entrance of the cemetery where William, Elizabeth, and my father, reposed. I entered it, and approached the tomb which marked their graves. Every thing was silent, except the leaves of the trees, which were gently agitated by the wind; the night was nearly dark; and the scene would have been solemn and affecting even to an uninterested observer. The spirits of the departed seemed to flit around, and to cast a shadow, which was felt but seen not, around the head of the mourner.

The deep grief which this scene had at first excited quickly gave way to rage and despair. They were dead, and I lived; their murderer also lived, and to destroy him I must drag out my weary existence. I knelt on the grass, and kissed the earth, and with quivering lips exclaimed, "By the sacred earth on which I kneel, by the shades[1] that wander near me, by the deep and eternal grief that I feel, I swear; and by thee, O Night, and by the spirits that preside over thee, I swear to pursue the dæmon, who caused this misery, until he or I shall perish in mortal conflict. For this purpose I will preserve my life: to execute this dear revenge, will I again behold the sun, and tread the green herbage of earth, which otherwise should vanish from my eyes for ever. And I call on you, spirits of the dead; and on you, wandering ministers of vengeance, to aid and conduct me in my work. Let the cursed and hellish

---

1. Disembodied spirits.

monster drink deep of agony; let him feel the despair that now torments me."

I had begun my adjuration with solemnity, and an awe which almost assured me that the shades of my murdered friends heard and approved my devotion; but the furies possessed me as I concluded, and rage choaked my utterance.

I was answered through the stillness of night by a loud and fiendish laugh. It rung on my ears long and heavily; the mountains re-echoed it, and I felt as if all hell surrounded me with mockery and laughter. Surely in that moment I should have been possessed by phrenzy, and have destroyed my miserable existence, but that my vow was heard, and that I was reserved for vengeance. The laughter died away, when a well-known and abhorred voice, apparently close to my ear, addressed me in an audible whisper — "I am satisfied: miserable wretch! you have determined to live, and I am satisfied."

I darted towards the spot from which the sound proceeded; but the devil eluded my grasp. Suddenly the broad disk of the moon arose, and shone full upon his ghastly and distorted shape, as he fled with more than mortal speed.

I pursued him; and for many months this has been my task. Guided by a slight clue, I followed the windings of the Rhone, but vainly. The blue Mediterranean appeared; and, by a strange chance, I saw the fiend enter by night, and hide himself in a vessel bound for the Black Sea. I took my passage in the same ship; but he escaped, I know not how.

Amidst the wilds of Tartary and Russia, although he still evaded me, I have ever followed in his track. Sometimes the peasants, scared by this horrid apparition, informed me of his path; sometimes he himself, who feared that if I lost all trace I should despair and die, often left some mark to guide me. The snows descended on my head, and I saw the print of his huge step on the white plain. To you first entering on life, to whom care is new and agony unknown, how can you understand what I have felt, and still feel. Cold, want, and fatigue, were the least pains which I was destined to endure. I was cursed by some devil, and carried about with me my eternal hell;[2] yet still a spirit of good followed and directed my steps, and, when I most murmured, would suddenly extricate me from seemingly insurmountable difficulties. Sometimes, when nature overcome by hunger, sunk under the exhaustion, a repast was prepared for me in the desert, that restored and inspirited me. The fare was indeed coarse, such as the peasants of the country ate; but I may not doubt that it was set there by the spirits that I had invoked to aid me. Often, when all was dry, the heavens cloudless, and I was parched by thirst, a slight cloud would bedim the sky, shed the few drops that revived me, and vanish.

2. See p. 92 and n. 1, above.

I followed, when I could, the courses of the rivers; but the dæmon generally avoided these, as it was here that the population of the country chiefly collected. In other places human beings were seldom seen; and I generally subsisted on the wild animals that crossed my path. I had money with me, and gained the friendship of the villagers by distributing it, or bringing with me some food that I had killed, which, after taking a small part, I always presented to those who had provided me with fire and utensils for cooking.

My life, as it passed thus, was indeed hateful to me, and it was during sleep alone that I could taste joy. O blessed sleep! often, when most miserable, I sank to repose, and my dreams lulled me even to rapture. The spirits that guarded me had provided these moments, or rather hours, of happiness that I might retain strength to fulfil my pilgrimage. Deprived of this respite, I should have sunk under my hardships. During the day I was sustained and inspirited by the hope of night: for in sleep I saw my friends, my wife, and my beloved country; again I saw the benevolent countenance of my father, heard the silver tones of my Elizabeth's voice, and beheld Clerval enjoying health and youth. Often, when wearied by a toilsome march, I persuaded myself that I was dreaming until night should come, and that I should then enjoy reality in the arms of my dearest friends. What agonizing fondness did I feel for them! how did I cling to their dear forms, as sometimes they haunted even my waking hours, and persuade myself that they still lived! At such moments vengeance, that burned within me, died in my heart, and I pursued my path towards the destruction of the dæmon, more as a task enjoined by heaven, as the mechanical impulse of some power of which I was unconscious, than as the ardent desire of my soul.

What his feelings were whom I pursued, I cannot know. Sometimes, indeed, he left marks in writing on the barks of the trees, or cut in stone, that guided me, and instigated my fury. "My reign is not yet over," (these words were legible in one of these inscriptions); "you live, and my power is complete. Follow me; I seek the everlasting ices of the north, where you will feel the misery of cold and frost, to which I am impassive. You will find near this place, if you follow not too tardily, a dead hare; eat, and be refreshed. Come on, my enemy; we have yet to wrestle for our lives; but many hard and miserable hours must you endure, until that period shall arrive."

Scoffing devil! Again do I vow vengeance; again do I devote thee, miserable fiend, to torture and death. Never will I omit my search, until he or I perish; and then with what ecstacy shall I join my Elizabeth, and those who even now prepare for me the reward of my tedious toil and horrible pilgrimage.

As I still pursued my journey to the northward, the snows thickened, and the cold increased in a degree almost too severe to support. The peasants were shut up in their hovels, and only a few of the most hardy ventured forth to seize the animals whom starvation had forced from their hiding-places to seek for prey. The rivers were covered with ice, and no fish could be procured; and thus I was cut off from my chief article of maintenance.

The triumph of my enemy increased with the difficulty of my labours. One inscription that he left was in these words: "Prepare! your toils only begin: wrap yourself in furs, and provide food, for we shall soon enter upon a journey where your sufferings will satisfy my everlasting hatred."

My courage and perseverance were invigorated by these scoffing words; I resolved not to fail in my purpose; and, calling on heaven to support me, I continued with unabated fervour to traverse immense deserts, until the ocean appeared at a distance, and formed the utmost boundary of the horizon. Oh! how unlike it was to the blue seas of the south! Covered with ice, it was only to be distinguished from land by its superior wildness and ruggedness. The Greeks wept for joy when they beheld the Mediterranean from the hills of Asia, and hailed with rapture the boundary of their toils.[3] I did not weep; but I knelt down, and, with a full heart, thanked my guiding spirit for conducting me in safety to the place where I hoped, notwithstanding my adversary's gibe, to meet and grapple with him.

Some weeks before this period I had procured a sledge and dogs, and thus traversed the snows with inconceivable speed. I know not whether the fiend possessed the same advantages; but I found that, as before I had daily lost ground in the pursuit, I now gained on him; so much so, that when I first saw the ocean, he was but one day's journey in advance, and I hoped to intercept him before he should reach the beach. With new courage, therefore, I pressed on, and in two days arrived at a wretched hamlet on the seashore. I inquired of the inhabitants concerning the fiend, and gained accurate information. A gigantic monster, they said, had arrived the night before, armed with a gun and many pistols; putting to flight the inhabitants of a solitary cottage, through fear of his terrific appearance. He had carried off their store of winter food, and, placing it in a sledge, to draw which he had seized on a numerous drove of trained dogs, he had harnessed them, and the same night, to the joy of the horror-struck villagers, had pursued his journey across the sea in a direction that led to no land; and they conjectured that he must speedily be destroyed by the breaking of the ice, or frozen by the eternal frosts.

On hearing this information, I suffered a temporary access of despair. He had escaped me; and I must commence a destructive and almost endless journey across the mountainous ices of the ocean, — amidst cold

3. A reference to the 401–399 B.C. Greek expedition to and from Persia, known as "the March of the Ten Thousand"; see book IV of the *Anabasis* of Xenophon (431–362 B.C.).

that few of the inhabitants could long endure, and which I, the native of a genial and sunny climate, could not hope to survive. Yet at the idea that the fiend should live and be triumphant, my rage and vengeance returned, and, like a mighty tide, overwhelmed every other feeling. After a slight repose, during which the spirits of the dead hovered round, and instigated me to toil and revenge, I prepared for my journey.

I exchanged my land sledge for one fashioned for the inequalities of the frozen ocean; and, purchasing a plentiful stock of provisions, I departed from land.

I cannot guess how many days have passed since then; but I have endured misery, which nothing but the eternal sentiment of a just retribution burning within my heart could have enabled me to support. Immense and rugged mountains of ice often barred up my passage, and I often heard the thunder of the ground sea, which threatened my destruction. But again the frost came, and made the paths of the sea secure.

By the quantity of provision which I had consumed I should guess that I had passed three weeks in this journey; and the continual protraction of hope, returning back upon the heart, often wrung bitter drops of despondency and grief from my eyes. Despair had indeed almost secured her prey, and I should soon have sunk beneath this misery; when once, after the poor animals that carried me had with incredible toil gained the summit of a sloping ice mountain, and one sinking under his fatigue died, I viewed the expanse before me with anguish, when suddenly my eye caught a dark speck upon the dusky plain. I strained my sight to discover what it could be, and uttered a wild cry of ecstacy when I distinguished a sledge, and the distorted proportions of a well-known form within. Oh! with what a burning gush did hope revisit my heart! warm tears filled my eyes, which I hastily wiped away, that they might not intercept the view I had of the dæmon; but still my sight was dimmed by the burning drops, until, giving way to the emotions that oppressed me, I wept aloud.

But this was not the time for delay; I disencumbered the dogs of their dead companion, gave them a plentiful portion of food; and, after an hour's rest, which was absolutely necessary, and yet which was bitterly irksome to me, I continued my route. The sledge was still visible; nor did I again lose sight of it, except at the moments when for a short time some ice rock concealed it with its intervening crags. I indeed perceptibly gained on it; and when, after nearly two days' journey, I beheld my enemy at no more than a mile distant, my heart bounded within me.

But now, when I appeared almost within grasp of my enemy, my hopes were suddenly extinguished, and I lost all trace of him more utterly than I had ever done before. A ground sea was heard; the thunder of its progress, as the waters rolled and swelled beneath me, became every moment more ominous and terrific. I pressed on, but in vain. The wind arose; the sea roared; and, as with the mighty shock of an earthquake, it split, and cracked with a tremendous and overwhelming sound. The work was soon finished: in a few minutes a tumultuous sea rolled between me and my enemy, and I was left drifting on a scattered piece of ice, that was continually lessening, and thus preparing for me a hideous death.

In this manner many appalling hours passed; several of my dogs died; and I myself was about to sink under the accumulation of distress, when I saw your vessel riding at anchor, and holding forth to me hopes of succour and life. I had no conception that vessels ever came so far north, and was astounded at the sight. I quickly destroyed part of my sledge to construct oars; and by these means was enabled, with infinite fatigue, to move my ice-raft in the direction of your ship. I had determined, if you were going southward, still to trust myself to the mercy of the seas, rather than abandon my purpose. I hoped to induce you to grant me a boat with which I could still pursue my enemy. But your direction was northward. You took me on board when my vigour was exhausted, and I should soon have sunk under my multiplied hardships into a death, which I still dread,—for my task is unfulfilled.

Oh! when will my guiding spirit, in conducting me to the dæmon, allow me the rest I so much desire; or must I die, and he yet live? If I do, swear to me, Walton, that he shall not escape; that you will seek him, and satisfy my vengeance in his death. Yet, do I dare ask you to undertake my pilgrimage, to endure the hardships that I have undergone? No; I am not so selfish. Yet, when I am dead, if he should appear; if the ministers of vengeance should conduct him to you, swear that he shall not live—swear that he shall not triumph over my accumulated woes, and live to make another such a wretch as I am. He is eloquent and persuasive; and once his words had even power over my heart: but trust him not. His soul is as hellish as his form, full of treachery and fiend-like malice. Hear him not; call on the manes[4] of William, Justine, Clerval, Elizabeth, my father, and of the wretched Victor, and thrust your sword into his heart. I will hover near, and direct the steel aright.

WALTON, in continuation.

August 26th, 17—.

You have read this strange and terrific story, Margaret; and do you not feel your blood congealed with horror, like that which even now curdles mine? Sometimes, seized with sudden agony, he could not continue his tale; at others, his voice broken, yet piercing, uttered with difficulty the words so replete with agony. His fine and lovely eyes were now lighted up with indignation, now subdued to downcast sorrow, and

4. Spirits of the dead.

quenched in infinite wretchedness. Sometimes he commanded his countenance and tones, and related the most horrible incidents with a tranquil voice, suppressing every mark of agitation; then, like a volcano bursting forth, his face would suddenly change to an expression of the wildest rage, as he shrieked out imprecations on his persecutor.

His tale is connected,[5] and told with an appearance of the simplest truth; yet I own to you that the letters of Felix and Safie, which he shewed me, and the apparition of the monster, seen from our ship, brought to me a greater conviction of the truth of his narrative than his asseverations, however earnest and connected. Such a monster has then really existence; I cannot doubt it; yet I am lost in surprise and admiration. Sometimes I endeavoured to gain from Frankenstein the particulars of his creature's formation; but on this point he was impenetrable.

"Are you mad, my friend?" said he, "or whither does your senseless curiosity lead you? Would you also create for yourself and the world a demoniacal enemy? Or to what do your questions tend? Peace, peace! learn my miseries, and do not seek to increase your own."

Frankenstein discovered that I made notes concerning his history: he asked to see them, and then himself corrected and augmented them in many places; but principally in giving the life and spirit to the conversations he held with his enemy. "Since you have preserved my narration," said he, "I would not that a mutilated one should go down to posterity."

Thus has a week passed away, while I have listened to the strangest tale that ever imagination formed. My thoughts, and every feeling of my soul, have been drunk up by the interest for my guest, which this tale, and his own elevated and gentle manners have created. I wish to soothe him; yet can I counsel one so infinitely miserable, so destitute of every hope of consolation, to live? Oh, no! the only joy that he can now know will be when he composes his shattered feelings to peace and death. Yet he enjoys one comfort, the offspring of solitude and delirium: he believes, that, when in dreams he holds converse with his friends, and derives from that communion consolation for his miseries, or excitements to his vengeance, that they are not the creations of his fancy, but the real beings who visit him from the regions of a remote world. This faith gives a solemnity to his reveries that render them to me almost as imposing and interesting as truth.

Our conversations are not always confined to his own history and misfortunes. On every point of general literature he displays unbounded knowledge, and a quick and piercing apprehension. His eloquence is forcible and touching; nor can I hear him, when he relates a pathetic incident, or endeavours to move the passions of pity or love, without tears. What a glorious creature must he have been in the days of his

5. Sequential and coherent.

prosperity, when he is thus noble and godlike in ruin. He seems to feel his own worth, and the greatness of his fall.

"When younger," said he, "I felt as if I were destined for some great enterprise. My feelings are profound; but I possessed a coolness of judgment that fitted me for illustrious achievements. This sentiment of the worth of my nature supported me, when others would have been oppressed; for I deemed it criminal to throw away in useless grief those talents that might be useful to my fellow-creatures. When I reflected on the work I had completed, no less a one than the creation of a sensitive and rational animal, I could not rank myself with the herd of common projectors.[6] But this feeling, which supported me in the commencement of my career, now serves only to plunge me lower in the dust. All my speculations and hopes are as nothing; and, like the archangel who aspired to omnipotence, I am chained in an eternal hell. My imagination was vivid, yet my powers of analysis and application were intense; by the union of these qualities I conceived the idea, and executed the creation of a man. Even now I cannot recollect, without passion, my reveries while the work was incomplete. I trod heaven in my thoughts, now exulting in my powers, now burning with the idea of their effects. From my infancy I was imbued with high hopes and a lofty ambition; but how am I sunk! Oh! my friend, if you had known me as I once was, you would not recognize me in this state of degradation. Despondency rarely visited my heart; a high destiny seemed to bear me on, until I fell, never, never again to rise."

Must I then lose this admirable being? I have longed for a friend; I have sought one who would sympathize with and love me. Behold, on these desert seas I have found such a one; but, I fear, I have gained him only to know his value, and lose him. I would reconcile him to life, but he repulses the idea.

"I thank you, Walton," he said, "for your kind intentions towards so miserable a wretch; but when you speak of new ties, and fresh affections, think you that any can replace those who are gone? Can any man be to me as Clerval was; or any woman another Elizabeth? Even where the affections are not strongly moved by any superior excellence, the companions of our childhood always possess a certain power over our minds, which hardly any later friend can obtain. They know our infantine dispositions, which, however they may be afterwards modified, are never eradicated; and they can judge of our actions with more certain conclusions as to the integrity of our motives. A sister or a brother can never, unless indeed such symptoms have been shewn early, suspect the other of fraud or false dealing, when another friend, however strongly he may be attached, may, in spite of himself, be invaded with suspicion. But I enjoyed friends, dear not only through habit

6. Schemers and speculators.

and association, but from their own merits; and, wherever I am, the soothing voice of my Elizabeth, and the conversation of Clerval, will be ever whispered in my ear. They are dead; and but one feeling in such a solitude can persuade me to preserve my life. If I were engaged in any high undertaking or design, fraught with extensive utility to my fellow-creatures, then could I live to fulfil it. But such is not my destiny; I must pursue and destroy the being to whom I gave existence; then my lot on earth will be fulfilled, and I may die."

September 2d.

MY BELOVED SISTER,

I write to you, encompassed by peril, and ignorant whether I am ever doomed to see again dear England, and the dearer friends that inhabit it. I am surrounded by mountains of ice, which admit of no escape, and threaten every moment to crush my vessel. The brave fellows, whom I have persuaded to be my companions, look towards me for aid; but I have none to bestow. There is something terribly appalling in our situation, yet my courage and hopes do not desert me. We may survive; and if we do not, I will repeat the lessons of my Seneca,[7] and die with a good heart.

Yet what, Margaret, will be the state of your mind? You will not hear of my destruction, and you will anxiously await my return. Years will pass, and you will have visitings of despair, and yet be tortured by hope. Oh! my beloved sister, the sickening failings of your heart-felt expectations are, in prospect, more terrible to me than my own death. But you have a husband, and lovely children; you may be happy: heaven bless you, and make you so!

My unfortunate guest regards me with the tenderest compassion. He endeavours to fill me with hope; and talks as if life were a possession which he valued. He reminds me how often the same accidents have happened to other navigators, who have attempted this sea, and, in spite of myself, he fills me with cheerful auguries. Even the sailors feel the power of his eloquence: when he speaks, they no longer despair; he rouses their energies, and, while they hear his voice, they believe these vast mountains of ice are mole-hills, which will vanish before the resolutions of man. These feelings are transitory; each day's expectation delayed fills them with fear, and I almost dread a mutiny caused by this despair.

September 5th.

A scene has just passed of such uncommon interest, that although it is highly probable that these papers may never reach you, yet I cannot forbear recording it.

---

7. Lucius Annaeus Seneca (c. 4 B.C.–A.D. 65), Roman Stoic philosopher and poet (see p. 46 and n. 1, above).

We are still surrounded by mountains of ice, still in imminent danger of being crushed in their conflict. The cold is excessive, and many of my unfortunate comrades have already found a grave amidst this scene of desolation. Frankenstein has daily declined in health: a feverish fire still glimmers in his eyes; but he is exhausted, and, when suddenly roused to any exertion, he speedily sinks again into apparent lifelessness.

I mentioned in my last letter the fears I entertained of a mutiny. This morning, as I sat watching the wan countenance of my friend — his eyes half closed, and his limbs hanging listlessly, — I was roused by half a dozen of the sailors, who desired admission into the cabin. They entered; and their leader addressed me. He told me that he and his companions had been chosen by the other sailors to come in deputation to me, to make me a demand, which, in justice, I could not refuse. We were immured in ice, and should probably never escape; but they feared that if, as was possible, the ice should dissipate, and a free passage be opened, I should be rash enough to continue my voyage, and lead them into fresh dangers, after they might happily have surmounted this. They desired, therefore, that I should engage with a solemn promise, that if the vessel should be freed, I would instantly direct my course southward.

This speech troubled me. I had not despaired; nor had I yet conceived the idea of returning, if set free. Yet could I, in justice, or even in possibility, refuse this demand? I hesitated before I answered; when Frankenstein, who had at first been silent, and, indeed, appeared hardly to have force enough to attend, now roused himself, his eyes sparkled, and his cheeks flushed with momentary vigour. Turning towards the men, he said —

"What do you mean? What do you demand of your captain? Are you then so easily turned from your design? Did you not call this a glorious expedition? and wherefore was it glorious? Not because the way was smooth and placid as a southern sea but because it was full of dangers and terror; because, at every new incident, your fortitude was to be called forth and your courage exhibited; because danger and death surrounded, and these dangers you were to brave and overcome. For this was it a glorious, for this was it an honourable undertaking. You were hereafter to be hailed as the benefactors of your species; your name adored, as belonging to brave men who encountered death for honour and the benefit of mankind. And now, behold, with the first imagination of danger, or, if you will, the first mighty and terrific trial of your courage, you shrink away, and are content to be handed down as men who had not strength enough to endure cold and peril; and so, poor souls, they were chilly, and returned to their warm fire-sides. Why, that requires not this preparation; ye need not have come thus far, and dragged your captain to the shame of a defeat, merely to prove yourselves cowards. Oh! be men, or be more than men. Be steady to your purposes, and firm as a rock. This ice is not made of such stuff as your hearts might be; it is mutable, cannot withstand you, if you say that it shall not. Do not return to your families with the stigma of disgrace marked on your brows. Return as heroes who have fought and conquered, and who know not what it is to turn their backs on the foe."

He spoke this with a voice so modulated to the different feelings expressed in his speech, with an eye so full of lofty design and heroism, that can you wonder that these men were moved. They looked at one another, and were unable to reply. I spoke; I told them to retire, and consider of what had been said: that I would not lead them further north, if they strenuously desired the contrary; but that I hoped that, with reflection, their courage would return.

They retired, and I turned towards my friend; but he was sunk in languor, and almost deprived of life.

How all this will terminate, I know not; but I had rather die, than return shamefully, — my purpose unfulfilled. Yet I fear such will be my fate; the men, unsupported by ideas of glory and honour, can never willingly continue to endure their present hardships.

September 7th.

The die is cast; I have consented to return, if we are not destroyed. Thus are my hopes blasted by cowardice and indecision; I come back ignorant and disappointed. It requires more philosophy than I possess, to bear this injustice with patience.

September 12th.

It is past; I am returning to England. I have lost my hopes of utility and glory; — I have lost my friend. But I will endeavour to detail these bitter circumstances to you, my dear sister; and, while I am wafted towards England, and towards you, I will not despond.

September 19th,[8] the ice began to move, and roarings like thunder were heard at a distance, as the islands split and cracked in every direction. We were in the most imminent peril; but, as we could only remain passive, my chief attention was occupied by my unfortunate guest, whose illness increased in such a degree, that he was entirely confined to his bed. The ice cracked behind us, and was driven with force towards the north; a breeze sprung from the west, and on the 11th the passage towards the south became perfectly free. When the sailors saw this, and that their return to their native country was apparently assured, a shout of tumultuous joy broke from them, loud and long-continued. Frankenstein, who was dozing, awoke, and asked the

8. Corrected in 1831 to "September 9th."

cause of the tumult. "They shout," I said, "because they will soon return to England."

"Do you then really return?"

"Alas! yes; I cannot withstand their demands. I cannot lead them unwillingly to danger, and I must return."

"Do so, if you will; but I will not. You may give up your purpose; but mine is assigned to me by heaven, and I dare not. I am weak; but surely the spirits who assist my vengeance will endow me with sufficient strength." Saying this, he endeavoured to spring from the bed, but the exertion was too great for him; he fell back, and fainted.

It was long before he was restored; and I often thought that life was entirely extinct. At length he opened his eyes, but he breathed with difficulty, and was unable to speak. The surgeon gave him a composing draught,[9] and ordered us to leave him undisturbed. In the mean time he told me, that my friend had certainly not many hours to live.

His sentence was pronounced; and I could only grieve, and be patient. I sat by his bed watching him; his eyes were closed, and I thought he slept; but presently he called to me in a feeble voice, and, bidding me come near, said — "Alas! the strength I relied on is gone; I feel that I shall soon die, and he, my enemy and persecutor, may still be in being. Think not, Walton, that in the last moments of my existence I feel that burning hatred, and ardent desire of revenge, I once expressed, but I feel myself justified in desiring the death of my adversary. During these last days I have been occupied in examining my past conduct; nor do I find it blameable. In a fit of enthusiastic madness I created a rational creature, and was bound towards him, to assure, as far as was in my power, his happiness and well-being. This was my duty; but there was another still paramount to that. My duties towards my fellow-creatures had greater claims to my attention, because they included a greater proportion of happiness or misery. Urged by this view, I refused, and I did right in refusing, to create a companion for the first creature. He shewed unparalleled malignity and selfishness, in evil: he destroyed my friends; he devoted to destruction beings who possessed exquisite sensations, happiness, and wisdom; nor do I know where this thirst for vengeance may end. Miserable himself, that he may render no other wretched, he ought to die. The task of his destruction was mine, but I have failed. When actuated by selfish and vicious motives, I asked you to undertake my unfinished work; and I renew this request now, when I am only induced by reason and virtue.

"Yet I cannot ask you to renounce your country and friends, to fulfil this task; and now, that you are returning to England, you will have little chance of meeting with him. But the consideration of these points,

9. Restorative liquid.

and the well-balancing of what you may esteem your duties, I leave to you; my judgment and ideas are already disturbed by the near approach of death. I dare not ask you to do what I think right, for I may still be misled by passion.

"That he should live to be an instrument of mischief disturbs me; in other respects this hour, when I momentarily expect my release, is the only happy one which I have enjoyed for several years. The forms of the beloved dead flit before me, and I hasten to their arms. Farewell, Walton! Seek happiness in tranquillity, and avoid ambition, even if it be only the apparently innocent one of distinguishing yourself in science and discoveries. Yet why do I say this? I have myself been blasted in these hopes, yet another may succeed."

His voice became fainter as he spoke; and at length, exhausted by his effort, he sunk into silence. About half an hour afterwards he attempted again to speak, but was unable; he pressed my hand feebly, and his eyes closed for ever, while the irradiation[1] of a gentle smile passed away from his lips.

Margaret, what comment can I make on the untimely extinction of this glorious spirit? What can I say, that will enable you to understand the depth of my sorrow? All that I should express would be inadequate and feeble. My tears flow; my mind is overshadowed by a cloud of disappointment. But I journey towards England, and I may there find consolation.

I am interrupted. What do these sounds portend? It is midnight; the breeze blows fairly, and the watch on deck scarcely stir. Again; there is a sound as of a human voice, but hoarser; it comes from the cabin where the remains of Frankenstein still lie. I must arise, and examine. Good night, my sister.

Great God! what a scene has just taken place! I am yet dizzy with the remembrance of it. I hardly know whether I shall have the power to detail it; yet the tale which I have recorded would be incomplete without this final and wonderful[2] catastrophe.

I entered the cabin, where lay the remains of my ill-fated and admirable friend. Over him hung a form which I cannot find words to describe; gigantic in stature, yet uncouth and distorted in its proportions. As he hung over the coffin, his face was concealed by long locks of ragged hair; but one vast hand was extended, in colour and apparent texture like that of a mummy. When he heard the sound of my approach, he ceased to utter exclamations of grief and horror, and sprung towards the window. Never did I behold a vision so horrible as his face, of such loathsome, yet appalling hideousness. I shut my eyes involuntarily, and endeavoured to recollect what were my duties with regard to this destroyer. I called on him to stay.

1. Shining forth.
2. I.e., to be wondered at.

He paused, looking on me with wonder; and, again turning towards the lifeless form of his creator, he seemed to forget my presence, and every feature and gesture seemed instigated by the wildest rage of some uncontrollable passion.

"That is also my victim!" he exclaimed; in his murder my crimes are consummated; the miserable series of my being is wound to its close! Oh, Frankenstein! generous and self-devoted being! what does it avail that I now ask thee to pardon me? I, who irretrievably destroyed thee by destroying all thou lovedst. Alas! he is cold; he may not answer me."

His voice seemed suffocated; and my first impulses, which had suggested to me the duty of obeying the dying request of my friend, in destroying his enemy, were now suspended by a mixture of curiosity and compassion. I approached this tremendous being; I dared not again raise my looks upon his face, there was something so scaring and unearthly in his ugliness. I attempted to speak, but the words died away on my lips. The monster continued to utter wild and incoherent self-reproaches. At length I gathered resolution to address him, in a pause of the tempest of his passion: "Your repentance," I said, "is now superfluous. If you had listened to the voice of conscience, and heeded the stings of remorse, before you had urged your diabolical vengeance to this extremity, Frankenstein would yet have lived."

"And do you dream?" said the dæmon; "do you think that I was then dead to agony and remorse?—He," he continued, pointing to the corpse, "he suffered not more in the consummation of the deed;—oh! not the ten-thousandth portion of the anguish that was mine during the lingering detail of its execution. A frightful selfishness hurried me on, while my heart was poisoned with remorse. Think ye that the groans of Clerval were music to my ears? My heart was fashioned to be susceptible of love and sympathy; and, when wrenched by misery to vice and hatred, it did not endure the violence of the change without torture, such as you cannot even imagine.

"After the murder of Clerval, I returned to Switzerland, heart-broken and overcome. I pitied Frankenstein; my pity amounted to horror: I abhorred myself. But when I discovered that he, the author at once of my existence and of its unspeakable torments, dared to hope for happiness; that while he accumulated wretchedness and despair upon me, he sought his own enjoyment in feelings and passions from the indulgence of which I was for ever barred, then impotent envy and bitter indignation filled me with an insatiable thirst for vengeance. I recollected my threat, and resolved that it should be accomplished. I knew that I was preparing for myself a deadly torture; but I was the slave, not the master of an impulse, which I detested, yet could not disobey. Yet when she died!—nay, then I was not miserable. I had cast off all feeling, subdued all anguish to riot in the excess of my despair. Evil thenceforth became my good.[3] Urged thus far, I had no choice but to adapt my nature to an element which I had willingly chosen. The completion of my demoniacal design became an insatiable passion. And now it is ended; there is my last victim!"

I was at first touched by the expressions of his misery; yet when I called to mind what Frankenstein had said of his powers of eloquence and persuasion, and when I again cast my eyes on the lifeless form of my friend, indignation was re-kindled within me. "Wretch!" I said, "it is well that you come here to whine over the desolation that you have made. You throw a torch into a pile of buildings, and when they are consumed you sit among the ruins, and lament the fall. Hypocritical fiend! if he whom you mourn still lived, still would he be the object, again would he become the prey of your accursed vengeance. It is not pity that you feel; you lament only because the victim of your malignity is withdrawn from your power."

"Oh, it is not thus — not thus," interrupted the being; "yet such must be the impression conveyed to you by what appears to be the purport of my actions. Yet I seek not a fellow-feeling in my misery. No sympathy may I ever find. When I first sought it, it was the love of virtue, the feelings of happiness and affection with which my whole being over-flowed, that I wished to be participated.[4] But now, that virtue has become to me a shadow, and that happiness and affection are turned into bitter and loathing despair, in what should I seek for sympathy? I am content to suffer alone, while my sufferings shall endure: when I die, I am well satisfied that abhorrence and opprobrium should load my memory. Once my fancy was soothed with dreams of virtue, of fame, and of enjoyment. Once I falsely hoped to meet with beings, who, pardoning my outward form, would love me for the excellent qualities which I was capable of bringing forth. I was nourished with high thoughts of honour and devotion. But now vice has degraded me beneath the meanest animal. No crime, no mischief, no malignity, no misery, can be found comparable to mine. When I call over the frightful catalogue of my deeds, I cannot believe that I am he whose thoughts were once filled with sublime and transcendant visions of the beauty and the majesty of goodness. But it is even so; the fallen angel becomes a malignant devil. Yet even that enemy of God and man had friends and associates in his desolation; I am quite alone.

"You, who call Frankenstein your friend, seem to have a knowledge of my crimes and his misfortunes. But, in the detail which he gave you of them, he could not sum up the hours and months of misery which I endured, wasting in impotent passions. For whilst I destroyed his hopes, I did not satisfy my own desires. They were for ever ardent and craving; still I desired love and fellowship, and I was still spurned. Was

3. Cf. Satan in *Paradise Lost*: "all Good to me is lost; / Evil be thou my Good" (IV.109–10).
4. Shared.

there no injustice in this? Am I to be thought the only criminal, when all human kind sinned against me? Why do you not hate Felix, who drove his friend from his door with contumely?[5] Why do you not execrate the rustic who sought to destroy the saviour of his child? Nay, these are virtuous and immaculate beings! I, the miserable and the abandoned, am an abortion,[6] to be spurned at, and kicked, and trampled on. Even now my blood boils at the recollection of this injustice.

"But it is true that I am a wretch. I have murdered the lovely and the helpless; I have strangled the innocent as they slept, and grasped to death his throat who never injured me or any other living thing. I have devoted my creator, the select specimen of all that is worthy of love and admiration among men, to misery; I have pursued him even to that irremediable ruin. There he lies, white and cold in death. You hate me; but your abhorrence cannot equal that with which I regard myself. I look on the hands which executed the deed; I think on the heart in which the imagination of it was conceived, and long for the moment when they will meet my eyes, when it will haunt my thoughts, no more.

"Fear not that I shall be the instrument of future mischief. My work is nearly complete. Neither your's nor any man's death is needed to consummate the series of my being, and accomplish that which must be done; but it requires my own. Do not think that I shall be slow to perform this sacrifice. I shall quit your vessel on the ice-raft which brought me hither, and shall seek the most northern extremity of the globe; I shall collect my funeral pile, and consume to ashes this miserable frame, that its remains may afford no light to any curious and unhallowed wretch, who would create such another as I have been. I shall die. I shall no longer feel the agonies which now consume me, or be the prey of feelings unsatisfied, yet unquenched. He is dead who called me into being; and when I shall be no more, the very remembrance of us both will speedily vanish. I shall no longer see the sun or stars, or feel the winds play on my cheeks. Light, feeling, and sense, will pass away; and in this condition must I find my happiness. Some years ago, when the images which this world affords first opened upon me, when I felt the cheering warmth of summer, and heard the rustling of the leaves and the chirping of the birds, and these were all to me, I should have wept to die; now it is my only consolation. Polluted by crimes, and torn by the bitterest remorse, where can I find rest but in death?

"Farewell! I leave you, and in you the last of human kind whom these eyes will ever behold. Farewell, Frankenstein! If thou wert yet alive, and yet cherished a desire of revenge against me, it would be better satiated in my life than in my destruction. But it was not so; thou

5. Humiliating contempt.
6. "Any dwarfed and misshapen product of generation" (*OED*).

didst seek my extinction, that I might not cause greater wretchedness; and if yet, in some mode unknown to me, thou hast not yet ceased to think and feel, thou desirest not my life for my own misery. Blasted as thou wert, my agony was still superior to thine; for the bitter sting of remorse may not cease to rankle in my wounds until death shall close them for ever.

"But soon," he cried, with sad and solemn enthusiasm, "I shall die, and what I now feel be no longer felt. Soon these burning miseries will be extinct. I shall ascend my funeral pile triumphantly, and exult in the agony of the torturing flames. The light of that conflagration will fade away; my ashes will be swept into the sea by the winds. My spirit will sleep in peace; or if it thinks, it will not surely think thus. Farewell."

He sprung from the cabin-window, as he said this, upon the ice-raft which lay close to the vessel. He was soon borne away by the waves, and lost in darkness and distance.

THE END.

Composition and Revision

M. K. JOSEPH

The Composition of Frankenstein†

The volume of Mary Shelley's own journal covering the period 14 May 1815–20 July 1816, during which *Frankenstein* originated, is missing.

The earlier preface to the novel, dated September 1817, was written by Shelley.[1] It states simply that the story was begun in the summer of 1816, at Geneva; that, during a time of cold and rainy weather, the anonymous author and friends would meet of an evening by the fire, and would 'occasionally' read German ghost stories. Out of a 'playful desire of imitation', the author and two other friends (sc. Byron and Shelley) agreed each to write a supernatural tale; but the two friends left on 'a journey among the Alps', and the author's tale was the only one completed.

Mary Shelley's own account, written fourteen years later for the revised edition of 1831,[2] is much fuller, but is certainly inaccurate in some details. The sequence here is: the summer of 1816 — fine weather and 'pleasant hours on the lake', followed by 'incessant rain' which 'often confined us for days to the house'; the reading of the book of German ghost stories; Byron's proposal, taken up by himself, Shelley, Mary, and Polidori, that each should write a ghost story; and the prolonged search for a story which, it is implied, went on for some days. Meantime Mary had been listening to 'many and long . . . conversations' between Byron and Shelley: one of these was the discussion on 'the nature of the principle of life', which led immediately to Mary's dream and to the beginning of the novel on the very next day.

Byron's unfinished vampire-story, dated 17 June 1816, was published with *Mazeppa* in 1819, and suggested Polidori's novelette, *The Vampyre*, later published in dubious circumstances and attributed to Byron. Of Polidori's 'skull-headed lady', there is no further trace; his novel, *Ernestus Berchtold* (1819), has no reference to her.

---

† From Mary Shelley, *Frankenstein*, ed. James Kinsley and M. K. Joseph (Oxford: Oxford UP, 1969) 224–27. Reprinted by permission.
1. See pp. 5–6, above [*Editor*].
2. See pp. 169–73, below [*Editor*].

Thomas Moore's account of these events in his *Life of Lord Byron* (1830) is slightly earlier, and presumably based largely on Mary Shelley's recollections. According to Moore, the regular routine while Byron was at Diodati included an evening excursion on the lake when the weather was fine; when it was bad, the Shelleys 'passed their evenings at Diodati; and, when the rain rendered it inconvenient for them to return home, remained there to sleep'. It was during 'a week of rain' that the party agreed to write their ghost stories, and *Frankenstein* resulted.[3]

The impression given by these accounts is of a leisurely time-scheme, yet it must in fact have been fairly brief: Byron met Shelley's party at Sécheron on 27 May, and did not move to the Villa Diodati until 10 June; the journey round Lake Leman began on 22 June, and the novel must have been started between these last two dates.

For more detailed information, we must turn to the brief and cryptic entries in the diary of Dr. Polidori. These confirm that Byron and Shelley's party met regularly in the evenings from 29 May onward, often for boating on the lake; these expeditions were interrupted for the first time by rain on 8 June. After the removal to Diodati on 10 June, evening meetings were resumed there. Then come three significant entries:

> June 15. . . . Shelley and I had a conversation about principles, —whether man was to be thought merely an instrument . . .
> June 16. . . . Shelley came, and dined and slept here, with Mrs. S[helley] and Miss Clare Clairmont . . .
> June 17. . . . The ghost-stories are begun by all but me.[4]

The 'conversation about principles' is likely to be the same as Mary's discussion on 'the principle of life', and it would be typical of Polidori to make himself a principal speaker rather than Byron. James Rieger, in an important article, would go further, and argue that in fact Mary gives the reverse order of events; that the 'conversation about principles' occurred first, followed next night by the stay at Diodati and the beginning of the ghost stories (including Mary's) next morning. Certainly, Mary's memory for detail, especially of the *Fantasmagoriana* stories, can be shown to be imperfect; but is Polidori's record any more reliable? We have no certainty that the hasty entries were made day-by-day as they occurred, and soon after he makes errors in dates. Polidori was himself absent from Diodati on the nights of 12 and 13 June, and on the latter a thunderstorm occurred; it is possible that the scheme of

---

3. Thomas Moore, *Letters and Journals of Lord Byron: with Notices of his Life* (1830), ii. 31. [Moore, Irish poet, was a friend and biographer of Byron—*Editor*.]
4. *The Diary of Dr. John William Polidori*, ed. W. M. Rossetti (1911), pp. 122–5. [Polidori was Byron's twenty-year-old physician and traveling companion. Claire Clairmont was Mary Shelley's stepsister—*Editor*.]

writing ghost stories was proposed then, and that Polidori joined in later. This would agree with Mary's order of events and, at least minimally, with her time scheme.

Incidentally, one would like to know whether, by 'instrument', Polidori meant 'mechanism', and whether anyone in the party had read de la Mettrie's *L'Homme Machine*, which also uses the phrase 'a new Prometheus'.

Mary began her story with the words, 'It was a dreary night of November . . .', which now form the opening of Chapter V (Chapter IV in the 1818 edition). In late July occurred the excursion to Chamonix and the Mer de Glace which gave her the impressive scenery for Chapters IX and X; when her journal resumes, we find her writing at Chamonix on 24 July, and the work went on in earnest after her return to Geneva on the 27th.[5] What had been originally designed as a story of 'a few pages' was being developed, on Shelley's urging, into a full-length novel. Journal entries show her at work on at least half the days in August, and on one occasion discussing the story with Shelley. Writing was interrupted by their departure from Geneva and return to England, and possibly not resumed in earnest until mid-December; the work seems to have been virtually complete when it was suspended for the visit to London and her marriage to Shelley.[6]

Except for a few days early in 1817, Mary's journal gives no indications of further writing until late February or March. For a week from 10 April 1817, the entries read 'Correct "Frankenstein"'; transcription went on, with some interruptions, until about the middle of May. On 14 May, 'Shelley . . . corrects "Frankenstein"'; on the 22nd, the Shelleys went to London to submit the manuscript to John Murray. Murray refused—on Gifford's advice, or so Mary believed; Ollier also turned it down in August; but the book was accepted by Lackington, Allen and Company a month later. It was seen through the press, with some emendation, by Shelley, who wrote that he had 'paid considerable attention to the correction of such few instances of baldness of style as necessarily occur in the production of a very young writer'. He also busied himself in having copies sent out to friends and others whose opinions might be useful; and *Frankenstein* finally appeared in March 1818.[7]

The reviewers were impressed in spite of themselves by a book which they found rather shocking; with partial truth, they sensed the Godwinian influence in it, but believed it to have been written by a man,

5. *Mary Shelley's Journal*, ed. Frederick L. Jones (Norman: U of Oklahoma P, 1974), p. 53. For what follows, see subsequent entries in the journal.
6. *The Letters of Mary W. Shelley*, ed. Frederick L. Jones (Norman: U of Oklahoma P, 1944), i. 14.
7. *Journal*, 78, 79, and 80; *Letters*, i. 29, 31; *The Letters of Percy Bysshe Shelley*, ed. Frederick L. Jones (1964), i. 564–5.

possibly Shelley himself. Mary's authorship, which was at first intended to be a secret known only to a few friends like Moore and Byron, gradually became common knowledge.[8]

ANNE K. MELLOR

Choosing a Text of *Frankenstein* to Teach[†]

Which edition of *Frankenstein* should I teach? This question is more complicated than it might at first appear. There are critically significant differences among the manuscript of *Frankenstein* in the Bodleian Library, the first edition of the novel in 1818, and the second and heavily revised edition of 1831. Since current text-editing theory and practice no longer assume that the author's final word is definitive, we cannot select the final edition for that reason alone. Nor should we be unduly swayed by the fact that the 1831 edition in the Signet-NAL paperback costs less than two dollars.

I strongly believe that the text of preference should be the 1818 edition, for the same reasons that students of Romanticism prefer the 1805 edition of Wordsworth's *Prelude* to the final 1850 edition. The first completed versions of both works have greater internal philosophical coherence, are closest to the authors' original conceptions, and are more convincingly related to their historical contexts. In *Frankenstein*, these contexts are biographical (the recent death of Mary Shelley's first baby and her dissatisfactions with Percy Shelley's Romantic ideology), political (her observations of the aftermath of the French Revolution in 1814–16), and scientific (the experiments with galvanic electricity in the first decade of the nineteenth century).

The most striking thematic differences between the two published versions of the novel concern the role of fate, the degree of Frankenstein's responsibility for his actions, the representation of nature, the role of Clerval, and the representation of the family. I discuss these issues in more detail later in this essay, but here I must make two preliminary observations. Even the first published text of *Frankenstein* has moved away from Mary Shelley's original style and conception, insofar as we can determine these from the surviving sections of the manuscript in the Abinger Shelley Collection in the Bodleian Library (these sections constitute page 30, line 13, through page 109, line 9, plus page 117, line 17, to page 221, line 12, in the Rieger edition of the 1818 text). Furthermore, the account given of this manuscript by

8. *Quarterly Review*, Jan. 1818; *Edinburgh Magazine*, Mar. 1818; *Blackwood's Edinburgh Magazine*, Mar. 1818. R. Glynn Grylls, *Mary Shelley*, pp. 315–18.
† From *Approaches to Teaching Shelley's* Frankenstein (New York: MLA, 1990) 31–37. Reprinted by permission of the Modern Language Association of America.

James Rieger, the editor of the only available reprint of the 1818 text of *Frankenstein*,[1] is so inaccurate and so prejudiced in favor of Percy Shelley that students must be warned against its misleading combination of truths, half-truths, and unwarranted speculations.

As Mary Shelley wrote her story of Frankenstein, she gave it to her husband to edit. She rightly claimed that she "did not owe the suggestion of one incident, nor scarcely of one train of feeling" to Percy Shelley (Rieger 229), with one minor exception: it was Percy who suggested that Frankenstein's trip to England be proposed by Victor himself, rather than by his father. Yet Percy Shelley made numerous corrections, about a thousand in all, on the surviving manuscript pages, almost all of which Mary Shelley accepted.

James Rieger credits Percy Shelley with wording the descriptions of contrasts between the personalities of Frankenstein and Elizabeth and between the governments of the Swiss republic and less fortunate nations, with coining the metaphoric description of the power within Mont Blanc, with conceiving the "idea that Frankenstein journey to England for the purpose of creating a female Monster," with making the "final revisions" of the last pages, and with correcting Mary Shelley's "frequent grammatical solecisms, her spelling, and her awkward phrasing." He then concludes that Percy Shelley's "assistance at every point in the book's manufacture was so extensive that one hardly knows whether to regard him as editor or minor collaborator" (Rieger xviii).

Close examination of the surviving manuscript fragments shows that Percy Shelley's numerous revisions of Mary's original text damaged as well as improved it. To dispose of Rieger's misinformation, Percy did expand, although he did not initiate, the comparison of Elizabeth's character to Victor Frankenstein's; and he did interpolate a favorable comparison of Switzerland's republicanism with the tyranny of other nations. However, the descriptions of Mont Blanc and the Mer de Glace in the novel are based primarily on Mary Shelley's own observations, which she made in July 1816 and recorded both in her journal entries for 22–26 July and in her letters to Fanny Imlay; these letters were later published in her *History of a Six Weeks' Tour* (1817). As already noted, Percy suggested merely that Victor rather than Alphonse Frankenstein propose the trip to England. We might pass over Rieger's annoying habit of referring to Percy Shelley only by his last name and to Mary Shelley by her first, or his failure to acknowledge, in his assertion that Percy corrected "her frequent grammatical solecisms, her spelling, and her awkward phrasing," that Mary's grammatical errors or misspellings were infrequent, while her phrasings were often more graceful than her husband's revised versions. Rieger's concluding suggestion that Percy Shelley can be regarded as a "minor collaborator"

---

1. Originally published by Bobbs-Merrill (Indianapolis) in 1974 and reprinted by U of Chicago P in 1982 [*Editor*].

or even as one of the two authors of the novel (xliv) is not only unjus-
tified by the evidence. It is also, as we can now recognize, explicitly
sexist, since it implies that Mary Shelley could not have created her
story alone. Rieger thus does a great disservice to Mary Shelley's genius.

Percy Shelley did improve the manuscript of *Frankenstein* in several
minor ways: he corrected three factual errors, eliminated a few grammatical mistakes, occasionally clarified the text, substituted more pre-
cise technical terms for Mary's cruder ones, smoothed out a few
paragraph transitions, and enriched the thematic resonance of the text.
But Percy Shelley misunderstood his wife's intentions. He tended to
see the Creature as more monstrous and less human than Mary did,
and he frequently underestimated the flaws in Victor Frankenstein's
personality. Furthermore, he introduced into the text his own philosophical and political opinions, opinions that were often at variance
with his wife's beliefs. For instance, throughout her manuscript Mary
assumes the existence of a sacred animating principle, call it Nature or
Life or God, which Frankenstein usurps at his peril. But Percy under-
mined her notion that Frankenstein's pursuit of his Creature was "a
task enjoined by heaven" by adding his atheistic concept of a universe
mechanistically determined by necessity or power, "the mechanical impulse of some power of which I was unconscious" (Rieger 202). Percy
also introduced all the references to Victor Frankenstein as the "author"
of the Creature (see Reiger 87, 96) and thus may be largely responsible
for recent discussions of Mary Shelley's anxiety of authorship (see Gilbert and Gubar 49; Poovey, chs. 4 and 5).

More important, Percy changed the last line of the novel in a way
that potentially alters its meaning. Mary had penned Walton's final
vision of the Creature thus:

> He sprung from the cabin window as he said this upon an ice raft
> that lay close to the vessel & pushing himself off he was carried
> away by the waves and I soon lost sight of him in the darkness and
> distance.

But Percy changed this to

> He sprung from the cabin-window, as he said this, upon the ice-
> raft which lay close to the vessel. He was soon borne away by the
> waves, and lost in darkness and distance. (Rieger 221)

Mary's version, by suggesting that Walton has only lost sight of the
Creature, leaves open the troubling possibility that the Creature may
still be alive, while Percy's flat assertion that the Creature is lost provides
the reader a more comforting closure of the novel's monstrous threats.

By far the largest number of Percy's revisions were stylistic. He typically changed Mary's simple, Anglo-Saxon diction and straightforward
or colloquial sentence structures into more refined, complex, and Lat-

inate equivalents. He is thus largely responsible for the stilted, ornate, putatively Ciceronian prose style about which so many students complain. Mary's voice tended to utter a sentimental, rather abstract, and generalized rhetoric, typically energized with a brisk stylistic rhythm. Here, for instance, is Mary on Frankenstein's fascination with supernatural phenomena:

> Nor were these my only visions. The raising of ghosts or devils was also a favorite pursuit and if I never saw any I attributed it rather to my own inexperience and mistakes than want of skill in my instructors.

And here is Percy's revision:

> Nor were these my only visions. The raising of ghosts or devils was a promise liberally accorded by my favourite authors, the fulfillment of which I most eagerly sought; and if my incantations were always unsuccessful, I attributed the failure rather to my own inexperience and mistakes, than to a want of skill or fidelity in my instructors. (Rieger 34)

Percy's preference for more learned, polysyllabic terms was obsessive; in addition, he rigorously eliminated Mary's colloquial phrases, as the following lists indicate.

Mary Shelley's manuscript	*Percy Shelley's revision*
have	possess
wish	desire, purpose
caused	derive their origin from
a painting	a representation
place	station
plenty of	sufficient
time	period
felt	endured
hope	confidence
had	experienced
stay	remain
took away	extinguish
talked	conversed
hot	inflamed
smallness	minuteness
end	extinction
inside	within
tired	fatigued
die	perish
leave out	omit
add to	augment

Mary Shelley's manuscript	*Percy Shelley's revision*
poverty	penury
mind	understanding
ghost-story	a tale of superstition
about on a par	of nearly equal interest and utility
we were all equal	neither of us possessed the slightest pre-eminence over the other
it was safe	the danger of infection was past
bear to part	be persuaded to part
the use I should make of it	the manner in which I should employ it
eyes were shut to	eyes were insensible to
do not wish to hate you	will not be tempted to set myself in opposition to thee
wrapping the rest	depositing the remains
it was a long time	a considerable period elapsed
had a means	possessed a method
how my disposition and habits were altered	the alteration perceptible in my disposition and habits
whatever I should afterwards think it right to do	whatever course of conduct I might hereafter think it right to pursue
what to say	what manner to commence the interview

I wish to claim not that Mary Shelley is a great prose stylist but only that her language, despite its tendency toward the abstract, sentimental, and even banal, is more direct and forceful than her husband's. (For a more detailed discussion of Percy Shelley's revisions of the manuscript of *Frankenstein*, see Mellor, *Mary Shelley*, ch. 3 and app.)[2]

Turning now to the differences between the first and second published editions of *Frankenstein*, we must recognize that between 1818 and 1831, Mary Shelley's philosophical views changed radically, primarily as a result of the pessimism generated by the deaths of Clara, William, and Percy Shelley; by the betrayals of Byron and Jane Williams; and by her severely straitened economic circumstances. These events convinced Mary Shelley that human events are decided not by personal choice or free will but by an indifferent destiny or fate. The values implicitly espoused in the first edition of *Frankenstein* — that nature is a nurturing and benevolent life force that punishes only those

2. *Mary Shelley: Her Life, Her Fiction, Her Monsters* (New York: Methuen, 1988) [*Editor*].

who transgress against its sacred rights, that Victor is morally responsible for his acts, that the Creature is potentially good but driven to evil by social and parental neglect, that a family like the De Laceys that loves all its children equally offers the best hope for human happiness, and that human egotism causes the greatest suffering in the world—are all rejected in the 1831 revisions.

In the 1818 version, Victor Frankenstein possessed free will: he could have abandoned his quest for the "principle of life," he could have cared for his Creature, he could have protected Elizabeth. But in the 1831 edition, he is the pawn of forces beyond his knowledge or control. As he comments, "Destiny was too potent, and her immutable laws had decreed my utter and terrible destruction" (Rieger, app. 239). Elizabeth also subscribes to this rhetoric of fatalism: "I think our placid home, and our contented hearts are regulated by the same immutable laws" (Rieger, app. 243).

In the 1831 edition, Mary Shelley replaces her earlier organic conception of nature with a mechanistic one. She now portrays nature as a mighty machine, a juggernaut, an "imperial" tyrant (Rieger, app. 249). Since human beings are now but puppets ("one by one the various keys were touched which formed the mechanism of my being," says Victor [Rieger, app. 241]), Victor's downfall is caused not so much by his egotistical "presumption and rash ignorance" as by bad influences, whether his father's ignorance or Professor Waldman's Mephistophelian manipulations. Victor's only sin is not his failure to love and care for his Creature but his original decision to construct a human being. His scientific experiments themselves are now described as "unhallowed arts" (Rieger, app. 247).

Not only is Frankenstein portrayed in 1831 as a victim rather than an originator of evil, but Clerval—who had functioned in the first edition as the touchstone of moral virtue against which Victor's fall was measured—is now portrayed as equally ambitious of fame and power, as a future colonial imperialist who will use his "mastery" of Oriental languages to exploit the natural resources of the East (Rieger, app. 243, 253). Furthermore, the ideology of the egalitarian and loving bourgeois family that Mary Shelley had inherited from her mother's writings and that sustained the first edition of *Frankenstein* is now undercut. Maternal love is identified with self-destruction when Caroline Beaufort deliberately sacrifices her life to nurse Elizabeth. And Elizabeth Lavenza has become a passive "angel in the house," no longer able to speak out in the law courts against Justine's execution.

By coming to construe nature in the 1831 edition as only Waldman and Frankenstein had done in the first edition, as a mighty and amoral machine, Mary Shelley significantly decreased the critical distance between herself and her protagonist. In the "Author's Introduction" added to the novel in 1831, Mary Shelley presents herself as she now represents Frankenstein, as a victim of destiny. She is "compelled" to write (Rieger 222); her imagination "unbidden" possessed and guided her (Rieger 227). She ends with a defensive lie: "I have changed no portion of the story, nor introduced any new ideas or circumstances" (Rieger 229). Thus in the final version of her novel, Mary Shelley disclaims responsibility for her hideous progeny and at the same time insists that she has remained passive before it, "leaving the core and substance of it untouched" (Rieger 229). For invention "can give form to dark, shapeless substances, but cannot bring into being the substance itself" (Rieger 226). Imperial nature, the thing-in-itself, is now triumphant. Before it, Mary Shelley's human imagination can only mold shapeless darkness into a hideous monster. Like Victor Frankenstein, she has become the unwilling "author of unalterable evils." (For a more detailed description of Mary Shelley's revisions of *Frankenstein* in 1831, see Mellor, *Mary Shelley*, ch. 9.)

The remarkable shifts in both diction and philosophical conception between the three versions of *Frankenstein*—the manuscript, the 1818 edition, and the 1831 edition—make this an ideal text for use in courses in either text editing or the theory of the text itself. From the perspective of deconstructive literary criticism, *Frankenstein* exemplifies what Julia Kristeva has called "the questionable subject-in-process," both a text and an author without stable boundaries. For students who have time to consult only one text, the 1818 text alone presents a stable and coherent conception of the character of Victor Frankenstein and of Mary Shelley's political and moral ideology. It is a pity that the significantly higher price of the Rieger edition often proves decisive in persuading teachers to opt for the cheaper editions of the revised 1831 *Frankenstein*, editions that cannot do justice to Mary Shelley's powerful originating vision.

CONTEXTS

MARY SHELLEY

Introduction to *Frankenstein*, Third Edition (1831)†

The Publishers of the Standard Novels, in selecting 'Frankenstein' for one of their series, expressed a wish that I should furnish them with some account of the origin of the story. I am the more willing to comply, because I shall thus give a general answer to the question, so very frequently asked me — 'How I, then a young girl, came to think of, and to dilate upon, so very hideous an idea?' It is true that I am very averse to bringing myself forward in print; but as my account will only appear as an appendage to a former production, and as it will be confined to such topics as have connection with my authorship alone, I can scarcely accuse myself of a personal intrusion.

It is not singular that, as the daughter of two persons of distinguished literary celebrity, I should very early in life have thought of writing. As a child I scribbled; and my favourite pastime, during the hours given me for recreation, was to 'write stories.' Still I had a dearer pleasure than this, which was the formation of castles in the air — the indulging in waking dreams — the following up trains of thought, which had for their subject the formation of a succession of imaginary incidents. My dreams were at once more fantastic and agreeable than my writings. In the latter I was a close imitator — rather doing as others had done, than putting down the suggestions of my own mind. What I wrote was intended at least for one other eye — my childhood's companion and friend; but my dreams were all my own; I accounted for them to nobody; they were my refuge when annoyed — my dearest pleasure when free.

I lived principally in the country as a girl, and passed a considerable time in Scotland. I made occasional visits to the more picturesque parts; but my habitual residence was on the blank and dreary northern shores of the Tay, near Dundee. Blank and dreary on retrospection I call them; they were not so to me then. They were the eyry of freedom, and the pleasant region where unheeded I could commune with the creatures of my fancy. I wrote then — but in a most common-place style. It was beneath the trees of the grounds belonging to our house, or on the bleak sides of the woodless mountains near, that my true compositions, the airy flights of my imagination, were born and fostered. I did not make myself the heroine of my tales. Life appeared to me too common-place an affair as regarded myself. I could not figure to myself that

† From *Frankenstein: or, The Modern Prometheus* (London: Henry Colburn and Richard Bentley, 1831) v–xii.

romantic woes or wonderful events would ever be my lot; but I was not confined to my own identity, and I could people the hours with creations far more interesting to me at that age, than my own sensations.

After this my life became busier, and reality stood in place of fiction. My husband, however, was, from the first, very anxious that I should prove myself worthy of my parentage, and enrol myself on the page of fame. He was for ever inciting me to obtain literary reputation, which even on my own part I cared for then, though since I have become infinitely indifferent to it. At this time he desired that I should write, not so much with the idea that I could produce any thing worthy of notice, but that he might himself judge how far I possessed the promise of better things hereafter. Still I did nothing. Travelling, and the cares of a family, occupied my time; and study, in the way of reading, or improving my ideas in communication with his far more cultivated mind, was all of literary employment that engaged my attention.

In the summer of 1816, we visited Switzerland, and became the neighbours of Lord Byron. At first we spent our pleasant hours on the lake, or wandering on its shores; and Lord Byron, who was writing the third canto of Childe Harold, was the only one among us who put his thoughts upon paper. These, as he brought them successively to us, clothed in all the light and harmony of poetry, seemed to stamp as divine the glories of heaven and earth, whose influences we partook with him.

But it proved a wet, ungenial summer, and incessant rain often confined us for days to the house. Some volumes of ghost stories, translated from the German into French, fell into our hands. There was the History of the Inconstant Lover, who, when he thought to clasp the bride to whom he had pledged his vows, found himself in the arms of the pale ghost of her whom he had deserted. There was the tale of the sinful founder of his race, whose miserable doom it was to bestow the kiss of death on all the younger sons of his fated house, just when they reached the age of promise. His gigantic, shadowy form, clothed like the ghost in Hamlet, in complete armour, but with the beaver up, was seen at midnight, by the moon's fitful beams, to advance slowly along the gloomy avenue. The shape was lost beneath the shadow of the castle walls; but soon a gate swung back, a step was heard, the door of the chamber opened, and he advanced to the couch of the blooming youths, cradled in healthy sleep. Eternal sorrow sat upon his face as he bent down and kissed the forehead of the boys, who from that hour withered like flowers snapt upon the stalk. I have not seen these stories since then; but their incidents are as fresh in my mind as if I had read them yesterday.

'We will each write a ghost story,' said Lord Byron; and his proposition was acceded to. There were four of us. The noble author began a tale, a fragment of which he printed at the end of his poem of Mazeppa. Shelley, more apt to embody ideas and sentiments in the radiance of brilliant imagery, and in the music of the most melodious verse that adorns our language, than to invent the machinery of a story, commenced one founded on the experiences of his early life. Poor Polidori had some terrible idea about a skull-headed lady, who was so punished for peeping through a key-hole — what to see I forget — something very shocking and wrong of course; but when she was reduced to a worse condition than the renowned Tom of Coventry, he did not know what to do with her, and was obliged to despatch her to the tomb of the Capulets, the only place for which she was fitted. The illustrious poets also, annoyed by the platitude of prose, speedily relinquished their uncongenial task.

I busied myself *to think of a story,* — a story to rival those which had excited us to this task. One which would speak to the mysterious fears of our nature, and awaken thrilling horror — one to make the reader dread to look round, to curdle the blood, and quicken the beatings of the heart. If I did not accomplish these things, my ghost story would be unworthy of its name. I thought and pondered — vainly. I felt that blank incapability of invention which is the greatest misery of authorship, when dull Nothing replies to our anxious invocations. *Have you thought of a story?* I was asked each morning, and each morning I was forced to reply with a mortifying negative.

Every thing must have a beginning, to speak in Sanchean phrase; and that beginning must be linked to something that went before. The Hindoos give the world an elephant to support it, but they make the elephant stand upon a tortoise. Invention, it must be humbly admitted, does not consist in creating out of void, but out of chaos; the materials must, in the first place, be afforded: it can give form to dark, shapeless substances, but cannot bring into being the substance itself. In all matters of discovery and invention, even of those that appertain to the imagination, we are continually reminded of the story of Columbus and his egg. Invention consists in the capacity of seizing on the capabilities of a subject, and in the power of moulding and fashioning ideas suggested to it.

Many and long were the conversations between Lord Byron and Shelley, to which I was a devout but nearly silent listener. During one of these, various philosophical doctrines were discussed, and among others the nature of the principle of life, and whether there was any probability of its ever being discovered and communicated. They talked of the experiments of Dr. Darwin, (I speak not of what the Doctor really did, or said that he did, but, as more to my purpose, of what was then spoken of as having been done by him,) who preserved a piece of vermicelli in a glass case, till by some extraordinary means it began to move with voluntary motion. Not thus, after all, would life be given. Perhaps a corpse would be re-animated; galvanism had given token of

such things: perhaps the component parts of a creature might be manufactured, brought together, and endued with vital warmth.

Night waned upon this talk, and even the witching hour had gone
by, before we retired to rest. When I placed my head on my pillow, I
did not sleep, nor could I be said to think. My imagination, unbidden,
possessed and guided me, gifting the successive images that arose in
my mind with a vividness far beyond the usual bounds of reverie. I
saw — with shut eyes, but acute mental vision, — I saw the pale student
of unhallowed arts kneeling beside the thing he had put together. I saw
the hideous phantasm of a man stretched out, and then, on the working
of some powerful engine, show signs of life, and stir with an uneasy,
half vital motion. Frightful must it be; for supremely frightful would be
the effect of any human endeavour to mock the stupendous mechanism
of the Creator of the world. His success would terrify the artist; he
would rush away from his odious handy-work, horror-stricken. He
would hope that, left to itself, the slight spark of life which he had
communicated would fade; that this thing, which had received such
imperfect animation, would subside into dead matter; and he might
sleep in the belief that the silence of the grave would quench for ever
the transient existence of the hideous corpse which he had looked upon
as the cradle of life. He sleeps; but he is awakened; he opens his eyes;
behold the horrid thing stands at his bedside, opening his curtains, and
looking on him with yellow, watery, but speculative eyes.

I opened mine in terror. The idea so possessed my mind, that a thrill
of fear ran through me, and I wished to exchange the ghastly image of
my fancy for the realities around. I see them still; the very room, the
dark *parquet*, the closed shutters, with the moonlight struggling
through, and the sense I had that the glassy lake and white high Alps
were beyond. I could not so easily get rid of my hideous phantom; still
it haunted me. I must try to think of something else. I recurred to my
ghost story, — my tiresome unlucky ghost story! O! if I could only con-
trive one which would frighten my reader as I myself had been frightened that night!

Swift as light and as cheering was the idea that broke in upon me.
'I have found it! What terrified me will terrify others; and I need only
describe the spectre which had haunted my midnight pillow.' On the
morrow I announced that I had *thought of a story*. I began that day
with the words, *It was on a dreary night of November*, making only a
transcript of the grim terrors of my waking dream.

At first I thought but of a few pages — of a short tale; but Shelley
urged me to develope the idea at greater length. I certainly did not owe
the suggestion of one incident, nor scarcely of one train of feeling, to
my husband, and yet but for his incitement, it would never have taken
the form in which it was presented to the world. From this declaration

I must except the preface. As far as I can recollect, it was entirely written by him.

And now, once again, I bid my hideous progeny go forth and prosper. I have an affection for it, for it was the offspring of happy days, when death and grief were but words, which found no true echo in my heart. Its several pages speak of many a walk, many a drive, and many a conversation, when I was not alone; and my companion was one who, in this world, I shall never see more. But this is for myself; my readers have nothing to do with these associations.

I will add but one word as to the alterations I have made. They are principally those of style. I have changed no portion of the story, nor introduced any new ideas or circumstances. I have mended the language where it was so bald as to interfere with the interest of the narrative; and these changes occur almost exclusively in the beginning of the first volume. Throughout they are entirely confined to such parts as are mere adjuncts to the story, leaving the core and substance of it untouched.

M.W.S.

London, October 15, 1831

MARY SHELLEY

Letter to [?Fanny Imlay]†

Campagne C[hapuis], near Coligny.
1 June 1816[1]

You will perceive from my date that we have changed our residence since my last letter. We now inhabit a little cottage on the opposite shore of the lake, and have exchanged the view of Mont Blanc and her snowy <u>aiguilles</u> for the dark frowning Jura, behind whose range we every evening see the sun sink, and darkness approaches our valley from behind the Alps, which are then tinged by that glowing rose-like hue which is observed in England to attend on the clouds of an autumnal sky when day-light is almost gone. The lake is at our feet, and a little harbour contains our boat, in which we still enjoy our evening excur-

† From Betty T. Bennett, ed., *The Letters of Mary Wollstonecraft Shelley*, vol. 1 (Baltimore: The Johns Hopkins UP, 1980) 20–21. Reprinted by permission of The Johns Hopkins University Press. See also the letter of 17 May 1816. Fanny Imlay was Mary Shelley's half-sister.
1. By the end of May Shelley and his party had moved to a cottage variously called Montalègre, Maison Chapuis, or Campagne Chapuis. On 10 June Byron rented the Villa Diodati, a short walk away (H. W. Häusermann, *The Genevese Background* [London: Routledge and Kegan Paul, 1952]). The two poets and their companions spent the summer in each other's company. The Shelley party remained at Lake Geneva until 29 August.

sions on the water. Unfortunately we do not now enjoy those brilliant skies that hailed us on our first arrival to this country. An almost perpetual rain confines us principally to the house; but when the sun bursts forth it is with a splendour and heat unknown in England. The thunder storms that visit us are grander and more terrific than I have even seen before. We watch them as they approach from the opposite side of the lake, observing the lightning play among the clouds in various parts of the heavens, and dart in jagged figures upon the piny heights of Jura, dark with the shadow of the overhanging cloud, while perhaps the sun is shining cheerily upon us. One night we enjoyed a finer storm than I had ever before beheld. The lake was lit up — the pines on Jura made visible, and all the scene illuminated for an instant, when a pitchy blackness succeeded, and the thunder came in frightful bursts over our heads amid the darkness.[2]

But while I still dwell on the country around Geneva, you will expect me to say something of the town itself: there is nothing, however, in it that can repay you for the trouble of walking over its rough stones. The houses are high, the streets narrow, many of them on the ascent, and no public building of any beauty to attract your eye, or any architecture to gratify your taste. The town is surrounded by a wall, the three gates of which are shut exactly at ten o'clock, when no bribery (as in France) can open them. To the south of the town is the promenade of the Genevese, a grassy plain planted with a few trees, and called Plainpalais. Here a small obelisk is erected to the glory of Rousseau, and here (such is the mutability of human life) the magistrates, the successors of those who exiled him from his native country, were shot by the populace during that revolution, which his writings mainly contributed to mature, and which, notwithstanding the temporary bloodshed and injustice with which it was polluted, has produced enduring benefits to mankind, which all the chicanery of statesmen, nor even the great conspiracy of kings, can entirely render vain. From respect to the memory of their predecessors, none of the present magistrates ever walk in Plainpalais. Another Sunday recreation for the citizens is an excursion to the top of Mont Salêve. This hill is within a league of the town, and rises perpendicularly from the cultivated plain. It is ascended on the other side, and I should judge from its situation that your toil is rewarded by a delightful view of the course of the Rhone and Arve, and of the shores of the lake. We have not yet visited it.

There is more equality of classes here than in England. This occasions a greater freedom and refinement of manners among the lower orders than we meet with in our own country. I fancy the haughty English ladies are greatly disgusted with this consequence of republican institutions, for the Genevese servants complain very much of their

2. Byron described such a storm in *Childe Harold* 3.92 (see pp. 180–82, below) [*Editor*].

scolding, an exercise of the tongue, I believe, perfectly unknown here. The peasants of Switzerland may not however emulate the vivacity and grace of the French. They are more cleanly, but they are slow and inapt. I know a girl of twenty, who although she had lived all her life among vineyards, could not inform me during what month the vintage took place, and I discovered she was utterly ignorant of the order in which the months succeed one another. She would not have been surprised if I had talked of the burning sun and delicious fruits of December, or of the frosts of July. Yet she is by no means deficient in understanding.

The Genevese are also much inclined to puritanism. It is true that from habit they dance on a Sunday, but as soon as the French government was abolished in the town, the magistrates ordered the theatre to be closed, and measures were taken to pull down the building.

We have latterly enjoyed fine weather, and nothing is more pleasant than to listen to the evening song of the vine-dressers. They are all women, and most of them have harmonious although masculine voices. The theme of their ballads consists of shepherds, love, flocks, and the sons of kings who fall in love with beautiful shepherdesses. Their tunes are monotonous, but it is sweet to hear them in the stillness of evening, while we are enjoying the sight of the setting sun, either from the hill behind our house or from the lake.

Such are our pleasures here, which would be greatly increased if the season had been more favourable, for they chiefly consist in such enjoyments as sunshine and gentle breezes bestow. We have not yet made any excursion in the environs of the town, but we have planned several, when you shall again hear of us; and we will endeavour, by the magic of words, to transport the ethereal part of you to the neighbourhood of the Alps, and mountain streams, and forests, which, while they clothe the former, darken the latter with their vast shadows. — Adieu!

M.

PERCY BYSSHE SHELLEY

Mont Blanc[1]

Lines Written in the Vale of Chamouni

I.

The everlasting universe of things
Flows through the mind, and rolls its rapid waves,

---

1. The highest peak in Europe. Its snows melt into the River Arve and the Chamonix Valley in France, near the borders of Switzerland and Italy.

Now dark — now glittering — now reflecting gloom —
Now lending splendour, where from secret springs
The source of human thought its tribute brings
Of waters, — with a sound but half its own,
Such as a feeble brook will oft assume
In the wild woods, among the mountains lone,
Where waterfalls around it leap for ever,
Where woods and winds contend, and a vast river
Over its rocks ceaselessly bursts and raves.

                              II.

Thus thou, Ravine of Arve — dark, deep Ravine —
Thou many-coloured, many-voiced vale,
Over whose pines and crags and caverns sail
Fast clouds, shadows, and sunbeams; awful scene,
Where Power in likeness of the Arve comes down
From the ice-gulfs that gird his secret throne,
Bursting through these dark mountains like the flame
Of lightning through the tempest; — thou dost lie,
The giant brood of pines around thee clinging,
Children of elder time, in whose devotion
The chainless winds still come and ever came
To drink their odours, and their mighty swinging
To hear — an old and solemn harmony:
Thine earthly rainbows stretched across the sweep
Of the ethereal waterfall, whose veil
Makes some unsculptured image; the strange sleep
Which, when the voices of the desert fail,
Wraps all in its own deep eternity; —
Thy caverns echoing to the Arve's commotion
A loud, lone sound, no other sound can tame;
Thou art pervaded with that ceaseless motion,
Thou art the path of that unresting sound —
Dizzy Ravine! and when I gaze on thee
I seem as in a trance sublime and strange
To muse on my own separate fantasy,
My own, my human mind, which passively
Now renders and receives fast influencings,
Holding an unremitting interchange
With the clear universe of things around;
One legion of wild thoughts, whose wandering wings
Now float above thy darkness, and now rest
Where that or thou art no unbidden guest,
In the still cave of the witch Poesy,
Seeking among the shadows that pass by
Ghosts of all things that are, some shade of thee,

Some phantom, some faint image; till the breast
From which they fled recalls them, thou art there!

III.

Some say that gleams of a remoter world
Visit the soul in sleep, — that death is slumber,
And that its shapes the busy thoughts outnumber
Of those who wake and live. — I look on high;
Has some unknown omnipotence unfurled
The veil of life and death? or do I lie
In dream, and does the mightier world of sleep
Speed far around and inaccessibly
Its circles? For the very spirit fails,
Driven like a homeless cloud from steep to steep
That vanishes among the viewless[2] gales!
Far, far above, piercing the infinite sky,
Mount Blanc appears, — still, snowy, and serene —
Its subject mountains their unearthly forms
Pile around it, ice and rock; broad vales between
Of frozen floods, unfathomable deeps,
Blue as the overhanging heaven, that spread
And wind among the accumulated steeps;
A desert peopled by the storms alone,
Save when the eagle brings some hunter's bone,
And the wolf tracks her there — how hideously
Its shapes are heaped around! rude, bare, and high,
Ghastly, and scarred, and riven. — Is this the scene
Where the old Earthquake-demon taught her young
Ruin? Were these their toys? or did a sea
Of fire envelope once this silent snow?[3]
None can reply — all seems eternal now.
The wilderness has a mysterious tongue
Which teaches awful doubt, or faith so mild,
So solemn, so serene, that man may be
But for such faith with nature reconciled;
Thou hast a voice, great Mountain, to repeal
Large codes of fraud and woe; not understood,
By all, but which the wise, and great, and good,
Interpret, or make felt, or deeply feel.

IV.

The fields, the lakes, the forests, and the streams,
Ocean, and all the living things that dwell

2. Invisible.
3. According to scientific theories of Shelley's time, the earth was originally round and smooth,
  and mountains resulted from floods, earthquakes, or fires erupting from the earth's center.

Within the dædal[4] earth; lightning, and rain,
Earthquake, and fiery flood, and hurricane,
The torpor of the year when feeble dreams
Visit the hidden buds, or dreamless sleep
Holds every future leaf and flower; — the bound
With which from that detested trance they leap;
The works and ways of man, their death and birth,
And that of him and all that his may be;
All things that move and breathe with toil and sound
Are born and die, revolve, subside, and swell.
Power dwells apart in its tranquillity
Remote, serene, and inaccessible:
And *this*, the naked countenance of earth,
On which I gaze, even these primæval mountains,
Teach the adverting mind. The glaciers creep
Like snakes that watch their prey, from their far fountains,
Slowly rolling on; there, many a precipice
Frost and the Sun in scorn of mortal power
Have piled — dome, pyramid, and pinnacle,
A city of death, distinct with many a tower
And wall impregnable of beaming ice.
Yet not a city, but a flood of ruin
Is there, that from the boundaries of the sky
Rolls its perpetual stream; vast pines are strewing
Its destined path, or in the mangled soil
Branchless and shattered stand; the rocks, drawn down
From yon remotest waste, have overthrown
The limits of the dead and living world,
Never to be reclaimed. The dwelling-place
Of insects, beasts, and birds, becomes its spoil;
Their food and their retreat for ever gone,
So much of life and joy is lost. The race
Of man flies far in dread; his work and dwelling
Vanish, like smoke before the tempest's stream,
And their place is not known. Below, vast caves
Shine in the rushing torrent's restless gleam,
Which from those secret chasms in tumult welling
Meet in the vale, and one majestic River,
The breath and blood of distant lands, for ever
Rolls its loud waters to the ocean waves,
Breathes its swift vapours to the circling air.

V.

Mont Blanc yet gleams on high: — the power is there,
The still and solemn power of many sights

4. Varied.

And many sounds, and much of life and death.
In the calm darkness of the moonless nights,
In the lone glare of day, the snows descend
Upon that Mountain; none beholds them there,
Nor when the flakes burn in the sinking sun,
Or the star-beams dart through them: — Winds contend
Silently there, and heap the snow with breath
Rapid and strong, but silently! Its home
The voiceless lightning in these solitudes
Keeps innocently, and like vapour broods
Over the snow. The secret strength of things
Which governs thought, and to the infinite dome
Of heaven is as a law, inhabits thee!
And what were thou, and earth, and stars, and sea,
If to the human mind's imaginings
Silence and solitude were vacancy?

SWITZERLAND, *June 23, 1816.*

PERCY BYSSHE SHELLEY

[The Sea of Ice]†

Chamouni, July 25th [1817].

We have returned from visiting the glacier of Montanvert, or as it is called, the Sea of Ice, a scene in truth of dizzying wonder. The path that winds to it along the side of a mountain, now clothed with pines, now intersected with snowy hollows, is wide and steep. The cabin of Montanvert is three leagues from Chamouni, half of which distance is performed on mules, not so sure footed but that on the first day the one which I rode fell in what the guides call a *mauvais pas*, so that I narrowly escaped being precipitated down the mountain. We passed over a hollow covered with snow, down which vast stones are accustomed to roll. One had fallen the preceding day, a little time after we had returned: our guides desired us to pass quickly, for it is said that sometimes the least sound will accelerate their descent. We arrived at Montanvert, however, safe.

On all sides precipitous mountains, the abodes of unrelenting frost, surround this vale: their sides are banked up with ice and snow, broken, heaped high, and exhibiting terrific chasms. The summits are sharp and naked pinnacles, whose overhanging steepness will not even permit snow to rest upon them. Lines of dazzling ice occupy here and there their perpendicular rifts, and shine through the driving vapours with

† From *History of a Six Weeks' Tour* (London: T. Hookham & C. & J. Oliver, 1817).

inexpressible brilliance: they pierce the clouds like things not belonging to this earth. The vale itself is filled with a mass of undulating ice, and has an ascent sufficiently gradual even to the remotest abysses of these horrible desarts. It is only half a league (about two miles) in breadth, and seems much less. It exhibits an appearance as if frost had suddenly bound up the waves and whirlpools of a mighty torrent. We walked some distance upon its surface. The waves are elevated about 12 or 15 feet from the surface of the mass, which is intersected by long gaps of unfathomable depth, the ice of whose sides is more beautifully azure than the sky. In these regions every thing changes, and is in motion. This vast mass of ice has one general progress, which ceases neither day nor night; it breaks and bursts for ever: some undulations sink while others rise; it is never the same. The echo of rocks, or of the ice and snow which fall from their overhanging precipices, or roll from their aerial summits, scarcely ceases for one moment. One would think that Mont Blanc, like the god of the Stoics, was a vast animal, and that the frozen blood for ever circulated through his stony veins.

We dined (M***, C***,[1] and I) on the grass, in the open air, surrounded by this scene. The air is piercing and clear. We returned down the mountain, sometimes encompassed by the driving vapours, sometimes cheered by the sunbeams, and arrived at our inn by seven o'clock.

GEORGE GORDON, LORD BYRON

From Childe Harold's Pilgrimage, *Canto III* (1817)

*   *   *

XCII.

The sky is changed!— and such a change! Oh night,
And storm, and darkness, ye are wondrous strong,
Yet lovely in your strength, as is the light
Of a dark eye in woman! Far along,
From peak to peak, the rattling crags among
Leaps the live thunder! Not from one lone cloud,
But every mountain now hath found a tongue,
And Jura answers, through her misty shroud,
Back to the joyous Alps, who call to her aloud!

1. Mary, Claire [Claremont].

XCIII.

And this is in the night: — Most glorious night!
Thou wert not sent for slumber! let me be
A sharer in thy fierce and far delight, —
A portion of the tempest and of thee!
How the lit lake shines, a phosphoric sea,
And the big rain comes dancing to the earth!
And now again 'tis black, — and now, the glee
Of the loud hills shakes with its mountain-mirth,
As if they did rejoice o'er a young earthquake's birth.

XCIV.

Now, where the swift Rhone cleaves his way between
Heights which appear as lovers who have parted
In hate, whose mining depths so intervene,
That they can meet no more, though broken-hearted;
Though in their souls, which thus each other thwarted,
Love was the very root of the fond rage
Which blighted their life's bloom, and then departed:
Itself expired, but leaving them an age
Of years all winters, — war within themselves to wage.

XCV.

Now, where the quick Rhone thus hath cleft his way,
The mightiest of the storms hath ta'en his stand:
For here, not one, but many, make their play,
And fling their thunder-bolts from hand to hand,
Flashing and cast around: of all the band,
The brightest through these parted hills hath fork'd
His lightnings, — as if he did understand,
That in such gaps as desolation work'd,
There the hot shaft should blast whatever therein lurk'd.

XCVI.

Sky, mountains, river, winds, lake, lightnings! ye!
With night, and clouds, and thunder, and a soul
To make these felt and feeling, well may be
Things that have made me watchful; the far roll
Of your departing voices, is the knoll[1]
Of what in me is sleepless, — if I rest.
But where of ye, O tempests! is the goal?

1. Knell (old form).

Are ye like those within the human breast?
Or do ye find, at length, like eagles, some high nest?

XCVII.

Could I embody and unbosom now
That which is most within me, — could I wreak
My thoughts upon expression, and thus throw
Soul, heart, mind, passions, feelings, strong or weak,
All that I would have sought, and all I seek,
Bear, know, feel, and yet breathe — into *one* word,
And that one word were Lightning, I would speak;
But as it is, I live and die unheard,
With a most voiceless thought, sheathing it as a sword.

*   *   *

[JOHN WILLIAM POLIDORI]

Letter Prefaced to *The Vampyre* (1819)

It appears that one evening Lord B., Mr. P. B. Shelly, the two ladies
and the gentleman before alluded to,[1] after having perused a German
work, which was entitled Phantasmagoriana, began relating ghost stories; when his lordship having recited the beginning of Christabel, then
unpublished, the whole took so strong a hold of Mr. Shelly's mind,
that he suddenly started up and ran out of the room. The physician
and Lord Byron followed, and discovered him leaning against a mantlepiece, with cold drops of perspiration trickling down his face. After
having given him something to refresh him, upon enquiring into the
cause of his alarm, they found that his wild imagination // having pic-
tured to him the bosom of one of the ladies with eyes (which was
reported of a lady in the neighbourhood where he lived) he was obliged
to leave the room in order to destroy the impression. It was afterwards
proposed, in the course of conversation, that each of the company present should write a tale depending upon some supernatural agency,
which was undertaken by Lord B., the physician, and Miss M. W.
Godwin.[2] * * *

1. Mary Shelley, Claire Clairmont, and Polidori himself.
2. Since published under the title of "Frankenstein; or, The Modern Prometheus" [Polidori's
   note].

NINETEENTH-CENTURY RESPONSES

PERCY BYSSHE SHELLEY

On *Frankenstein*†

The novel of 'Frankenstein; or, the Modern Prometheus,' is undoubtedly, as a mere story, one of the most original and complete productions
of the day. We debate with ourselves in wonder, as we read it, what
could have been the series of thoughts—what could have been the
peculiar experiences that awakened them—which conduced, in the
author's mind, to the astonishing combinations of motives and incidents, and the startling catastrophe, which compose this tale. There are,
perhaps, some points of subordinate importance, which prove that it is
the author's first attempt. But in this judgment, which requires a very
nice discrimination, we may be mistaken; for it is conducted throughout with a firm and steady hand. The interest gradually accumulates
and advances towards the conclusion with the accelerated rapidity of a
rock rolled down a mountain. We are led breathless with suspense and
sympathy, and the heaping up of incident on incident, and the working
of passion out of passion. We cry "hold, hold! enough!"—but there is
yet something to come; and, like the victim whose history it relates, we
think we can bear no more, and yet more is to be borne. Pelion is
heaped on Ossa, and Ossa on Olympus. We climb Alp after Alp, until
the horizon is seen blank, vacant, and limitless; and the head turns
giddy, and the ground seems to fail under our feet.

This novel rests its claim on being a source of powerful and profound
emotion. The elementary feelings of the human mind are exposed to
view; and those who are accustomed to reason deeply on their origin
and tendency will, perhaps, be the only persons who can sympathize,
to the full extent, in the interest of the actions which are their result.
But, founded on nature as they are, there is perhaps no reader, who
can endure anything beside a new love story, who will not feel a re-
sponsive string touched in his inmost soul. The sentiments are so affectionate and so innocent—the characters of the subordinate agents
in this strange drama are clothed in the light of such a mild and gentle
mind—the pictures of domestic manners are of the most simple and
attaching character: the father's is irresistible and deep. Nor are the
crimes and malevolence of the single Being, though indeed withering
and tremendous, the offspring of any unaccountable propensity to evil,
but flow irresistibly from certain causes fully adequate to their production. They are the children, as it were, of Necessity and Human Nature.

† Written in 1817; published (posthumously) in *The Athenæum Journal of Literature, Science
and the Fine Arts,* Nov. 10, 1832.

In this the direct moral of the book consists; and it is perhaps the most important, and of the most universal application, of any moral that can be enforced by example. Treat a person ill, and he will become wicked. Requite affection with scorn; — let one being be selected, for whatever cause, as the refuse of his kind — divide him, a social being, from society, and you impose upon him the irresistible obligations — malevolence and selfishness. It is thus that, too often in society, those who are best qualified to be its benefactors and its ornaments, are branded by some accident with scorn, and changed, by neglect and solitude of heart, into a scourge and a curse.

The Being in 'Frankenstein' is, no doubt, a tremendous creature. It was impossible that he should not have received among men that treatment which led to the consequences of his being a social nature. He was an abortion and an anomaly; and though his mind was such as its first impressions framed it, affectionate and full of moral sensibility, yet the circumstances of his existence are so monstrous and uncommon, that, when the consequences of them became developed in action, his original goodness was gradually turned into inextinguishable misanthropy and revenge. The scene between the Being and the blind De Lacey in the cottage, is one of the most profound and extraordinary instances of pathos that we ever recollect. It is impossible to read this dialogue, — and indeed many others of a somewhat similar character, — without feeling the heart suspend its pulsations with wonder, and the "tears stream down the cheeks." The encounter and argument between Frankenstein and the Being on the sea of ice, almost approaches, in effect, to the expostulations of Caleb Williams with Falkland. It reminds us, indeed, somewhat of the style and character of that admirable writer, to whom the author has dedicated his work, and whose productions he seems to have studied.

There is only one instance, however, in which we detect the least approach to imitation; and that is the conduct of the incident of Frankenstein's landing in Ireland. The general character of the tale, indeed, resembles nothing that ever preceded it. After the death of Elizabeth, the story, like a stream which grows at once more rapid and profound as it proceeds, assumes an irresistible solemnity, and the magnificent energy and swiftness of a tempest.

The churchyard scene, in which Frankenstein visits the tombs of his family, his quitting Geneva, and his journey through Tartary to the shores of the Frozen Ocean, resemble at once the terrible reanimation of a corpse and the supernatural career of a spirit. The scene in the cabin of Walton's ship — the more than mortal enthusiasm and grandeur of the Being's speech over the dead body of his victim — is an exhibition of intellectual and imaginative power, which we think the reader will acknowledge has seldom been surpassed.

[JOHN CROKER]

From the *Quarterly Review* (January 1818)†

Frankenstein, a Swiss student at the university of Ingolstadt, is led by a
peculiar enthusiasm to study the structure of the human frame, and to
attempt to follow to its recondite sources 'the stream of animal being.'
In examining the causes of *life*, he informs us, antithetically, that he
had first recourse to *death*. — He became acquainted with anatomy; but
that was not all; he traced through vaults and charnel-houses the decay
and corruption of the human body, and whilst engaged in this agreeable
pursuit, examining and analyzing the minutiæ of mortality, and the
phenomena of the change from life to death and from death to life, a
sudden light broke in upon him —

> 'A light so brilliant and wondrous, yet so simple, that while I
> became dizzy with the immensity of the prospect which it illus-
> trated, I was surprized that among so many men of genius, who
> had directed their inquiries towards the same science, I alone
> should be reserved to discover so astonishing a secret.
>
> 'Remember, I am NOT recording the vision of a madman. The
> sun does not more certainly shine in the heavens, than that which
> I now affirm is true. Some miracle might have produced it, yet
> the stages of the discovery were distinct and probable. After days
> and nights of incredible labour and fatigue, I succeeded in dis-
> covering the cause of generation and life; nay, more, I became
> myself capable of bestowing animation upon lifeless matter.'

Having made this wonderful discovery, he hastened to put it in practice; by plundering graves and stealing, not bodies, but parts of bodies,
from the church-yard: by dabbling (as he delicately expresses it) with
the unhallowed damps of the grave, and torturing the living animal to
animate lifeless clay, our modern Prometheus formed a filthy image to
which the last step of his art was to communicate being: — for the convenience of the process of his animal manufacture, he had chosen to
form his figure about eight feet high, and he endeavoured to make it
as handsome as he could — he succeeded in the first object and failed
in the second; he made and animated his giant; but by some little
mistake in the artist's calculation, the intended beauty turned out the
ugliest monster that ever deformed the day. The creator, terrified at his
own work, flies into one wood, and the work, terrified at itself, flies into
another. Here the monster, by the easy process of listening at the win-

† 36 (January 1818): 379–85.

dow of a cottage, acquires a complete education: he learns to think, to
talk, to read prose and verse; he becomes acquainted with geography,
history, and natural philosophy, in short, 'a most delicate monster.' This
credible course of study, and its very natural success, are brought about
by a combination of circumstances almost as natural. In the aforesaid
cottage, a young *Frenchman* employed his time in teaching an *Arabian*
girl all these fine things, utterly unconscious that while he was

> 'whispering soft lessons in his fair one's ear,'

he was also tutoring Frankenstein's hopeful son. The monster, however,
by due diligence, becomes highly accomplished: he reads Plutarch's
Lives, Paradise Lost, Volney's Ruin of Empires, and the Sorrows of
Werter. Such were the works which constituted the Greco-Anglico-
Germanico-Gallico-Arabic library of a Swabian hut, which, if not numerous, was at least miscellaneous, and reminds us, in this particular,
of Lingo's famous combination of historic characters — 'Mahomet, Hel-
iogabalus, Wat Tyler, and Jack the Painter.' He learns also to decypher
some writings which he carried off from the laboratory in which he was
manufactured; by these papers he becomes acquainted with the name
and residence of Frankenstein and his family, and as his education has
given him so good a taste as to detest himself, he has also the good
sense to detest his creator for imposing upon him such a horrible burden as conscious existence, and he therefore commences a series of
bloody persecutions against the unhappy Frankenstein — he murders his
infant brother, his young bride, his bosom friend; even the very nursery
maids of the family are not safe from his vengeance, for he contrives
that they shall be hanged for robbery and murder which he himself
commits.

The monster, however, has some method in his madness: he meets
his Prometheus in the valley of Chamouny, and, in a long conversation,
tells him the whole story of his adventures and his crimes, and declares,
that he will 'spill much more blood and become worse,' unless Frankenstein will *make* (we should perhaps say *build*) a wife for him; the
Sorrows of Werter had, it seems, given him a strange longing to find a
Charlotte, of a suitable size, and it is plain that none of Eve's daughters,
not even the enormous Charlotte[1] of the Variétés herself, would have
suited this stupendous fantoccino. A compliance with this natural desire
his kind-hearted parent most reasonably promises; but, on further consideration, he becomes alarmed at the thoughts of reviving the race of
Anak, and he therefore resolves to break his engagement, and to defeat
the procreative propensities of his ungracious child — hence great wrath
and new horrors — parental unkindness and filial ingratitude. The mon-

---

1. In the parody of Werter, at the Variétés in Paris, the Charlotte is ludicrously corpulent.

ster hastens to execute his promised course of atrocity, and the monster-maker hurries after to stab or shoot him, and so put an end to his proceedings. This chase leads Frankenstein through Germany and France, to England, Scotland, and Ireland, in which latter country, he is taken up by a constable called Daniel Nugent, and carried before Squire Kirwan a magistrate, and very nearly hanged for a murder committed by the monster. We were greatly edified with the laudable minuteness which induces the author to give us the names of these officers of justice; it would, however, have been but fair to have given us also those of the impartial judge and enlightened jury who acquitted him, for acquitted, as our readers will be glad to hear, honourably acquitted, he was at the assizes of Donegal. — Escaped from this peril, he renews the chase, and the monster, finding himself hard pressed, resolves to fly to the most inaccessible point of the earth; and, as our Review had not yet enlightened mankind upon the real state of the North Pole, he directs his course thither as a sure place of solitude and security; but Frankenstein, who probably had read Mr. Daines Barrington and Colonel Beaufoy on the subject, was not discouraged, and follows him with redoubled vigour, the monster flying on a sledge drawn by dogs, according to the Colonel's proposition, and Prometheus following in another — the former, however, had either more skill or better luck than the latter, whose dogs died, and who must have been drowned on the breaking up of the ice, had he not been fortunately picked up in the nick of time by Mr. Walton, the master of an English whaler, employed on a voyage of discovery towards the North Pole. On board this ship poor Frankenstein, after telling his story to Mr. Walton, who has been so kind as to write it down for our use, dies of cold, fatigue, and horror; and soon after, the monster, who had borrowed (we presume from the flourishing colony of East Greenland) a kind of raft, comes alongside the ship, and notwithstanding his huge bulk, jumps in at Mr. Walton's cabin window, and is surprized by that gentleman pronouncing a funeral oration over the departed Frankenstein; after which, declaring that he will go back to the Pole, and there burn himself on a funeral pyre (of ice, we conjecture) of his own collecting, he jumps again out of the window into his raft, and is out of sight in a moment.

Our readers will guess from this summary, what a tissue of horrible and disgusting absurdity this work presents. — It is piously dedicated to Mr. Godwin, and is written in the spirit of his school. The dreams of insanity are embodied in the strong and striking language of the insane, and the author, notwithstanding the rationality of his preface, often leaves us in doubt whether he is not as mad as his hero. Mr. Godwin is the patriarch of a literary family, whose chief skill is in delineating the wanderings of the intellect, and which strangely delights in the most afflicting and humiliating of human miseries. His disciples are a kind of *out-pensioners of Bedlam*, and, like 'Mad Bess' or 'Mad Tom,' are occasionally visited with paroxysms of genius and fits of expression, which make sober-minded people wonder and shudder.

We shall give our readers a very favourable specimen of the vigour of fancy and language with which this work is written, by extracting from it the three passages which struck us the most on our perusal of it. The first is the account of the animation of the image.[2]

The next is the description of the meeting in the valley of Chamouny.[3]

The last with which we shall agitate the nerves of our readers is Captain Walton's description of the monster he found in his cabin.[4]

It cannot be denied that this is nonsense — but it is nonsense decked out with circumstances and clothed in language highly terrific: it is, indeed,

> _____'a tale
> Told by an ideot, full of sound and fury,
> Signifying nothing—'

but still there is something tremendous in the unmeaning hollowness of its sound, and the vague obscurity of its images.

But when we have thus admitted that Frankenstein has passages which appal the mind and make the flesh creep, we have given it all the praise (if praise it can be called) which we dare to bestow. Our taste and our judgment alike revolt at this kind of writing, and the greater the ability with which it may be executed the worse it is — it inculcates no lesson of conduct, manners, or morality; it cannot mend, and will not even amuse its readers, unless their taste have been deplorably vitiated — it fatigues the feelings without interesting the understanding; it gratuitously harasses the heart, and wantonly adds to the store, already too great, of painful sensations. The author has powers, both of conception and language, which employed in a happier direction might, perhaps, (we speak dubiously,) give him a name among those whose writings amuse or amend their fellow-creatures; but we take the liberty of assuring him, and hope that he may be in a temper to listen to us, that the style which he has adopted in the present publication merely tends to defeat his own purpose, if he really had any other object in view than that of leaving the wearied reader, after a struggle between laughter and loathing, in doubt whether the head or the heart of the author be the most diseased.

2. See p. 35, above [Editor].
3. See p. 65, above [Editor].
4. See p. 152, above [Editor].

ANONYMOUS

From *Edinburgh Magazine* (March 1818)†

Here is one of the productions of the modern school in its highest style of caricature and exaggeration. It is formed on the Godwinian manner, and has all the faults, but many likewise of the beauties of that model. In dark and gloomy views of nature and of man, bordering too closely on impiety, — in the most outrageous improbability, — in sacrificing everything to effect, — it even goes beyond its great prototype; but in return, it possesses a similar power of fascination, something of the same mastery in harsh and savage delineations of passion, relieved in like manner by the gentler features of domestic and simple feelings. There never was a wilder story imagined, yet, like most of the fictions of this age, it has an air of reality attached to it, by being connected with the favourite projects and passions of the times. The real events of the world have, in our day, too, been of so wondrous and gigantic a kind, — the shiftings of the scenes in our stupendous drama have been so rapid and various, that Shakespeare himself, in his wildest flights, has been completely distanced by the eccentricities of actual existence. Even he would scarcely have dared to have raised, in one act, a private adventurer to the greatest of European thrones, — to have conducted him, in the next, victorious over the necks of emperors and kings, and then, in a third, to have shewn him an exile, in a remote speck of an island, some thousands of miles from the scene of his triumphs; and the chariot which bore him along covered with glory, quietly exhibited to a gaping mechanical rabble under the roof of one of the beautiful buildings on the North Bridge of Edinburgh, — (which buildings we heartily pray may be brought as low as the mighty potentate whose Eagles are now to be seen looking out of their windows, like the fox from the ruins of Balclutha.) Our appetite, we say, for every sort of wonder and vehement interest, has in this way become so desperately inflamed, that especially as the world around us has again settled into its old dull state of happiness and legitimacy, we can be satisfied with nothing in fiction that is not highly coloured and exaggerated; we even like a story the better that it is disjointed and irregular, and our greatest inventors, accordingly, have been obliged to accommodate themselves to the taste of the age, more, we believe, than their own judgment can, at all times, have approved of. The very extravagance of the present production will now, therefore, be, perhaps, in its favour, since the events which have actually passed before our eyes have made the atmosphere of miracles that in which we most readily breathe.

† March 1818: 249–53.

The story opens with a voyage of discovery to the North Pole. A young Englishman, whose mind had long been inflamed with this project, sets sail from Archangel, soon gets inclosed, as usual, among ice mountains, and is beginning to despair of success, when all his interest and thoughts are diverted suddenly into another channel, in consequence of a very singular adventure. One day a gigantic figure was seen moving northwards on a sledge, drawn by dogs, and a short time afterwards a poor emaciated wretch was picked up from a sledge that drifted close to the vessel. The Englishman soon formed a violent friendship for this stranger, and discovers him to be a person of the greatest virtues, talents, and acquirements, which are only rendered the more admirable and interesting, from the deep cloud of melancholy which frequently overshadowed them. After a time, he gets so far into his confidence, as to obtain from him the story of his life and misfortunes. His name was Frankenstein, son of a Syndic of Geneva, and of an amiable mother, who very properly dies at the beginning of the book, to leave her son and a young female cousin, who resided in the family, so disconsolate, that they could find no comfort except by falling in love. Frankenstein had been left much to his own disposal in the conduct of his studies, and, at a very early period, he had become quite *entêté* with some of the writings of the alchemists, on which he accidentally lighted; and we were at first in expectation that, like St Leon, he was to become possessed of the philosopher's stone, or of the *elixir vitae*. He is destined, however, to obtain a still more extraordinary power, but not from the alchemists, of the futility of whose speculations he soon became convinced, but whose wild conceptions continued to give to his mind a strong and peculiar bias.

At the university, stimulated by the encouragement of some distinguished philosophers, he applied himself, with the utmost perseverance and ability, to every department of natural science, and soon became the general object of envy and admiration. His researches led him to investigate the principle of life, which he did in the old and approved manner by dissecting living animals, groping into all the repositories of the dead, and making himself acquainted with life and death in all their forms. The result was a most wonderful discovery, — quite simple, he says, when it was made, but yet one which he very wisely does not communicate to his English acquaintance, and which, of course, must remain a secret to the world, — no less than the discovery of the means of communicating life to an organized form. With this our young philosopher sets himself to make a man, and that he might make no blunder from taking too small a scale, unfortunately, as it turns out, his man is a giant. In a garret of his apartments, to which none but himself was ever admitted, he employs four months on this wonderful production. Many of the ingredients seem to have been of a very disgusting description, since he passed whole nights in sepulchres raking them out; he thought, however, that he had succeeded in making a giant, as gainly in appearance at least as O'Brien, or the Yorkshire Boy, and every thing was now ready for the last touch of the master, the infusion of life into the inanimate mass. In breathless expectation, in the dead of night, he performed this last momentous act of creation; and the creature opened upon him two immense ghastly yellow eyes, which struck him with instant horror. He immediately hated himself and his work, and flew, in a state of feverish agony, to his room below; but, finding himself followed thither by the monster, he rushed out into the streets, where he walked about in fearful agitation, till the morning dawned, and they began to be frequented by their inhabitants. Passing along, he saw step from a coach an intimate friend of his from Geneva. For the moment he forgot every thing that had happened, was delighted to find that his friend had come to pursue his studies along with him, and was conducting him to his apartments, when on a sudden he recollected the dreadful inmate who would probably be found in them. He ran up and examined them, and, on finding that the monster had disappeared, his joy became quite foolish and outrageous; he danced about like a madman, and his friend was not surprised when immediately after he was seized by a delirious fever, which confined him for some weeks, alleviated, however, by all the attentions which friendship could bestow.

Scarcely had he recovered, when a sad piece of intelligence arrives from home. His father writes him that his little brother had strayed from them in an evening walk, and was at last found dead, and apparently strangled. He flies home to comfort his family, but it is night ere he reaches Geneva, and the gates being shut, he remains in the neighbourhood, and walks out in the dark towards the hills. The monster on a sudden stalks past him, and moving with inconceivable rapidity, is seen by him perched on one of the highest cliffs. The thought instantly strikes him, that this fiend, the creation of his own hand, must have been the murderer of his brother, and he feels all the bitterness of despair. Very ill able to comfort others, he next morning went to his father's house, and learns, as an additional misery, that a young servant girl, who had been beloved as a friend in the family, was taken up on suspicion of the murder, and was to be tried for her life. A picture, which the child had worn on the fatal night, was found in her pocket. Though, in his own mind, he could not doubt of the real author of the murder, and his beloved Elizabeth was equally convinced that it could not be her favourite Justine, still circumstances were so strong against her, that the poor girl was condemned and executed. No wonder that Frankenstein now fell into a deep melancholy; to relieve him from which, his father took him and Elizabeth on a tour to the valley of Chamounix. This part of the book is very beautifully written; the description of the mountain scenery, and of its effect on Frankenstein's mind, is finely given. One rainy day they did not proceed on their journey, but Frankenstein, in a state of more than common depression, left them early in the inn, for the purpose of scaling the summit of Montarvet.[1]

Frankenstein at first addresses him in words of violent rage, — the monster, however, endeavours to soften him.[2]

The monster now begins his story, and a very amiable personage he makes himself to be. The story is well fancied and told. Immediately on his creation he wandered out into the forest of Ingolstadt, where he remained for some days, till his different senses learnt to perform their appropriate functions, and he discovered the use of fire and various other rudiments of knowledge; and thus accomplished, he ventured forth into the great world. But in the first village that he reached he was hooted and stoned, and was obliged to take shelter in a hovel at the back of a cottage. Through a crevice in the wall, he soon became intimate with all the operations in the cottage, the inhabitants of which were an old blind man, his son and daughter. After the reception he had met with in the village, he kept himself very snug in his hole through the day, but being really a good-natured monster, and finding the young man was much overwrought in cutting fuel for the family, what does he, but betake him to the wood in the night time, and collect quantities of fuel, which he piles up beside the door? The good people think themselves the favourites of some kind spirit or *brownie*. In the mean time, he learns how to apply their language, which he found he could imitate tolerably well. He gradually, too, becomes acquainted with more of their circumstances and feelings; and there was so much affection between the venerable blind man (who moreover played beautifully on a musical instrument) and his children, and they were so loving to each other, — and they were so interesting withal from their poverty, that the worthy monster took a vehement passion for them, and had the greatest inclination to make himself agreeable to them. By close study, and the occurrence of favourable opportunities, he also acquires a knowledge of written language; and one day on his rambles, lighting on a portmanteau, which contained the Sorrows of Werter, a volume of Plutarch, and Milton's Paradise Lost, — he becomes quite an adept in German sentiment, ancient heroism, and Satanic sturdiness. He now thought himself qualified to make himself acquainted with the family, — though aware of his hideous appearance, he very wisely began with the blind gentleman, on whom he ventured to make a call when the rest of the family were out of doors. He had just begun to interest the old man in his favour, when their *tête-a-tête* is unluckily interrupted, and the poor monster is abused and maltreated as heretofore by the villagers. He flies to the woods, furious with rage, and disappointed affection; and, finding on his return that the cottagers had forsaken the

1. See p. 63, above [*Editor*].
2. See p. 65, above [*Editor*].

place, scared by his portentous visit, he amuses himself in his rage with setting it on fire, and then sets out in search of his creator. Other circumstances occur in his journey to give him a greater antipathy to the human race. He confesses the murder of the boy, whom, lighting upon, he wished to carry off, in the hope that he might find in him an object to attach himself to; — the murder was partly accidental, — but the slipping the picture into Justine's pocket was a piece of devilish malice. He concludes with denouncing vengeance against Frankenstein and all his race, if he does not agree to one request, to create a female companion for him like himself, with whom he proposes to retire to the wilds of North America, and never again to come into contact with man.

It is needless to go minutely through the remainder of this wild fiction. After some demurring, Frankenstein at last accedes to the demand, and, begins a second time the abhorred creation of a human being, — but again repents, and defies the demon; who thenceforth recommences his diabolical warfare against the unhappy philosopher, — destroys his friends and relations one by one, and finally murders his beloved Elizabeth, on the very evening of their marriage. Frankenstein, alive only to vengeance, now pursues the fiend over the world, — and it was in this chace that he had got into the neighbourhood of the North Pole, where he was but a little way behind him, but had quite spent himself in the pursuit. So ends the narrative of Frankenstein, and worn out nature soon after yields to the bitterness of his thoughts and his exhausted frame. He dies, and, to the astonishment of our Englishman and the crew, the monster makes his appearance, — laments the fate of his creator, — says that his feelings of vengeance are for ever at an end, — departs, and is heard of no more.

Such is a sketch of this singular performance, in which there is much power and beauty, both of thought and expression, though, in many parts, the execution is imperfect, and bearing the marks of an unpractised hand. It is one of those works, however, which, when we have read, we do not well see why it should have been written; — for a *jeu d'esprit* it is somewhat too long, grave, and laborious, — and some of our highest and most reverential feelings receive a shock from the conception on which it turns, so as to produce a painful and bewildered state of mind while we peruse it. We are accustomed, happily, to look upon the creation of a living and intelligent being as a work that is fitted only to inspire a religious emotion, and there is an impropriety, to say no worse, in placing it in any other light. It might, indeed, be the author's view to shew that the powers of man have been wisely limited, and that misery would follow their extension, — but still the expression "Creator," applied to a mere human being, gives us the same sort of shock with the phrase, "the Man Almighty," and others of the same kind, in Mr Southey's "Curse of Kehama." All these monstrous conceptions are the consequences of the wild and irregular theories of the age; though we do not at all mean to infer that the authors who give into such freedoms have done so with any bad intentions. This incongruity, however, with our established and most sacred notions, is the chief fault in such fictions, regarding them merely in a critical point of view. Shakespeare's Caliban (though his simplicity and suitableness to the place where he is found are very delightful) is, perhaps, a more *hateful* being than our good friend in this book. But Caliban comes into existence in the received way which common superstition had pointed out; we should not have endured him if Prospero had created him. Getting over this original absurdity, the character of our monster is in good keeping; — there is a grandeur, too, in the scenery in which he makes his appearances, — the ice-mountains of the Pole, or the glaciers of the Alps; — his natural tendency to kind feelings, and the manner in which they were blighted, — and all the domestic picture of the cottage, are very interesting and beautiful. We hope yet to have more productions, both from this author and his great model, Mr Godwin; but they would make a great improvement in their writings, if they would rather study the established order of nature as it appears, both in the world of matter and of mind, than continue to revolt our feelings by hazardous innovations in either of these departments.

ANONYMOUS

From *Gentleman's Magazine* (April 1818)†

This Tale [*Frankenstein*] is evidently the production of no ordinary Writer; and, though we are shocked at the idea of the event on which the fiction is founded, many parts of it are strikingly good, and the description of the scenery is excellent.

In the pride of Science, the Hero of the Tale presumes to take upon himself the structure of a human being; in which, though he in some degree is supposed to have succeeded, he forfeits every comfort of life, and finally even life itself.

> "The event," we are told, "has been supposed, by Dr. Darwin, and some of the physiological writers of Germany, as not of impossible occurrence. I shall not be supposed as according the remotest degree of serious faith to such an imagination; yet, in assuming it as the basis of a work of fancy, I have not considered myself as merely weaving a series of supernatural terrors. The event on which the interest of the story depends is exempt from the disadvantages of a mere tale of spectres or enchantment. It was

† April 1818: 334–35.

recommended by the novelty of the situations which it developes; and, however impossible as a physical fact, affords a point of view to the imagination for the delineating of human passions more comprehensive and commanding than any which the ordinary relations of existing events can yield. — The story was begun in the majestic region where the scene is principally laid, and in society which cannot cease to be regretted. I passed the summer of 1816 in the environs of Geneva. The season was cold and rainy, and in the evenings we crowded around a blazing wood fire, and occasionally amused ourselves with some German stories of ghosts, which happened to fall into our hands. These tales excited in us a playful desire of imitation. Two other friends (a tale from the pen of one of whom would be far more acceptable to the publick than any thing I can ever hope to produce) and myself agreed to write each a story, founded on some supernatural occurrence. The weather, however, suddenly became serene; and my two friends left me on a journey among the Alps, and lost, in the magnificent scenes which they present, all memory of their ghostly visions. The following tale is the only one which has been completed."

If we mistake not, this friend was a Noble Poet.

ANONYMOUS

From *Knight's Quarterly* (Aug.–Nov. 1824)†

I do not think I ever was so much disappointed in any book as in Valperga; I had the very highest expectations of the maturing of the genius which could produce such a work as Frankenstein. The faults of Frankenstein were occasional extravagance and *over-writing*; — it was, therefore, natural to suppose that the interval of between four and five years would correct this, without impairing its freshness, force, and vigour. But in Valperga there is not the slightest trace of the same hand — instead of the rapidity and enthusiastic energy which hurries you forward in Frankenstein, every thing is cold, crude, inconsecutive, and wearisome; — not one flash of imagination, not one spark of passion — opening it as I did, with eager expectation, it must indeed have been bad for me after toiling a week to send the book back without having finished the first volume. This induced me to read Frankenstein again — for I thought I must have been strangely mistaken in my original judgment. So far, however, from this, a second reading has confirmed it. I think Frankenstein possesses extreme power, and displays

† 3 (Aug.–Nov. 1824): 195–99.

capabilities such as I did hope would have produced far different things from Castruccio.

*   *   *

Frankenstein is, I think, the best instance of natural passions applied to supernatural events that I ever met with. Grant that it is possible for one man to create another, and the rest is perfectly natural and in course. I do not allude to the incidents, for they are thrown together with a haste and carelessness so apparent as to be almost confessed; but the sentiments — both of thought and passion — are given with a truth which is equal to their extraordinary vigour. I am surprised to see by the preface that Dr. Darwin, and some of the physiological writers of Germany supposed the creation of a human being "as not of impossible occurrence." I can understand that it might be possible to put together a human frame — though with the very greatest difficulty — both from the intricacy and minuteness of the conformation, the most trifling error in which would be fatal, and from the difficulty of preventing putrescence during the process, without drying up the form like a mummy, which would incapacitate it from all purposes of *life*. But, granting that a frame could be so constructed, I cannot conceive how Dr. Darwin, who, however over-rated by his friends, was certainly a man of considerable powers of mind, I cannot conceive, I say, how he could contemplate the possibility of infusing the principle of life, when of such principle we are wholly ignorant. Many attempts have been made to say where life dwells — to prove that such or such a part is infallibly vital; but whoever could say what life itself was? This is one of the most strange of those mysteries which are hidden from human reason. The simplest operations of nature are, in their cause and process, equally inscrutable; — the whole progress and vegetation from the seed rotting in the earth, to the shoot, the sapling, the tree, the blossom, the fruit — is as utterly inscrutable by man as are the causes of his own production and existence.

The most unskilful thing in the book is the extreme ugliness of the being whom Frankenstein creates. It is not natural, that to save himself additional trouble from the minuteness of the parts, he should create a giant. He must have known the vast danger of forming one of such bodily power, whose mind it would take a considerable time to mould into humanity. Besides, though it is highly natural that the features which had been chosen individually as perfect, and which appeared so even when conjoined in the lifeless figure, should, on their being vivified, have an incongruous and unearthly aspect; yet, it is not at all probable, that one with Frankenstein's science should have formed a creature of such "appalling hideousness." It is utterly inconceivable also, that he should have let the monster (as he is somewhat unfairly called) escape; — one of the thoughts which must, one would imagine, have been uppermost in his mind during his labours, would have been

the instructing his creature intellectually as he had formed him physically.

In the account which the creature gives of his instruction by means
of watching the polished cottagers, the hastiness of the composition is
the most apparent. Indeed, nothing would require such extreme trouble
and carefulness as a correct representation of the mind of one who had
(from whatever circumstances) reached maturity without any acquired
knowledge. Those things which, from having been known to us before
the period to which our remembrances reach, appear to be part of our
innate consciousness, would be perfect novelty to such a being. Not
only speech would be non-existent but even sight would be imperfect
in him. In short, it would require much thought and some physical
knowledge, joined (as I before said) to the greatest care, to render such
a description at once full and accurate. In Frankenstein what there is
of it is sufficiently interesting in itself, but it suggests so frequently how
much more it might be wrought out, that it brings strongly into view
its own imperfectness.

For my own part, I confess that *my* interest in the book is entirely
on the side of the monster. His eloquence and persuasion, of which
Frankenstein complains, are so because they are truth. The justice is
indisputably on his side, and his sufferings are, to me, touching to the
last degree. Are there are any sufferings, indeed, so severe as those
which arise from the sensation of dereliction, or, (as in this case) of
isolation? Even the slightest tinge of those feelings, arising as they often
do from trivial circumstances, as from passing a solitary evening in a
lone and distant situation — even these, are bitter to a severe degree.
What it must be, then, — what *is* it to feel oneself *alone in the world!*
Fellow-feeling is the deepest of all the needs which Nature has im-
planted within us. The impulses which lead us to the physical preservation of our life are scarcely stronger than those which impel us to
communion with our fellows. Alas! then to have no fellows! — to be,
with feelings of kindliness and beneficence, the object of scorn and
hate to every one whose eyes lighted on us! — to be repaid with blows
and wounds for the very benefits we confer! — The poor monster always,
for these reasons, touched me to the heart. Frankenstein ought to have
reflected on the means of giving happiness to the being of his creation,
before he *did* create him. Instead of that, he heaps on him all sorts of
abuse and contumely for his *ugliness*, which was directly *his* work, and
for his crimes to which his neglect gave rise.

But whence arises the extreme inferiority of Valperga? I can account
for it only by supposing that Shelley wrote the first, though it was attributed to his wife, — and that she really wrote the last. Still I should
not, from internal evidence, suppose Frankenstein to be the work of
Shelley. It has much of his poetry and vigour — but it is wholly free
from those philosophical opinions from which scarcely any of his works

are free, and for which there are many fair openings in Frankenstein. It is equally to be observed that there are no religious reflections — and that there are many circumstances in which a mind at all religiously inclined would not have failed to have expressed some sentiments of that nature. It may be, that Mrs. Shelley wrote Frankenstein — but, knowing that its fault was extravagance, determined to be careful and correct in her next work; and, thence, as so many do from the same cause, became cold and common-place. At all events, the difference of the two books is very remarkable.

HUGH REGINALD HAWEIS

Introduction to the Routledge World Library Edition (1886)

I issue "Frankenstein" with some degree of hesitation, but after mature reflection.

The subject is somewhat revolting, the treatment of it somewhat hideous. The conception is powerful, but the execution very unequal.

The *mise-en-scène* of this appalling story is admirable. It ranges from the ice drifts in Polar seas to Alpine valleys and the steppes of Asia; but the local outlines are sharp, the colouring is faithful.

It is in her natural descriptions, as well as her subtle analysis of moods, that Mrs. Shelley proves herself to be an imaginative writer of no mean order.

It is in her construction and plot that she is weak.

The manufacturer of the human monster, since no mortal could say how such a thing should be done, is slurred over in a few hasty but ghastly paragraphs.

When this nameless demon stalks forth and is shunned by his terrified creator, what becomes of him, how he develops, why he is let go free, is not sufficiently made clear.

When the figure begins to talk, all the show of probability at once vanishes, more completely than in "Gulliver's Travels" or the "Arabian Nights' Entertainments."

The general conception of a creature created non-natural by the appliance of art and science, and impelled into crime after crime simply by a despairing contest with a world into which he should never have been introduced at all, is certainly powerful; but the tale of horror is unrelieved by any real poetical justice, and the moral threat — if there is any — is vague and indeterminate.

Still "Frankenstein" retains its popularity as the first of a class of fiction — not of a very high order — to which the genius of Edgar Allan

Poe has given an importance somewhat out of proportion to its merits.

The handling of horrors, like the practice of anatomy and vivisection, can only be justified by the supposed benefits conferred.

In the case of anatomy those benefits are physical, in the case of action they are moral. In cases where neither physical nor moral interests are furthered, many people think that such things had best be left alone.

"Frankenstein," with all its undoubted power, with its exquisite descriptions, its subtle analysis of feeling, its continual attempts at a moral, falls short of a *chef d-oeuvre* for want of workmanship and constructive power, or those qualities which reconcile us to the horrors of Poe's "M. Valdemar" and the ghastly solution of the "Murders in the Rue Morgue."

Still the reader will begin "Frankenstein" excited by the leading idea, and he will read it to the end, not only on account of its accumulation of horrors, but for the sake of its fine and varied scenes — I had almost said atmospheric effects — and its deep insight into the natural workings of the human heart.

✳   ✳   ✳

The actual occasion which gave rise to "Frankenstein" was this. One day Shelley and his wife, Lord Byron and Polidori, had been talking together, apparently about ghosts, when Lord Byron, before they separated, exclaimed, "We will each write a ghost story!" Although Lord Byron's "Vampire" remains an uncouth fragment of no great merit in prose, neither Shelley's nor Polidori's compositions seem to have come to anything; but Mrs. Shelley, who had always been what she calls a "scribbler" from her early girlhood, was more tenacious of the project, and urged on by both Shelley and Byron, she at last completed the ghastly and powerful narrative which, in spite of its technical imperfections, is certainly worth preserving, and will be undoubtedly read through by everyone who gets as far as the second letter. In that letter "so strange an accident happens," that a curiosity is then and there excited which is not finally satisfied until the horrid figure which haunts the remaining pages finally springs through the window of the ship's cabin "upon the ice-raft which lay close to the vessel, and is soon borne away by the waves and lost in darkness and distance."

MODERN CRITICISM

CHRISTOPHER SMALL

[Percy] Shelley and *Frankenstein*†

The two people directly responsible for Mary Shelley's writing *Frankenstein* were Byron and Shelley himself. It was Byron who suggested that everyone in the party at Geneva should "write a ghost story". It was the conversation between Byron and Shelley about "the principle of life" that gave Mary her starting point. For Byron the ghost story project was a diversion, and one he soon tired of. ("The illustrious poets", says Mary in her Introduction, ". . . annoyed by the platitude of prose, speedily relinquished their uncongenial task".) But for Shelley no kind of writing, least of all Mary's, could be regarded merely as a diversion. His own story aborted, but he took the keenest interest in hers; it was he who encouraged her, gave her the continued stimulus that (if Godwin was right) she needed, and helped her at every point up to and including negotiation with the publishers and provision of the original anonymous Preface. How far his help went in actual composition we cannot be sure. According to Mary, she owed her expansion of the idea into a novel to his "incitement". ("At first I thought of but a few pages . . . but Shelley urged me to develop the idea at greater length".) But she was clear and insistent that not "the suggestion of one incident, nor scarcely of one train of feeling" was his. Shelley's own references to the book, in dealing with the publishers, indicate that he did nothing more than make a few corrections in proof[1] and some earlier corrections in his hand appear in the original manuscript. The actual writing seems to have been done mostly when Shelley was not there. Entries in Mary's *Journal* show that she usually worked on the story when he was out of the house; two years later, when they were living in Italy and Shelley, being away for a few days, wrote to Mary urging her to employ the time on another work, he spoke of *Frankenstein* as "fruits of my absence."[2] It is curious that he should describe it in such a way; for he did very much more than push Mary into writing. He provided the subject.

Frankenstein himself is clearly and to some extent must intentionally have been a portrayal of Shelley, and Shelley can scarcely have been unaware of it, if only on account of his name. Frankenstein's first name is Victor, the same (presumably in earnest of a life of mental fight and

---

† From *Ariel Like a Harpy: Shelley, Mary and* Frankenstein (London: Victor Gollancz, 1972) 100–104. Reprinted by permission of the publisher.
1. Shelley, letter to Lackington Allen and Company (the eventual publishers of *Frankenstein*, after Ollier had turned it down) 22 August, 1817.
2. Shelley, letter to Mary, 20 August, 1818.

spiritual conquest) that Shelley took for himself on a number of occasions in boyhood and later. His first published work was the volume
of poems shared with his sister Elizabeth (and also, if inadvertently,
with "Monk" Lewis) printed as by "Victor and Cazire"; the hero of
another poem of this time, "*The Wandering Jew*", was called Victorio;
even the pseudonymous "editor" of the anti-monarchical burlesque,
The Posthumous Fragments of Margaret Nicholson, published while
Shelley was at Oxford, was "John Fitzvictor". To these may be added
a feminine version, Victoria, who briefly appears as a murdered sister
in the early prose-romance, *St Irvyne*.

Shelley dropped the pseudonym soon, of course, and nearly all his
published work, these juvenilia apart, appeared either anonymously or
under his own name. But the name Victor was absorbed, so to speak,
into the work itself. "Victory" is a word that occurs with striking fre-
quency in his poetry, especially in the later period. Almost every one
of what may for the moment — if very roughly — be called his "political"
poems includes at some point aspiration towards or invocation of "Victory". It is the last word of *Prometheus Unbound*, and it sounds, though
more ambiguously, all through *Hellas*, of which the epigraph is a line
from Sophocles, the *Oedipus Colonnus*: "I am a prophet of a victorious
contest." What it meant for him we shall try to see later; in the meantime it can be asserted that anyone who knew Shelley or his writings
well could scarcely have thought of victory or a victor without thinking
of him.

But it is not only in name that Frankenstein resembles Shelley. It
cannot be said, perhaps, that their characters are alike, since Frankenstein has scarcely any character in the ordinary sense, and the very fact
of his inadequacy in this respect, his want of solidity in fictional terms,
is something that must be taken into account. But if he does not appear
in the story as a "real" human being, he very vividly is there (if one
may make such distinctions within a work of art) as an "ideal" one;
and the ideal he represents is in many very striking ways a Shelleyan
one. If he is not Shelley he is a dream of Shelley, and one that he
would not have been averse to dreaming himself, as an improvement,
up to a point, on experience.

Frankenstein, like Shelley, is an ardent and high-spirited youth, of
early promise and "vehement passions". If his upbringing does not
much resemble what we know of Shelley's early years at Field Place,
it is possible to see in it, in its atmosphere of perfect love, harmony,
and parental indulgence — "I was their plaything and their idol, and
something better — their child, the innocent and helpless creature bestowed on them by Heaven . . . to bring up to good" — not only a stock
model of romantic family principles but also an idealised and transformed version of Shelley's childhood, the childhood that he felt and
must often have said that he ought to have had. No doubt it was also

a compensation for some of Mary's deprivations as a child: as in this beginning, so throughout, the story of Frankenstein serves for both, he is a visible sign of their identification with each other.

There is no physical description of Frankenstein, and again one might say that he has no physical body, he is all spirit and restless, inquiring mind. These are sufficiently described, in childhood and later. As a child, he says, "my temper was sometimes violent, and my passions vehement; but by some law in my temperature they were turned, not towards childish pursuits, but to an eager desire to learn, and not to learn all things indiscriminately". Compare the impressions of Shelley's boyhood collected by Hogg and given in his *Life*:

> From his earliest years, all his amusements and occupations were of a daring and, in one sense of the term, lawless nature. He delighted to exert his powers, not as a boy, but as a man. . . . His understanding and early development of imagination never permitted him to mingle in childish players. . . . But he was always actively employed; and although his endeavours were prosecuted with puerile precipitancy, yet his aim and his thoughts were constantly directed to those great objects which have employed the thoughts of the greatest among men.[3]

Frankenstein is brought up with his "more than sister", Elizabeth, the name also of Shelley's mother and of his favourite sister. Frankenstein's elderly father, on the other hand, the revered, high-principled learned Syndic, entirely mild and benevolent, is an exact reverse image of the tyrannical father who, to whatever extent he existed in real life, haunted Shelley's imagination. In fact this sort of wise, kindly, silver-haired old man, altogether un-authoritarian, the somewhat enfeebled counter-balance to the hated Lord God Father Almighty — too old, it may be observed, to be any sort of rival to a young man — crops up again and again in Shelley's writings, most notably in *The Revolt of Islam* (1817): the aged "hermit", "grand and mild" who rescues the hero, Laon, from prison, cares for him and instructs him, though only as his "passive instrument".

In the biographical (apart from the psychological) ancestry of this ideal father William Godwin undoubtedly had a share; but more probably was owed, both in Shelley's and Mary's representations of him, to Dr Lind, the elderly savant who befriended Shelley at Eton and who, in one of the ill-attested stories of his schooldays — one can never be sure how far Shelley's accounts of persecution were founded on fact — is said to have intervened with his actual father to prevent his being sent to a madhouse. Whether or not this incident was pure fantasy on Shelley's part is immaterial in the present context; it clearly established a connection between the "hermit" and Dr Lind, and that the "hermit"

3. Thomas Jefferson Hogg, *Life of Shelley*, London 1858.

was a "memorial" to him is indeed testified in Mary Shelley's own notes to *The Revolt of Islam.* Dr Lind, "exactly what an old man ought to be. Free, calm-spirited, full of benevolence and even of grateful ardour", as Shelley described him, according to Hogg, is also very like the elder Frankenstein, of "upright mind" and calm integrity, whom his son loves and reveres. He also enters into the person of Waldman, the second of Frankenstein's professors at Ingolstadt, of "mild and attractive" manners, dignity and kindliness, who is chiefly responsible for engaging Frankenstein in the study of science.

At this point the parallel between Shelley and the young Frankenstein becomes even more evident. Shelley, like Victor Frankenstein, had an early passion to learn "the secrets of heaven and earth": one may say that in both the drive was inherent (like Caleb Williams's "curiosity", and possibly of the same unconscious origins), although in Frankenstein's case the particular direction it takes is the result of small original accidents, "ignoble and almost forgotten sources". Oddly enough, and with a logic by no means immediately apparent, the first of these is a chance exchange between Victor and his father which confirms him, not in scientific pursuits but in his interest in magic and alchemy. It seems less odd when we remember that Shelley too had the same interest: when Frankenstein describes his compulsion to penetrate the "secrets" both of the material and immaterial worlds — "whether it was the outward substance of things, or the inner spirit of nature and the mysterious soul of man that occupied me, still my enquiries were directed to the metaphysical or, in its highest sense, the physical secrets of the world" — it might be Shelley speaking.

* * *

GEORGE LEVINE

Frankenstein and the Tradition of Realism†

* * *

Frankenstein is one of the first in a long tradition of fictional overreachers, of characters who act out in various ways the myth of Faust, and transport it from the world of mystery and miracle to the commonplace. He is destroyed not by some metaphysical agency, some supernatural intervention — as God expelled Adam from Eden or Mephistopheles collected his share of the bargain (though echoes of these events are everywhere) — but by his own nature and the consequences of living in or rejecting human community. Frankenstein is in a way the indirect

† From *Novel: A Forum on Fiction*, vol. 7, no. 1 (Fall 1973) 17–23. Reprinted with permission.

father of lesser, more humanly recognizable figures, like Becky Sharp or Pip or Lydgate, people who reject the conventional limits imposed upon them by society and who are punished for their troubles. *Frankenstein* embodies one of the central myths of realistic fiction in the nineteenth century, even in the contrast between its sensational style and its apparently explicit moral implications. It embodies characteristically a simultaneous awe and reverence toward greatness of ambition, and fear and distrust of those who act on such ambition. That ambivalence is almost always disguised in realistic fiction, where the manner itself seems to reject the possibility of greatness and the explicit subject is frequently the evil of aspiring to it; in gothic fiction the energies to be suppressed by the realist ideal, by the model of Flemish painting, by worldly wise compromise with the possible, are released. Gothic fiction, as Lowry Nelson has observed, "by its insistence on singularity and exotic setting . . . seems to have freed the minds of readers from direct involvement of their superegos and allowed them to pursue daydreams and wish fulfillment in regions where inhibitions and guilt could be suspended" (*Yale Review*, 1962–63, p. 238). The mythology of virtue rewarded, which was curiously central to English realism, is put to question in the gothic landscape where more powerful structures than social convention give shape to wish; and, as Nelson suggests, reader and writer alike were freed to pursue the possibilities of their own potential evil. It is striking how difficult it is to locate in realistic fiction any positive and active evil. The central realist mythology is spelled out in characters like George Eliot's Tito Melema, whose wickedness is merely a gradual sliding into the consequences of a natural egoism. In gothic fiction, but more particularly in *Frankenstein*, evil is both positively present and largely inexplicable. Although ostensibly based on the ideas of Godwin's rationalist ethics which see evil as a consequence of maltreatment or injustice, there is no such comfortable explanation for the evil of Frankenstein himself. Where did his decision to create the monster come from? Mere chance. Evil is a deadly and fascinating mystery originating in men's minds as an inexplicable but inescapable aspect of human goodness.

It is a commonplace of criticism of *Frankenstein*, as of Conrad's *The Secret Sharer*, that the hero and his antagonist are one. Leggatt is the other side of the captain; the monster and Frankenstein are doubles, two aspects of the same being. This seems an entirely just reading given that Frankenstein creates the monster and that, as they pursue their separate lives, they increasingly resemble and depend upon each other so that by the end Frankenstein pursues his own monster, their positions reversed, and the monster plants clues to keep Frankenstein in pursuit. As Frankenstein's creation, the monster can be taken as an expression of an aspect of Frankenstein's self: the monster is a sort of New Critical art object, leading an apparently independent organic life of its own and yet irremediably and subtly tied to its creator, re-enacting in mildly disguised ways, his creator's feelings and experiences. * * *

The world of *Frankenstein* has a kind of objective existence which only partially disguises — much less convincingly than a realistic novel would — its quality as projection of a subjective state. The laws governing this world are almost the laws of dream in which the control of action is only partially, if at all, ordinary causation. Characters and actions move around central emotional preoccupations. Clearly, for example, Walton is an incipient Frankenstein, in his lesser way precisely in Frankenstein's position: ambitious for glory, embarked on a voyage of scientific discovery, putting others to risk for his work, isolated from the rest of mankind by his ambition, and desperately lonely. Frankenstein becomes his one true friend, and he is a friend who dies just at the point when their friendship is becoming solidified. And, of course, he is the man to whom Frankenstein tells his story, partly, like the Ancient Mariner, to keep him from the same fate. Moreover, the lesson he learns is not merely the explicit one, that he must sacrifice his ambition to others, but that he must also reject the vengeance that Frankenstein wishes upon him. Frankenstein's last wish is that Walton promise to destroy the monster; yet when the monster appears, Walton does not kill him but rather listens to his story and is moved to compassion which he tries to force himself to reject. He cannot kill the monster, who speaks in a way that echoes Frankenstein's own ideas and sentiments; and, though this is not stated, in rejecting the vengeance which consumed Frankenstein, he is finally freed into a better (and perhaps a lesser) life — but one to which he returns in bitterness and dejection.

Clerval, too, Frankenstein's friend from boyhood, echoes an aspect of Frankenstein's self. Clerval is, surely, Frankenstein without the monster. Frankenstein describes himself as having been committed from his youth to the "metaphysical, or, in its highest sense, the physical secrets of the world." Meanwhile, Clerval occupied himself, so to speak, "with the moral relations of things. The busy stage of life, the virtues of heroes, and actions of men, were his theme; and his hope and his dream was to become one among those whose names are recorded in story, as the gallant and adventurous benefactors of our species" (pp. 37–38).[1] Except, of course, for the emphasis on political action, this description would serve for Frankenstein as well. Moreover, as Frankenstein himself notes, both he and Clerval were softened into gentleness and generosity by the influence of Elizabeth: "I might have become sullen in my study, rough through the ardour of my nature, but that she was there to subdue me to a semblance of her own gentleness. And Clerval . . . might not have been so perfectly humane . . . so full of kindness

1. Mary Shelley, *Frankenstein*, ed. James Kinsley and M. K. Joseph (Oxford: Oxford UP, 1969).

and tenderness amidst his passion for adventurous exploit, had she not unfolded to him the real loveliness of beneficence, and made the doing good the end and aim of his soaring ambition" (p. 38). Clerval, whose father denies him a university education, feels, like Frankenstein himself, a repugnance to the meanness of business. On the night Frankenstein is to depart for Ingolstadt and the university, he reads in Clerval's "kindling eye and in his animated glance a firm but restrained resolve, not to be chained to the miserable details of commerce" (p. 44). Both men reject the occupations of ordinary life, both are consumed with great ambitions, both are kept humane by the influence of the same woman, and, in the end, both are destroyed by Frankenstein's own creation, by the aspect of Frankenstein which ignores "the moral relations of things." Moreover, when Clerval dies, Frankenstein is not only accused of the murder (and seems unwilling to exculpate himself though he knows he has evidence that will do so), but he falls almost mortally ill — as though he himself has been the victim.

These kinds of redoublings are characteristic of the whole novel. Not only all the major characters, but the minor characters as well seem to be echoes of each other. Every story seems a variation on every other. Both Elizabeth and Justine are found by the Frankenstein family and rescued from poverty, and both accuse themselves, in different ways, of the murder of Frankenstein's youngest brother. When she hears of his death, Elizabeth exclaims, "O God, I have murdered my darling child" (p. 72). Justine, too, is a kind of sister of Frankenstein. She so adored Madame Frankenstein that she "endeavoured to imitate her phraseology and manners, so that even now," Elizabeth writes, "she often reminds me of her" (p. 65). And after she is convicted, Justine "confesses" to the murder.

And then there are the parents. Frankenstein himself is a father, the creator of the monster, and the novel is in part an examination of the responsibility of the father to the son. The monster asks Frankenstein for the gift of a bride to alleviate his solitude. Frankenstein's father in effect gives Frankenstein a bride, and a sister. The night before Elizabeth is brought into the Frankenstein house, his mother "had said playfully, — 'I have a pretty present for my Victor — tomorrow he shall have it.' And when, on the morrow, she presented Elizabeth to me as her promised gift, I, with childish seriousness, interpreted her words literally, and looked upon Elizabeth as mine — mine to protect, love, and cherish. All praises bestowed on her, I received as made to a possession of my own. We called each other familiarly by the name of cousin. No word, no expression could body forth the kind of relation in which she stood to me — my more than sister, since till death she was to be mine only" (pp. 35–36). Frankenstein's father, in bestowing the gift and in caring for him, behaves to his son as the monster would have Frankenstein behave. Interestingly, in this extraordinary novel of intricate relations, when Frankenstein's father arrives after Clerval's death to help his son, Frankenstein at first assumes that his visitor is to be the murderer: "Oh take him away! I cannot see him," he cries. "For God's sake, do not let him enter." This strange hallucination focuses again on the bond that connects all the characters in the novel, and suggests how deeply incestuous and Oedipal the relationships are. It suggests, too, how close to the surface of this world are motives derived not from external experience, but from emotional and psychic energies beneath the surface of things.

Despite the potentially easy patterning, there is no simple way to define the relation between parents and offspring in this novel. Frankenstein's father is loved and generous, and marries the daughter of an unsuccessful merchant who, in his pride, almost brings his whole family down. The father of Safie betrays his daughter and her lover and is the cause of the fall of the DeLacey family. Felix DeLacey, in order to save Safie, brings his whole family to the brink of ruin. Frankenstein ignores his creation and, in effect, destroys his family as a consequence. Father and sons are almost equally responsible and irresponsible: what is consistent is only the focal concern on the relationship itself.

Within the novel, almost all relations have the texture of blood kinship. Percy Shelley's notorious preoccupation with incest is manifest in Mary's work. The model is Eden, where Eve is an actual physical part of Adam, and the monster's situation is caused precisely because he has no blood relations, no kinship. Frankenstein, on his death bed, makes clear why there is such an intense, reduplicative obsession throughout the novel on the ties of kinship:

> I thank you Walton . . . for your kind intentions towards so miserable a wretch; but when you speak of new ties, and fresh affections, think you that any can replace those who are gone? Can any man be to me as Clerval was; or any woman another Elizabeth? Even where the affections are not strongly moved by any superior excellence, the companions of our childhood always possess a certain power over our minds, which hardly any later friend can obtain. They know our infantine dispositions, which, however they may be afterwards modified, are never eradicated; and they can judge of our actions with more certain conclusions as to the integrity of our motives. A sister or a brother can never, unless indeed such symptoms have been shown early, suspect the other of fraud or false dealing, when another friend, however strongly he may be attached, may, in spite of himself, be contemplated with suspicion. (pp. 211–212)

In the original version of the novel, Elizabeth was, as the Oxford editor M. K. Joseph points out, Frankenstein's cousin, "the daughter of his father's sister" (p. 236n), and throughout the revised version, Frank-

enstein continues to refer to her as cousin. Every death in the novel is
a death in the family, literal or figurative: what Frankenstein's ambition
costs him is the family connection which makes life humanly possible.
William is his brother. Justine looks like his mother, and is another
kind of sister, though a subservient one. Clerval is a "brother." Elizabeth is both bride and sister (and cousin). And as a consequence of
these losses, his father dies as well. Frankenstein kills his family, and
is, in his attempt to obliterate his own creation, his own victim. As he
dies, he severs the monster's last link with life so that, appropriately,
the monster then moves out across the frozen wastes to immolate himself. The family is an aspect of the self and the self cannot survive bereft
of its family.

Thus, even while it wanders across the Alps, to the northern islands
of Scotland, to the frozen wastes of the Arctic, *Frankenstein* is a claustrophobic novel. It presents us not with the landscape of the world but
of a single mind, and its extraordinary power, despite its grotesqueness
and the awkwardness of so much of its prose, resides in its mythic
exploration of that mind, and of the consequences of its choices, the
mysteries of its impulses. Strangely, the only figure who stands outside
of that mind is Walton, who is nevertheless, as I have already argued,
another "double" of Frankenstein. Walton provides the frame which
allows us to glimpse Frankenstein's story. He is the "wedding guest,"
who can hear the story only because he is so similar to Frankenstein,
and who can engage us because while he is outside the story he is still,
like us, implicated in it. He is the link between our world and Frankenstein's, and he is saved by Frankenstein and by his difference from
him, to return to his country and, significantly, his sister — his one connection with the human community.

The apparent simplicity and order of Mary Shelley's story only in-
tensifies its extraordinary emotional energy and complexity. Although,
for example, it is not unreasonable to argue, as Shelley did, that it aims
at exhibiting "the amiableness of domestic affection, and the excellence
of universal virtue," we can see that the strongly ordering hand of the
novelist has allowed the expression of powerful tensions and energies
which realistic techniques would tend to repress and, which, having
their source in the irrational, will not resolve themselves into any simple
meanings. * * *

Frankenstein, like other great romances, notably *Wuthering Heights*, is
a more shapely and orderly book than most realistic novels, but the
order is the means by which Mary's "readiness to accept what her
imagination offered" is expressed. As Northrop Frye has suggested, the
freer the imagination is allowed to roam, the more formally shapely
will be the structure of the work. Imagination is structural power. Or
at least it is that in *Frankenstein* and *Wuthering Heights* which, freed

from the initial commitment to plausibility and to reason, take the shape of the writers' most potent imaginations and desires.

The simplicity of the structure, Walton's tale enfolding Franken-stein's, which, in turn, enfolds that of the monster, implies a clarity and firmness of moral ordering which is not present in the actual texture of the novel. Walton would seem the ultimate judge of the experience, as the outsider: yet he explicitly accepts Frankenstein's judgment of it, and largely exculpates him. The monster's own defense and explana-tion, lodged in the center of the story, is, however, by far the most convincing—though it is also a special—reading, and Frankenstein himself confesses that he has failed in his responsibility to his creature. In the end, however, we are not left with a judgment but with Walton's strangely uncolored report of the monster's last speech and last action. If anyone, the monster has the last word: and that word expresses a longing for self-destruction, for the pleasure which will come in the agony of self-immolation, and for an ultimate peace in extinction.

*　　*　　*

ELLEN MOERS

Female Gothic: The Monster's Mother†

What I mean by Female Gothic is easily defined: the work that women writers have done in the literary mode that, since the eighteenth cen-tury, we have called the Gothic. But what I mean—or anyone else means—by "the Gothic" is not so easily stated except that it has to do with fear. In Gothic writings fantasy predominates over reality, the strange over the commonplace, and the supernatural over the natural, with one definite auctorial intent: to scare. Not, that is, to reach down into the depths of the soul and purge it with pity and terror (as we say tragedy does), but to get to the body itself, its glands, epidermis, mus-cles, and circulatory system, quickly arousing and quickly allaying the physical reactions to fear.

Certainly the earliest tributes to the power of Gothic writers tended to emphasize the physiological. Jane Austen has Henry Tilney say, in *Northanger Abbey*, that he could not put down Mrs. Radcliffe's *Mys-teries of Udolpho*: "I remember finishing it in two days—my hair stand-ing on end the whole time." For Hazlitt Ann Radcliffe had mastered "the art of freezing the blood": "harrowing up the soul with imaginary horrors, and making the flesh creep and the nerves thrill." Mary Shelley

† From the *New York Review of Books*. Reprinted with permission. Later incorporated in some-what different form in Moers's *Literary Women* (Garden City: Doubleday, 1976).

said she intended *Frankenstein* to be the kind of ghost story that would "curdle the blood, and quicken the beatings of the heart." Why such claims? Presumably because readers enjoyed these sensations. For example, in Joanna Baillie's verse play on the theme of addiction to artificial fear, the heroine prevails upon a handmaiden, against the best advice, to tell a horror story:

> . . . Tell it, I pray thee.
> And let me cow'ring stand, and be my touch
> The valley's ice: there is a pleasure in it.
> Yea, when the cold blood shoots through every vein;
> When every pore upon my shrunken skin
> A knotted knoll becomes, and to mine ears
> Strange inward sounds awake, and to mine eyes
> Rush stranger tears, there is a joy in fear.[1]

At the time when literary Gothic was born, religious fears were on the wane, giving way to that vague paranoia of the modern spirit for which Gothic mechanisms seem to have provided welcome therapy. Walter Scott compared reading Mrs. Radcliffe to taking drugs, dangerous when habitual "but of most blessed power in those moments of pain and languor, when the whole head is sore, and the whole heart sick. If those who rail indiscriminately at this species of composition, were to consider the quantity of actual pleasure which it produces, and the much greater proportion of real sorrow and distress which it alleviates, their philanthropy ought to moderate their critical pride, or religious intolerance." A grateful public rewarded Mrs. Radcliffe, according to her most recent biographer,[2] by making her the most popular and best paid English novelist of the eighteenth century. Her preeminence among the "Terrorists," as they were called, was hardly challenged in her own day, and modern readers of *Udolpho* and *The Italian* continue to hail her as mistress of the pure Gothic form.

The secrets of Mrs. Radcliffe's power over the reader seem to be her incantatory prose style, her artful stretching of suspense over long periods of novelistic time, her pictorial and musical imagination which verges on the surreal. But the reasons for her own manipulation of that power remain mysterious, and there is no sign that any more will ever be known of her life and personality than the sparse facts we now have. She was married, childless, shy, sensitive to criticism of her respectability as woman and author, and addicted to travel—an addiction she

---

1. *Orra: A Tragedy*, published in 1812 in the third volume of *Plays On the Passions*, was one of the works read and reread by Mary and Percy Bysshe Shelley in their early years together. Its author, an earnestly moral and wistfully melodramatic Scottish spinster, was then famous and hyperbolically praised, especially in Scotland, as a Shakespeare *rediviva*.
2. E. B. Murray, *Ann Radcliffe* (Twayne, 1972).

was able to satisfy more through reading and imagining than through experience.

Ann Radcliffe's novels suggest that, for her, Gothic was a device to set maidens on distant and exciting journeys without offending the proprieties. In the power of villains, her heroines are forced to scurry up the top of pasteboard Alps and penetrate bandit-infested forests. They can scuttle miles along castle corridors, descend into dungeons, and explore secret chambers without a chaperone, because the Gothic castle, however ruined, is an indoor and therefore freely female space. In Mrs. Radcliffe's hands the Gothic novel became a feminine substitute for the picaresque, where heroines could enjoy all the adventures and alarms that masculine heroes had long experienced, far from home, in fiction.

She also made the Gothic novel into a make-believe puberty rite for young women. Her heroines are always good daughters, her villains bad, cruel, painfully attractive father figures, for which her lovers are at last accepted as palely satisfactory substitutes, but only after paternal trials and tortures are visited upon the heroine. When satirizing the form, Jane Austen wisely refrained from tampering with this essential feature of Mrs. Radcliffe's Gothic: the father in *Northanger Abbey* is one of Austen's nastiest.

As early as the 1790s, then, Ann Radcliffe firmly set the Gothic in one of the ways it would go ever after: a novel in which the central figure is a young woman who is simultaneously persecuted victim and courageous heroine. But what are we to make of the next major turning of the Gothic tradition that a woman brought about a generation later? Mary Shelley's *Frankenstein*, in 1818, made over the Gothic novel into what today we call science fiction. *Frankenstein* brought a new sophistication to literary terror, and it did so without a heroine, without even an important female victim. Paradoxically, however, no other Gothic work by a woman writer, perhaps no other literary work of any kind by a woman, better repays examination in the light of the sex of its author. For *Frankenstein* is a birth myth, and one that was lodged in the novelist's imagination, I am convinced, by the fact that she was herself a mother.

Much in Mary Shelley's life was remarkable. She was the daughter of a brilliant mother (Mary Wollstonecraft) and father (William Godwin). She was the mistress and then wife of the poet Shelley. She read widely in five languages, including Latin and Greek. She had easy access to the writings and conversation of some of the most original minds of her age. But nothing so sets her apart from the generality of writers of her own time, and before, and for long afterward, than her early and chaotic experience, at the very time she became an author, with motherhood. Pregnant at sixteen, and almost constantly pregnant throughout the following five years; yet not a secure mother, for she lost most of her babies soon after they were born; and not a lawful mother, for she was not married—not at least when, at the age of eighteen, Mary Godwin began to write *Frankenstein*. So are monsters born.

What in fact has the experience of giving birth to do with women's literature? In the eighteenth and nineteenth centuries very few important women writers, except for Mary Shelley, bore children; most of them, in England and America, were spinsters and virgins. With the coming of Naturalism late in the century, and the lifting of the Victorian taboo against writing about physical sexuality (including pregnancy and labor), the subject of birth was first brought to literature in realistic form by male novelists, from Tolstoy and Zola to William Carlos Williams.[3] Tolstoy was the father of thirteen babies born at home; Williams, as well as a poet and a Naturalist, was a small-town doctor with hundreds of deliveries to his professional credit. For knowledge of the sort that makes half-a-dozen pages of obstetrical detail, they had the advantage over women writers until relatively recent times.[4]

Mary Shelley was a unique case, in literature as in life. She brought birth to fiction not as realism but as Gothic fantasy, and thus contributed to Romanticism a myth of genuine originality. She invented the mad scientist who locks himself in his laboratory and secretly, guiltily, works at creating human life, only to find that he has made a monster.

> It was on a dreary night of November, that I beheld the accomplishment of my toils. With an anxiety that almost amounted to agony, I collected the instruments of life around me, that I might infuse a spark of being into the lifeless thing that lay at my feet. . . . The rain pattered dismally against the panes, and my candle was nearly burnt out, when, by the glimmer of the half-extinguished light, I saw the dull yellow eye of the creature open; it breathed hard, and a convulsive motion agitated its limbs. . . . His yellow skin scarcely covered the work of muscles and arteries beneath; his hair was of a lustrous black, and flowing . . . ; but these luxuriances only formed a more horrid contrast with his watery eyes, that seemed almost of the same colour as the dun white

3. Williams's remarkable account of a birth, the opening chapter of *The White Mule*, is one of a number of unusual selections included by Michèle Murray in her anthology *A House of Good Proportion: Images of Women in Literature* (Simon and Schuster, 1973).
4. Two very popular women novelists (and Nobel laureates), Pearl Buck and Sigrid Undset, were probably responsible for establishing pregnancy, labor, and breast feeding as themes belonging to twentieth century "women's literature." But Colette's note of skepticism may be worth recalling. In *La Maison de Claudine* she tells of fainting away in horror when, as a girl, she first came upon a gruesome birth scene in Zola. "*Ce n'est pas si terrible, va, l'arrivée d'un enfant*," she has her mother comment. ". . . *La preuve que toutes les femmes l'oublient, c'est qu'il n'y a jamais que les hommes—est-ce que ça le regardait, voyons, ce Zola?—qui en font des histoires.*"

sockets in which they were set, his shrivelled complexion and straight black lips.

That is very good horror, but what follows is more horrid still: Frankenstein, the scientist, runs away and abandons the newborn monster, who is and remains nameless. Here, I think, is where Mary Shelley's book is most interesting, most powerful, and most feminine: in the motif of revulsion against newborn life, and the drama of guilt, dread, and flight surrounding birth and its consequences. Most of the novel, roughly two of its three volumes, can be said to deal with the retribution visited upon monster and creator for deficient infant care. *Frankenstein* seems to be distinctly a woman's mythmaking on the subject of birth precisely because its emphasis is not upon what precedes birth, not upon birth itself, but upon what follows birth: the trauma of the afterbirth.

Fear and guilt, depression and anxiety are commonplace reactions to the birth of a baby, and well within the normal range of experience. But more deeply rooted in our cultural mythology, and certainly in our literature, are the happy maternal reactions: ecstasy, a sense of fulfillment, and the rush of nourishing love which sweep over the new mother when she first holds her baby in her arms. Thackeray's treatment of the birth of a baby in *Vanity Fair* is the classic of this genre. Gentle Amelia is pregnant when her adored husband dies on the field of Waterloo, a tragedy which drives the young woman into a state of comatose grief until the blessed moment when her baby is born. "Heaven had sent her consolation," writes Thackeray. "A day came — of almost terrified delight and wonder — when the poor widowed girl pressed a child upon her breast . . . a little boy, as beautiful as a cherub. . . . Love, and hope, and prayer woke again in her bosom. . . . She was safe."

Thackeray was here recording a reality, as well as expressing a sentiment. But he himself was under no illusion that happiness was the only possible maternal reaction to giving birth, for his own wife had become depressed and hostile after their first baby was born, and suicidal and insane after the last. At the time of *Vanity Fair*, Thackeray had already had to place her in a sanitarium, and he was raising their two little girls himself. So, in *Vanity Fair*, he gives us not only Amelia as a mother, but also Becky Sharp. Becky's cold disdain toward her infant son, her hostility and selfishness as a mother, are perhaps a legacy of Thackeray's experience; they are also among the finest things in the novel.

From what we know about the strange young woman who wrote *Frankenstein*, Mary Shelley was in this respect nothing like Becky Sharp. She rejoiced at becoming a mother and loved and cherished her babies as long as they lived. But her journal is a chilly and laconic document, mostly concerned with the extraordinary reading program she put herself through at Shelley's side. Her own emphasis on books in the journal has set the tone of most of the discussion of the genesis of *Frankenstein*. Mary Shelley is said — and rightly — to have based her treatment of the life of her monster on the ideas about education, society, and morality held by her father and her mother. She is shown to have been influenced directly by Shelley's genius, and by her reading of Coleridge and Wordsworth and the Gothic novelists. She learned from Sir Humphry Davy's book on chemistry and Erasmus Darwin on biology. In Switzerland, during the summer she began *Frankenstein*, she sat by while Shelley, Byron, and Polidori discussed the new sciences of mesmerism, electricity, and galvanism, which promised to unlock the riddle of life, and planned to write ghost stories.

Mary Shelley herself was the first to point to her fortuitous immersion in the romantic and scientific revolutions of her day as the source of *Frankenstein*. Her extreme youth, as well as her sex, has contributed to the generally held opinion that she was not so much an author in her own right as a transparent medium through which passed the ideas of those around her.[5] "All Mrs. Shelley did," writes Mario Praz, "was to provide a passive reflection of some of the wild fantasies which were living in the air about her."

Passive reflections, however, do not produce original works of literature, and *Frankenstein*, if not a great novel, was unquestionably an original one. The major Romantic and minor Gothic tradition to which it *should* have belonged was the literature of the overreacher: the superman who breaks through normal human limitations to defy the rules of society and infringe upon the realm of God. In the Faust story, hypertrophy of the individual will is symbolized by a pact with the devil. Byron's and Balzac's heroes; the rampaging monks of Mat Lewis and E. T. A. Hoffmann; the Wandering Jew and Melmoth the wanderer; the chained and unchained Prometheus: all are overreachers, all are punished by their own excesses — by a surfeit of sensation, of experience, of knowledge, and most typically, by the doom of eternal life.

---

5. Two new publications should provide a useful corrective to this common bias of Shelley scholarship. William A. Walling's *Mary Shelley* (Twayne, 1972) is mostly about the extensive literary career of Mary Shelley herself. Although Professor Walling's motive is to press the case for Byron rather than Shelley as the major influence on his subject, the result is an unusually sympathetic treatment of the five novels and numerous other works she published after Shelley's death. James Rieger's forthcoming scholarly edition of the little known 1818 text of *Frankenstein* (to be published by Bobbs-Merrill [published in 1974 and reprinted by the U of Chicago P in 1982]) will provide information about Mary's unused notes for revision and about Shelley's actual contribution, as an editor, to the publication of the novel. Throughout this article I am quoting from M. K. Joseph's edition of the 1831 text of *Frankenstein* (Oxford University Press, 1971), which is available in paper.

But Mary Shelley's overreacher is different. Frankenstein's exploration of the forbidden boundaries of human science does not cause the prolongation and extension of his own life, but the creation of a new one. He defies mortality not by living forever, but by giving birth. That this original twist to an old myth should have been the work of a young woman who was also a young mother seems to me, after all, not a very surprising answer to the question that, according to Mary Shelley herself, was asked from the start: "How I, then a young girl, came to think of, and to dilate upon, so very hideous an idea?"

Birth is a hideous thing in *Frankenstein*, even before there is a monster. For Frankenstein's procedure, once he has determined to create new life, is to frequent the vaults and charnel houses and study the human corpse in all its loathsome stages of decay and decomposition. "To examine the causes of life," he says, "we must first have recourse to death." His purpose is to "bestow animation upon lifeless matter," so that he might "in process of time renew life where death had apparently devoted the body to corruption." Frankenstein collects bones and other human parts from the slaughterhouse and the dissecting room, and through long months of feverish activity sticks them together in a frame of gigantic size in what he calls "my workshop of filthy creation."

It is in her journal and her letters that Mary Shelley reveals the workshop of her own creation, where she pieced together the materials for a new species of romantic mythology. They record a horror story of maternity such as literary biography hardly provides again until Sylvia Plath.

As far as I can figure out, she was pregnant, barely pregnant but aware of the fact, when at the age of sixteen she ran off with Shelley in July, 1814.[6] Also pregnant at the same time was Shelley's legal wife

6. Swift conceiving, and mysteriously early consciousness of the fact, seem to be keynotes of Mary Shelley's experience as reflected in her journal and letters (both edited by Frederick L. Jones and published by the University of Oklahoma Press in 1944 and 1947). Her first child was born on February 22, 1815: "A female child . . . not quite seven months . . . not expected to live," Shelley noted that day in her journal. The opening entry in her journal, also in Shelley's hand, records the event of their elopement on July 28, 1814, or not quite seven months before the birth, as well as Shelley's odd comment on Mary's feeling ill and faint as they traveled: "in that illness what pleasure and security did we not share!"

What strange ideas about conception and gestation lay behind these journal entries, not only in Shelley's mind but in the medical opinion of the day? For strange they probably were. Erasmus Darwin's *Zoonomia* proclaimed that the "embryo" was "a living filament" and "secreted from the blood of the male," and that the sex of the baby was determined by what passed through the imagination of the male at the moment of conception. "The world has long been mistaken in ascribing great power to the imagination of the female," Dr. Darwin wrote; but he puzzled over the fact that there were not immeasurably more female than male births, considering that the copulating male was rather likely to imagine "the idea of form and features" of a female at that interesting moment.

Harriet, who gave birth in November to a "son and heir," as Mary noted in her journal. In February, 1815, Mary gave birth to a daughter, illegitimate, premature, and sickly. There is nothing in the journal about domestic help or a nurse in attendance. Mary notes that she breast fed the baby; that Fanny, her half-sister, came to call; that Mrs. Godwin, her stepmother, sent over some linen; that Claire Clairmont, Mrs. Godwin's daughter who had run off with Mary, kept Shelley amused. Bonaparte invaded France, the journal tells us, and Mary took up her incessant reading program: this time, Mme. de Staël's *Corinne*. The baby died in March. "Find my baby dead," Mary wrote. "A miserable day."

In April, 1815, she was pregnant again, about eight weeks after the birth of her first child. In January, 1816, she gave birth to a son: more breast feeding, more reading. In March, Claire Clairmont sought out Lord Byron and managed to get herself pregnant by him within a couple of weeks. This pregnancy would be a subject of embarrassment and strain to Mary and Shelley, and it immediately changed their lives, for Byron left England in April, and Claire, Shelley, Mary, and her infant pursued him to Switzerland in May. There is nothing yet in Mary's journal about a servant, but a good deal about mule travel in the mountains. In June they all settled near Byron on the shores of Lake Geneva.

In June, 1816, also, Mary began *Frankenstein*. And during the year of its writing the following events ran their swift and sinister course: In October, Fanny Imlay, Mary's half-sister, committed suicide after discovering that she was not Godwin's daughter but Mary Wollstonecraft's daughter by her American lover. (The suicide was not only a tragedy but an embarrassment to all. Godwin refused even to claim Fanny's body, which was thrown nameless into a pauper's grave.) In early December Mary was pregnant again, which she seems to have sensed almost the day it happened. (See her letter to Shelley of December 5, in which she also announced completion of chapter 4 of her novel.) In mid-December, Harriet Shelley drowned herself in the Serpentine, she was pregnant by someone other than Shelley. In late December Mary married Shelley. In January, 1817, Mary wrote Byron that Claire had borne him a daughter. In May she finished *Frankenstein*, published the following year.

Death and birth were thus as hideously mixed in the life of Mary Shelley as in Frankenstein's "workshop of filthy creation." Who can read without shuddering, and without remembering her myth of the birth of a nameless monster, Mary's journal entry of March 19, 1815, which records the trauma of her loss, when she was seventeen, of her first baby, the little girl who did not live long enough to be given a name.

"Dream that my little baby came to life again," Mary wrote; "that it had only been cold, and that we rubbed it before the fire, and it lived. Awake and find no baby. I think about the little thing all day. Not in good spirits."[7] ("*I thought, that if I could bestow animation upon lifeless matter, I might in process of time renew life where death had apparently devoted the body to corruption.*")

So little use has been made of this material by writers about *Frankenstein* that it may be worth emphasizing how important, because how unusual, was Mary Shelley's experience as a woman.[8] The harum-scarum circumstances surrounding her maternity have no parallel until our own time, which in its naïve cerebrations upon family life (and in much else, except genius) resembles the generation of the Shelleys. Mary Godwin sailed into teenage motherhood without any of the financial or social or familial supports that made bearing and rearing children a relaxed experience for the normal middle-class woman of her day (as Jane Austen, for example, described her). She was an unwed mother, responsible for breaking up the marriage of a young woman just as much a mother as she. The father whom she adored broke furiously with her when she eloped; and Mary Wollstonecraft, the mother whose memory she revered, and whose books she was rereading throughout her teenage years, had died in childbirth — died giving birth to Mary herself.

Surely no outside influence need be sought to explain Mary Shelley's fantasy of the newborn as at once monstrous agent of destruction and piteous victim of parental abandonment. "I, the miserable and the abandoned," cries the monster at the end of *Frankenstein*, "I am an abortion to be spurned at, and kicked, and trampled on. . . . I have

---

7. Her dream of "the dead being alive" recurred along with "bitter" reflections on death during the period of *Frankenstein*, as she wrote Leigh Hunt on March 5, 1817.

8. I cannot think of another important woman writer of the nineteenth century or before who began to write for publication while she was learning, at a very early age, to be a mother. Harriet Beecher Stowe and Elizabeth Cleghorn Gaskell were two of the rare Victorian writers who were mothers; in both cases, the death of one of their babies also played a decisive role in their literary careers. But Mrs. Stowe and Mrs. Gaskell were about twice Mary Shelley's age when their babies died, and both were respectably settled middle-class women, wives of ministers. The young women novelists and poets today who are finding in the subject of inexperienced and unassisted motherhood a mine of troubled fantasy and black humor are themselves a new breed of writer reacting to a trauma they share with almost no writer before them but Mary Shelley. The newborn returns again to literature as a monster:

> At six months he grew big as six years
> . . . One day he swallowed
> Her whole right breast. . . .
> . . . both died,
> She inside him, curled like an embryo.
> — Cynthia Macdonald, "The Insatiable Baby," *Amputations*
> (George Braziller, 1972)

But the literary use of monstrous size to express anxieties about feeding and cleaning a baby need not, of course, be exclusively feminine, as Dr. Phyllis Greenacre's study of Gulliver convincingly demonstrates (*Swift and Carroll: A Psychoanalytic Study of Two Lives*, International Universities Press, Inc., 1955).

murdered the lovely and the helpless. . . . I have devoted my creator to misery; I have pursued him even to that irremediable ruin."

In the century and a half since its publication, *Frankenstein* has spawned innumerable interpretations among the critics, and among the novelists, playwrights, and filmmakers who have felt its influence. The idea, though not the name, of the robot originated with Mary Shelley's novel, and her title character became a byword for the dangers of scientific knowledge. But the work has also been read as an existential fable; as a commentary on the split between reason and feeling, in both philosophical thought and educational theory; as a parable of the excesses of idealism and genius; as a dramatization of the divided self; as an attack on the stultifying force of social convention.[9]

The versatility of Mary Shelley's myth is due to the brilliance of her mind and the range of her learning, as well as to the influence of the circle in which she moved as a young writer. But *Frankenstein* was most original in its dramatization of dangerous oppositions through the struggle of a creator with monstrous creation. The sources of this Gothic conception, which still has power to "curdle the blood, and quicken the beatings of the heart," were surely the anxieties of a woman who, as daughter, mistress, and mother, was a bearer of death.

Robert Kiely's suggestive new study, *The Romantic Novel in England* (Harvard, 1972), includes one of the rare serious discussions of *Frankenstein* as a woman's work. For Professor Kiely does more than interpret; he also responds, as one must in reading *Frankenstein*, to what he calls the "mundane side to this fantastic tale."

> In making her hero the creator of a monster, she does not necessarily mock idealistic ambition, but in making that monster a poor grotesque patchwork, a physical mess of seams and wrinkles, she introduces a consideration of the material universe which challenges and undermines the purity of idealism. In short, the sheer concreteness of the ugly thing which Frankenstein has created often makes his ambitions and his character—however sympathetically described—seem ridiculous and even insane. The arguments on behalf of idealism and unworldly genius are seriously presented, but the controlling perspective is that of an earthbound woman.

The "mundane side" to *Frankenstein* is one of its richest aspects. Mary Shelley came honestly to grips with the dilemma of a newly

9. Including even racial prejudice. Has it been noticed how much Stephen Crane's "The Monster" owes to *Frankenstein*? In this eerie novella of 1899, Crane comments obliquely on the relations between black man and white in the civilized, middle-class North by portraying the community persecution of a doctor, a man of science and social justice, after he brings to life as a monster a Negro who has done a heroic deed as a man. The germ of this idea may have come to Crane from the metaphorical cakewalk with which Mark Twain began his celebrated polemic of 1893, "In Defense of Harriet Shelley."

created human being, a giant adult male in shape, who must swiftly recapitulate, and without the assistance of his terrified parent, the infantile and adolescent stages of human development. She even faces squarely the monster's sexual needs, for the denouement of the story hangs on his demand that Frankenstein create a female monster partner, and Frankenstein's refusal to do so.

But more than mundane is Mary Shelley's concern with the emotions surrounding the parent-child and child-parent relationship. Here her intention to underline the birth myth in *Frankenstein* becomes most evident, quite apart from biographical evidence about its author. She provides an unusual thickening of the background of the tale with familial fact and fantasy, from the very opening of the story in the letters a brother addresses to his sister of whom he is excessively fond, because they are both orphans. There is Frankenstein's relationship to his doting parents, and his semi-incestuous love for an abandoned orphan girl brought up as his sister. There is the first of the monster's murder victims, Frankenstein's infant brother (precisely drawn, even to his name, after Mary Shelley's baby); and the innocent young girl wrongly executed for the infant's murder, who is also a victim of what Mary Shelley calls that "strange perversity," a mother's hatred. (Justine accepts guilt with docility: "I almost began to think that I was the monster that my confessor said I was. . . .") The abundant material in *Frankenstein* about the abnormal, or monstrous, manifestations of the child-parent tie justifies as much as does its famous monster Mary Shelley's reference to the novel as "my hideous progeny."

What Mary Shelley actually did in *Frankenstein* was to transform the standard Romantic matter of incest, infanticide, and patricide into a phantasmagoria of the nursery. Nothing quite like it was done again in English literature until that Victorian novel by a woman, which we also place uneasily in the Gothic tradition: *Wuthering Heights*.

SANDRA M. GILBERT AND SUSAN GUBAR

Mary Shelley's Monstrous Eve†

The nature of a Female Space is this: it shrinks the Organs
Of Life till they become Finite & Itself seems Infinite
And Satan vibrated in the immensity of the Space! Limited
To those without but Infinite to those within . . .
　　　　　　　　　　　　　　　　　　—William Blake

The woman writes as if the Devil was in her; and that is the only condition
under which a woman ever writes anything worth reading.
　　　　　　　　　　—Nathaniel Hawthorne, on Fanny Fern

　　　　　I probed Retrieveless things
　　　　　My Duplicate—to borrow—
　　　　　A Haggard Comfort springs

　　　　　From the belief that Somewhere—
　　　　　Within the Clutch of Thought—
　　　　　There dwells one other Creature
　　　　　Of Heavenly Love—forgot—

　　　　　I plucked at our Partition
　　　　　As One should pry the Walls—
　　　　　Between Himself—and Horror's Twin—
　　　　　Within Opposing Cells—‡
　　　　　　　　　—Emily Dickinson

　　　　　　　*　*　*　*

Many critics have noticed that *Frankenstein* (1818) is one of the key
Romantic "readings" of *Paradise Lost.*[1] Significantly, however, as a
woman's reading it is most especially the story of hell: hell as a dark
parody of heaven, hell's creations as monstrous imitations of heaven's
creations, and hellish femaleness as a grotesque parody of heavenly
maleness. But of course the divagations of the parody merely return to
and reinforce the fearful reality of the original. For by parodying *Paradise Lost* in what may have begun as a secret, barely conscious attempt
to subvert Milton, Shelley ended up telling, too, the central story of

† From *The Madwoman in the Attic* (New Haven: Yale UP, 1979) 213, 221–27, 230–41. Originally published in *Feminist Studies*. Reprinted with permission.
‡ Reprinted by permission of the publishers and the Trustees of Amherst College from *The Poems of Emily Dickinson*, Thomas H. Johnson, ed., Cambridge, Mass.: The Belknap Press of Harvard University Press, Copyright © 1951, 1955, 1979, 1983 by the President and Fellows of Harvard College.
1. See, for instance, Harold Bloom, "Afterword," *Frankenstein* (New York and Toronto: New American Library, 1965), p. 214.

Paradise Lost, the tale of "what misery th' inabstinence of Eve / Shall bring on men."

Mary Shelley herself claims to have been continually asked "how I . . . came to think of and to dilate upon so very hideous an idea" as that of *Frankenstein*, but it is really not surprising that she should have formulated her anxieties about femaleness in such highly literary terms. For of course the nineteen-year-old girl who wrote *Frankenstein* was no ordinary nineteen-year-old but one of England's most notable literary heiresses. Indeed, as "the daughter of two persons of distinguished literary celebrity," and the wife of a third, Mary Wollstonecraft Godwin Shelley was the daughter and later the wife of some of Milton's keenest critics, so that Harold Bloom's useful conceit about the family romance of English literature is simply an accurate description of the reality of her life.[2]

In acknowledgment of this web of literary/familial relationships, critics have traditionally studied *Frankenstein* as an interesting example of Romantic myth-making, a work ancillary to such established Promethean masterpieces as Shelley's *Prometheus Unbound* and Byron's *Manfred*. ("Like almost everything else about [Mary's] life," one such critic remarks, *Frankenstein* "is an instance of genius observed and admired but not shared."[3]) Recently, however, a number of writers have noticed the connection between Mary Shelley's "waking dream" of monster-manufacture and her own experience of awakening sexuality, in particular the "horror story of Maternity" which accompanied her precipitous entrance into what Ellen Moers calls "teen-age motherhood."[4] Clearly they are articulating an increasingly uneasy sense that, despite its male protagonist and its underpinning of "masculine" philosophy, *Frankenstein* is somehow a "woman's book," if only because its author was caught up in such a maelstrom of sexuality at the time she wrote the novel.

In making their case for the work as female fantasy, though, critics like Moers have tended to evade the problems posed by what we must define as *Frankenstein*'s literariness. Yet, despite the weaknesses in those traditional readings of the novel that overlook its intensely sexual materials, it is still undeniably true that Mary Shelley's "ghost story," growing from a Keatsian (or Coleridgean) waking dream, is a Romantic novel about — among other things — Romanticism, as well as a book about books and perhaps, too, about the writers of books. Any theorist of the novel's femaleness and of its significance as, in Moers's phrase,

---

2. Author's introduction to *Frankenstein* (1818; Toronto, New York, London: Bantam Pathfinder Edition, 1967), p. xi. Hereafter page references to this edition will follow quotations, and we will also include chapter references for those using other editions. For a basic discussion of the "family romance" of literature, see Harold Bloom, *The Anxiety of Influence*.
3. Robert Kiely, *The Romantic Novel in England* (Cambridge, Mass.: Harvard University Press, 1972), p. 161.
4. Moers, *Literary Women*, pp. 95–97.

a "birth myth" must therefore confront this self-conscious literariness. For as was only natural in "the daughter of two persons of distinguished literary celebrity," Mary Shelley explained her sexuality to herself in the context of her reading and its powerfully felt implications.

For this orphaned literary heiress, highly charged connections between femaleness and literariness must have been established early, and established specifically in relation to the controversial figure of her dead mother. As we shall see, Mary Wollstonecraft Godwin read her mother's writings over and over again as she was growing up. Perhaps more important, she undoubtedly read most of the reviews of her mother's *Posthumous Works*, reviews in which Mary Wollstonecraft was attacked as a "philosophical wanton" and a monster, while her *Vindication of the Rights of Woman* (1792) was called "A scripture, archly fram'd for propagating w[hore]s."[5] But in any case, to the "philosophical wanton's" daughter, all reading about (or of) her mother's work must have been painful, given her knowledge that that passionate feminist writer had died in giving life to *her*, to bestow upon Wollstonecraft's death from complications of childbirth the melodramatic cast it probably had for the girl herself. That Mary Shelley was conscious, moreover, of a strangely intimate relationship between her feelings toward her dead mother, her romance with a living poet, and her own sense of vocation as a reader and writer is made perfectly clear by her habit of "taking her books to Mary Wollstonecraft's grave in St. Pancras' Churchyard, there," as Muriel Spark puts it, "to pursue her studies in an atmosphere of communion with a mind greater than the second Mrs. Godwin's [and] to meet Shelley in secret."[6]

Her mother's grave: the setting seems an unusually grim, even ghoulish locale for reading, writing, or lovemaking. Yet, to a girl with Mary Shelley's background, literary activities, like sexual ones, must have been primarily extensions of the elaborate, gothic psychodrama of her family history. If her famous diary is largely a compendium of her reading lists and Shelley's that fact does not, therefore, suggest unusual reticence on her part. Rather, it emphasizes the point that for Mary, even more than for most writers, reading a book was often an emotional as well as an intellectual event of considerable magnitude. Especially because she never knew her mother, and because her father seemed so definitively to reject her after her youthful elopement, her principal mode of self-definition — certainly in the early years of her life with Shelley, when she was writing *Frankenstein* — was through reading, and to a lesser extent through writing.

Endlessly studying her mother's works and her father's, Mary Shelley may be said to have "read" her family and to have been related to her

5. See Ralph Wardle, *Mary Wollstonecraft* (Lincoln, Neb.: University of Nebraska Press, 1951), p. 322, for more detailed discussion of these attacks on Wollstonecraft.
6. Muriel Spark, *Child of Light* (Hodleigh, Essex: Tower Bridge Publications, 1951), p. 21.

reading, for books appear to have functioned as her surrogate parents, pages and words standing in for flesh and blood. That much of her reading was undertaken in Shelley's company, moreover, may also help explain some of this obsessiveness, for Mary's literary inheritance was obviously involved in her very literary romance and marriage. In the years just before she wrote *Frankenstein*, for instance, and those when she was engaged in composing the novel (1816–17), she studied her parents' writings, alone or together with Shelley, like a scholarly detective seeking clues to the significance of some cryptic text.[7]

To be sure, this investigation of the mysteries of literary genealogy was done in a larger context. In these same years, Mary Shelley recorded innumerable readings of contemporary gothic novels, as well as a program of study in English, French, and German literature that would do credit to a modern graduate student. But especially, in 1815, 1816, and 1817, she read the works of Milton: *Paradise Lost* (twice), *Paradise Regained*, *Comus*, *Areopagitica*, *Lycidas*. And what makes the extent of this reading particularly impressive is the fact that in these years, her seventeenth to her twenty-first, Mary Shelley was almost continuously pregnant, "confined," or nursing. At the same time, it is precisely the coincidence of all these disparate activities — her family studies, her initiation into adult sexuality, and her literary self-education — that makes her vision of *Paradise Lost* so significant. For her developing sense of herself as a literary creature and/or creator seems to have been inseparable from her emerging self-definition as daughter, mistress, wife, and mother. Thus she cast her birth myth — her myth of origins — in precisely those cosmogenic terms to which her parents, her husband, and indeed her whole literary culture continually alluded: the terms of *Paradise Lost*, which (as she indicates even on the title page of her novel), she saw as preceding, paralleling, and commenting upon the Greek cosmogeny of the Prometheus play her husband had just translated. It is as a female fantasy of sex and reading, then, a gothic psychodrama reflecting Mary Shelley's own sense of what we might call bibliogenesis, that *Frankenstein* is a version of the misogynistic story implicit in *Paradise Lost*.

It would be a mistake to underestimate the significance of *Frankenstein*'s title page, with its allusive subtitle ("The Modern Prometheus") and carefully pointed Miltonic epigraph ("Did I request thee, Maker,

---

7. See *Mary Shelley's Journal*, ed. Frederick L. Jones (Norman, Okla.: University of Oklahoma Press, 1947), esp. pp. 32–33, 47–49, 71–73, and 88–90, for the reading lists themselves. Besides reading Wollstonecraft's *Maria*, her *Vindication of the Rights of Woman*, and three or four other books, together with Godwin's *Political Justice* and his *Caleb Williams*, Mary Shelley also read parodies and criticisms of her parents' works in these years, including a book she calls *Anti-Jacobin Poetry*, which may well have included that periodical's vicious attack on Wollstonecraft. To read, for her, was not just to read her family, but to read *about* her family.

from my clay / To mould me man? Did I solicit thee / From darkness to promote me?"). But our first really serious clue to the highly literary nature of this history of a creature born outside history is its author's use of an unusually *evidentiary* technique for conveying the stories of her monster and his maker. Like a literary jigsaw puzzle, a collection of apparently random documents from whose juxtaposition the scholar-detective must infer a meaning, *Frankenstein* consists of three "concentric circles" of narration (Walton's letters, Victor Frankenstein's recital to Walton, and the monster's speech to Frankenstein), within which are embedded pockets of digression containing other miniature narratives (Frankenstein's mother's story, Elizabeth Lavenza's and Justine's stories, Felix's and Agatha's story, Safie's story), etc.[8] * * * Reading and assembling documentary evidence, examining it, analyzing it and researching it comprised for Shelley a crucial if voyeuristic method of exploring origins, explaining identity, understanding sexuality. Even more obviously, it was a way of researching and analyzing an emotionally unintelligible text, like *Paradise Lost*. In a sense, then, even before *Paradise Lost* as a central item on the monster's reading list becomes a literal event in *Frankenstein*, the novel's literary structure prepares us to confront Milton's patriarchal epic, both as a sort of research problem and as the framework for a complex system of allusions.

The book's dramatic situations are equally resonant. Like Mary Shelley, who was a puzzled but studious Miltonist, this novel's key characters—Walton, Frankenstein, and the monster—are obsessed with problem-solving. "I shall satiate my ardent curiosity with the sight of a part of the world never before visited," exclaims the young explorer, Walton, as he embarks like a child "on an expedition of discovery up his native river" (2, letter 1). "While my companions contemplated . . . the magnificent appearance of things," declares Frankenstein, the scientist of sexual ontology, "I delighted in investigating their causes" (22, chap. 2). "Who was I? What was I? Whence did I come?" (113–15, chap. 15) the monster reports wondering, describing endless speculations cast in Miltonic terms. All three, like Shelley herself, appear to be trying to understand their presence in a fallen world, and trying at the same time to define the nature of the lost paradise that must have existed before the fall. But unlike Adam, all three characters seem to have fallen not merely from Eden but from the earth, fallen directly into hell, like Sin, Satan, and—by implication—Eve. Thus their questionings are in some sense female, for they belong in that line of literary women's questionings of the fall into

8. Marc A. Rubenstein suggests that throughout the novel "the act of observation, passive in one sense, becomes covertly and symbolically active in another: the observed scene becomes an enclosing, even womb-like container in which a story is variously developed, preserved, and passed on. Storytelling becomes a vicarious pregnancy." " 'My Accursed Origin': The Search for the Mother in *Frankenstein,*" *Studies in Romanticism* 15, no. 2 (Spring 1976): 173.

gender which goes back at least to Anne Finch's plaintive "How are we fal'n?" and forward to Sylvia Plath's horrified "I have fallen very far!"⁹

From the first, however, *Frankenstein* answers such neo-Miltonic questions mainly through explicit or implicit allusions to Milton, retelling the story of the fall not so much to protest against it as to clarify its meaning. The parallels between those two Promethean overreachers Walton and Frankenstein, for instance, have always been clear to readers. But that both characters can, therefore, be described (the way Walton describes Frankenstein) as "fallen angels" is not as frequently remarked. Yet Frankenstein himself is perceptive enough to ask Walton "Do you share my madness?" at just the moment when the young explorer remarks Satanically that "One man's life or death were but a small price to pay . . . for the dominion I [wish to] acquire" (13, letter 4). Plainly one fallen angel can recognize another. Alienated from his crew and chronically friendless, Walton tells his sister that he longs for a friend "on the wide ocean," and what he discovers in Victor Frankenstein is the fellowship of hell.

In fact, like the many other secondary narratives Mary Shelley offers in her novel, Walton's story is itself an alternative version of the myth of origins presented in *Paradise Lost*. Writing his ambitious letters home from St. Petersburgh [*sic*], Archangel, and points north, Walton moves like Satan away from the sanctity and sanity represented by his sister, his crew, and the allegorical names of the places he leaves. Like Satan, too, he seems at least in part to be exploring the frozen frontiers of hell in order to attempt a return to heaven, for the "country of eternal light" he envisions at the Pole (1, letter 1) has much in common with Milton's celestial "Fountain of Light" (*PL* 3. 375).¹ Again, like Satan's (and Eve's) aspirations, his ambition has violated a patriarchal decree: his father's "dying injunction" had forbidden him "to embark on a seafaring life." Moreover, even the icy hell where Walton encounters Frankenstein and the monster is Miltonic, for all three of these diabolical wanderers must learn, like the fallen angels of *Paradise Lost*, that "Beyond this flood a frozen Continent / Lies dark and wild . . . / Thither by harpy-footed Furies hal'd, / At certain revolutions all the damn'd / Are brought . . . From Beds of raging Fire to starve in Ice" (*PL* 2. 587–600).

Finally, another of Walton's revelations illuminates not only the likeness of his ambitions to Satan's but also the similarity of his anxieties

9. See Anne Finch, "The Introduction," in *The Poems of Anne Countess of Winchilsea*, pp. 4–6, and Sylvia Plath, "The Moon and the Yew Tree," in *Ariel*, p. 41.
1. Speaking of the hyperborean metaphor in *Frankenstein*, Rubenstein argues that Walton (and Mary Shelley) seek "the fantasied mother locked within the ice . . . the maternal Paradise beyond the frozen north," and asks us to consider the pun implicit in the later meeting of Frankenstein and his monster on the *mer* (or *Mère*) *de Glace* at Chamonix (Rubenstein " 'My Accursed Origin,' " pp. 175–76).

to those of his female author. Speaking of his childhood, he reminds his sister that, because poetry had "lifted [my soul] to heaven," he had become a poet and "for one year lived in a paradise of my own creation." Then he adds ominously that "You are well-acquainted with my failure and how heavily I bore the disappointment" (2–3, letter 1). But of course, as she confesses in her introduction to *Frankenstein*, Mary Shelley, too, had spent her childhood in "waking dreams" of literature; later, both she and her poet-husband hoped she would prove herself "worthy of [her] parentage and enroll [herself] on the page of fame" (xii). In a sense, then, given the Miltonic context in which Walton's story of poetic failure is set, it seems possible that one of the anxious fantasies his narrative helps Mary Shelley covertly examine is the fearful tale of a female fall from a lost paradise of art, speech, and autonomy into a hell of sexuality, silence, and filthy materiality, "A Universe of death, which God by curse / Created evil, for evil only good, / Where all life dies, death lives, and Nature breeds, / Perverse, all monstrous, all prodigious things" (*PL* 2. 622–25).

*   *   *

On the surface, Victor seems at first more Adamic than Satanic or Eve-like. His Edenic childhood is an interlude of prelapsarian innocence in which, like Adam, he is sheltered by his benevolent father as a sensitive plant might be "sheltered by the gardener, from every rougher wind" (19–20, chap. 1). When cherubic Elizabeth Lavenza joins the family, she seems as "heaven-sent" as Milton's Eve, as much Victor's "possession" as Adam's rib is Adam's. Moreover, though he is evidently forbidden almost nothing ("My parents [were not] tyrants . . . but the agents and creators of many delights"), Victor hints to Walton that his deific father, like Adam's and Walton's, did on one occasion arbitrarily forbid him to pursue his interest in arcane knowledge. Indeed, like Eve and Satan, Victor blames his own fall at least in part on his father's apparent arbitrariness. "If . . . my father had taken the pains to explain to me that the principles of Agrippa had been entirely exploded. . . . It is even possible that the train of my ideas would never have received the fatal impulse that led to my ruin" (24–25, chap. 2). And soon after asserting this he even associates an incident in which a tree is struck by Jovian thunder bolts with his feelings about his forbidden studies.

As his researches into the "secrets of nature" become more feverish, however, and as his ambition "to explore unknown powers" grows more intense, Victor begins to metamorphose from Adam to Satan, becoming "as Gods" in his capacity of "bestowing animation upon lifeless matter," laboring like a guilty artist to complete his false creation. Finally, in his conversations with Walton he echoes Milton's fallen angel, and Marlowe's, in his frequently reiterated confession that "I bore a hell within me which nothing could extinguish" (72, chap. 8). Indeed, as the "true murderer" of innocence, here cast in the form of the child William, Victor perceives himself as a diabolical creator whose mind has involuntarily "let loose" a monstrous and "filthy demon" in much the same way that Milton's Satan's swelled head produced Sin, the disgusting monster he "let loose" upon the world. Watching a "noble war in the sky" that seems almost like an intentional reminder that we are participating in a critical rearrangement of most of the elements of *Paradise Lost*, he explains that "I considered the being whom I had cast among mankind . . . nearly in the light of my own vampire, my own spirit let loose from the grave and forced to destroy all that was dear to me" (61, chap. 7).

Even while it is the final sign and seal of Victor's transformation from Adam to Satan, however, it is perhaps the Sin-ful murder of the child William that is our first overt clue to the real nature of the bewilderingly disguised set of identity shifts and parallels Mary Shelley incorporated into *Frankenstein*. For as we saw earlier, not just Victor and the monster but also Elizabeth and Justine insist upon responsibility for the monster's misdeed. Feeling "as if I had been guilty of a crime" (41, chap. 4) even before one had been committed, Victor responds to the news of William's death with the same self-accusations that torment the two orphans. And, significantly, for all three — as well as for the monster and little William himself — one focal point of both crime and guilt is an image of that other beautiful orphan, Caroline Beaufort Frankenstein. Passing from hand to hand, pocket to pocket, the smiling miniature of Victor's "angel mother" seems a token of some secret fellowship in sin, as does Victor's post-creation nightmare of transforming a lovely, living Elizabeth, with a single magical kiss, into "the corpse of my dead mother" enveloped in a shroud made more horrible by "grave-worms crawling in the folds of the flannel" (42, chap. 5). Though it has been disguised, buried, or miniaturized, femaleness — the gender definition of mothers and daughters, orphans and beggars, monsters and false creators — is at the heart of this apparently masculine book.

Because this is so, it eventually becomes clear that though Victor Frankenstein enacts the roles of Adam and Satan like a child trying on costumes, his single most self-defining act transforms him definitively into Eve. For as both Ellen Moers and Marc Rubenstein have pointed out, after much study of the "cause of generation and life," after locking himself away from ordinary society in the tradition of such agonized mothers as Wollstonecraft's Maria, Eliot's Hetty Sorel, and Hardy's Tess, Victor Frankenstein has a baby.[2] His "pregnancy" and childbirth

2. See Moers, *Literary Women*, "Female Gothic"; also Rubenstein, " 'My Accursed Origin,' "
pp. 165–166.

are obviously manifested by the existence of the paradoxically huge being who emerges from his "workshop of filthy creation," but even the descriptive language of his creation myth is suggestive: "incredible labours," "emaciated with confinement," "a passing trance," "oppressed by a slow fever," "nervous to a painful degree," "exercise and amusement would . . . drive away incipient disease," "the instruments of life" (39–41, chap. 4), etc. And, like Eve's fall into guilty knowledge and painful maternity, Victor's entrance into what Blake would call the realm of "generation" is marked by a recognition of the necessary interdependence of those complementary opposites, sex and death: "To examine the causes of life, we must first have recourse to death," he observes (36, chap. 4), and in his isolated workshop of filthy creation — filthy because obscenely sexual[3] — he collects and arranges materials furnished by "the dissecting room and the slaughterhouse." Pursuing "nature to her hiding places" as Eve does in eating the apple, he learns that "the tremendous secrets of the human frame" are the interlocked secrets of sex and death, although, again like Eve, in his first mad pursuit of knowledge he knows not "eating death." But that his actual orgasmic animation of his monster-child takes place "on a dreary night in November," month of All Souls, short days, and the year's last slide toward death, merely reinforces the Miltonic and Blakean nature of his act of generation.

Even while Victor Frankenstein's self-defining procreation dramatically transforms him into an Eve-figure, however, our recognition of its implications reflects backward upon our sense of Victor-as-Satan and our earlier vision of Victor-as-Adam. Victor as Satan, we now realize, was never really the masculine, Byronic Satan of the first book of *Paradise Lost*, but always, instead, the curiously female, outcast Satan who gave birth to Sin. In his Eve-like pride ("I was surprised . . . that I alone should be reserved to discover so astonishing a secret" [37, chap. 4]), this Victor-Satan becomes "dizzy" with his creative powers, so that his monstrous pregnancy, bookishly and solipsistically conceived, reenacts as a terrible bibliogenesis the moment when, in Milton's version, Satan "dizzy swum / In darkness, while [his] head flames thick and fast / Threw forth, till on the left side op'ning wide" and Sin, Death's mother-to-be, appeared like "a Sign / Portentous" (*PL* 2: 753–61). Because he has conceived — or, rather, misconceived — his monstrous offspring by brooding upon the *wrong* books, moreover, this Victor-Satan is paradigmatic, like the falsely creative fallen angel, of the female artist, whose anxiety about her own aesthetic activity is expressed, for instance, in Mary Shelley's deferential introductory phrase about her "hideous progeny," with its plain implication that in her alienated attic workshop of filthy creation she has given birth to a deformed book, a literary abor-

---

3. The *OED* gives "obscenity" and "moral defilement" among its definitions of "filth."

tion or miscarriage. "How [did] I, then a young girl, [come] to think of and to *dilate* upon so very hideous an idea?" is a key (if disingenuous) question she records. But we should not overlook her word play upon *dilate*, just as we should not ignore the anxious pun on the word *author* that is so deeply embedded in *Frankenstein.*

If the adult, Satanic Victor is Eve-like both in his procreation and his anxious creation, even the young, prelapsarian, and Adamic Victor is — to risk a pun — *curiously* female, that is, Eve-like. Innocent and guided by silken threads like a Blakeian lamb in a Godwinian garden, he is consumed by "a fervent longing to penetrate the secrets of nature," a longing which — expressed in his explorations of "vaults and charnel-houses," his guilty observations of "the unhallowed damps of the grave," and his passion to understand "the structure of the human frame" — recalls the criminal female curiosity that led Psyche to lose love by gazing upon its secret face, Eve to insist upon consuming "intellectual food," and Prometheus's sister-in-law Pandora to open the forbidden box of fleshly ills. But if Victor-Adam is also Victor-Eve, what is the real significance of the episode in which, away at school and cut off from his family, he locks himself into his workshop of filthy creation and gives birth by intellectual parturition to a giant monster? Isn't it precisely at this point in the novel that he discovers he is not Adam but Eve, not Satan but Sin, not male but female? If so, it seems likely that what this crucial section of *Frankenstein* really enacts is the story of Eve's discovery not that she must fall but that, having been created female, she *is* fallen, femaleness and fallenness being essentially synonymous. For what Victor Frankenstein most importantly learns, we must remember, is that he is the "author" of the monster — for him alone is "reserved . . . so astonishing a secret" — and thus it is he who is "the true murderer," he who unleashes Sin and Death upon the world, he who dreams the primal kiss that incestuously kills both "sister" and "mother." Doomed and filthy, is he not, then, Eve instead of Adam? In fact, may not the story of the fall be, for women, the story of the discovery that one is not innocent and Adam (as one had supposed) but Eve, and fallen? Perhaps this is what Freud's cruel but metaphorically accurate concept of penis-envy really means: the girl-child's surprised discovery that she is female, hence fallen, inadequate. Certainly the almost grotesquely anxious self-analysis implicit in Victor Frankenstein's (and Mary Shelley's) multiform relationships to Eve, Adam, God, and Satan suggest as much.

The discovery that one is fallen is in a sense a discovery that one is a monster, a murderer, a being gnawed by "the never-dying worm" (72, chap. 8) and therefore capable of any horror, including but not limited to sex, death, and filthy literary creation. More, the discovery that one is fallen — self-divided, murderous, material — is the discovery that one has released a "vampire" upon the world, "forced to destroy all that [is] dear" (61, chap. 7). For this reason — because *Frankenstein* is a story of woman's fall told by, as it were, an apparently docile daughter to a censorious "father" — the monster's narrative is embedded at the heart of the novel like the secret of the fall itself. Indeed, just as Franken-stein's workshop, with its maddening, riddling answers to cosmic ques-tions is a hidden but commanding attic womb/room where the young artist-scientist murders to dissect and to recreate, so the murderous monster's single, carefully guarded narrative commands and controls Mary Shelley's novel. Delivered at the top of Mont Blanc — like the North Pole one of the Shelley family's metaphors for the indifferently powerful source of creation and destruction — it is the story of deformed Geraldine in "Christabel," the story of the dead-alive crew in "The Ancient Mariner," the story of Eve in *Paradise Lost*, and of her de-graded double Sin — all secondary or female characters to whom male authors have imperiously denied any chance of self-explanation.[4] At the same time the monster's narrative is a philosophical meditation on what it means to be born without a "soul" or a history, as well as an explo-ration of what it feels like to be a "filthy mass that move[s] and talk[s]," a thing, an other, a creature of the second sex. In fact, though it tends to be ignored by critics (and film-makers), whose emphasis has always fallen upon Frankenstein himself as the archetypal mad scientist, the drastic shift in point of view that the nameless monster's monologue represents probably constitutes *Frankenstein*'s most striking technical *tour de force*, just as the monster's bitter self-revelations are Mary Shel-ley's most impressive and original achievement.[5]

Like Victor Frankenstein, his author and superficially better self, the monster enacts in turn the roles of Adam and Satan, and even even-tually hints at a sort of digression into the role of God. Like Adam, he recalls a time of primordial innocence, his days and nights in "the forest near Ingolstadt," where he ate berries, learned about heat and cold, and perceived "the boundaries of the radiant roof of light which can-opied me" (88, chap. 11). Almost too quickly, however, he metamor-phoses into an outcast and Satanic figure, hiding in a shepherd's hut which seems to him "as exquisite . . . a retreat as Pandemonium . . . after . . . the lake of fire" (90, chap. 11). Later, when he secretly sets up housekeeping behind the De Laceys' pigpen, his wistful obser-vations of the loving though exiled family and their pastoral abode ("Happy, happy earth! Fit habitation for gods . . ." [100, chap. 12]) recall Satan's mingled jealousy and admiration of that "happy rural seat

---

4. The monster's narrative also strikingly echoes Jemima's narrative in Mary Wollstonecraft's posthumously published novel, *Maria, or The Wrongs of Woman*. See *Maria* (1798; rpt. New York: Norton, 1975), pp. 52–69.
5. Harold Bloom does note that "the monster is . . . Mary Shelley's finest invention, and his narrative . . . forms the highest achievement of the novel." ("Afterword" to *Frankenstein*, p. 219.)

of various view" where Adam and Eve are emparadised by God and
Milton (*PL* 4. 247). Eventually, burning the cottage and murdering
William in demonic rage, he seems to become entirely Satanic: "I, like
the arch-fiend, bore a hell within me" (121, chap. 16); "Inflamed by
pain, I vowed eternal hatred . . . to all mankind" (126, chap. 16). At
the same time, in his assertion of power over his "author," his mental
conception of another creature (a female monster), and his implicit
dream of founding a new, vegetarian race somewhere in "the vast wilds
of South America," (131, chap. 17), he temporarily enacts the part of
a God, a creator, a master, albeit a failed one.

As the monster himself points out, however, each of these Miltonic
roles is a Procrustean bed into which he simply cannot fit. Where, for
instance, Victor Frankenstein's childhood really was Edenic, the monster's anxious infancy is isolated and ignorant, rather than insulated or
innocent, so that his groping arrival at self-consciousness — "I was a
poor, helpless, miserable wretch; I knew and could distinguish nothing;
but feeling pain invade me on all sides, I sat down and wept" (87–88,
chap. 11) — is a fiercely subversive parody of Adam's exuberant "all
things smil'd, / With fragrance and with joy my heart o'erflowed. /
Myself I then perus'd, and Limb by Limb / Survey'd, and sometimes
went, and sometimes ran / With supple joints, as lively vigor led" (*PL*
8. 265–69). Similarly, the monster's attempts at speech ("Sometimes I
wished to express my sensations in my own mode, but the uncouth and
inarticulate sounds which broke from me frightened me into silence
again" (88, chap. 11) parody and subvert Adam's ("To speak I tri'd, and
forthwith spake, / My Tongue obey'd and readily could name / What-
e'er I saw" (*PL* 8. 271–72). And of course the monster's anxiety and
confusion ("What was I? The question again recurred to be answered
only with groans" [106, chap. 13]) are a dark version of Adam's wondering bliss ("who I was, or where, or from what cause, / [I] Knew not.
. . . [But I] feel that I am happier than I know" (*PL* 8. 270–71, 282).

Similarly, though his uncontrollable rage, his alienation, even his
enormous size and superhuman physical strength bring him closer to
Satan than he was to Adam, the monster puzzles over discrepancies
between his situation and the fallen angel's. Though he is, for example,
"in bulk as huge / As whom the Fables name of monstrous size, /
Titanian, or *Earth-born*, that warr'd on *Jove*," and though, indeed, he
is fated to war like Prometheus on Jovean Frankenstein, this demon/
monster has fallen from no heaven, exercised no power of choice, and
been endowed with no companions in evil. "I found myself similar yet
at the same time strangely unlike to the beings concerning whom I
read and to whose conversation I was a listener," he tells Frankenstein,
describing his schooldays in the De Lacey pigpen (113, chap. 15). And,
interestingly, his remark might well have been made by Mary Shelley
herself, that "devout but nearly silent listener" (xiv) to masculine con-

versations who, like her hideous progeny, "continually studied and exercised [her] mind upon" such "histories" as *Paradise Lost*, Plutarch's *Lives*, and *The Sorrows of Werter* [*sic*] "whilst [her] friends were employed in their ordinary occupations" (112, chap. 15).

In fact, it is his intellectual similarity to his authoress (rather than his "author") which first suggests that Victor Frankenstein's male monster may really be a female in disguise. Certainly the books which educate him — *Werter*, Plutarch's *Lives*, and *Paradise Lost* — are not only books Mary had herself read in 1815, the year before she wrote *Frankenstein*, but they also typify just the literary categories she thought it necessary to study: the contemporary novel of sensibility, the serious history of Western civilization, and the highly cultivated epic poem. As specific works, moreover, each must have seemed to her to embody lessons a female author (or monster) must learn about a male-dominated society. Werter's story, says the monster — and he seems to be speaking for Mary Shelley — taught him about "gentle and domestic manners," and about "lofty sentiments . . . which had for their object something out of self." It functioned, in other words, as a sort of Romantic conduct book. In addition, it served as an introduction to the virtues of the proto-Byronic "Man of Feeling," for, admiring Werter and never mentioning Lotte, the monster explains to Victor that "I thought Werter himself a more divine being than I had ever . . . imagined," adding, in a line whose female irony about male self-dramatization must surely have been intentional, "I wept [his extinction] without precisely understanding it" (113, chap. 15).

If *Werter* introduces the monster to female modes of domesticity and self abnegation, as well as to the unattainable glamour of male heroism, Plutarch's *Lives* teaches him all the masculine intricacies of that history which his anomalous birth has denied him. Mary Shelley, excluding herself from the household of the second Mrs. Godwin and studying family as well as literary history on her mother's grave, must, again, have found in her own experience an appropriate model for the plight of a monster who, as James Rieger notes, is especially characterized by "his unique knowledge of what it is like to be born free of history."[6] In terms of the disguised story the novel tells, however, this monster is not unique at all, but representative, as Shelley may have suspected she herself was. For, as Jane Austen has Catherine Morland suggest in *Northanger Abbey*, what is woman but man without a history, at least without the sort of history related in Plutarch's *Lives*? "History, real solemn history, I cannot be interested in," Catherine declares ". . . the men all so good for nothing, and hardly any women at all — it is very tiresome" (*NA* I, chap. 14).

But of course the third and most crucial book referred to in the

6. James Rieger, "Introduction" to *Frankenstein*, (*the 1818 Text*) (Indianapolis: Bobbs-Merrill, 1974), p. xxx.

miniature *Bildungsroman* of the monster's narrative is *Paradise Lost*, an epic myth of origins which is of major importance to him, as it is to Mary Shelley, precisely because, unlike Plutarch, it does provide him with what appears to be a personal history. And again, even the need for such a history draws Shelley's monster closer not only to the realistically ignorant female defined by Jane Austen but also to the archetypal female defined by John Milton. For, like the monster, like Catherine Morland, and like Mary Shelley herself, Eve is characterized by her "unique knowledge of what it is like to be born free of history," even though as the "Mother of Mankind" she is fated to "make" history. It is to Adam, after all, that God and His angels grant explanatory visions of past and future. At such moments of high historical colloquy Eve tends to excuse herself with "lowliness Majestic" (before the fall) or (after the fall) she is magically put to sleep, calmed like a frightened animal "with gentle Dreams . . . and all her spirits compos'd / To meek submission" (*PL* 12. 595–96).

Nevertheless, one of the most notable facts about the monster's ceaselessly anxious study of *Paradise Lost* is his failure even to mention Eve. As an insistently male monster, on the surface of his palimpsestic narrative he appears to be absorbed in Milton's epic only because, as Percy Shelley wrote in the preface to *Frankenstein* that he drafted for his wife, *Paradise Lost* "most especially" conveys "the truth of the elementary principles of human nature," and conveys that truth in the dynamic tensions developed among its male characters, Adam, Satan, and God (xvii). Yet not only the monster's uniquely ahistorical birth, his literary anxieties, and the sense his readings (like Mary's) foster that he must have been parented, if at all, by *books*; not only all these facts and traits but also his shuddering sense of deformity, his nauseating size, his namelessness, and his orphaned, motherless isolation link him with Eve and with Eve's double, Sin. Indeed, at several points in his impassioned analysis of Milton's story he seems almost on the verge of saying so, as he examines the disjunctions among Adam, Satan, and himself:

> Like Adam, I was apparently united by no link to any other being in existence; but his state was far different from mine in every other respect. He had come forth from the hands of God a perfect creature, happy and prosperous, guided by the especial care of his Creator; he was allowed to converse with and acquire knowledge from beings of a superior nature, but I was wretched, helpless, and alone. Many times I considered Satan as the fitter emblem of my condition, for often, like him, when I viewed the bliss of my protectors, the bitter gall of envy rose within me. . . . Accursed creator! Why did you form a monster so hideous that even *you* turned from me in disgust? God, in pity, made man beautiful and alluring, after his own image; but my form is a filthy type of yours, more horrid even from the very resemblance. Satan had his com-

panions, fellow devils, to admire and encourage him, but I am
solitary and abhorred. [114–15, chap. 15]

It is Eve, after all, who languishes helpless and alone, while Adam
converses with superior beings, and it is Eve in whom the Satanically
bitter gall of envy rises, causing her to eat the apple in the hope of
adding "what wants / In Female Sex." It is Eve, moreover, to whom
deathly isolation is threatened should Adam reject her, an isolation
more terrible even than Satan's alienation from heaven. And finally it
is Eve whose body, like her mind, is said by Milton to resemble "less
/ His Image who made both, and less [to express] / The character of
that Dominion giv'n / O'er other Creatures . . ." (PL 8. 543–46). In
fact, to a sexually anxious reader, Eve's body might, like Sin's, seem
"horrid even from [its] very resemblance" to her husband's, a "filthy"
or obscene version of the human form divine.[7]

* * * Women have seen themselves (because they have been seen)
as monstrous, vile, degraded creatures, second-comers, and emblems of
filthy materiality, even though they have also been traditionally defined
as superior spiritual beings, angels, better halves. "Woman [is] a temple
built over a sewer," said the Church father Tertullian, and Milton
seems to see Eve as both temple and sewer, echoing that patristic mi-
sogyny.[8] Mary Shelley's conscious or unconscious awareness of the
monster woman implicit in the angel woman is perhaps clearest in the
revisionary scene where her monster, as if taking his cue from Eve in
Paradise Lost book 4, first catches sight of his own image: "I had admired the perfect forms of my cottagers . . . but how was I terrified
when I viewed myself in a transparent pool. At first I started back,
unable to believe that it was indeed I who was reflected in the mirror;
and when I became fully convinced that I was in reality the monster
that I am, I was filled with the bitterest sensations of despondence and
mortification" (98–99, chap. 12). In one sense, this is a corrective to
Milton's blindness about Eve. Having been created second, inferior, a
mere rib, how could she possibly, this passage implies, have seemed
anything but monstrous to herself? In another sense, however, the scene
supplements Milton's description of Eve's introduction to herself, for
ironically, though her reflection in "the clear / Smooth Lake" is as
beautiful as the monster's is ugly, the self-absorption that Eve's confessed passion for her own image signals is plainly meant by Milton to
seem morally ugly, a hint of her potential for spiritual deformity: "There
I had fixt / Mine eyes till now, and pin'd with vain desire, / Had not a

7. In Western culture the notion that femaleness is a deformity or obscenity can be traced back
   at least as far as Aristotle, who asserted that "we should look upon the female state as being
   as it were a deformity, though one which occurs in the ordinary course of nature." (The
   Generation of Animals, trans. A. L. Peck [London: Heinemann, 1943], p. 461.) For a brief
   but illuminating discussion of his theories see Katharine M. Rogers, The Troublesome
   Helpmate.
8. See de Beauvoir, The Second Sex, p. 156.

voice thus warn'd me, What thou seest, / What there thou seest fair
Creature is thyself . . ." (*PL* 4. 465–68).

The figurative monstrosity of female narcissism is a subtle deformity,
however, in comparison with the literal monstrosity many women are
taught to see as characteristic of their own bodies. Adrienne Rich's
twentieth-century description of "a woman in the shape of a monster /
A monster in the shape of a woman" is merely the latest in a long line
of monstrous female self-definitions that includes the fearful images in
Djuna Barnes's *Book of Repulsive Women*, Denise Levertov's "a white
sweating bull of a poet told us / our cunts are ugly" and Sylvia Plath's
"old yellow" self of the poem "In Plaster."[9] Animal and misshapen,
these emblems of self-loathing must have descended at least in part
from the distended body of Mary Shelley's darkly parodic Eve/Sin/Mon-
ster, whose enormity betokens not only the enormity of Victor Frankenstein's crime and Satan's bulk but also the distentions or deformities
of pregnancy and the Swiftian sexual nausea expressed in Lemuel Gulliver's horrified description of a Brobdignagian breast, a passage Mary
Shelley no doubt studied along with the rest of *Gulliver's Travels* when
she read the book in 1816, shortly before beginning *Frankenstein*.[1]

At the same time, just as surely as Eve's moral deformity is symbolized by the monster's physical malformation, the monster's physical
ugliness represents his social illegitimacy, his bastardy, his namelessness. Bitchy and dastardly as Shakespeare's Edmund, whose association
with filthy femaleness is established not only by his devotion to the
material/maternal goddess Nature but also by his interlocking affairs
with those filthy females Goneril and Regan, Mary Shelley's monster
has also been "got" in a "dark and vicious place." Indeed, in his vile
illegitimacy he seems to incarnate that bestial "unnameable" place.
And significantly, he is himself as nameless as a woman is in patriarchal
society, as nameless as unmarried, illegitimately pregnant Mary Wollstonecraft Godwin may have felt herself to be at the time she wrote
Frankenstein.

*   *   *

---

9. Adrienne Rich, "Planetarium," in *Poems: Selected and New* (New York: Norton, 1974), pp.
146–48; Djuna Barnes, *The Book of Repulsive Women* (1915; rpt. Berkeley, Calif., 1976);
Denise Levertov, "Hypocrite Women," *O Taste & See* (New York: New Directions, 1965);
Sylvia Plath, "In Plaster," *Crossing the Water* (New York: Harper & Row, 1971), p. 16.
1. See *Mary Shelley's Journal*, p. 73.

BARBARA JOHNSON

My Monster/My Self†

To judge from recent trends in scholarly as well as popular literature, three crucial questions can be seen to stand at the forefront of today's preoccupations: the question of mothering, the question of the woman writer, and the question of autobiography. Although these questions and current discussions of them often appear unrelated to each other, it is my intention here to explore some ways in which the three questions *are* profoundly interrelated, and to attempt to shed new light on each by approaching it via the others. I shall base my remarks upon two twentieth-century theoretical studies — Nancy Friday's *My Mother/My Self* and Dorothy Dinnerstein's *The Mermaid and the Minotaur* — and one nineteenth-century gothic novel, *Frankenstein; Or, the Modern Prometheus*, written by Mary Shelley, whose importance for literary history has until quite recently been considered to arise not from her own writings but from the fact that she was the second wife of poet Percy Bysshe Shelley and the daughter of political philosopher William Godwin and pioneering feminist Mary Wollstonecraft.

All three of these books, in strikingly diverse ways, offer a critique of the institution of parenthood. *The Mermaid and the Minotaur* is an analysis of the damaging effects of the fact that human infants are cared for almost exclusively by women. "What the book's title as a whole is meant to connote," writes Dinnerstein, "is both (a) our longstanding general awareness of our uneasy, ambiguous position in the animal kingdom, and (b) a more specific awareness: that until we grow strong enough to renounce the pernicious forms of collaboration between the sexes, both man and woman will remain semi-human, monstrous.[1]" Even as Dinnerstein describes convincingly the types of imbalance and injustice the prevailing asymmetry in gender relations produces, she also analyzes the reasons for our refusal to abandon the very modes of monstrousness from which we suffer most. Nancy Friday's book, which is subtitled "A Daughter's Search for Identity," argues that the mother's repression of herself necessitated by the myth of maternal love creates a heritage of self-rejection, anger, and duplicity that makes it difficult for the daughter to seek any emotional satisfaction other than the state of idealized symbiosis that both mother and daughter continue to punish themselves for never having been able to achieve. Mary Shelley's *Frankenstein* is an even more elaborate and unsettling formulation of

† From *Diacritics* 12 (1982): 2–10. Reprinted by permission of The Johns Hopkins University Press.
1. Dorothy Dinnerstein, *The Mermaid and the Minotaur* (New York: Harper/Colophon, 1976) 5. Further page references appear in the text.

the relation between parenthood and monstrousness. It is the story of two antithetical modes of parenting that give rise to two increasingly parallel lives — the life of Victor Frankenstein, who is the beloved child of two doting parents, and the life of the monster he single-handedly creates, who is immediately spurned and abandoned by his creator. The fact that in the end both characters reach an equal degree of alienation and self-torture and indeed become indistinguishable as they pursue each other across the frozen polar wastes indicates that the novel is, among other things, a study of the impossibility of finding an adequate model for what a parent should be.

All three books agree, then, that in the existing state of things there is something inherently monstrous about the prevailing parental arrangements. While Friday and Dinnerstein, whose analyses directly address the problem of sexual difference, suggest that this monstrousness is curable, Mary Shelley, who does not explicitly locate the self's monstrousness in its gender arrangements, appears to dramatize divisions within the human being that are so much a part of being human that no escape from monstrousness seems possible.

What I will try to do here is to read these three books not as mere *studies* of the monstrousness of selfhood, not as mere *accounts* of human monsterdom in general, but precisely as autobiographies in their own right, as textual dramatizations of the very problems with which they deal. None of the three books, of course, presents itself explicitly as autobiography. Yet each includes clear moments of employment of the autobiographical — not the purely authorial — first person pronoun. In each case the autobiographical reflex is triggered by the resistance and ambivalence involved in the very writing of the book. What I shall argue here is that what is specifically feminist in each book is directly related to this struggle for feminine authorship.

The notion that *Frankenstein* can somehow be read as the autobiography of a woman would certainly appear at first sight to be ludicrous. The novel, indeed, presents not one but *three* autobiographies of men. Robert Walton, an arctic explorer on his way to the North Pole, writes home to his sister of his encounter with Victor Frankenstein, who tells Walton the story of his painstaking creation and unexplained abandonment of a nameless monster who suffers excruciating and fiendish loneliness, and who tells Frankenstein *his* life story in the middle pages of the book. The three male autobiographies motivate themselves as follows:

> Walton (to his sister): "You will rejoice to hear that no disaster has accompanied the commencement of an enterprise which you have regarded with such evil forebodings. I arrived here yesterday, and my first task is to assure my dear sister of my welfare."[2]

2. Mary Shelley, *Frankenstein: Or, The Modern Prometheus* (New York: Signet, 1965) 15. Further page references appear in the text.

Frankenstein (with his hands covering his face, to Walton, who has been speaking of his scientific ambition): "Unhappy man! Do you share my madness? Have you drunk also of the intoxicating draught? Hear me; let me reveal my tale, and you will dash the cup from your lips!" [p. 26]

Monster (to Frankenstein): "I entreat you to hear me before you give vent to your hatred on my devoted head." [Frankenstein:] "Begone! I will not hear you. There can be no community between you and me [. . .]" [Monster places his hands before Frankenstein's eyes]: "Thus I take from thee a sight which you abhor. Still thou canst listen to me and grant me thy compassion . . . God, in pity, made man beautiful and alluring, after his own image; but my form is a filthy type of yours, more horrid even from the very resemblance." [pp. 95, 96, 97, 125]

All three autobiographies here are clearly attempts at persuasion rather than simple accounts of facts. They all depend on a presupposition of *resemblance* between teller and addressee: Walton assures his sister that he has not really left the path she would wish for him, that he still resembles *her*. Frankenstein recognizes in Walton an image of himself and rejects in the monster a resemblance he does not wish to acknowledge. The teller is in each case speaking into a mirror of his own transgression. The tale is designed to reinforce the resemblance between teller and listener so that somehow transgression can be eliminated. Yet the desire for resemblance, the desire to create a being like oneself — which is the autobiographical desire par excellence — is also the *central* transgression in Mary Shelley's novel. What is at stake in Frankenstein's workshop of filthy creation is precisely the possibility of shaping a life in one's own image: Frankenstein's monster can thus be seen as a figure for autobiography as such. Victor Frankenstein, then, has twice obeyed the impulse to construct an image of himself: on the first occasion he creates a monster, and on the second he tries to explain to Walton the causes and consequences of the first. *Frankenstein* can be read as the story of autobiography as the attempt to neutralize the monstrosity of autobiography. Simultaneously a revelation and a cover-up, autobiography would appear to constitute itself as in some way a repression of autobiography.

These three fictive male autobiographies are embedded within a thin introductory frame, added in 1831, in which Mary Shelley herself makes the repression of her own autobiographical impulse explicit:

The publishers of the standard novels, in selecting *Frankenstein* for one of their series, expressed a wish that I should furnish them with some account of the origin of the story. [. . .] It is true that I am very averse to bringing myself forward in print, but as my account will only appear as an appendage to a former production, and as it will be continued to such topics as have connection with my authorship alone, I can scarcely accuse myself of a personal intrusion.[3]

Mary Shelley, here, rather than speaking *into* a mirror, is speaking as an appendage to a text. It might perhaps be instructive to ask whether this change of status has anything to do with the problem of specifically *feminine* autobiography. In a humanistic tradition in which *man* is the measure of all things, how does an appendage go about telling the story of her life?

Before pursuing this question further, I would like to turn to a more explicit version of surreptitious feminine autobiography. Of the three books under discussion, Nancy Friday's account of the mother/daughter relationship relies the most heavily on the facts of the author's life in order to demonstrate its thesis. Since the author grew up without a father, she shares with Frankenstein's monster some of the problems of coming from a single-parent household. The book begins with a chapter entitled "Mother Love," of which the first two sentences are: "I have always lied to my mother. And she to me" [p. 19].[4] Interestingly, the book carries the following dedication: "When I stopped seeing my mother with the eyes of a child, I saw the woman who helped me give birth to myself. This book is for Jane Colbert Friday Scott." How, then, can we be sure that this huge book is not itself another lie to the mother it is dedicated to? Is autobiography somehow always in the process of symbolically killing the mother off by telling her the lie that we have given birth to ourselves? On page 460, Nancy Friday is still not sure what kind of lie she has told. She writes: "I am suddenly afraid that the mother I have depicted throughout this book is false." Whose life is this, anyway? This question cannot be resolved by a book that sees the "daughter's search for identity" as the necessity of choosing *between* symbiosis and separation, *between* the mother and the autonomous self. As long as this polarity remains unquestioned, the autobiography of Nancy Friday becomes the drawing and redrawing of the portrait of Jane Colbert Friday Scott. The most truly autobiographical moments occur not in expressions of triumphant separation but in descriptions of the way the book itself attempts to resist its own writing. At the end of the chapter on loss of virginity, Nancy Friday writes:

> It took me twenty-one years to give up my virginity. In some similar manner I am unable to let go of this chapter.[. . .]
>   It is no accident that wrestling with ideas of loss of virginity immediately bring me to a dream of losing my mother. This chap-

3. See above, p. 169 [*Editor*].
4. Nancy Friday, *My Mother/My Self* (New York: Dell, 1977) vii. Further page references appear in the text.

ter has revealed a split in me. Intellectually, I think of myself as a
sexual person, just as I had intellectually been able to put my ideas
for this chapter down on paper. Subjectively, I don't want to face
what I have written: that the declaration of full sexual independence is the declaration of separation from my mother. As long as
I don't finish this chapter, as long as I don't let myself understand
the implications of what I've written, I can maintain the illusion,
at least, that I can be sexual and have my mother's love and approval too. [pp. 331–333]

As long as sexual identity and mother's judgment are linked as antithetical and exclusive poles of the daughter's problem, the "split" she
describes will prevent her from ever completing her declaration of sexual independence. "Full sexual independence" is shown by the book's
own resistance to be as illusory and as mystifying an ideal as the notion
of "mother love" that Friday so lucidly rejects.

Dinnerstein's autobiographical remarks are more muted, although
her way of letting the reader know that the book was written partly in
mourning for her husband subtly underlies its persuasive seriousness.
In her gesture of rejecting more traditional forms of scholarship, she
pleads not for the validity but for the urgency of her message:

Right now, what I think is that the kind of work of which this is
an example is centrally necessary work. Whether our understanding makes a difference or not, we must try to understand what is
threatening to kill us off as fully and clearly as we can. [. . .]
What [this book] is, then, is not a scholarly book. it makes no
effort to survey the relevant literature. Not only would that task be
(for me) unmanageably huge. It would also be against my principles. I *believe* in reading unsystematically and taking notes er-
ratically. Any effort to form a rational policy about what to take
in, out of the inhuman flood of printed human utterance that
pours over us daily, feels to me like a self-deluded exercise in
pseudomastery. [pp. viii–ix]

The typographical form of this book bears out this belief in renouncing the appearance of mastery: there are two kinds of footnotes, some
at the foot of the page and some at the back of the book; there are
sections between chapters with unaligned right-hand margins which are
called "Notes toward the next chapter." And there are bold-face inserts
which dialogue with the controversial points in the main exposition.
Clearly, great pains have been taken to let as many seams as possible
show in the fabric of the argument. The preface goes on:

I mention these limitations in a spirit not of apology but of warning. To the extent that it succeeds in communicating its point at
all, this book will necessarily enrage the reader. What it says is

emotionally threatening. *(Part of why it has taken me so long to finish it is that I am threatened by it myself.)* [p. ix; emphasis mine]

My book is roughly sutured, says Dinnerstein, and it is threatening. This description sounds uncannily like a description of Victor Frankenstein's monster. Indeed, Dinnerstein goes on to warn the reader not to be tempted to avoid the threatening message by pointing to superficial flaws in its physical make-up. The reader of *Frankenstein*, too, would be well advised to look beyond the monster's physical deformity, both for his fearsome power and for his beauty. There are indeed numerous ways in which *The Mermaid and the Minotaur* can be seen as a modern rewriting of *Frankenstein*.

Dinnerstein's book situates its plea for two-sex parenting firmly in an apparently twentieth-century double bind: the realization that the very technological advances that make it possible to change the structure of parenthood also threaten to extinguish earthly life altogether. But it is startling to note that this seemingly contemporary pairing of the question of parenthood with a love-hate relation to technology is already at work in Mary Shelley's novel, where the spectacular scientific discovery of the secrets of animation produces a terrifyingly vengeful creature who attributes his evil impulses to his inability to find or to become a parent. Subtitled "The Modern Prometheus," *Frankenstein* itself indeed refers back to a myth that already links scientific ambivalence with the origin of mankind. Prometheus, the fire bringer, the giver of both creation and destruction, is also said by some accounts to be the father of the human race. Ambivalence toward technology can thus be seen as a displaced version of the love-hate relation we have toward our own children.

It is only recently that critics have begun to see Victor Frankenstein's disgust at the sight of his creation as a study of postpartum depression, as a representation of maternal rejection of a newborn infant, and to relate the entire novel to Mary Shelley's mixed feelings about motherhood.[5] Having lived through an unwanted pregnancy from a man married to someone else only to see that baby die, followed by a second baby named William — which is the name of the Monster's first murder victim — Mary Shelley, at the age of only eighteen, must have had excruciatingly divided emotions. Her own mother, indeed, had died upon giving her birth. The idea that a mother can loathe, fear, and reject her baby has until recently been one of the most repressed of psychoanalytical insights, although it is of course already implicit in the story

---

5. See Ellen Moers, "Female Gothic" and U. C. Knoepflmacher, "Thoughts on the Aggression of Daughters," in *The Endurance of Frankenstein*, ed. Levine and Knoepflmacher (Berkeley: University of California Press, 1979). Other related and helpful studies include S. M. Gilbert and S. Gubar, "Horror's Twin," in *The Madwoman in the Attic* (New Haven: Yale University Press, 1979) and Mary Poovey, "My Hideous Progeny: Mary Shelley and the Feminization of Romanticism," *PMLA*, 95 (May 1980).

of Oedipus, whose parents cast him out as an infant to die. What is threatening about each of these books is the way in which its critique of the *role* of the mother touches on primitive terrors of the mother's rejection of the child. Each of these women writers *does* in her way reject the child as part of her coming to grips with the untenable nature of mother love: Nancy Friday decides not to have children, Dorothy Dinnerstein argues that men as well as women should do the mothering, and Mary Shelley describes a parent who flees in disgust from the repulsive being to whom he has just given birth.

Yet it is not merely in its depiction of the ambivalence of motherhood that Mary Shelley's novel can be read as autobiographical. In the introductory note added in 1831, she writes:

> The publishers of the standard novels, in selecting *Frankenstein* for one of their series, expressed a wish that I should furnish them with some account of the origin of the story. I am the more willing to comply because I shall thus give a general answer to the question so very frequently asked me — how I, then a young girl, came to think of and to *dilate upon* so very hideous an idea. [p. vii, emphasis mine]

As this passage makes clear, readers of Mary Shelley's novel had frequently expressed the feeling that a young girl's fascination with the idea of monstrousness was somehow monstrous in itself. When Mary ends her introduction to the re-edition of her novel with the words: "And now, once again, I bid my hideous progeny go forth and prosper," the reader begins to suspect that there may perhaps be meaningful parallels between Victor's creation of his monster and Mary's creation of her book.

Such parallels are indeed unexpectedly pervasive. The impulse to write the book and the desire to search for the secrets of animation both arise under the same seemingly trivial circumstances: the necessity of finding something to read on a rainy day. During inclement weather on a family vacation, Victor Frankenstein happens upon the writings of Cornelius Agrippa, and is immediately fired with the longing to penetrate the secrets of life and death. Similarly, it was during a wet, ungenial summer in Switzerland that Mary, Shelley, Byron, and several others picked up a volume of ghost stories and decided to write a collection of spine-tingling tales of their own. Moreover, Mary's discovery of the subject she would write about is described in almost exactly the same words as Frankenstein's discovery of the principle of life: "Swift as light and as cheering was the idea that broke in upon me" [p. xi], writes Mary in her introduction, while Frankenstein says: "From the midst of this darkness a sudden light broke in upon me" [p. 51]. In both cases the sudden flash of inspiration must be supported by the meticulous gathering of heterogeneous, ready-made materials: Frankenstein collects bones and organs; Mary records overheard discussions of scientific questions that lead her to her sudden vision of monstrous creation. "Invention," she writes of the process of writing, but her words apply equally well to Frankenstein's labors. "Invention . . . does not consist in creating out of the void, but out of chaos; the materials must, in the first place, be afforded: it can give form to dark, shapeless substances but cannot bring into being the substance itself" [p. x]. Perhaps the most revealing indication of Mary's identification of Frankenstein's activity with her own is to be found in her use of the word "artist" on two different occasions to qualify the "pale student of unhallowed arts": "His success would terrify the *artist*" [p. xi], she writes of the catastrophic moment of creation, while Frankenstein confesses to Walton: "I appeared rather like one doomed by slavery to toil in the mines, or any other unwholesome trade than an *artist* occupied by his favorite employment" [p. 55].

Frankenstein, in other words, can be read as the story of the experience of writing *Frankenstein*. What is at stake in Mary's introduction as well as in the novel is the description of a *primal scene of creation*. *Frankenstein* combines a monstrous answer to two of the most fundamental questions one can ask: where do babies come from? and where do stories come from? In both cases, the scene of creation is described, but the answer to these questions is still withheld.

But what can Victor Frankenstein's workshop of filthy creation teach us about the specificity of *female* authorship? At first sight, it would seem that *Frankenstein* is much more striking for its avoidance of the question of femininity than for its insight into it. All the interesting, complex characters in the book are male, and their deepest attachments are to other males. The females, on the other hand, are beautiful, gentle, selfless, boring nurturers and victims who never experience inner conflict or true desire. Monstrousness is so incompatible with femininity that Frankenstein cannot even complete the female companion that his creature so eagerly awaits.

On the other hand, the story of Frankenstein is, after all, the story of a man who usurps the female role by physically giving birth to a child. It would be tempting, therefore, to conclude that Mary Shelley, surrounded as she then was by the male poets Byron and Shelley, and mortified for days by her inability to think of a story to contribute to their ghost-story contest, should have fictively transposed her own frustrated female pen envy into a tale of catastrophic male womb envy. In this perspective, Mary's book would suggest that a woman's desire to write and a man's desire to give birth would both be capable only of producing monsters.

Yet clearly things cannot be so simple. As the daughter of a famous feminist whose *Vindication of the Rights of Woman* she was in the process of rereading during the time she was writing *Frankenstein*, Mary

Shelley would have no reason to believe that writing was not proper for a woman. Indeed, as she says in her introduction, Mary was practically born with ink flowing through her veins:

> It is not singular that, as the daughter of two persons of distinguished literary celebrity, I should very early in life have thought of writing. (. . .) My husband (. . .) was from the first very anxious that I should prove myself worthy of my parentage and enroll myself on the page of fame. [pp. vii–viii]

In order to prove herself worthy of her parentage, Mary, paradoxically enough, must thus usurp the parental role and succeed in giving birth to *herself* on paper. Her declaration of existence as a writer must therefore figuratively repeat the matricide that her physical birth all too literally entailed. The connection between literary creation and the death of a parent is in fact suggested in the novel by the fact that, immediately after the monster's animation, Victor Frankenstein dreams that he holds the corpse of his dead mother in his arms. It is also suggested by the juxtaposition of two seemingly unrelated uses of italics in the novel: Mary's statement that she had *thought of a story* (which she inexplicably underlines twice) and the monster's promise to Frankenstein, *I will be with you on your wedding night*, which is repeatedly italicized. Both are eliminations of the mother, since the story Mary writes is a tale of motherless birth, and the wedding night marks the death of Frankenstein's bride, Elizabeth. Indeed, Mary herself was in fact the unwitting murderous intruder present on her own parents' wedding night: their decision to marry was due to the fact that Mary Wollstonecraft was already carrying the child that was to kill her. When Mary, describing her waking vision of catastrophic creation, affirms that "His success would terrify the artist," she is not giving vent to any ordinary fear-of-success syndrome. Or rather, what her book suggests is that what is at stake behind what is currently being banalized under the name of female fear of success is nothing less than the fear of somehow effecting the death of one's own parents.

It is not, however, the necessary murderousness of any declaration of female subjectivity that Mary Shelley's novel is proposing as its most troubling message of monsterdom. For, in a strikingly contemporary sort of predicament, Mary had not one but *two* mothers, each of whom consisted in the knowledge of the unviability of the other. After the death of Mary Wollstonecraft, Mary's father William Godwin married a woman as opposite in character and outlook as possible, a staunch housewifely mother of two who clearly preferred her own children to Godwin's. Between the courageous, passionate, intelligent, and suicidal mother Mary knew only through her writings, and the vulgar, repressive "pustule of vanity" whose dislike she resented and returned, Mary must have known at first hand a whole gamut of feminine contradictions, impasses, and options. For the complexities of the demands, desires, and sufferings of Mary's life as a woman were staggering. Her father, who had once been a vehement opponent of the institution of marriage, nearly disowned his daughter for running away with Shelley, an already married disciple of Godwin's own former views. Shelley himself, who believed in multiple love objects, amicably fostered an erotic correspondence between Mary and his friend Thomas Jefferson Hogg, among others. For years, Mary and Shelley were accompanied everywhere by Mary's stepsister Claire, whom Mary did not particularly like, who had a child by Byron, and who maintained an ambiguous relation with Shelley. During the writing of *Frankenstein*, Mary learned of the suicide of her half-sister Fanny Imlay, her mother's illegitimate child by an American lover, and the suicide of Shelley's wife Harriet, who was pregnant by a man other than Shelley. By the time she and Shelley married, Mary had had two children; she would have two more by the time of Shelley's death, and would watch as all but one of the children died in infancy. Widowed at age 24, she never remarried. It is thus indeed perhaps the very hiddenness of the question of femininity in *Frankenstein* that somehow proclaims the painful message not of female monstrousness but of female contradictions. For it is the fact of self-contradiction that is so vigorously repressed in women. While the story of a man who is haunted by his own contradictions is representable as an allegory of monstrous doubles, how indeed would it have been possible for Mary to represent feminine contradiction *from the point of view of its repression* otherwise than precisely in the *gap* between angels of domesticity and an uncompleted monsteress, between the murdered Elizabeth and the dismembered Eve?

It is perhaps because the novel does succeed in conveying the unresolvable contradictions inherent in being female that Shelley himself felt compelled to write a prefatory disclaimer in Mary's name before he could let loose his wife's hideous progeny upon the world. In a series of denials jarringly at odds with the daring negativity of the novel, Shelley places the following words in Mary's mouth:

> I am by no means indifferent to the manner in which whatever moral tendencies exist in the sentiments or characters it contains shall affect the reader; yet my chief concern in this respect has been limited to (. . .) the exhibition of the amiableness of domestic affection, and the excellence of universal virtue. The opinions which naturally spring from the character and situation of the hero are by no means to be conceived as existing always in my own conviction; nor is any inference justly to be drawn from the following pages as prejudicing any philosophical doctrine of whatever kind. [pp. xiii–xiv]

How is this to be read except as a gesture of repression of the very specificity of the power of feminine contradiction, a gesture reminiscent of Frankenstein's destruction of his nearly-completed female monster? What is being repressed here is the possibility that a woman can write anything that would *not* exhibit "the amiableness of domestic affection," the possibility that for women as well as for men the home can be the very site of the *unheimlich*.

It can thus be seen in all three of the books we have discussed that the monstrousness of selfhood is intimately embedded within the question of female autobiography. Yet how could it be otherwise, since the very notion of a self, the very shape of human life stories, has always, from St. Augustine to Freud, been modeled on the man? Rousseau's — or any man's — autobiography consists precisely in the story of the difficulty of conforming to the standard of what a *man* should be. The problem for the female autobiographer is, on the one hand, to resist the pressure of masculine autobiography as the only literary genre available for her enterprise, and, on the other, to describe a difficulty in conforming to a female ideal which is largely a fantasy of the masculine, not the feminine, imagination. The fact that these three books deploy a *theory* of autobiography as monstrosity within the framework of a less overtly avowed struggle with the raw materials of the authors' own lives and writing is perhaps, in the final analysis, precisely what is most autobiographically fertile and *telling* about them.

MARY POOVEY

"My Hideous Progeny": The Lady and the Monster†

*   ✧   ✧

When she was in Switzerland in the summer of 1816, Mary Shelley's creative energies were finally rerouted from "travelling, and the cares of a family" (*F*, p. 223)[1] to this all-important activity of writing. Living next to Lord Byron, listening to — though not participating in — the conversations of the two poets ("incapacity and timidity always prevented my mingling in the nightly conversations," she said [*MSJ*, p. 184]),[2] and no doubt inspired by Percy's example, Mary Shelley began to compose steadily. After 24 July 1816, her journal frequently contains the important monosyllable, "Write," and the attention Percy devoted to the novel's progress, its revisions, and, eventually, its publication reveals that his support for the project was as enthusiastic as Mary could have

† From *The Proper Lady and the Woman Writer* (Chicago: U of Chicago P, 1984) 121–31. Reprinted by permission.
1. *F* = James Rieger, ed., *Frankenstein* (Chicago: U of Chicago P, 1978).
2. *MSJ* = Frederick L. Jones, ed., *Mary Shelley's Journal* (Norman: U of Oklahoma P, 1947).

wished. But the narrative that Mary Shelley wrote between that "eventful" summer and the following April was less a wholehearted celebration of the imaginative enterprise she had undertaken in order to prove her worth to Percy than a troubled, veiled exploration of the price she had already begun to fear such egotistical self-assertion might exact. *Frankenstein* occupies a particularly important place in Shelley's career, not only because it is by far her most famous work, but because, in 1831, she prepared significant revisions and an important introduction, both of which underscore and elaborate her initial ambivalence. By tracing first the contradictions already present in the 1818 edition and then the revisions she made after Percy's death and her return to England, we can begin to see the roots and progress of Shelley's growing desire to accommodate her adolescent impulses to conventional propriety. Taken together, the two editions of *Frankenstein* provide a case study of the tensions inherent in the confrontation between the expectations Shelley associated, on the one hand, with her mother and Romantic originality and, on the other, with a textbook Proper Lady.

Even though they praised the power and stylistic vigor of *Frankenstein*, its first reviewers sharply criticized the anonymous novelist's failure to moralize about the novel's startling, even blasphemous, subject. The reviewer for the *Quarterly Review*, for example, complained that

> Our taste and our judgment alike revolt at this kind of writing, and the greater the ability with which it may be executed the worse it is — it inculcates no lesson of conduct, manners, or morality; it cannot mend, and will not even amuse its readers, unless their taste have been deplorably vitiated — it fatigues the feelings without interesting the understanding; it gratuitously harasses the heart, and only adds to the store, already too great, of painful sensations.

Presumably because it was unthinkable that a woman should refuse to moralize, most critics automatically assumed that the author of *Frankenstein* was a man — no doubt a "follower of Godwin," according to *Blackwood's*, or even Percy Shelley himself, as the *Edinburgh Magazine* surmised. These reviewers, however, were too preoccupied with the explicit unorthodoxy of *Frankenstein's* subject to attend carefully to the undercurrents in it that challenged their opinion. Like her mother and many male Romantics, Mary Shelley had chosen to focus on the theme of Promethean desire, which has implications for both the development of culture and the individual creative act; but when *Frankenstein* is considered alongside contemporary works that display even some degree of confidence in imaginative power, it proves to be more conservative than her first readers realized. Indeed, *Frankenstein* calls into question, not the social conventions that inhibit creativity, but rather the egotism that Mary Shelley associates with the artist's monstrous self-assertion.

Like Wollstonecraft and most male Romantics, Shelley discusses desire explicitly within a paradigm of individual maturation: *Frankenstein*
is Shelley's version of the process of identity-formation that Wollstonecraft worked out in her two *Vindications*. Keats called this maturation
"soul-making," and Wordsworth devoted his longest completed poem
to it. In the 1818 text, Shelley's model of maturation begins with a
realistic depiction of Lockean psychology; young Victor Frankenstein
is a *tabula rasa* whose character is formed by his childhood experiences.
The son of loving, protective parents, the companion of affectionate
friends, he soon finds the harmony of his childhood violated by what
he calls a "predilection" for natural philosophy. Yet even though this
"predilection" seems to be innate, Frankenstein locates its origin not
in his own disposition but in a single childhood event—the accidental
discovery of a volume of Cornelius Agrippa's occult speculations. The
"fatal impulse" this volume sparks is then kindled into passionate enthusiasm by other accidents: Frankenstein's father neglects to explain
Agrippa's obsolescence, a discussion provoked by a lightning bolt un-
dermines his belief in the occult, and "some accident" prevents him
from attending lectures on natural philosophy. Left with a craving for
knowledge but no reliable guide to direct it, Frankenstein's curiosity is
kept within bounds only by the "mutual affection" of his domestic
circle.

In this dramatization of Victor Frankenstein's childhood, Mary Shelley fuses mechanistic psychological theories of the origin and development of character with the more organic theories generally associated
with the Romantics. Like most contemporary Lockean philosophers,
she asserts that circumstances activate and direct an individual's capacity for imaginative activity; the inclination or predilection thus formed
then constitutes the basis of identity. But when Shelley combines this
model with the notion (implied by Wollstonecraft's *Letters Written . . .
in Sweden* and by the poetry of Wordsworth, Coleridge, Byron, and
Percy Shelley) that an individual's desire, once aroused, has its own
impetus and logic, she comes up with a model of maturation that con-
tradicts the optimism of both mechanists and organicists. More in keeping with eighteenth-century moralists than with either William Godwin
or Percy Shelley, Mary Shelley characterizes innate desire not as neu-
tral or benevolent but as quintessentially egotistical. And, unlike Mary
Wollstonecraft, she does not conceive of imaginative activity as leading
through intimations of mortality to new insight or creativity. Instead,
she sees imagination as an appetite that can and must be regulated—
specifically, by the give-and-take of domestic relationships. If it is
aroused but is not controlled by human society, it will project itself into
the natural world, becoming voracious in its search for objects to conquer and consume. This principle, which draws both mechanistic and
organic models under the mantle of conventional warnings to women,

constitutes the major dynamic of *Frankenstein's* plot. As long as domestic relationships govern an individual's affections, his or her desire
will turn outward as love. But when the individual loses or leaves the
regulating influence of relationship with others, imaginative energy always threatens to turn back on itself, to "mark" all external objects as
its own and to degenerate into "gloomy and narrow reflections upon
self" (*F*, p. 32).

Shelley's exposition of the degeneration of incipient curiosity into
full-fledged egotism begins when Frankenstein leaves his childhood
home for the University of Ingolstadt. At the university he is left to
"form [his] own friends, and be [his] own protector" (p. 40), and, given
this freedom, his imagination is liberated to follow its natural course.
To the young scholar, this energy seems well-directed, for Frankenstein
assumes that his ambition to conquer death through science is fundamentally unselfish. With supreme self-confidence, he "penetrate[s] into
the recesses of nature" in search of the secret of life. What he discovers
in the "vaults and charnel houses" he visits, however, is not life but
death, the "natural decay and corruption of the human body." In pursuing his ambition even beyond this grisly sight, Frankenstein proves
unequivocally that his "benevolent" scheme actually acts out the imagination's essential and deadly self-devotion. For what he really wants
is not to serve others but to assert himself. Indeed, he wants ultimately
to defy mortality, to found a "new species" that would "bless [him] as
its creator and source." "No father could claim the gratitude of his
child so completely as I should deserve their's," he boasts (p. 49).

Frankenstein's particular vision of immortality and the vanity that it
embodies have profound social consequences, both because Frankenstein would deny relationships (and women) any role in the conception
of children and because he would reduce all domestic ties to those that
center on and feed his selfish desires. Given the egotism of his ambition, it comes as no surprise that Frankenstein's love for his family is
the first victim of his growing obsession; "supernatural enthusiasm"
usurps the place of his previous domestic love. "I wished, as it were, to
procrastinate all that related to my feelings of affection until the great
object, which swallowed up every habit of my nature, should be completed" (p. 50). Frankenstein isolates himself in a "solitary chamber,"
refuses to write even to his fiancée, Elizabeth, and grows "insensible to
the charms of nature." "I became as timid as a love-sick girl," he realizes, in retrospect, "and alternate tremor and passionate ardour took
the place of wholesome sensation and regulated ambition" (p. 51).

Despite what the reviewers thought, in her dramatization of the imaginative quest Mary Shelley is actually more concerned with this anti-
social dimension than with its metaphysical implications. In chapter 5,
for example, at the heart of her story, she elaborates the significance of
Frankenstein's self-absorption primarily in terms of his social relation-

ships. After animating the monster, product and symbol of self-serving desire, Frankenstein falls asleep, only to dream the true meaning of his accomplishment: having denied domestic relationships by indulging his selfish passions, he has, in effect, murdered domestic tranquillity.

> I thought I saw Elizabeth, in the bloom of health, walking in the streets of Ingolstadt. Delighted and surprised, I embraced her; but as I imprinted the first kiss on her lips, they became livid with the hue of death; her features appeared to change, and I thought that I held the corpse of my dead mother in my arms; a shroud enveloped her form, and I saw the grave-worms crawling in the folds of the flannel. [P. 53]

Lover and mother, as the presiding female guardians of Frankenstein's "secluded and domestic" youth, are conflated in this tableau of the enthusiast's guilt. Only now, when Frankenstein starts from his sleep to find the misshapen creature hanging over his bed (as he himself will later hang over Elizabeth's) does he recognize his ambition for what it really is: a monstrous urge, alien and threatening to all human intercourse.

In effect, animating the monster completes and liberates Frankenstein's egotism, for his indescribable experiment gives explicit and autonomous form to his ambition and desire. Paradoxically, in this incident Shelley makes the ego's destructiveness literal by setting in motion the figurative, symbolic character of the monster. We will see later the significance of this event for the monster; for Frankenstein, this moment, which aborts his maturation, has the dual effect of initiating self-consciousness and, tragically, perfecting his alienation. Momentarily "restored to life" by his childhood friend Clerval, Frankenstein rejects the "selfish pursuit [that] had cramped and narrowed" him and returns his feeling to its proper objects, his "beloved friends." But ironically, the very gesture that disciplines his desire has already destroyed the possibility of reestablishing relationships with his loved ones. Liberating the monster allows Frankenstein to see that personal fulfillment results from self-denial rather than self-assertion, but it also condemns him to perpetual isolation and, therefore, to permanent incompleteness.

This fatal paradox, the heart of Mary Shelley's waking nightmare, gives a conventionally "feminine" twist to the argument that individuals mature through imaginative projection, confrontation, and self-consciousness. In the version of maturation that Wollstonecraft sketched out in her two *Vindications* and in *Letters Written . . . in Sweden* and that Wordsworth set out more fully in *The Prelude*, the child's innate desires, stirred and nurtured by the mother's love, are soon projected outward toward the natural world. Desire takes this aggressive turn because in maternal love and in the receptivity this love cultivates "there exists / A virtue which irradiates and exalts / All objects through all intercourse of sense" (1805 *Prelude*, book 2, lines 258–60). As a result of both the child's growing confidence in the beneficence of the questing imagination and nature's generous response, the child is able to effect a radical break with the mother without suffering irretrievable loss.

> No outcast he, bewildered and depressed;
> Along his infant veins are interfused
> The gravitation and the filial bond
> Of Nature that connect him with the world.
> [*Prelude*, 2.261–64]

The heightened images of the self cast back from nature then help the child internalize a sense of autonomous identity and personal power.

In marked contrast, Mary Shelley distrusts both the imagination *and* the natural world. The imagination, as it is depicted in Frankenstein's original transgression, is incapable of projecting an irradiating virtue, for, in aiding and abetting the ego, the imagination expands the individual's self-absorption to fill the entire universe, and, as it does so, it murders everyone in its path. In *Frankenstein*, the monster simply acts out the implicit content of Frankenstein's desire: just as Frankenstein figuratively murdered his family, so the monster literally murders Frankenstein's domestic relationships, blighting both the memory and the hope of domestic harmony with the "black mark" of its deadly hand. William Frankenstein, Justine Moritz, Henry Clerval, even Elizabeth Lavenza are, as it were, literally *possessed* by this creature; but, as Frankenstein knows all too well, its victims are by extension his own: Justine is *his* "unhappy victim" (p. 80); *he* has murdered Clerval (p. 174); and the creature consummates *his* deadly desire on "*its* bridal bier" (p. 193).

By the same token, Mary Shelley also distrusts nature, for, far from curbing the imagination, nature simply encourages imaginative projection. Essentially, Mary Shelley's understanding of nature coincides with those of Wordsworth, Wollstonecraft, and Percy Shelley. But where these three trust the imagination to disarm the natural world of its meaninglessness by projecting human content into it, Mary Shelley's anxiety about the imagination bleeds into the world it invades. In the inhospitable world most graphically depicted in the final setting of *Frankenstein*, nature is "terrifically desolate," frigid, and fatal to human beings and human relationships. These fields of ice provide a fit home only for the monster, that incarnation of the imagination's ugly and deadly essence.

Thus Shelley does not depict numerous natural theaters into which the individual can project his or her growing desire and from which affirmative echoes will return to hasten the process of maturation. Instead, she continues to dramatize personal fulfillment strictly in terms of the child's original domestic harmony, with the absent mother now replaced by the closest female equivalent: ideally, Elizabeth would link Frankenstein's maturity to his youth, just as Mrs. Saville should anchor the mariner Walton. Ideally, in other words, the beloved object would be sought and found only within the comforting confines of preexisting domestic relationships. In this model, Shelley therefore ties the formation of personal identity to self-denial rather than self-assertion; personal identity for her entails defining oneself in terms of relationships (not one but many) — not, as Wollstonecraft and Wordsworth would have it, in terms of self-assertion, confrontation, freedom, and faith in the individualistic imaginative act.

Shelley repeatedly stresses the fatal kinship between the human imagination, nature, and death by the tropes of natural violence that describe all kinds of desire. Passion is like nature internalized, as even Frankenstein knows:

> When I would account to myself for the birth of that passion, which afterwards ruled my destiny, I find it arise, like a mountain river, from ignoble and almost forgotten sources; but, swelling as it proceeded, it became the torrent which, in its course, has swept away all my hopes and joys. [*F*, p. 32]

Ambition drives Frankenstein "like a hurricane" as he engineers the monster (p. 49) and, after its liberation, he is a "blasted tree," "utterly destroyed" by a lightning blast to his soul. Through these metaphoric associations, Shelley is laying the groundwork for the pattern acted out by the monster. Like forces in the natural world, Frankenstein's unregulated desire gathers strength until it erupts in the monster's creation; then the creature actualizes, externalizes, the pattern of nature — Frankenstein's nature and the natural world, now explicitly combined — with a power that destroys all society. In other words, the pattern inherent in the natural world and figuratively ascribed to the individual becomes, through the monster, Frankenstein's literal "fate" or "destiny."

The individual's fatal relationship to nature is further complicated by the egotistical impulse to deny this kinship. In retrospect, Frankenstein knows that the winds will more likely yield a storm than calm, but in the blindness of his original optimism he believes that nature is hospitable to humanity, that it offers a Wordsworthian "ennobling interchange" that consoles and elevates the soul. Still trusting himself and the natural world, Frankenstein cries out with "something like joy" to the spirit of the Alps, as if it were a compassionate as well as a natural parent: "Wandering spirits . . . allow me this faint happiness, or take me, as your companion, away from the joys of life." But Frankenstein's belief in natural benevolence, like his earlier confidence in the benevolence of his desire, proves a trick of the wishful imagination. His request is answered by the true spirit of this and every place untamed by social conventions — the "superhuman," "unearthly" monster. Lulled once more by vanity and desire, Frankenstein recognizes the character of his bond with nature only when it again stands incarnate before him.

In order to understand why Mary Shelley's first readers did not fully appreciate what seems, in comparison to Romantic optimism, to be an unmistakable distrust of the imagination, we must turn to the monster's narrative. For Shelley's decision to divide the novel into a series of first-person narratives instead of employing a single perspective, whether first-person or omniscient, has the effect of qualifying her judgment of egotism. Because she dramatizes in the monster — not in Franken-stein — the psychological consequences of imaginative self-assertion, the reader is encouraged to participate not only in Frankenstein's desire for innate and natural benevolence but also in the agonizing repercussions of this misplaced optimism.

In the monster's narrative, Shelley both recapitulates Frankenstein's story and, ingeniously, completes it. Influenced by external circum-stances that arouse, then direct, their desire for knowledge, both beings find that their imaginative quests yield only the terrible realization of an innate grotesqueness. But, unlike Frankenstein, the monster is de-nied the luxury of an original domestic harmony. The monster is "made" not born, and, as the product of the unnatural coupling of nature and the imagination, it is caught in the vortex of death that will ultimately characterize Frankenstein as well. Moreover, as the product, then the agent of Frankenstein's egotism, the monster is merely a link in the symbolic "series" of Frankenstein's "self-devoted being," not an autonomous member of a natural, organic family. Given a human's nobler aspirations without the accompanying power, the monster strug-gles futilely to deny both its status as a function of Frankenstein and the starkness of its circumscribed domain; the creature yearns to ex-perience and act upon its own desires and to break free into the realistic frame that Frankenstein occupies. But the monster cannot have inde-pendent desires or influence its own destiny because, as the projection of Frankenstein's indulged desire and nature's essence, the creature *is* destiny. Moreover, because the monster's physical form literally em-bodies its essence, it cannot pretend to be something it is not; it cannot enter the human community it longs to join, and it cannot earn the sympathy it can all too vividly imagine. Paradoxically, the monster is the victim of both the symbolic and the literal. And, as such, it is doubly like a woman in patriarchal society — forced to be a symbol of (and vehicle for) someone else's desire, yet exposed (and exiled) as the deadly essence of passion itself.

For the monster, then, self-consciousness comes with brutal speed, for it depends, not on an act of transgression, but on literal self-perception.

An old man's terror, a pool of water, a child's fear, all are nature's mirrors, returning the monster repeatedly to its grotesque self, "a figure hideously deformed and loathsome . . . a monster, a blot upon the earth" (pp. 115–16). When the creature discovers its true origin — not in the literary works it finds and learns to read but in the records of Frankenstein's private experiments — it can no longer deny the absolute "horror" of its being, the monstrous singularity of egotism: "the minutest description of my odious and loathsome person is given, in language which painted your own horrors, and rendered mine ineffaceable" (p. 126). From this moment on, the monster's attempts to deny its nature are as futile as they are desperate. In its most elaborate scheme, the creature hides in a womblike hovel, as if it could be born again into culture by aping the motions of the family it spies upon. Although the monster tries to disguise its true nature by confronting only the blind old father, De Lacey's children return and recognize the creature's "ineffaceable" monstrosity for what it literally is. Their violent reaction, which the monster interprets as rejection by its "adopted family," at last precipitates the creature's innate nature; abandoning humanity's "godlike science" — the language of society it so diligently learned — for its natural tongue — the nonsignifying "fearful howlings" of beasts — the monster embarks on its systematic destruction of domestic harmony. The creature makes one final attempt to form a new society; but when Frankenstein refuses to create a female monster, it is condemned, like its maker, to a single bond of hatred. After Frankenstein's death, the monster disappears into the darkness at the novel's end, vowing to build its own funeral pyre; for it is as immune to human justice as it was repulsive to human love.

The monster carries with it the guilt and alienation that attend Frankenstein's self-assertion; yet, because Shelley realistically details the stages by which the creature is driven to act out its symbolic nature from *its* point of view, the reader is compelled to identify with its anguish and frustration. This narrative strategy precisely reproduces Mary Shelley's profound ambivalence toward Frankenstein's creative act; for by separating self-assertion from its consequences, she is able to dramatize both her conventional judgment of the evils of egotism and her emotional engagement in the imaginative act. Indeed, the pathos of the monster's cry suggests that Shelley identified most strongly with the product (and the victim) of Frankenstein's transgression: the objectified imagination, helpless and alone.

Although in an important sense, objectifying Frankenstein's imagination in the symbolic form of the monster delimits the range of connotations the imagination can have (it eliminates, for example, the possibilities of transcendent power or beneficence), this narrative strategy allows Shelley to express her ambivalence toward the creative act because a symbol is able to accommodate different, even contradictory, meanings. It is important to recognize that Shelley is using symbolism in a quite specific way here, a way that differs markedly from Percy Shelley's description of symbolism in his preface to the 1818 *Frankenstein*. In his justification for the central scene, Percy stresses not the ambivalence of the symbol but its comprehensiveness: "However impossible as a physical fact, [this incident] affords a point of view to the imagination for the delineating of human passions more comprehensive and commanding than any which the ordinary relations of existing events can yield" (p. 6). Although we know from the Shelleys' letters and from the surviving manuscript of *Frankenstein* that Percy was instrumental in promoting and even revising the text, Mary did not uncritically or wholeheartedly accept the aesthetic program of which this self-confident use of symbolism was only one part. Instead, she transforms Percy's version of the Romantic aesthetic in such a way as to create for herself a nonassertive, and hence acceptable, voice.

Percy Shelley defended his aesthetic doctrines, as part of his political and religious beliefs, with a conviction Mary later called a "resolution firm to martyrdom." Scornful of public opinion, he maintained that a true poet may be judged only by his legitimate peers, a jury "impaneled by Time from the selectest of the wise of many generations." Society's accusation that an artist is "immoral," he explains in the "Defence of Poetry" (1821), rests on "a misconception of the manner in which poetry acts to produce the moral improvement of man." The audience's relationship to poetry is based not on reason but on the imagination; true poetry does not encourage imitation or judgment but participation. It strengthens the individual's moral sense because it exercises and enlarges the capacity for sympathetic identification, that is, for establishing relationships. Following Plato, Percy declares that the primary reflex of the moral imagination is the outgoing gesture of love.

> The great secret of morals is Love; or a going out of our own nature, and an identification of ourselves with the beautiful which exists in thought, action, or person, not our own. A man, to be greatly good, must imagine intensely and comprehensively; he must put himself in the place of another and of many others; the pains and pleasures of his species must become his own. The great instrument of moral good is the imagination; and poetry administers to the effect by acting upon the cause.

Each of Percy Shelley's aesthetic doctrines comes to rest on this model of the imagination as an innately moral, capacious faculty. Because the imagination, if unrestrained, naturally supersedes relative morals (and in so doing compensates for the inhumaneness of the natural world), the poet should not discipline his or her poetic efforts according to a particular society's conceptions of right and wrong. Because the imagination tends to extend itself, through sympathy, to truth, the poet should simply depict examples of truth, thus drawing the audience into a relationship that simultaneously feeds and stimulates humanity's appetite for "thoughts of ever new delight."

This model of the artwork as an arena for relationships is the only aspect of Percy's aesthetics that Mary Shelley adopts without reservation. It seems to have been particularly appealing to her not only because it conforms to Percy's ideal but also because it satisfies society's conventional definition of proper feminine identity and proper feminine self-assertion. In doing so, it also answered needs and assuaged fears that seem to have been very pressing for Mary Shelley. As we have seen, she did not agree with Percy that the imagination is inherently moral. By the same token, she seems to have doubted that the abstract controls that Wollstonecraft described in her two *Vindications* and her *Letters Written . . . in Sweden* were capable of governing an individual's desire or disciplining the imagination. The factors that reinforced Shelley's doubts were probably as complicated as the anxieties themselves, but we can surmise that Percy Shelley's outspoken atheism helped undermine Mary's confidence in orthodox religion, that society's denigration of women's reasoning ability weakened her trust in that faculty, and that society's judgment and her own conflicting emotions conspired to make her doubt the morality of female feeling. For Mary Shelley, then, the only acceptable or safe arena in which to articulate her feelings, exercise her reason, and act out her unladylike ambition was that of personal relationships. In addition to the aesthetic purpose it serves, the narrative strategy of *Frankenstein* also provides just such a network of relationships. Because of its three-part narrative arrangement, Shelley's readers are drawn into a relationship with even the most monstrous part of the young author; Shelley is able to create her artistic persona through a series of relationships rather than a single act of self-assertion; and she is freed from having to take a single, definitive position on her unladylike subject. In other words, the narrative strategy of *Frankenstein*, like the symbolic presentation of the monster, enables Shelley to express and efface herself at the same time and thus, at least partially, to satisfy her conflicting desires for self-assertion and social acceptance.

*   *   *

GAYATRI CHAKRAVORTY SPIVAK

[*Frankenstein* and a Critique of Imperialism]†

It should not be possible to read nineteenth-century British literature without remembering that imperialism, understood as England's social mission, was a crucial part of the cultural representation of England to the English. The role of literature in the production of cultural representation should not be ignored. These two obvious "facts" continue to be disregarded in the reading of nineteenth-century British literature. This itself attests to the continuing success of the imperialist project, displaced and dispersed into more modern forms.

If these "facts" were remembered, not only in the study of British literature but in the study of the literatures of the European colonizing cultures of the great age of imperialism, we would produce a narrative, in literary history, of the "worlding" of what is now called "the Third World." To consider the Third World as distant cultures, exploited but with rich intact literary heritages waiting to be recovered, interpreted, and curricularized in English translation fosters the emergence of "the Third World" as a signifier that allows us to forget that "worlding," even as it expands the empire of the literary discipline.[1]

* * *

Mary Shelley's *Frankenstein* [is] a text of nascent feminism that remains cryptic, I think, simply because it does not speak the language of feminist individualism which we have come to hail as the language of high feminism within English literature. It is interesting that Barbara Johnson's brief study tries to rescue this recalcitrant text for the service of feminist autobiography.[2] Alternatively, George Levine reads *Frankenstein* in the context of the creative imagination and the nature of the hero. He sees the novel as a book about its own writing and about writing itself, a Romantic allegory of reading within which Jane Eyre as unself-conscious critic would fit quite nicely.[3]

I propose to take *Frankenstein* out of this arena and focus on it in terms of that sense of English cultural identity which I invoked at the opening of this essay. Within that focus we are obliged to admit that,

† From *Critical Inquiry* 12 (Autumn 1985): 243–61. Original title = "Three Women's Texts and a Critique of Imperialism." *F* = Mary Shelley, *Frankenstein* (New York, 1965). Reprinted by permission of the author.

1. My notion of the "worlding of a world" upon what must be assumed to be uninscribed earth is a vulgarization of Martin Heidegger's idea; see "The Origin of the Work of Art," *Poetry, Language, Thought*, trans. Albert Hofstadter (New York, 1977), pp. 17–87.
2. See Barbara Johnson, "My Monster/My Self," *Diacritics* 12 (Summer 1982): 2–10.
3. See George Levine, *The Realistic Imagination: English Fiction from Frankenstein to Lady Chatterley* (Chicago, 1981), pp. 23–35.

although *Frankenstein* is ostensibly about the origin and evolution of man in society, it does not deploy the axiomatics of imperialism.

Let me say at once that there is plenty of incidental imperialist sentiment in *Frankenstein*. My point, within the argument of this essay, is that the discursive field of imperialism does not produce unquestioned ideological correlatives for the narrative structuring of the book. The discourse of imperialism surfaces in a curiously powerful way in Shelley's novel, and I will later discuss the moment at which it emerges.

Frankenstein is not a battleground of male and female individualism articulated in terms of sexual reproduction (family and female) and social subject-production (race and male). That binary opposition is undone in Victor Frankenstein's laboratory—an artificial womb where both projects are undertaken simultaneously, though the terms are never openly spelled out. Frankenstein's apparent antagonist is God himself as Maker of Man, but his real competitor is also woman as the maker of children. It is not just that his dream of the death of mother and bride and the actual death of his bride are associated with the visit of his monstrous homoerotic "son" to his bed. On a much more overt level, the monster is a bodied "corpse," unnatural because bereft of a determinable childhood: "No father had watched my infant days, no mother had blessed me with smiles and caresses; or if they had, all my past was now a blot, a blind vacancy in which I distinguished nothing" (*F*, pp. 57, 115). It is Frankenstein's own ambiguous and miscued understanding of the real motive for the monster's vengefulness that reveals his own competition with woman as maker:

> I created a rational creature and was bound towards him to assure, as far as was in my power, his happiness and well-being. This was my duty, but there was another still paramount to that. My duties towards the beings of my own species had greater claims to my attention because they included a greater proportion of happiness or misery. Urged by this view, I refused, and I did right in refusing, to create a companion for the first creature. [*F*, p. 206]

It is impossible not to notice the accents of transgression inflecting Frankenstein's demolition of his experiment to create the future Eve. Even in the laboratory, the woman-in-the-making is not a bodied corpse but "a human being." The (il)logic of the metaphor bestows on her a prior existence which Frankenstein aborts, rather than an anterior death which he reembodies: "The remains of the half-finished creature, whom I had destroyed, lay scattered on the floor, and I almost felt as if I had mangled the living flesh of a human being" (*F*, p. 163).

In Shelley's view, man's hubris as soul maker both usurps the place of God and attempts—vainly—to sublate woman's physiological prerogative.[4] Indeed, indulging a Freudian fantasy here, I could urge that, if to give and withhold to/from the mother a phallus is *the* male fetish, then to give and withhold to/from the man a womb might be the female fetish.[5] The icon of the sublimated womb in man is surely his productive brain, the box in the head.

In the judgment of classical psychoanalysis, the phallic mother exists only by virtue of the castration-anxious son; in *Frankenstein's* judgment, the hysteric father (Victor Frankenstein gifted with his laboratory — the womb of theoretical reason) cannot produce a daughter. Here the language of racism — the dark side of imperialism understood as social mission — combines with the hysteria of masculism into the idiom of (the withdrawal of) sexual reproduction rather than subject-constitution. The roles of masculine and feminine individualists are hence reversed and displaced. Frankenstein cannot produce a "daughter" because "she might become ten thousand times more malignant than her mate . . . [and because] one of the first results of those sympathies for which the demon thirsted would be children, and a race of devils would be propagated upon the earth who might make the very existence of the species of man a condition precarious and full of terror" (F, p. 158). This particular narrative strand also launches a thoroughgoing critique of the eighteenth-century European discourses on the origin of society through (Western Christian) man. Should I mention that, much like Jean-Jacques Rousseau's remark in his *Confessions*, Frankenstein declares himself to be "by birth a Genevese" (F, p. 31)?

In this overly didactic text, Shelley's point is that social engineering should not be based on pure, theoretical, or natural-scientific reason alone, which is her implicit critique of the utilitarian vision of an engineered society. To this end, she presents in the first part of her deliberately schematic story three characters, childhood friends, who seem to represent Kant's three-part conception of the human subject: Victor Frankenstein, the forces of theoretical reason or "natural philosophy"; Henry Clerval, the forces of practical reason or "the moral relations of things"; and Elizabeth Lavenza, that aesthetic judgment — "the aerial creation of the poets" — which, according to Kant, is "a suitable mediating link connecting the realm of the concept of nature and that of the concept of freedom . . . (which) promotes . . . *moral* feeling" (F, pp. 37, 36).[6]

4. Consult the publications of the Feminist International Network for the best overview of the current debate on reproductive technology.
5. For the male fetish, see Sigmund Freud, "Fetishism," *The Standard Edition of the Complete Psychological Works of Sigmund Freud*, ed. and trans. James Strachey et al., 24 vols. (London, 1953–74), 21:152-57. For a more "serious" Freudian study of *Frankenstein*, see Mary Jacobus, "Is There a Woman in This Text?" *New Literary History* 14 (Autumn 1982): 117–41. My "fantasy" would of course be disproved by the "fact" that it is more difficult for a woman to assume the position of fetishist than for a man; see Mary Ann Doane, "Film and the Masquerade: Theorising the Female Spectator," *Screen* 23 (Sept.–Oct. 1982): 74-87.
6. Kant, *Critique of Judgement*, trans. J. H. Bernard (New York, 1951), p. 39.

This three-part subject does not operate harmoniously in *Franken-stein*. That Henry Clerval, associated as he is with practical reason, should have as his "design . . . to visit India, in the belief that he had in his knowledge of its various languages, and in the views he had taken of its society, the means of materially assisting the progress of European colonization and trade" is proof of this, as well as part of the incidental imperialist sentiment that I speak of above (*F*, pp. 151–52). I should perhaps point out that the language here is entrepreneurial rather than missionary:

> He came to the university with the design of making himself com-plete master of the Oriental languages, as thus he should open a field for the plan of life he had marked out for himself. Resolved to pursue no inglorious career, he turned his eyes towards the East as affording scope for his spirit of enterprise. The Persian, Arabic, and Sanskrit languages engaged his attention. [*F*, pp. 66–67]

But it is of course Victor Frankenstein, with his strange itinerary of obsession with natural philosophy, who offers the strongest demonstra-tion that the multiple perspectives of the three-part Kantian subject cannot co-operate harmoniously. Frankenstein creates a putative hu-man subject out of natural philosophy alone. According to his own miscued summation: "In a fit of enthusiastic madness I created a ra-tional creature" (*F*, p. 206). It is not at all farfetched to say that Kant's categorical imperative can most easily be mistaken for the hypothetical imperative — a command to ground in cognitive comprehension what can be apprehended only by moral will — by putting natural philosophy in the place of practical reason.

I should hasten to add here that just as readings such as this one do not necessarily accuse Charlotte Brontë the named individual of har-boring imperialist sentiments [in *Jane Eyre*], so also they do not nec-essarily commend Mary Shelley the named individual for writing a successful Kantian allegory. The most I can say is that it is possible to read these texts, within the frame of imperialism and the Kantian eth-ical moment, in a politically useful way. Such an approach presupposes that a "disinterested" reading attempts to render transparent the inter-ests of the hegemonic readership. (Other "political" readings — for in-stance, that the monster is the nascent working class — can also be advanced.)

Frankenstein is built in the established epistolary tradition of multiple frames. At the heart of the multiple frames, the narrative of the monster (as reported by Frankenstein to Robert Walton, who then recounts it in a letter to his sister) is of his almost learning, clandestinely, to be human. It is invariably noticed that the monster reads *Paradise Lost* as true history. What is not so often noticed is that he also reads Plutarch's *Lives*, "the histories of the first founders of the ancient republics," which he compares to "the patriarchal lives of my protectors" (F, pp. 123, 124). And his *education* comes through "Volney's *Ruins of Empires*," which purported to be a prefiguration of the French Revolution, published after the event and after the author had rounded off his theory with practice (F, p. 113). It is an attempt at an enlightened universal secular, rather than a Eurocentric Christian, history, written from the perspective of a narrator "from below," somewhat like the attempts of Eric Wolf or Peter Worsley in our own time.[7]

This Caliban's education in (universal secular) humanity takes place through the monster's eavesdropping on the instruction of an Ariel—Safie, the Christianized "Arabian" to whom "a residence in Turkey was abhorrent" (F, p. 121). In depicting Safie, Shelley uses some commonplaces of eighteenth-century liberalism that are shared by many today: Safie's Muslim father was a victim of (bad) Christian religious prejudice and yet was himself a wily and ungrateful man not as morally refined as her (good) Christian mother. Having tasted the emancipation of woman, Safie could not go home. The confusion between "Turk" and "Arab" has its counterpart in present-day confusion about Turkey and Iran as "Middle Eastern" but not "Arab."

Although we are a far cry here from the unexamined and covert axiomatics of imperialism in *Jane Eyre*, we will gain nothing by celebrating the time-bound pieties that Shelley, as the daughter of two antievangelicals, produces. It is more interesting for us that Shelley differentiates the Other, works at the Caliban/Ariel distinction, and *cannot* make the monster identical with the proper recipient of these lessons. Although he had "heard of the discovery of the American hemisphere and *wept with Safie* over the helpless fate of its original inhabitants," Safie cannot reciprocate his attachment. When she first catches sight of him, "Safie, unable to attend to her friend [Agatha], rushed out of the cottage" (F, pp. 114 [my emphasis], 129).

In the taxonomy of characters, the Muslim-Christian Safie belongs with Rhys' Antoinette/Bertha [in *Wide Sargasso Sea*]. And indeed, like Christophine the good servant, the subject created by the fiat of natural philosophy is the tangential unresolved moment in *Frankenstein*. The simple suggestion that the monster is human inside but monstrous out-

---

7. See [Constantin François Chasseboeuf de Volney], *The Ruins; or, Meditations on the Revolutions of Empires*, trans. pub. (London, 1811). Johannes Fabian has shown us the manipulation of time in "new" secular histories of a similar kind; see *Time and the Other: How Anthropology Makes Its Object* (New York, 1983). See also Eric R. Wolf, *Europe and the People without History* (Berkeley and Los Angeles, 1982), and Peter Worsley, *The Third World*, 2d ed. (Chicago, 1973); I am grateful to Dennis Dworkin for bringing the latter book to my attention. The most striking ignoring of the monster's education through Volney is in Gilbert's otherwise brilliant "Horror's Twin: Mary Shelley's Monstrous Eve," *Feminist Studies* 4 (June 1980): 48–73. Gilbert's essay reflects the absence of race-determinations in a certain sort of feminism. Her present work has most convincingly filled in this gap; see, e.g., her recent piece on H. Rider Haggard's *She* ("Rider Haggard's Heart of Darkness," *Partisan Review* 50, no. 3 [1983]: 444–53).

side and only provoked into vengefulness is clearly not enough to bear the burden of so great a historical dilemma.

At one moment, in fact, Shelley's Frankenstein does try to tame the monster, to humanize him by bringing him within the circuit of the Law. He "repair[s] to a criminal judge in the town and . . . relate[s his] history briefly but with firmness" — the first and disinterested version of the narrative of Frankenstein — "marking the dates with accuracy and never deviating into invective or exclamation. . . . When I had concluded my narration I said, 'This is the being whom I accuse and for whose seizure and punishment I call upon you to exert your whole power. It is your duty as a magistrate' " (*F*, pp. 189, 190). The sheer social reasonableness of the mundane voice of Shelley's "Genevan magistrate" reminds us that the absolutely Other cannot be selfed, that the monster has "properties" which will not be contained by "proper" measures:

> "I will exert myself [he says], and if it is in my power to seize the monster, be assured that he shall suffer punishment proportionate to his crimes. But I fear, from what you have yourself described to be his properties, that this will prove impracticable; and thus, while every proper measure is pursued, you should make up your mind to disappointment." [*F*, p. 190]

In the end, as is obvious to most readers, distinctions of human individuality themselves seem to fall away from the novel. Monster, Frankenstein, and Walton seem to become each others' relays. Frankenstein's story comes to an end in death; Walton concludes his own story within the frame of his function as letter writer. In the *narrative* conclusion, he is the natural philosopher who learns from Frankenstein's example. At the end of the *text*, the monster, having confessed his guilt toward his maker and ostensibly intending to immolate himself, is borne away on an ice raft. We do not see the conflagration of his funeral pile — the self-immolation is not consummated in the text: he too cannot be contained by the text. In terms of narrative logic, he is "lost in darkness and distance" (*F*, p. 211) — these are the last words of the novel — into an existential temporality that is coherent with neither the territorializing individual imagination (as in the opening of *Jane Eyre*) nor the authoritative scenario of Christian psychobiography (as at the end of Brontë's work). The very relationship between sexual reproduction and social subject-production — the dynamic nineteenth-century topos of feminism-in-imperialism — remains problematic within the limits of Shelley's text and, paradoxically, constitutes its strength.

Earlier, I offered a reading of woman as womb holder in *Frankenstein*. I would now suggest that there is a framing woman in the book who is neither tangential, nor encircled, nor yet encircling. "Mrs. Sa-

ville," "excellent Margaret," "beloved Sister" are her address and kinship inscriptions (*F*, pp. 15, 17, 22). She is the occasion, though not
the protagonist, of the novel. She is the feminine *subject* rather than
the female individualist: she is the irreducible *recipient*-function of the
letters that constitute *Frankenstein*. * * * Here the reader must read
with Margaret Saville in the crucial sense that she must *intercept* the
recipient-function, read the letters *as* recipient, in order for the novel
to exist.[8] Margaret Saville does not respond to close the text as „frame.
The frame is thus simultaneously not a frame, and the monster can
step "beyond the text" and be "lost in darkness." Within the allegory
of our reading, the place of both the English lady and the unnamable
monster are left open by this great flawed text. It is satisfying for a
postcolonial reader to consider this a noble resolution for a nineteenth-
century English novel. This is all the more striking because, on the
anecdotal level, Shelley herself abundantly "identifies" with Victor
Frankenstein.[9]

*   *   *

Postscript[1]

I "chose" to study English Literature at University because I was not
good enough in Science. I must confess I rather like the so-called English classics — shamefacedly in the way of a Kipling Bengali — and I
don't want to stop liking them. Over the years I have developed, without
stopping much to think about it, a new way of ranking them: in terms
of how they acommodate(d) conquest.

Making public this private shift, I wrote an essay called "Three Wom-
en's Texts and A Critique of Imperialism" a little over ten years ago.
In it I wrote in praise of Mary Shelley's *Frankenstein* because, in my
estimation, Shelley had attempted to come to terms with the making
of the colonial subject. Sympathetic yet monstrous, clandestinely reared
on sacred and profane histories of salvation and empire, shunned by
the civilisation which produced his subjectivity, this creature's destruc-

8. "A letter is always and *a priori* intercepted, . . . the 'subjects' are neither the senders nor the
   receivers of messages. . . . The letter is constituted . . . by its interception" (Jacques Derrida,
   "Discussion," after Claude Rabant, "Il n'a aucune chance de l'entendre," in *Affranchissement:
   Du transfert et de la lettre*, ed. René Major [Paris, 1981], p. 106; my translation). Margaret
   Saville is not made to appropriate the reader's "subject" into the signature of her own
   "individuality."
9. The most striking "internal evidence" is the admission in the "Author's Introduction" that,
   after dreaming of the yet-unnamed Victor Frankenstein figure and being terrified (through,
   yet not quite through, him) by the monster in a scene she later reproduced in Frankenstein's
   story, Shelley began her tale "on the morrow . . . with the words 'It was on a dreary night of
   November' " (*F*, p. xi). Those are the opening words of chapter 5 of the finished book, where
   Frankenstein begins to recount the actual making of his monster (see *F*, p. 56).
1. The following is a slightly revised extract from Spivak, *Thinking Academic Freedom in Gendered Post-Coloniality* (Cape Town, 1992), 28–32. [It was appended to "Three Women's Texts
   and a Critique of Imperialism" after its original publication in *Critical Inquiry — Editor*.]

tive rage propels him out of the novel into an indefinite future. But what of his history? The feminist dimension of the novel provides a frame that is critical of the effort to construct a creature without womb-life and infancy. But when it comes to the colonial subject's prehistory, Shelley's political imagination fails. (We have seen that in postcoloniality, the subject mourns the unlamented death of this previous history.)

Thus Shelley's emancipatory vision cannot extend beyond the speculary situation of the colonial enterprise, where the master alone has a history, master and subject locked up in the cracked mirror of the present, and the subject's future, although indefinite, is vectored specifically toward and away from the master. Within this restricted vision, Shelley gives to the monster the right to refuse the withholding of the master's returned gaze — to refuse an *apartheid* of speculation, as it were:

> "I will not be tempted to set myself in opposition to thee. . . . How can I move thee?" . . . [He] placed his hated hands before my [Frankenstein's] eyes, which I flung from me with violence, "thus I take from thee a sight which you abhor. Still thou canst listen to me . . ."[2]

His request, not granted, is for a gendered future, for the colonial female subject.

I want now to advance the argument just a bit further, and make a contrastive point. The task of the post-colonial writer, the descendant of the colonial female subject that history did in fact produce, cannot be restrained within the specular master-slave enclosure so powerfully staged in *Frankenstein*. I turn to Mahasweta Devi's "Pterodactyl, Pirtha, and Puran Sahay" to measure out some of the differences between the sympathetic and supportive colonial staging of the situation of the refusal of the withholding of specular exchange in favour of the monstrous colonial subject; and the post-colonial performance of the construction of the constitutional subject of the new nation.[3]

Devi stages the workings of the post-colonial state with minute knowledge, anger, and loving despair. There are suppressed dissident radicals, there is the national government seeking electoral publicity, there are systemic bureaucrats beneath good and evil, subaltern state functionaries to whom the so-called Enlightenment principles of democracy are counter-intuitive. Then there is the worst product of post-coloniality, the Indian who uses the alibis of Development to exploit the tribals

---

2. Mary Wollstonecraft Shelley, *Frankenstein, or the Modern Prometheus (the 1818 text)*, ed. James Rieger (1974), pp. 95, 96.
3. Mahasweta Devi, "Pterodactyl, Pirtha, and Puran Sahay," in *Imaginary Maps*, trans. Gayatri Chakravorty Spivak (New York, forthcoming).

and destroy their life-system. Over against him is the handful of conscientious and understanding government workers who operate through a system of official sabotage and small compromises. The central figure is Puran Sahay, a journalist. (Devi herself, in addition to being an ecology-health-literacy activist and a fiction writer, is also an indefatigable interventionist journalist.)

The post-colonial state gives the frame-narrative. At the heart of the novella is an act of mourning. A tribal boy has drawn the picture of a pterodactyl on the cave-wall. Puran and a "good" government officer do not allow this to become public. Through his unintentionally successful "prediction" of rain, Puran becomes part of the tribe's ongoing historical record. He sees the pterodactyl.

If the exchange between the nameless monster (without history) and Victor Frankenstein is a finally futile refusal of withheld specularity, the situation of the gaze between pterodactyl (before history) and a "national" history that holds tribal and non-tribal together, is somewhat different.[4] There can be no speculation here; in a textual space rhetorically separated from the counter-factual funeral, the tribal and the non-tribal must pull together, both modern:

> You are moveless with your wings folded, I do not wish to touch you, you are outside my wisdom, reason, and feelings, who can place his hand on the axial moment of the end of the third phase of the Mesozoic and the beginnings of the Kenozoic geological ages? . . . What do its eyes want to tell Puran? . . . There is no communication between eyes. Only a dusky waiting, without end. What does it want to tell? We are extinct by the inevitable natural geological evolution. You too are endangered. You too will become extinct in nuclear explosions, or in war, or in the aggressive advance of the strong as it obliterates the weak, . . . think if you are going forward or back. . . . What will you finally grow in the soil, having murdered nature in the application of man-imposed substitutes? . . . The dusky lidless eyes remain unresponsive.

For the modern Indian the pterodactyl is an empirical impossibility. For the modern tribal Indian the pterodactyl is the soul of the ancestors. The fiction does not judge between the registers of truth and exactitude, simply stages them in separate spaces. This is not science fiction. And the pterodactyl is not a symbol.

To read *Frankenstein* and "Pterodactyl" together is an act of supplementation that leads us into the history of the present.

---

4. This is of course rigorously to be distinguished from a romanticisation of the *tribal* as prehistory (or the "unconscious") that Kuman Sangari correctly deplores in "Figures of the Unconscious," *Journal of Arts and Ideas* (1991).

WILLIAM VEEDER

The Women of *Frankenstein*†

*   *   *

Mary Shelley's very sense of the weakness in herself and womanhood makes her defensive in *Frankenstein*. After admitting that women are no more immune than men to weakness, she insists self-justifyingly that women are less weak. What destroys them is not effeminacy but a world impossibly strong. Thus as we explore Mary's demonstrations of weakness in *Frankenstein*, we must be more attuned than most criticism has been to the careful controls which prevent readers from responding to women in the severe and even derisive way we did to Victor the anxious bridegroom. We must be particularly careful because extreme weakness is the very thing which critics charge Mary's women with. Justine, Caroline, and Elizabeth all act in ways which leave them open to criticism; none exhibits the perfection conventional with the good women of melodrama. In defining their weaknesses, however, we must avoid melodramatic simplifications.

With Justine the question is not whether she is weak but whether Mary Shelley sees that weakness as Justine's critics do, as symptomatic of the inadequacies of true womanhood. "Justine and Elizabeth have learned well the lessons of submissiveness and devotion . . . Their model behavior similarly lowers their resistance to the forces that kill them."[1] The lumping together of two characters as different as Justine and Elizabeth calls Ellis's criticism into doubt, and our experience of the text confirms that doubt. Before we learn of Justine's incriminating behavior, we are made to feel the weight of evidence against her. "This picture . . . was doubtless the temptation which urged the murderer to the deed. . . . even now Elizabeth will not be convinced [of Justine's guilt], notwithstanding all the evidence. . . . several circumstances came out, that have almost forced conviction upon us" (67–68, 74). My point is not that we, who already know of Justine's excellence, are persuaded of her guilt, but that the Genevese are. The cards seem stacked formidably against Justine from the start.

Then, the courtroom scene minimizes her weakness.

> The appearance of Justine was calm. . . . she appeared confident in innocence, and did not tremble, although gazed on and exe-

---

† From *Mary Shelley and Frankenstein: The Fate of Androgyny* (Chicago: U of Chicago P, 1988) 182–85. Reprinted by permission. Parenthetical page numbers refer to James Rieger, ed., *Frankenstein* (Chicago: U of Chicago P, 1982).
1. Kate Ellis, "Monsters in the Garden: Mary Shelley and the Bourgeois Family," in George Levine and U.C. Knoepflmacher, *The Endurance of Frankenstein*, (Berkeley: U of California P, 1982) 123–42.

crated by thousands. . . . She was tranquil, yet her tranquility was
evidently constrained; and as her confusion had before been adduced as a proof of her guilt, she worked up her mind to an
appearance of courage. . . . A tear seemed to dim her eye when
she saw us; but she quickly recovered herself, and a look of sorrowful affection seemed to attest to her utter guiltlessness. . . .
Justine was called on for her defence. As the trial had proceeded,
her countenance had altered. Surprise, horror, and misery were
strongly expressed. Sometimes she struggled with her tears; but
when she was desired to plead, she collected her powers, and spoke
in an audible although variable voice. (77, 78)

Besides bearing up well under considerable pressure, Justine explains
part of what seemed weak in her previous conduct. Her initial bewil-
derment "was not surprising, since she had passed a sleepless night,
and the fate of poor William was yet uncertain" (78–79).

Our primary experience in the courtroom is not of Justine as weak,
but of Justine as victim. Arrayed against her are five formidable forces.
Besides the populace incensed by "the enormity she was supposed to
have committed" (77) and the "timorous" friends who "supposed her
guilty" (79), there are the plot of the novel, the power of the church,
and the machinery of the law.

"I know . . . how heavily and fatally this one circumstance [the
miniature] weighs against me, but I have no power of explaining
it . . . when I have expressed my utter ignorance, I am only left to
conjecture concerning the probabilities by which it might have been
placed in my pocket. But here also I am checked" (79). Justine proves
incapable of saving herself, but the cause of her failure affects our
response to it. Her bafflement confirms less her analytical weakness
than the weakness of analysis itself. Justine has been victimized by the
very plot of the novel. How could she imagine that an eight-foot-tall,
man-made monster had sneaked up and slipped the miniature into her
pocket? Mary's structuring of the action is also a factor when we reach
Justine's weakest moment. That she might have shown spunk enough
to refuse to confess, is true; but Mary does here what she need not—
delays the confession until *after* the verdict. Had she wanted to indict
true woman for passive weakness, Mary would have made Justine's fate
dependent upon her giving in. Instead the young woman holds out as
long as acquittal remains a possibility.

Moreover, Justine's giving in seems less weak when we learn of the
other forces arrayed against her. "My confessor has besieged me; he
threatened . . . excommunication and hell fire in my last moments"
(82). Focus shifts away from the nature of true woman and onto that
conventional target of gothic opprobrium, the Romish clergy. (How far
Mary is going out of her way to invoke conventional anti-Catholic responses is shown by the illogic of events here: the last thing we would

expect to encounter in Geneva, the bastion of John Calvin, is Catholic coerciveness.) Justine seems doubly beset because the clerical Father is carrying on the browbeating practiced by her fanatical mother. That sympathy which a victim of Catholicism is guaranteed with British readers is, moreover, augmented by Mary's implication of another force which her audience traditionally distrusts, the judiciary.

> "When one creature is murdered [says Elizabeth], another is immediately deprived of life in a slow torturing manner; then the executioners, their hands yet reeking with the blood of innocence, believe that they have done a great deed. They call this *retribution*. Hateful name! When that word is pronounced, I know greater and more horrid punishments are going to be inflicted than the gloomiest tyrant has ever invented to satiate his utmost revenge." (83)

Set off against state and church and venal individuals, true woman is presented not as debilitatingly weak but as touchingly vulnerable. Justine sounds like Mary Shelley herself when she cries out, "I had none to support me" (82).

While recognizing the force of external coercion we must, however, be careful of simplification. Justine's confession is not superfluous. By making it indispensable to the young woman's sentencing ("none of our judges like to condemn a criminal upon circumstantial evidence" [81]), Mary Shelley reveals in true woman not a "feminine" weakness which destroys her but a radical purposiveness which releases her. Woman in the spirit of Eros spites and flees what Justine calls in 1831 "a sad and bitter world" (246). Rather than finding with Moers that Justine "accepts guilt with docility" (99), I agree with Knoepflmacher that Justine's "passive death becomes . . . a retaliation" (11).

There is thus in true womanhood an inevitable mix to which our response has been carefully controlled. Justine does not seem self-destructive in any simple, petulant sense; she is only self-victimized enough to be understandably human. Confronted with a plot as perfect in its criminal as in its novelistic aspect, Justine is a sympathetic sacrifice to forces inhumanly powerful. When she asks "what could I do?" (82), Mary Shelley has made sure that we can only answer, Not enough, poor thing.

* * *

ANNE K. MELLOR

Possessing Nature: The Female in *Frankenstein*†

When Victor Frankenstein identifies Nature as female — "I pursued nature to *her* hiding places"[1] — he participates in a gendered construction of the universe whose ramifications are everywhere apparent in *Frankenstein*. His scientific penetration and technological exploitation of female nature, which I have discussed elsewhere,[2] is only one dimension of a more general cultural encoding of the female as passive and possessable, the willing receptacle of male desire. The destruction of the female implicit in Frankenstein's usurpation of the natural mode of human reproduction symbolically erupts in his nightmare following the animation of his creature, in which his bride-to-be is transformed in his arms into the corpse of his dead mother — "a shroud enveloped her form, and I saw the grave-worms crawling in the folds of the flannel" (p. 53). By stealing the female's control over reproduction, Frankenstein has eliminated the female's primary biological function and source of cultural power. Indeed, for the simple purpose of human survival, Frankenstein has eliminated the necessity to have females at all. One of the deepest horrors of this novel is Frankenstein's implicit goal of creating a society for men only: his creature is male; he refuses to create a female; there is no reason that the race of immortal beings he hoped to propagate should not be exclusively male.[3]

On the cultural level, Frankenstein's scientific project — to become the sole creator of a human being — supports a patriarchal denial of the value of women and of female sexuality. Mary Shelley, doubtless inspired by her mother's *A Vindication of the Rights of Woman*, specifically portrays the consequences of a social construction of gender that values the male above the female. Victor Frankenstein's nineteenth-century Genevan society is founded on a rigid division of sex roles: the

† From *Romanticism and Feminism*, ed. Anne K. Mellor (Bloomington: Indiana UP, 1988) 220–32. Reprinted by permission.
1. Mary W. Shelley, *Frankenstein, or The Modern Prometheus* (London: Lackington, Hughes, Harding, Mavor and Jones, 1818); all further references to *Frankenstein* will be to Rieger, ed. (New York: Bobbs-Merrill, 1974; reprinted, Chicago: University of Chicago Press, 1982), and will be cited by page number only in the text. This phrase occurs on page 49.
2. Anne K. Mellor, "*Frankenstein*: A Feminist Critique of Science," in *One Culture: Essays on Literature and Science*, ed. George Levine (Madison: University of Wisconsin Press, 1988), pp. 287–312.
3. Mary Shelley thus heralds a tradition of literary utopias and dystopias that depict single-sex societies, a tradition most recently appropriated by feminist writers to celebrate exclusively female societies. For an analysis of the strengths and weaknesses of such feminist utopian writing, in which female societies are reproduced by parthenogenesis, see my "On Feminist Utopias," *Women's Studies* (1982): 241–62. Leading examples of this genre include Charlotte Perkins Gilman's *Herland*, Sally Miller Gearhart's *The Wanderground*, Joanna Russ's *The Female Man*, James Tiptree, Jr.'s "Houston, Houston Do You Read?" and Suzy McKee Charnas's trilogy *The Vampire Tapestry*.

male inhabits the public sphere, the female is relegated to the private or domestic sphere.[4] The men in Frankenstein's world all work outside the home, as public servants (Alphonse Frankenstein), as scientists (Victor), as merchants (Clerval and his father), or as explorers (Walton). The women are confined to the home; Elizabeth, for instance, is not permitted to travel with Victor and "regretted that she had not the same opportunities of enlarging her experience and cultivating her understanding" (151). Inside the home, women are either kept as a kind of pet (Victor "loved to tend" on Elizabeth "as I should on a favorite animal" [p. 30]); or they work as house wives, childcare providers, and nurses (Caroline Beaufort Frankenstein, Elizabeth Lavenza, Margaret Saville) or as servants (Justine Moritz).

As a consequence of this sexual division of labor, masculine work is kept outside of the domestic realm; hence intellectual activity is segregated from emotional activity. Victor Frankenstein cannot do scientific research and think lovingly of Elizabeth and his family at the same time. His obsession with his experiment has caused him "to forget those friends who were so many miles absent, and whom I had not seen for so long a time" (p. 50). This separation of masculine work from the domestic affections leads directly to Frankenstein's downfall. Because Frankenstein cannot work and love at the same time, he fails to feel empathy for the creature he is constructing and callously makes him eight feet tall simply because "the minuteness of the parts formed a great hindrance to my speed" (p. 49). He then fails to love or feel any parental responsibility for the freak he has created. And he remains so fixated on himself that he cannot imagine his monster might threaten someone else when he swears to be with Victor "on his wedding-night."

This separation of the sphere of public (masculine) power from the sphere of private (feminine) affection also causes the destruction of many of the women in the novel. Caroline Beaufort dies unnecessarily

---

4. On the gender division of nineteenth-century European culture, see Jean Elshtain, *Public Man, Private Woman: Women in Social and Political Thought* (Oxford: Robertson, 1981); and *Victorian Women: A Documentary Account of Women's Lives in Nineteenth-Century England, France, and the United States,* ed. E. Hellerstein, L. Hume, and K. Offen (Stanford: Stanford University Press, 1981). For a study of sex roles in *Frankenstein,* see Kate Ellis, "Monsters in the Family: Mary Shelley and the Bourgeois Family," in *The Endurance of Frankenstein,* ed. George Levine and U. C. Knoepflmacher (Berkeley, Los Angeles, London: University of California Press, 1979), pp. 123–42; and Anca Vlasopolos, "*Frankenstein's* Hidden Skeleton: The Psycho-Politics of Oppression," *Science-Fiction Studies* 10 (1983): 125–36.

   William Veeder, in his insightful but occasionally reductive psychological study of Mary and Percy Shelley and *Frankenstein, Mary Shelley and Frankenstein: The Fate of Androgyny* (1986), wishes to define masculinity and femininity as the complementary halves of an ideally balanced androgynous or agapic personality that is destroyed or bifurcated by erotic self-love; his book traces the reasons why Mary Shelley's fictional characters realize or fail to achieve her androgynous ideal. While he is right to argue that Mary Shelley believed in balancing "masculine" and "feminine" characteristics, he consistently defines as innate psychological characteristics those patterns of learned behavior (masculinity, femininity) that I prefer to see as socially constructed gender roles. His readings thus unintentionally reinforce an oppressive biological determinism and sex-stereotyping, even as they call attention to the dangers of extreme masculine and feminine behaviors.

because she feels obligated to nurse her favorite Elizabeth during a smallpox epidemic; she thus incarnates a patriarchal ideal of female self-sacrifice (this suggestion is strengthened in the 1831 revisions where she eagerly risks her life to save Elizabeth). She is a woman who is devoted to her father in wealth and in poverty, who nurses him until his death, and then marries her father's best friend to whom she is equally devoted.

The division of public man from private woman also means that women cannot function effectively in the public realm. Despite her innocence of the crime for which she is accused, Justine Moritz is executed for the murder of William Frankenstein (and is even half-persuaded by her male confessor that she is responsible for William's death). And Elizabeth, fully convinced of Justine's innocence, is unable to save her: the impassioned defense she gives of Justine arouses public approbation of Elizabeth's generosity but does nothing to help Justine, "on whom the public indignation was turned with renewed violence, charging her with the blackest ingratitude" (p. 80). Nor can Elizabeth save herself on her wedding night. Both these deaths are of course directly attributable to Victor Frankenstein's self-devoted concern for his own suffering (the creature will attack only him) and his own reputation (people would think him mad if he told them his own monster had killed his brother).

Mary Shelley underlines the mutual deprivation inherent in a family and social structure based on rigid and hierarchical gender divisions by portraying an alternative social organization in the novel: the De Lacey family. The political situation of the De Lacey family, exiled from their native France by the manipulations of an ungrateful Turkish merchant and a draconian legal system, points up the injustice that prevails in a nation where masculine values of competition and chauvinism reign. Mary Shelley's political critique of a society founded on the unequal distribution of power and possessions is conveyed not only through the manifest injustice of Justine's execution and of France's treatment first of the alien Turkish merchant and then of the De Lacey family, but also through the readings in political history that she assigns to the creature. From Plutarch's *Parallel Lives of the Greeks and Romans* and from Volney's *Ruins, or Meditations on the Revolutions of Empires*, the creature learns both of masculine virtue and of masculine cruelty and injustice. "I heard of the division of property, of immense wealth and squalid poverty; . . . I learned that the possessions most esteemed . . . were high and unsullied descent united with riches" (p. 115). "Was man, indeed, at once so powerful, so virtuous, and magnificent, yet so vicious and base?" the creature asks incredulously. Implicit in Mary Shelley's attack on the social injustice of established political systems is the suggestion that the separation from the public realm of feminine affections and compassion has caused much of this social evil. Had

Elizabeth Lavenza's plea for mercy for Justine, based on her intuitively correct knowledge of Justine's character, been heeded, Justine would not have been wrongly murdered by the courts. As Elizabeth exclaims,

> how I hate [the] shews and mockeries [of this world]! when one creature is murdered, another is immediately deprived of life in a slow torturing manner; then the executioners, their hands yet reeking with the blood of innocence, believe that they have done a great deed. They call this *retribution*. Hateful name! when the word is pronounced, I know greater and more horrid punishments are going to be inflicted than the gloomiest tyrant has ever invented to satiate his utmost revenge. (p. 83)

In contrast to this pattern of political inequality and injustice, the De Lacey family represents an alternative ideology: a vision of a social group based on justice, equality, and mutual affection. Felix willingly sacrificed his own welfare to ensure that justice was done to the Turkish merchant. More important, the structure of the De Lacey family constitutes Mary Shelley's ideal, an ideal derived from her mother's *A Vindication of the Rights of Woman*. In the impoverished De Lacey household, all work is shared equally in an atmosphere of rational companionship, mutual concern, and love. As their symbolic names suggest, Felix embodies happiness, Agatha goodness. They are then joined by Safie (*sophia* or wisdom). Safie, the daughter of the Turkish merchant, is appalled both by her father's betrayal of Felix and by the Islamic oppression of women he endorses; she has therefore fled from Turkey to Switzerland, seeking Felix. Having reached the De Lacey household, she promptly becomes Felix's beloved companion and is taught to read and write French. Safie, whose Christian mother instructed her "to aspire to higher powers of intellect, and an independence of spirit, forbidden to the female followers of Mahomet" (p. 119), is the incarnation of Mary Wollstonecraft in the novel. Wollstonecraft too traveled alone through Europe and Scandinavia; more important, she advocated in *A Vindication* that women be educated to be the "companions" of men and be permitted to participate in the public realm by voting, working outside the home, and holding political office.

But this alternative female role-model of an independent, well-educated, self-supporting, and loving companion, and this alternative nuclear family structure based on sexual equality and mutual affection, is lost in the novel, perhaps because the De Lacey family lacks the mother who might have been able to welcome the pleading, pitiable creature. When Safie flees with the De Lacey family, we as readers are deprived of the novel's only alternative to a rigidly patriarchal construction of gender and sex roles, just as Mary Shelley herself was deprived of a feminist role-model when her mother died and was subsequently denounced in the popular British press as a harlot, atheist, and anarchist. Safie's disappearance from the novel reflects Mary Shelley's own predicament. Like Frankenstein's creature, she has no positive prototype she can imitate, no place in history. That unique phenomenon envisioned by Mary Wollstonecraft, the wife as the lifelong intellectual equal and companion of her husband, does not exist in the world of nineteenth-century Europe experienced by Mary Shelley.

The doctrine of the separate spheres that Victor Frankenstein endorses encodes a particular attitude to female sexuality that Mary Shelley subtly exposes in her novel. This attitude is manifested most vividly in Victor's response to the creature's request for a female companion, an Eve to comfort and embrace him. After hearing his creature's autobiographical account of his sufferings and aspirations, Frankenstein is moved by an awakened conscience to do justice toward his Adam and promises to create a female creature, on condition that both leave forever the neighborhood of mankind. After numerous delays, Frankenstein finally gathers the necessary instruments and materials together into an isolated cottage on one of the Orkney Islands off Scotland and proceeds to create a female being. Once again he becomes ill: "my heart often sickened at the work of my hands. . . . my spirits became unequal; I grew restless and nervous" (p. 162).

Disgusted by his enterprise, Frankenstein finally determines to stop his work, rationalizing his decision to deprive his creature of a female companion in terms that repay careful examination. Here is Frankenstein's meditation:

> I was now about to form another being, of whose dispositions I was alike ignorant; she might become ten thousand times more malignant than her mate, and delight, for its own sake, in murder and wretchedness. He had sworn to quit the neighborhood of man, and hide himself in deserts; but she had not; and she, who in all probability was to become a thinking and reasoning animal, might refuse to comply with a compact made before her creation. They might even hate each other; the creature who already lived loathed his own deformity, and might he not conceive a greater abhorrence for it when it came before his eyes in the female form? She also might turn with disgust from him to the superior beauty of man; she might quit him, and he be again alone, exasperated by the fresh provocation of being deserted by one of his own species.
>
> Even if they were to leave Europe, and inhabit the deserts of the new world, yet one of the first results of those sympathies for which the daemon thirsted would be children, and a race of devils would be propagated upon the earth, who might make the very existence of the species of man a condition precarious and full of terror. Had I a right, for my own benefit, to inflict this curse upon everlasting generations? . . . I shuddered to think that future ages might curse me as their pest, whose selfishness had not hesitated

to buy its own peace at the price perhaps of the existence of the whole human race. (p. 163)

What does Victor Frankenstein truly fear, which causes him to end his creation of a female? First, he is afraid of an independent female will, afraid that his female creature will have desires and opinions that cannot be controlled by his male creature. Like Rousseau's natural man, she might refuse to comply with a social contract made before her birth by another person; she might assert her own integrity and the revolutionary right to determine her own existence. Moreover, those uninhibited female desires might be sadistic: Frankenstein imagines a female "ten thousand times" more evil than her mate, who would "delight" in murder for its own sake. Third, he fears that his female creature will be more ugly than his male creature, so much so that even the male will turn from her in disgust. Fourth, he fears that she will prefer to mate with ordinary males; implicit here is Frankenstein's horror that, given the gigantic strength of this female, she would have the power to seize and even rape the male she might choose. And finally, he is afraid of her reproductive powers, her capacity to generate an entire race of similar creatures. What Victor Frankenstein truly fears is female sexuality as such. A woman who is sexually liberated, free to choose her own life, her own sexual partner (by force, if necessary), and to propagate at will can appear only monstrously ugly to Victor Frankenstein, for she defies that sexist aesthetic that insists that women be small, delicate, modest, passive, and sexually pleasing—but available only to their lawful husbands.

Horrified by this image of uninhibited female sexuality, Victor Frankenstein violently reasserts a male control over the female body, penetrating and mutilating the female creature at his feet in an image that suggests a violent rape: "trembling with passion, [I] tore to pieces the thing on which I was engaged" (p. 164). The morning after, when he returns to the scene, "The remains of the half-finished creature, whom I had destroyed, lay scattered on the floor, and I almost felt as if I had mangled the living flesh of a human being" (p. 167). However he has rationalized his decision to murder the female creature, Frankenstein's "passion" is here revealed as a fusion of fear, lust, and hostility, a desire to control and even destroy female sexuality.

Frankenstein's fear of female sexuality is endemic to a patriarchal construction of gender. Uninhibited female sexual experience threatens the very foundation of patriarchal power: the establishment of patrilineal kinship networks together with the transmission of both status and property by inheritance entailed upon a male line. Significantly, in the patriarchal world of Geneva in the novel, female sexuality is strikingly repressed. All the women are presented as sexless: Caroline Beaufort is a devoted daughter and chaste wife while Elizabeth Lavenza's relationship with Victor is that of a sister.

In this context, the murder of Elizabeth Lavenza on her wedding night becomes doubly significant. The scene of her death is based on a painting Mary Shelley knew well, Henry Fuseli's famous "The Nightmare." The corpse of Elizabeth lies in the very attitude in which Fuseli placed his succubus-ridden woman: "She was there, lifeless and inanimate, thrown across the bed, her head hanging down, and her pale and distorted features half covered by her hair" (p. 193). Fuseli's woman is an image of female erotic desire, both lusting for and frightened of the incubus (or male demon) that rides upon her, brought to her bedchamber by the stallion that leers at her from the foot of her bed; both the presence of this incubus and the woman's posture of open sexual acceptance leave Fuseli's intentions in no doubt.[5] Evoking this image, Mary Shelley alerted us to what Victor fears most: his bride's sexuality.[6] Significantly, Elizabeth would not have been killed had Victor not sent her into their wedding bedroom *alone*. Returning to the body of the murdered Elizabeth, Victor "embraced her with ardour; but the deathly languor and coldness of the limbs told me, that what I now held in my arms had ceased to be the Elizabeth whom I had loved and cherished" (p. 193). Victor most ardently desires his bride when he knows she is dead; the conflation with his earlier dream, when he thought to embrace the living Elizabeth but instead held in his arms the corpse of his mother, signals Victor's most profound erotic desire, a necrophiliac and incestuous desire to possess the dead female, the lost mother.

To put this point another way, we might observe that Victor Frankenstein's most passionate relationships are with men rather than with women. He sees Clerval as "the image of my former self" (p. 155), as his "friend and dearest companion" (p. 181), as his true soul mate. His

5. Henry Fuseli, *The Nightmare*, first version, 1781; The Detroit Institute of Art. This famous painting was widely reproduced throughout the early nineteenth century and was of particular interest to Mary Shelley, who knew of her mother's early passionate love for Fuseli. H. W. Janson has suggested that Fuseli's representation of the nightmare is a projection of his unfulfilled passion for Anna Landolt, whose portrait is drawn on the reverse side (H. W. Janson, "Fuseli's *Nightmare*," *Arts and Sciences* 2 [1963]: 23–28). When Fuseli learned that Anna Landolt had married, he wrote to her uncle and his good friend Johann Lavater from London on 16 June 1779 that he had dreamed of lying in her bed and fusing "her body and soul" together with his own. Fuseli's painting is thus a deliberate allusion to traditional images of Cupid and Psyche meeting in her bedroom at night; here the welcomed god of love has been transformed into a demonic incubus of erotic lust (see also Peter Tomory, *The Life and Art of Henry Fuseli*, London: 1972, pp. 92ff.; and the Catalogue Raisonnée by Gert Schiff, *Johann Heinrich Fussli*, Zurich: 1973, pp. 757–59).

   Gerhard Joseph first noted the allusion to Fuseli's painting, "Frankenstein's Dream: The Child Is Father of the Monster," *Hartford Studies in Literature* 7 (1975): 97–115, 109. William Veeder denies the association (*Mary Shelley and Frankenstein*, 192–93) on the grounds that Elizabeth's hair half-covers her face; in this regard, it may be significant that Fuseli's woman's face is half-covered in shadow.
6. Paul A. Cantor has discussed Frankenstein's rejections both of normal sexuality and of the bourgeois lifestyle, in *Creature and Creator: Myth-making and English Romanticism* (New York: Cambridge University Press, 1984), pp. 109–15.

description of Clerval's haunting eyes — "languishing in death, the dark orbs covered by the lids, and the long black lashes that fringed them" (p. 179) — verges on the erotic. Similarly, Walton responds to Frankenstein with an ardor that borders on the homoerotic. Having desired "the company of a man who could sympathize with me; whose eyes would reply to mine" (p. 13), Walton eagerly embraces Frankenstein as "a celestial spirit" (p. 23) whose death leaves him inarticulate with grief: "what can I say," Walton writes to his sister, "that will enable you to understand the depth of my sorrow?" (p. 216). Finally, Frankenstein dedicates himself to his scientific experiment with a passion that can be described only as erotic: as Mary Shelley originally described Frankenstein's obsession, "I wished, as it were, to procrastinate my feelings of affection, until the great object of my affection was compleated." Frankenstein's homoerotic fixation upon his creature, whose features he had selected as "beautiful" (p. 52) in a parody of Pygmalion and Galatea, was underlined by Mary Shelley in a revision she made in the Thomas copy of *Frankenstein*. Describing his anxious enslavement to his task, Frankenstein confesses: "my voice became broken, my trembling hands almost refused to accomplish their task; I became as timid as a lovesick girl, and alternate tremor and passionate ardour took the place of wholesome sensation and regulated ambition" (51:31–35). In place of a normal heterosexual attachment to Elizabeth, Victor Frankenstein has substituted a homosexual obsession with his creature,[7] an obsession that in his case is energized by a profound desire to reunite with his dead mother, by becoming himself a mother.

To sum up, at every level Victor Frankenstein is engaged upon a rape of nature, a violent penetration and usurpation of the female's "hiding places," of the womb. Terrified of female sexuality and the power of human reproduction it enables, both he and the patriarchal society he represents use the technologies of science and the laws of the polis to manipulate, control, and repress women. Thinking back on Elizabeth Lavenza strangled on her bridal bier and on Fuseli's image of female erotic desire that she replicates, we can now see that at this level Victor's creature, his monster, realizes his own most potent lust. The monster, like Fuseli's incubus, leers over Elizabeth, enacting Victor's own repressed desire to rape, possess, and destroy the female. Vic-

---

7. William Veeder has emphasized the homosexual bond between Frankenstein and his monster (*Mary Shelley and Frankenstein*, pp. 89–92). Eve Kosofsky Sedgwick arrives at this conclusion from a different direction. In her *Between Men: English Literature and Male Homosocial Desire* (New York: Columbia University Press, 1985), she observes in passing that *Frankenstein*, like William Godwin's *Caleb Williams*, is "about one or more males who not only is persecuted by, but considers himself transparent to and often under the compulsion of, another male. If we follow Freud [in the case of Dr. Schreber] in hypothesizing that such a sense of persecution represents the fearful, phantasmic rejection by recasting of an original homosexual (or even merely homosocial) desire, then it would make sense to think of this group of novels as embodying strongly homophobic mechanisms" (pp. 91–92).

tor's creature here becomes just that, his "creature," the instrument of his most potent desire: to destroy female reproductive power so that only men may rule.

However, in Mary Shelley's feminist novel, Victor Frankenstein's desire is portrayed not only as horrible and finally unattainable but also as self-destructive. For Nature is not the passive, inert, or "dead" matter that Frankenstein imagines.[8] Frankenstein assumes that he can violate Nature and pursue her to her hiding places with impunity. But Nature both resists and revenges herself upon his attempts. During his research, Nature denies to Victor Frankenstein both mental and physical health: "my enthusiasm was checked by my anxiety, and I appeared rather like one doomed by slavery to toil in the mines, or any other unwholesome trade, than an artist occupied by his favourite employment. Every night I was oppressed by a slow fever, and I became nervous to a most painful degree" (p. 51). When his experiment is completed, Victor has a fit that renders him "lifeless" for "a long, long time" and that marks the onset of a "nervous fever" that confines him for many months (p. 57). Victor continues to be tormented by anxiety attacks, bouts of delirium, periods of distraction and madness. As soon as he determines to blaspheme against Nature a second time, by creating a female human being, Nature punishes him: "the eternal twinkling of the stars weighed upon me, and . . . I listened to every blast of wind, as if it were a dull ugly siroc on its way to consume me" (p. 145). His mental illness returns: "Every thought that was devoted to it was an extreme anguish, and every word that I spoke in allusion to it caused my lips to quiver and my heart to palpitate" (p. 156); "my spirits became unequal; I grew restless and nervous" (p. 162). Finally, Frankenstein's obsession with destroying his creature exposes him to such mental and physical fatigue that he dies at the age of twenty-five.

Appropriately, Nature prevents Frankenstein from constructing a normal human being: an unnatural method of reproduction produces an unnatural being, in this case a freak of gigantic stature, watery eyes, a shriveled complexion, and straight black lips. This physiognomy causes Frankenstein's instinctive withdrawal from his child, and sets in motion the series of events that produces the monster who destroys Frankenstein's family, friends, and self.

Moreover, Nature pursues Victor Frankenstein with the very electricity he has stolen: lightning, thunder, and rain rage around him. The November night on which he steals the "spark of being" from Nature is dreary, dismal, and wet: "the rain . . . poured from a black and comfortless sky" (p. 54). He next glimpses his creature during a flash

---

8. While I largely agree with Mary Poovey's intelligent and sensitive analysis of Frankenstein's egotistic desire (in *The Proper Lady and the Woman Writer*, pp. 123–33), I do not share her view that the nature we see in the novel is "fatal to human beings and human relationships." Poovey fails to distinguish between Frankenstein's view of nature and the author's and between the first and third editions of the novel in this regard.

of lightning as a violent storm plays over his head at Plainpalais (p. 71); significantly, the almighty Alps, and in particular Mont Blanc, are represented in this novel as female, as an image of omnipotent fertility[9] — on his wedding day, Victor admires "the beautiful Mont Blanc, and the assemblage of snowy mountains that in vain endeavour to emulate *her*" (p. 190; my italics). Before Frankenstein's first encounter with his creature among the Alps, "the rain poured down in torrents, and thick mists hid the summits of the mountains" (p. 91). Setting sail from the Orkney island where he has destroyed his female creature, planning to throw her mangled remains into the sea, Frankenstein wakes to find his skiff threatened by a fierce wind and high waves that portend his own death: "I might be driven into the wide Atlantic, and feel all the tortures of starvation, or be swallowed up in the immeasurable waters that roared and buffetted around me. I . . . felt the torment of a burning thirst; . . . I looked upon the sea, it was to be my grave" (p. 169). Frankenstein ends his life and his pursuit of the monster he has made in the arctic regions, surrounded by the aurora borealis, the electromagnetic field of the North Pole. The atmospheric effects of the novel, which most readers have dismissed as little more than the traditional trappings of Gothic fiction, in fact manifest the power of Nature to punish those who transgress her boundaries. The elemental forces that Victor has released pursue him to his hiding places, raging round him like avenging Furies.

Finally, Nature punishes Victor Frankenstein the life-stealer most justly by denying him the capacity for natural procreation. His bride is killed on their wedding night, cutting off his chance to engender his own children. His creature — that "great object, which swallowed up every habit of my nature" (50) — turns against him, destroying not only his brother William, his soul mate Clerval, his loyal servant Justine, his grief-stricken father, and his wife, but finally pursuing Victor himself to his death, leaving Frankenstein entirely without progeny. Nature's revenge is absolute: he who violates her sacred hiding places is destroyed.

Mary Shelley's novel thus portrays the penalties of raping Nature. But it also celebrates an all-creating Nature loved and revered by human beings. Those characters capable of deeply feeling the beauties of Nature are rewarded with physical and mental health. Even Frankenstein in his moments of tranquillity or youthful innocence can respond powerfully to the glory of Nature. As Walton notes, "the starry sky, the sea, and every sight afforded by these wonderful regions, seems still to have the power of elevating his soul from earth" (p. 23). In Clerval's company Victor becomes again

9. On Mary Shelley's subversive representation of the traditionally masculinized Alps as female, see Fred V. Randel, "*Frankenstein*, Feminism, and the Intertextuality of Mountains," *Studies in Romanticism* 23 (Winter, 1984): 515–33.

the same happy creature who, a few years ago, loving and beloved by all, had no sorrow or care. When happy, inanimate nature had the power of bestowing on me the most delightful sensations. A serene sky and verdant fields filled me with ecstasy. (p. 65)

Clerval's relationship to Nature represents one moral touchstone of the novel: since he "loved with ardour . . . the scenery of external nature" (p. 154), Nature endows him with a generous sympathy, a vivid imagination, a sensitive intelligence and an unbounded capacity for devoted friendship. His death annihilates the possibility that Victor Frankenstein might regain a positive relationship with Nature.

Mary Shelley envisions Nature as a sacred life-force in which human beings ought to participate in conscious harmony. Elizabeth Lavenza gives voice to this ideal in her choice of profession for Ernest Frankenstein:

I proposed that he should be a farmer. . . . A farmer's is a very healthy happy life; and the least hurtful, or rather the most beneficial profession of any. My uncle [wanted him] educated as an advocate . . . but . . . it is certainly more creditable to cultivate the earth for the sustenance of man, than to be the confidant, and sometimes the accomplice, of his vices. (p. 59)

Nature nurtures those who cultivate her; perhaps this is why, of all the members of Frankenstein's family, only Ernest survives. Mary Shelley shares Wordsworth's concept of a beneficial bond between the natural and the human world, which is broken only at man's peril. Had Victor Frankenstein's eyes not become "insensible to the charms of nature" (p. 50) and the affections of family and friends, he would not have defied Mary Shelley's moral credo:

A human being in perfection ought always to preserve a calm and peaceful mind, and never to allow passion or a transitory desire to disturb his tranquillity. I do not think that the pursuit of knowledge is an exception to this rule. If the study to which you apply yourself has a tendency to weaken your affections, and to destroy your taste for those simple pleasures in which no alloy can possibly mix [e.g., the "beautiful season"], then that study is certainly unlawful, that is to say, not befitting the human mind. (p. 51)

As an ecological system of interdependent organisms, Nature requires the submission of the individual ego to the welfare of the family and the larger community. Like George Eliot after her, Mary Shelley is profoundly committed to an ethic of cooperation, mutual dependence, and self-sacrifice. The Russian sea-master willingly sacrifices his own desires that his beloved and her lover may marry; Clerval immediately gives up his desire to attend university in order to nurse his dear friend Victor back to health; Elizabeth offers to release her beloved Victor from his engagement should he now love another. Mary Shelley's moral vision thus falls into that category of ethical thinking which Carol Gilligan has recently identified as more typically female than male. Where men have tended to identify moral laws as abstract principles that clearly differentiate right from wrong, women have tended to see moral choice as imbedded in an ongoing shared life. As Gilligan contrasts them, a male "ethic of justice proceeds from the premise of equality — that everyone should be treated the same" while a female "ethic of care rests on the premise of nonviolence — that no one should be hurt."[1] This traditional female morality can probably be traced to what Nancy Chodorow and Dorothy Dinnerstein have shown to be the daughter's greater identification with the mother.[2] Whereas the son has learned to assert his separateness from the mother (and the process of mothering), the daughter has learned to represent that gendered role and thus has felt more tightly (and ambivalently) bound to the mother. Less certain of her ego boundaries, the daughter has been more likely to engage in moral thinking which gives priority to the good of the family and the community rather than to the rights of the individual.

Insofar as the family is the basic social unit, it has historically represented the system of morality practiced by the culture at large. The hierarchical structure of the Frankenstein family embodies a masculine ethic of justice in which the rights of the individual are privileged: Frankenstein pursues his own interests in alchemy and chemistry, cheerfully ignoring his family obligations as he engages "heart and soul" in his research, and is moreover encouraged to leave his family and fiancée for two years ("for a more indulgent and less dictatorial parent did not exist upon earth" [p. 130]). In contrast, the egalitarian and interdependent structure of the De Lacey family ideologically encodes a female ethic of care in which the bonding of the family unit is primary. Felix blames himself most because his self-sacrificing action on behalf of the Turkish merchant involved his family in his suffering. Agatha and Felix perform toward their father "every little office of affection and duty with gentleness; and he rewarded them by his benevolent smiles"; they willingly starve themselves that their father may eat (106). Safie's arrival particularly delighted Felix but also "diffused gladness through the cottage, dispelling their sorrow as the sun dissipates the morning mists" (112). In portraying the De Laceys as an archetype of the egalitarian, benevolent, and mutually loving nuclear family, Mary Shelley clearly displayed her own moral purpose, which Percy Shelley

1. Carol Gilligan, *In a Different Voice: Psychological Theory and Women's Development* (Cambridge, Mass: Harvard University Press, 1982), p. 174.
2. See Nancy Chodorow, *The Reproduction of Mothering: Psychoanalysis and the Sociology of Gender* (Berkeley and Los Angeles: University of California Press, 1978); Dorothy Dinnerstein, *The Mermaid and the Minotaur: Sexual Arrangements and Human Malaise* (New York: Harper and Row, 1976); cf. Nancy Friday, *My Mother/My Self: The Daughter's Search for Identity* (New York: Dell, 1977).

rightly if somewhat vaguely described in his Preface as "the exhibition of the amiableness of domestic affection, and the excellence of universal virtue" (7).

Mary Shelley's grounding of moral virtue in the preservation of familial bonds (against which Frankenstein, in his failure to parent his own child, entirely transgresses) entails an aesthetic credo as well. While such romantic descendants as Walter Pater and Oscar Wilde would later argue that aesthetics and morality, art and life, are distinct, Mary Shelley endorsed a traditional mimetic aesthetic that exhorted literature to imitate ideal Nature and defined the role of the writer as a moral educator. Her novel purposefully identifies moral virtue, based on self-sacrifice, moderation, and domestic affection, with aesthetic beauty. Even in poverty, the image of the blind old man listening to the sweetly singing Agatha is "a lovely sight, even to me, poor wretch! who had never beheld aught beautiful before" (103). In contrast, Frankenstein's and Walton's dream of breaking boundaries is explicitly identified as both evil and ugly. As Walton acknowledges, "my day dreams are . . . extended and magnificent; but they want (as the painters call it) *keeping*" (p. 14). "Keeping," in painting, means "the maintenance of the proper relation between the representations of nearer and more distant objects in a picture"; hence, in a more general sense, "the proper subserviency of tone and colour in every part of a picture, so that the general effect is harmonious to the eye" (*OED*). Walton thus introduces Mary Shelley's ethical norm as an aesthetic norm; both in life and in art, her ideal is a balance or golden mean between conflicting demands, specifically here between large and small objects. In ethical terms, this means that Walton must balance his dreams of geographical discovery and fame against the reality of an already existing set of obligations (to his family, his crew, and the sacredness of Nature). Similarly, Frankenstein should have better balanced the obligations of great and small, of parent and child, of creator and creature. Frankenstein's failure to maintain *keeping*, to preserve "a calm and peaceful mind" (p. 51), is thus in Mary Shelley's eyes both a moral and an aesthetic failure, resulting directly in the creation of a hideous monster.

SUSAN WINNETT

Coming Unstrung: Women, Men, Narrative, and Principles of Pleasure†

Here are two sides, and only half the argument.
Athena, in The Eumenides

I would like to begin with the proposition that female orgasm is un-necessary. I am not, of course, saying that it is unnecessary to any particular woman that she experience orgasm or, for that matter, to any particular man that his female partner do so; rather, I mean that wom-en's orgasm and, by extension, women's pleasure can be extraneous to that culmination of heterosexual desire which is copulation. Women's pleasure can take place outside, or independent of, the male sexual economy whose pulsations determine the dominant culture, its repres-sions, its taboos, and its narratives, as well as the "human sciences" developed to explain them. Considering the last decade's preoccupa-tions with sexual difference and the pleasure of the text, it is surprising that theories concerned with the relation between narrative and pleas-ure have largely neglected to raise the issue of the difference between women's and men's reading pleasures. But this question seems to re-quire critical tools that, for reasons I explore in this essay, have not been available. Indeed, the same analytic paradigms that give us pro-fessional access to texts have already determined the terms in which we accede to, comply with, or resist the coercions of a cultural program for pleasure that is not interested in—and whose interests may be threatened by—the difference of women's pleasure. If this paper does no more than get us as far as the giddy brink of an alternative to this cultural program, it will, I hope, suggest the magnitude of the resis-tances to this alternative as well as possible strategies for engaging them.

I

But, first, let us return to the question of orgasm. We all know what male orgasm looks like. It is preceded by a visible "awakening, an arousal, the birth of an appetency, ambition, desire or intention." The male organ registers the intensity of this stimulation, rising to the oc-casion of its provocation, becoming at once the means of pleasure and culture's sign of power. This energy, "aroused into expectancy," takes its course toward "significant discharge" and shrinks into a state of qui-

† From *PMLA* (1990) 505–12, 515–16. Reprinted with permission of the Modern Language Association of America.

escence (or satisfaction) that, minutes before, would have been a sign
of impotence. The man must have this genital response before he can
participate, which means that something in the time before intercourse
must have aroused him. And his participation generally ceases with the
ejaculation that signals the end of his arousal. The myth of the
afterglow — so often a euphemism for sleep — seems a compensation for
the finality he has reached.

Before I proceed to hypothesize the pleasure of his female mate, I
must account for the quotation marks in the previous paragraph. The
words used to describe the trajectory of male arousal ("awakening, an
arousal, the birth of an appetency, ambition, desire or intention" on
the one hand and "significant discharge" on the other) are taken from
Peter Brooks's influential "Freud's Masterplot" (*Reading* 90–112),
which examines the relation between Freud's plotting of the life trajectory in *Beyond the Pleasure Principle* and the dynamics of beginnings,
middles, and ends in traditional narrative. Brooks's articulation of what
are ultimately the oedipal dynamics that structure and determine traditional fictional narratives and psychoanalytic paradigms is brilliant,
and it reminds us, in case we had forgotten, what men want, how they
go about trying to get it, and the stories they tell about this pursuit. But
it seems clear that a narratology based on the oedipal model would
have to be profoundly and vulnerably male in its assumptions about
what constitutes pleasure and, more insidiously, what this pleasure looks
like; even Freud was troubled by his theory's inadequate explanation of
female experience. Yet the gender bias of contemporary narratology
seems not to have troubled our profession's most prominent practition-
ers of narrative theory and advocates of textual pleasure. Is it that the
assumptions about narrative theory and the pleasure of the text that
seem obvious to me are somehow not available to them? If they were
conscious that the narrative dynamics and the erotics of reading they
were expounding were specifically tied to an ideology of representation
derivable only from the dynamics of male sexuality, would they not at
least feel uncomfortable making general statements about "narrative,"
"pleasure," and "us"?

When I came upon the following passage — thanks to Teresa de-
Lauretis, who cites it in *Alice Doesn't* — I realized that the problem was
not that the narratologists were blind but that I was naive. In "The
Orgastic Pattern of Fiction," Robert Scholes writes:

> The archetype of all fiction is the sexual act. In saying this I do
> not mean merely to remind the reader of the connection between
> all art and the erotic in human nature. . . . For what connects
> fiction — and music — with sex is the fundamental orgastic rhythm
> of tumescence and detumescence, of tension and resolution, of
> intensification to the point of climax and consummation. In the

sophisticated forms of fiction, as in the sophisticated practice of
sex, much of the art consists of delaying climax within the framework of desire in order to prolong the pleasurable act itself.

(Scholes, *Fabulation* 26; deLauretis 108)

It comes as no surprise that Scholes, after reminding us that all fictional
romance conforms to this model, crowns the novel as the "high art"
manifestation of this universal pattern and claims for that genre the task
of adapting the " 'low atavistic' form, the orgastic story, to the job of
spreading the news, telling the truth about man in society" (27). A
refresher course in the fundamentals of structuralism should suffice to
remind us that the "erotic in human nature" has to be understood
within its various determining contexts if the concept is to be productive
(what is "the erotic"? how do we define the "human nature" in which
we locate "the erotic"? is "human nature" a cultural ["human"] or a
biological ["nature"] construct?). And even if we have become wary of
the generic "man in society," we still might need to be reminded that
such generalizations in such contexts indicate that the pleasure the
reader is expected to take in the text is the pleasure of the man. This
would seem to be true even when — as [Italo] Calvino's great novel of
reading, *If on a winter's night a traveler,* suggests — the pleasure of the
(projected) male author (or his surrogate, the critic) is heightened by
the fantasy that the reader is a woman. Scholes continues:

> Like the sexual act, the act of fiction is a reciprocal relationship.
> It takes two. Granted, a writer can write for *his* own amusement,
> and a reader can read in the same way [note the finesse with which
> the male generic is suspended here]; but these are acts of mental
> masturbation, with all the limitations that are involved in narcis-
> sistic gratification of the self. . . . The meaning of the fictional act
> itself is something like love. The writer, at *his* best, respects the
> dignity of the reader. . . . (27; my emphasis)

Figures, of course, will insist on their own economies, and it is not
long before Scholes's reader becomes a man, and the act of pleasure
becomes, despite the orgastic language of his foreplay, a "marriage of
true minds," a platonized, legalized, entirely male circuit of desire:

> The reader . . . respects the dignity of the writer. He does not
> simply try to take *his* pleasure and *his* meaning from the book. He
> strives to mate with the writer, to share the writer's viewpoint, to
> come fully to terms with the sensibility and intelligence that have
> informed this particular work of fiction. When writer and reader
> make a "marriage of true minds," the act of fiction is perfect and
> complete. (27; *his* emphasis)

I doubt that Scholes is conscious of or celebrating the profound
homoerotic — or homoaesthetic — subtext in these passages, although its

emergence in his discussion precisely at the moment when he articulates the relation between his reading and sexual pleasures might explain why the issue of women's reading pleasure has not attracted the attention it should: for the male critic, the sexual pleasure of reading would seem to take place within a nexus of homosocial arrangements in which "the marriage of true minds" is an affair "between men," as Eve Sedgwick has put it. In this system, woman is neither an independent subjectivity nor a desiring agent but, rather, an enabling position organizing the social fiction of heterosexuality. In its honest outrageousness, Scholes's erotics of reading makes clearer than does Brooks's more subtle articulation that the patriarchy has a simultaneously blind and enlightened investment both in the forms of its pleasure and in its conscious valorization and less conscious mystification of them.[1] And this realization does nothing but make it all the more frightening to contemplate the obstacles our own education has placed in the way both of women's conceiving (of) their own pleasure and of men's conceding that female pleasure might have a different plot.

For if we do now pursue the analogy between the representability of the sex act and a possible erotics of reading, we find a woman's encounter with the text determined by a broad range of options for pleasure that have *nothing to do* (or can choose to have nothing to do) with the notions of representability crucial to the narratologies of Brooks, Scholes, and, I dare say, others. I might point out, however, that it is exactly what I see as a potentially — but not necessarily — liberating relation to representability that has allowed the entire issue of female pleasure to go unacknowledged or to be entirely misconstrued for as long as it has. Everything that the last two decades have taught us about human sexual response suggests that the female partner in intercourse has accesses to pleasure not open to her male partner. It is, of course, a commonplace that she can fake pleasure. But she can also (like Mme de Merteuil in Laclos's *Les liaisons dangereuses*) fake frigidity. Without endangering her partner's ultimate "success," she can begin her own arousal at whatever point in the intercourse her fantasy finds exciting. She can even take as her point of arousal the attained satisfaction of

1. This is the place to acknowledge Scholes's subsequent engagement with feminism; his "Reading like a Man" shows that he has paid careful attention to the feminist revolution in his field: "More than any other critical approach feminism has forced us to see the folly of thinking about reading in terms of a transcendental subject: the ideal reader reading a text that is the same for all" (206). It is interesting to note the continuities in his practice: "reading like a man," he still prefers to articulate his (feminist) position in dialogue with a man (Jonathan Culler). This approach is certainly preferable to trashing female feminists. Yet a question remains: Does such a dialogue place the question of feminism in the "traditional position of women in patriarchy — the ultimately expendable item of exchange that merely gets the conversation going" (Boone 170), or can it be seen as a welcome response to Alice Jardine's suggestions that men "read women's writing — write on it and teach it . . . recognize [their] debts to feminism in writing . . . critique [their] male colleagues on the issue of feminism" (60–61)?

her mate. Without defying the conventions dictating that sex be experienced more or less together, she can begin and end her pleasure according to a logic of fantasy and arousal that is totally unrelated to the functioning and representation of the "conventional" heterosexual sex act. Moreover, she can do so again. Immediately. And, we are told, again after that.

While the reader completes or continues this fantasy as desired, I would like to review how pleasure is defined and generated in Brooks's version of Freud's "Masterplot," a scheme that has no place for such "unruly" sexual dynamics as the ones I have just sketched. According to Brooks, Freud's discussion of the pleasure principle charts the route an organism takes when, stimulated out of quiescence, it strives to regain equilibrium by finding the appropriate means of discharging the energy invested in it. According to this scheme, desire would be, even at its inception, a desire for the end; birth (the moment at which the organism begins to dispose of its energies) would be evaluated proleptically through the significance it acquires in the light of the death that consummates and totalizes the life history. And pleasure would involve the recognitions and reproductions of the dynamics "of ends in relation to beginnings and the forces that animate the middle in between" (Brooks, *Reading* 299). In short, the pleasure principle seeks to overcome birth, to attain the quiescence that preceded the organism's delivery onto the stage of life. We remember, for example, how Mary Shelley describes the coming to life of Frankenstein's Monster, the moment when a being composed of inanimate matter assembled, significantly, from pieces of dead bodies — receives the dangerous spark of life: "I saw the dull yellow eyes of the creature open, it breathed hard, and a convulsive motion agitated its limbs" (56). The *Masterplot* of the novel would, according to the pleasure principle, be the chain of events that restores the creature to death while accounting for all the significances of its having come to life.

II

But just as *Frankenstein* does not get the Monster quite dead, it also seems not to account satisfactorily for all the significances that can be attributed to the creature's life. We need only to consider the kinds of major questions the novel raises to realize how successfully it avoids resolving any one of them.[2] This lack of resolution is often attributed to the young author's lack of skill, her inability, for all her imagination,

2. George Levine, for instance, writes, "[T]he text announces clearly . . . the terms of our modern crises," and goes on to discuss the "seven elements of the Frankenstein metaphor": "Birth and Creation"; "The Overreacher"; "Rebellion and Moral Isolation"; "The Unjust Society"; "The Defects of Domesticity"; "The Double"; "Technology, Entropy, and the Monstrous" (3–16).

to write a coherent plot (Rieger xxiv). And indeed, *Frankenstein's* narrative dynamics are not at all well explained by analogy with the pleasure principle, although both the problem of this model and its underlying oedipal scenario might be regarded as among the novel's most important thematic concerns. In its mise-en-scène of the fantasy of the pleasure principle, *Frankenstein* dramatizes the monstrosity of the relation the Freudian scheme posits between beginnings and endings; the detours and repetitions that a Freudian narratology would associate with the bindings (and sublimations) of life energy toward appropriate resolution pose and repose a question that traditional narrative is not plotted to answer.

I have been arguing that male narratology conceptualizes narrative dynamics in terms of an experience it so swiftly and seamlessly generalizes that we tend to forget that it has its source in experience — in fact, in experience of the body. Although I have stressed male and female sexualities' different relations to representability, I of course do not think that textual production and narrative dynamics are matters of sexuality alone; nor do I mean to trivialize Brooks's work by emphasizing its dependence on a physiological model. Yet this demonstration enables us to speculate about how another set of experiences might yield another set of generalizations, another theory as vulnerable to the introduction of a counterexample as the Masterplot itself. I would like to explore what would happen if, having recognized the Masterplot's reliance on male morphology and male experience, we retained the general narrative pattern of tension and resolution ("tumescence and detumescence," "arousal and significant discharge") and simply substituted for the male experience an analogously representable female one. I do not propose the hypothetical model that follows as *the* alternative to what I have called male narratology — indeed, it does not even hold up as a model for all "female" narrative. Rather, I see it as *an* alternative that, however useful in explaining *Frankenstein* (and perhaps other texts), is ultimately more valuable for its relativizing function than as a scheme competing for authority with the Masterplot. The existence of two models implies to me the possibility of many more; neither the schemes I am criticizing nor the one I develop here exhausts the possibilities offered by the psychoanalytic model.[3] Work, class, law, politics, ambition, domination, power, and geography — issues that involve gender but not necessarily sexuality — represent compelling and theoretically productive motivations for narrative outside a psychoanalytic

---

3. Leo Bersani's work represents a compelling reading of Freud in relation to questions of narrative dynamics. Edward Said's language often resembles Brooks's, although Said examines "incipience" within a broader philosophical context. Among the numerous excellent book-length feminist studies of the nineteenth-century novel, Margaret Homans's and Marianne Hirsch's invoke a specifically feminist psychoanalysis that, whatever its debts to traditional psychoanalysis, focuses on other experiences and relations.

paradigm that sees them as dramatizations of sexual drives (see, e.g., Beer, *Darwin's Plots*; Chambers; Gates; Jameson; and D. A. Miller).

Any narrative model can be shown to privilege a particular explanatory paradigm and thereby a particular thematics. Yet if my model, based on uniquely female experience, is to represent only a shift in *thematic* emphasis, we will not be meeting the Masterplot on the terrain it has staked out for itself—that of form. We will have to return to an examination of how the distinction between form and theme is drawn. First, I want to explore the different narrative logic—and the very different possibilities of pleasure—that emerge when issues such as incipience, repetition, and closure are reconceived in terms of *an* experience (not *the* experience) of the female body.

Female experience does indeed include two highly representable instances of "tumescence and detumescence," of "arousal and significant discharge," whose very issue might suggest why they have been ignored in conceptualizations of narrative dynamics.[4] Both birth and breast feeding manifest dynamic patterns not unlike those described in the various orgastic sequences I cite above. Yet because they do not culminate in a quiescence that can bearably be conceptualized as a simulacrum of death, they neither need nor can confer on themselves the kind of retrospective significance attained by analogy with the pleasure principle. Indeed, as sense-making operations, both are radically *prospective*, full of the incipience that the male model will see resolved in its images of detumescence and discharge. Their ends (in both senses of the word) are, quite literally, beginning itself. With this change of focus, the "middle" and its repetitions too must be conceptualized anew. Breast feeding involves much repetition without, I am told, all that much difference. Furthermore, it is stimulated by the demand of a very dependent other rather than by one's own desire. And its pleasure—which, I hear, is considerable—may well be why women keep doing it, but not why they are encouraged to.

Both breast feeding and birth involve the potentially—but not necessarily—satisfying presence of an other, and not simply the other who makes intercourse perhaps more gratifying than, but not essentially different from, masturbation. Now a woman whose mothering of this other was governed by an acute awareness of "ends in relation to beginnings" or, for that matter, beginnings in relation to ends would probably be both depressed and inefficient, whereas a man whose awareness of the logic of the pleasure principle inspired him to perfect his foreplay would be considered both a wise man and a good lover. We seem to

---

4. I am grateful to Susan Stanford Friedman for calling my attention to these issues, which my own lack of experience made me overlook in earlier versions of this paper. Further thanks to Marilyn Fries, Carolyn Heilbrun, Marianne Hirsch, Heidi Kruger, and Elaine Winnett, who have lent the authority of their experience to my subsequent attempts to do justice to the subject.

have arrived at a crucial asymmetry in our analogy. While the male scheme fantasizes a scene of coupling, it then privileges a simultaneity of sensation and representability that is appropriate to one partner only (assuming, of course, that we are still talking about a heterosexual couple). In neither of the scenes of female experience in which a bodily part gets visibly larger and then smaller again can we fail to recognize that these changes are governed by the will, desire, and rhythms of another human being. The woman's will or desire may play a role in these processes, but it need not. A pregnancy may be willed (the result of reproductive lovemaking) or not (the result of rape or defective contraception); the onset of birth, too, is out of the mother's conscious control, unless one regards a representative of the medical profession and its chemical apparatus as an extension of her control; and a mother whose baby is asleep or sated is going to have trouble satisfying a desire to nurse it. Most important for our narratological purposes, however, both childbirth and breast feeding force us to think forward rather than backward; whatever finality birth possesses as a physical experience pales in comparison with the exciting, frightening sense of the beginning of a new life. (We should also not forget that birth is *painful*; its promise is so powerful that women often seem to forget what they have been through.)

Keeping in mind the possibility of some relation between female experiences of "tumescence and detumescence" and a narrative sense-making operation, we can now return to the narrative dynamics of *Frankenstein* and the particular quality of its irresolution. Critics have called attention to the thematics of birth in *Frankenstein*, noting poignantly that Shelley was pregnant, nursing a child, or mourning its death during the entire gestation of the novel.[5] Ellen Moers sees *Frankenstein* as "distinctly a *woman*'s mythmaking on the subject of birth precisely because its emphasis is not upon what precedes birth, not upon birth itself, but upon what follows birth: the trauma of the afterbirth" (93). She reminds us that Shelley's experience as a mother was preceded by her experience as the daughter of a mother who died of poisoning when the placenta that had nourished the baby was not expelled and became septic. So Shelley's own experience of "beginnings in relation to ends" might itself be well described as the "trauma of the afterbirth."

Although Moers's analysis of the novel's focus on unsentimentalized motherhood is extraordinarily helpful, I am not sure I agree that Shelley set out to write a "horror story of maternity" (95). Moers overlooks that Frankenstein is a *male* mother; unlike the women in the novel, he is entirely unwilling to nurture the creature(s) dependent on him, al-

---

5. See Moers 90–99 and Rieger xi–xxiv. Johnson discusses *Frankenstein* as a narrative about maternity and female authorship.

though he all too readily sentimentalizes the creatures on whom he has been dependent. In other words, his indulgence in the retrospective mode of "male" sense making keeps him from acknowledging his on-going responsibility to the birth he clones as well as from seeing that henceforth his plot inevitably involves the consequences of an act of creation that he regards as a triumph in and of itself. That creation would demand anything of him *beyond* the moment when scientific genius culminates the trajectory of its intellectual self-stimulation seems never to have occurred to him. Instead, in his fantasy of motherhood (which he calls fatherhood), he dwells exclusively on his own demands: "A new species would bless me as its creator and source; many happy and excellent natures would owe their being to me. No father [!] could claim the gratitude of his child so completely as I should deserve theirs" (53). The text suggests that Frankenstein has got things backward when, unlike a pregnant woman, he becomes increasingly pale and emaciated as his "creation" nears completion. And as if in anticipation of all the alienations his creature's alienation will cause him to share, he cuts himself off from friends and family for the duration of the project:

> I wished, as it were, to procrastinate all that related to my feelings of affection until the great object, which swallowed up every habit of my nature, should be completed. . . . [T]he energy of my purpose alone sustained me; my labours would soon end, and I believed that exercise and amusement would then drive away incipient disease; and I promised myself both of these when my creation should be complete. (54–55)

What Shelley's text makes appallingly clear is that the end of Frankenstein's "labours" effects a change in "all that related to [his] feelings of affection," if not in the feelings themselves. The postpartum nightmare in which "Elizabeth, in the bloom of health, walking in the streets of Ingolstadt" becomes "the corpse of my dead mother in my arms" is, of course, a neat foreshadowing of disasters to come, but it is also a parody of the kinds of retrospection Frankenstein has been promising himself as a reward for completing his act. The dream identifies Frankenstein with his mother and Elizabeth, so that the moment of retrospection fantasized by the pleasure principle becomes a nightmarish identification with the object of that fantasy. Frankenstein's completed feat, "read . . . in anticipation of the structuring power of those endings that will retrospectively give [it] the order and significance of plot" (Brooks, *Reading* 94), is thus part of the wrong story, because it represents a beginning instead of an end. The dream concludes with an image of labor (". . . a cold dew covered my forehead, my teeth chattered, and every limb convulsed . . .") and culminates in a vision of the Monster: "I beheld the wretch—the miserable monster whom I had created" (57). The Monster's story not only emphasizes the disastrous consequences of confusing the accomplishment of fatherhood with the prospective relation of motherhood but involves them directly with issues of representability: it is the hideousness of his creation that triggers Frankenstein's abandonment of the Monster and leads to the series of brutal rejections that transform the creature's beautiful soul into a murderous one. The chain of monstrous acts that critics have had so much trouble accounting for within a traditional narratology seems to me to be about the inability of a male scheme to account for something it refuses to acknowledge. Shelley's use of the rhythms and dynamics of the experience of birth criticizes the culture's association of detumescence and "significant discharge" with ending and sense making. In its unrelenting insistence on the demands made by the figure whose existence turns the scientist's triumphant *consummatum est* into a new beginning, Shelley's narrative poses questions not accommodated in a *Master*plot and gestures toward an economy in which another consideration of the relations among beginnings, middles, and ends would yield radically different results.

III

From the way that both Brooks and Scholes implicate the scenario of male pleasure in the processes that determine narrative sequence as well as the narrative's aesthetic, erotic, and ethical yield, it would seem that the pleasure of the text depends on the gratification of the reader's erotic investment. Once we recognize how a psychoanalytic dynamics of reading assumes the universality of the male response, we have little difficulty noticing how arbitrary the foundations of its universalizations are. To examine how these assumptions make their way into critical practice, I want to return to Brooks's "dynamic model" for narrative and to the distinctions his discussion implies between properties of narrative that are formal (and that continue to be matters of form even when Brooks calls for a narrative "dynamics") and those that remain merely thematic. He specifically takes issue with a

> feminist criticism that needs to show how the represented female psyche (particularly of course as created by women authors) refuses and problematizes the dominant concepts of male psychological doctrine. Feminist criticism has in fact largely contributed to a new variant of the psychoanalytic study of fictive characters, a variant one might label the "situational-thematic": studies of Oedipal triangles in fiction, their permutations and evolution, of the role of mothers and daughters, of situations of nurture and bonding, and so forth. It is work often full of interest, but nonetheless methodologically disquieting in its use of Freudian analytic tools in a

wholly thematic way, as if the identification and labeling of human relations in a psychoanalytic vocabulary were the task of criticism. ("Idea" 335)[6]

I especially like the "so forth." What it indicates is the writer's sense of the inessentiality ("situationality") of the feminist critic's concerns; Brooks seems not to be able to imagine that the study of, for instance, mothers and daughters in fiction could generate anything as compellingly theoretical as the study of fathers and sons. And such issues do indeed remain irrelevant to a narrative model that speaks to and of male experience. But they are more than irrelevant to Brooks's system; they threaten it and its hegemony. Feminist scholarship has been particularly and systematically critical of traditional psychoanalysis and self-consciously uncomfortable when it invokes the Freudian apparatus. Moreover, having recognized the extent to which any theory remains blind to its own thematics, much feminist criticism strikes me as being far less thematic than Brooks's. In attending to other versions of the issues traditionally referred to as "man's place in the world," "man's narratives," "man's fate," and so on, feminist scholarship calls into question the authority of many of the assumptions that enable Brooks to write it off as he does.

It is, then, only in the context of the androcentric paradigm that Brooks's Freudian reading of the crisis of paternity articulated by male nineteenth-century novelists can be considered the model for all narrative — or even for all "traditional narrative." Yet this "situational-thematic" swiftly becomes a paradigm, and we are asked to regard it as an issue of form rather than of theme. It is easy to fall into the trap such a move represents, since traditional narrative and criticism generally assume the universality of the male paradigm. And it is correspondingly difficult to map a way out of this trap, since this effort requires paying attention to interpretational details that could easily be written off as "merely" thematic ("studies of Oedipal triangles in fiction, their permutations and evolution, of the role of mothers and daughters, of situations of nurture and bonding, and so forth"), as quibbles about a part rather than statements about the whole.

Nevertheless. In a passage reflecting on the plots of Stendhal's novels,

---

6. Earlier, in *Reading for the Plot*, Brooks had this to say: "The female plot is not unrelated to [male plots of ambition], but it takes a more complex stance toward ambition, the formation of an inner drive toward the assertion of selfhood in resistance to the overt and violating male plots of ambition, a counterdynamic which, from the prototype *Clarissa* to *Jane Eyre* and *To the Lighthouse*, is only superficially passive and in fact a reinterpretation of the vectors of plot" (39). Indeed, Brooks further describes the female plot as "a resistance and what we might call an 'endurance': a waiting (and suffering) until the woman's desire can be a permitted response to the expression of male desire" (*Reading* 330n3). See Hirsch, "Ideology," as well as Nancy K. Miller, *The Heroine's Text* and "Emphasis Added."

Brooks sees what he considers the major issues of nineteenth-century narrative:

> It is a fault inherent to fatherhood that to act toward the son, even with the intent of aiding him in *la chasse au bonheur*, is inevitably to exercise an illegitimate (because *too* legitimate) control, to impose a model that claims authoritative (because authorial) status. All Stendhal's novels record the failure of authoritative paternity in his protagonists' lives, and at the same time demonstrate the narrator's attempt to retrieve the failure by being himself the perfect father, he who can maintain the conversation with his son.
>
> (*Reading* 76)

This is, indeed, a formidable agenda, and Brooks's use of this situational-thematic to illuminate what is going on in *Le rouge et le noir* is masterful. But his analysis proceeds at the expense of precisely the figures at whose expense Stendhal's novel — and Julien Sorel's plot — proceeds: the women. Hence, it reproduces, rather than acts critically on, the cultural assumptions encoded into the narrative form. Brooks comments, "[N]o longer interested in ambition, [Julien] judges his whole Parisian experience to have been an error; no longer interested in [the pregnant] Mathilde and his worldly marriage, he returns to the explicitly maternal embrace of Mme de Rênal" (*Reading* 86). This passage has an endnote, and when I turned to the back of the book, hoping for a statement of discomfort about this sense-making operation, I found instead a long authorization, complete with references to the fathers of psychoanalysis and structural anthropology, of Julien's enactment of the oedipal story: ". . . not only does Julien want Mme de Rênal to be mother to his unborn child, Mme de Rênal herself earlier expresses the wish that Julien were father to her children . . ." (337n25). By accepting such a hornet's nest as an issue of form instead of as a particular situation and a particular thematic, however powerfully they may govern what gets told in our culture, Brooks seems to vitiate rather than to enhance the power of his interpretation. If he claims for the novel the project of cultural criticism — of the nineteenth-century ideology of pleasure and its intersection with political institutions and narrative practices — then it would seem necessary to interrogate what becomes the uninterrogated ground of this vast cultural project, the woman's body and a particular myth of her pleasure and power that Brooks lays bare and then refuses to examine critically.[7] In the erotics of oedipal transmission, the woman is always a stage (in both senses of the word) for or in the working out of a problem of paternal interdiction, toward

---

7. If we take the time to look at her now, we discover that she is either "impervious to desire, a smooth surface on which desire cannot take hold" (Balzac's Foedora [Brooks, *Reading* 57]) or a being (Zola's Nana) whose "sexual organ, which is nothing, absence, becomes a tool more powerful than all phallic engines, capable of supreme leverage on the world" (Brooks, *Reading* 47).

the moment of "significant discharge" when the son frees himself from the nets of paternal restriction and forges a self-creation — however ironized this process may be.

Like Scholes's homoaesthetic erotics of reading, then, Brooks's Masterplot occults the woman in such a way that the desire negotiated in the tug-of-war between men (here, fathers and sons) is played out, pleasured in, at her expense, without any acknowledgment of what her value outside this circuit of exchange might have been. *Le rouge et le noir*, *La peau de chagrin*, and *Nana* offer ample material for counterreadings, in which the text could be shown to be self-critically aware of the woman's presence as a function of its fantasy of the pleasure principle (Schor, *Breaking* and *Zola's Crowds*).

*   *   *

V

If we set out to seek women's pleasure in the text, there seems to have been scant yield of pleasure in our pursuit. And, indeed, neither the readings I have criticized nor those I have proposed entertain female pleasure as a representable option, although the former would hold out, I suspect, for the possibility of an accident, never recounted, in which the woman's desire would coincide exactly with the desire of the male protagonist and his official surrogate, the male reader. The meanings generated through the dynamic relations of beginnings, middles, and ends in traditional narrative and traditional narratology never seem to accrue directly to the account of the woman. At best, they point toward a rereading that evaluates the ideology of narrative dynamics according to whose desire they serve, rendering us suspicious of our complicity in what has presented itself to us as the pleasure of the text. We have been taught to read in drag and must begin to question seriously the determinants that govern the mechanics of our narratives, the notion of history as a sense-making operation, and the enormous investment the patriarchy has in maintaining them.

I would like to close with statements, roughly contemporaneous, from three figures central to our understanding of our culture and its narratives. Each was capable, despite his investment and powerful role in perpetuating the narratives of patriarchy from the nineteenth century into the twentieth, of glimpsing the utter arbitrariness of these constructs as well as the crucial role of gender in their formation and perpetuation. In 1900 Mrs. Everard Cotes sent Henry James a copy of her novel *His Honour and a Lady* and suggested that her writing was "like" his; in reply, James wrote:

> I think your drama lacks a little *line* — bony structure and palpable, as it were, tense cord — on which to string the pearls of detail. It's

the frequent fault of women's work — and *I* like a rope (the rope
of the direction *and march of the subject,* the action) pulled, like
a taut cable between a steamer and tug, from beginning to end.
[Your plot] lapses on a trifle too liquidly. (*Letters* 131)

Certainly this passage deserves any giggles it might provoke. But by
underlining the "I" ("*I* like a rope") and admitting, a week later in
another letter, that he "doubt[ed] if any man *ever* understands any woman's critical bias and method," James calls attention to the personal,
ultimately arbitrary, and male bias of his own structures (*Letters* 135).
And a reading of his last novel, *The Golden Bowl,* could show how he
addresses just this question of sexual difference by juxtaposing a man's
"critical bias and method" with a woman's, offering us a glimpse of the
kinds of pleasure narrative provides when the "pearls of detail" are
strung differently — or not strung at all.

In *The Education of Henry Adams,* a text whose mythical investment
in the figure of the virgin cannot be overstated, we read, "The study of
history is useful to the historian by teaching him his ignorance of
women; and the mass of this ignorance crushes one who is familiar
enough with what are called historical sources to realize how few
women have ever been known" (Adams 353). And even Freud, in a
rare moment of total divestiture, when he acknowledges his own
inability — and furthermore, his utter lack of desire — to "cure" a perfectly healthy lesbian, whose only problem it seems, is her father's violent opposition to her choice of object, is able to distance himself
from the Masterplot so crucial to his — and his followers' — construc-
tions of culture and its narratives. He writes:

So long as we trace the development from its final outcome back-
wards, the chain of events appears continuous and we feel we have
gained an insight which is completely satisfactory and even ex-
haustive. But if we proceed the reverse way, if we start from the
premises inferred from the analysis and try to follow them up to
the final result, then we no longer get the impression of an inevitable sequence of events which could not have been otherwise
determined. We notice at once that there might have been another
result, and that we might have been just as well able to understand
and explain the latter. The synthesis is thus not so satisfactory as
the analysis; in other words, from a knowledge of the premises we
could not have foretold the nature of the result. (154–55)[8]

8. The German, "so kommt uns der Eindruck einer notwendigen und auf keine andere Weise
   zu bestimmenden Verkettung ganz abhanden" (276–77), expresses better than the English
   translation the notion both of the narrative "chain" and the threat of things getting "out of
   hand."

It is time to start again, to see what comes of unstringing the Masterplot that wants to have told us in advance where it is that we should take our pleasures and what must inevitably come of them.

Works Cited

Adams, Henry. *The Education of Henry Adams*. Boston: Houghton, 1961.
Beer, Gillian. "Beyond Determinism: George Eliot and Virginia Woolf." *Arguing with the Past: Essays in Narrative from Woolf to Sidney*. London: Routledge, 1989. 117–37.
———. *Darwin's Plots: Evolutionary Narrative in Darwin, George Eliot and Nineteenth-Century Fiction*. London: Routledge, 1983.
Bersani, Leo. *The Freudian Body*. New York: Columbia UP, 1982.
Boone, Joseph Allen. "Me(n) and Feminism." *Gender and Theory: Dialogues on Feminist Criticism*. Ed. Linda Kauffman. Oxford: Blackwell, 1989. 158–80.
Brooks, Peter. "The Idea of a Psychoanalytic Literary Criticism." *Critical Inquiry* 13 (1987): 334–48.
———. *Reading for the Plot: Design and Intention in Narrative*. New York: Knopf, 1984.
Chambers, Ross. *Story and Situation: Narrative Seduction and the Power of Fiction*. Minneapolis: U of Minnesota P, 1984.
deLauretis, Teresa. *Alice Doesn't: Feminism, Semiotics, Cinema*. Bloomington: Indiana UP, 1984.
Eliot, George. *Middlemarch*. London: Penguin, 1985.
———. *Romola*. London: Penguin, 1980.
Freud, Sigmund. "The Psychogenesis of a Case of Homosexuality in a Woman." 1920. Trans. Barbara Low and R. Gabler. *Sexuality and the Psychology of Love*. New York: Collier, 1963. 133–59.
———. "Über die Psychogenese eines Falles von weiblicher Homosexualität." 1920. *Studienausgabe*. Vol. 7. Frankfurt: Fischer, 1982. 255–81.
Gates, Henry Louis, Jr. *The Signifying Monkey: A Theory of African-American Literary Criticism*. New York: Oxford UP, 1988.
Hirsch, Marianne. "Ideology, Form, and *Allerleihrauh*: Reflections on *Reading for the Plot*. *Children's Literature* 14 (1986): 163–68.
———. *The Mother/Daughter Plot: Narrative, Psychoanalysis, Feminism*. Bloomington: Indiana UP, 1989.
James, Henry. *Letters*. Ed. Leon Edel. Vol. 4. Cambridge: Harvard UP, 1984. 4 vols. 1977–84.
Jameson, Fredric. *The Political Unconscious: Narrative as a Socially Symbolic Act*. Ithaca: Cornell UP, 1981.
Jardine, Alice. "Men in Feminism: Odor di Uomo or Compagnons de Route?" Jardine and Smith 54–61.
Jardine, Alice, and Paul Smith, eds. *Men in Feminism*. New York: Methuen, 1987.
Johnson, Barbara. "My Monster/My Self." *Diacritics* 12.2 (1982): 2–10.
Levine, George. "The Ambiguous Heritage of *Frankenstein*." *The Endurance of Frankenstein: Essays on Mary Shelley's Novel*. Ed. George Levine and U.C. Knoepflmacher. Berkeley: U of California P, 1979. 3–18.
Miller, D. A. *The Novel and the Police*. Berkeley: U of California P, 1988.
Miller, Nancy K. "Emphasis Added: Plots and Plausibilities in Women's Fiction." *Subject to Change: Reading Feminist Writing*. New York: Columbia UP, 1988. 25–46.
———. *The Heroine's Text: Readings in the French and English Novel (1722–1782)*. New York: Columbia UP, 1980.
Moers, Ellen. *Literary Women*. Garden City: Doubleday, 1976.
Rieger, James, ed. *Frankenstein: Or, The Modern Prometheus (the 1818 Text)*. By Mary Shelley. New York: Bobbs, 1974.
Said, Edward. *Beginnings: Intention and Method*. New York: Columbia UP, 1975.
Scholes, Robert. *Fabulation and Metafiction*. Urbana: U of Illinois P, 1979.
———. "Reading like a Man." Jardine and Smith 204–18.
Schor, Naomi. *Breaking the Chain: Women, Theory, and French Realist Fiction*. New York: Columbia UP, 1985.
———. *Zola's Crowds*. Baltimore: Johns Hopkins UP, 1978.
Sedgwick, Eve Kosofsky. *Between Men: English Literature and Male Homosocial Desire*. New York: Columbia UP, 1985.
Shelley, Mary. *Frankenstein: Or, The Modern Prometheus*. New York: Dell, 1974.

MARILYN BUTLER

Frankenstein and Radical Science†

Mary Shelley's *Frankenstein* is famously reinterpretable. It can be a late version of the Faust myth, or an early version of the modern myth of the mad scientist; the id on the rampage, the proletariat running amok, or what happens when a man tries to have a baby without a woman.[1] Mary Shelley invites speculation, and in the last generation has been rewarded with a great deal of it.

From professionals, that is. Since 1823, the year when the novel's title, characters and plot first became public property, the general public has seemed remarkably little divided about what the action signifies. A Californian researcher recently employed to find out what the public thinks of scientists was able to summarise his findings wordlessly, with a quick sketch of Frankenstein's Monster. Readers, filmgoers, people who are neither, take the very word Frankenstein to convey an awful warning: don't usurp God's prerogative in the Creation-game, or don't get too clever with technology.

Yet this is by no means what knowledgeable first readers in 1818 were likely to think, or on the evidence of early press comment did think. All three serious reviews in 1818 mention that the novel is topical. No-one appears to discern, as some modern critics do, an allegory of revolution or popular unrest; instead they suspect it of covertly promoting 'favourite projects and passions of the times'. By 'projects' must be meant the novel's network of allusions to contemporary science — not science as formally taught, but current scientific activity as represented to the British public in the 1810s by lectures, newspapers, a few accessible books, above all the serious Reviews.

The idea Mary Shelley famously hit upon in a house rented by Byron beside the shores of Lake Geneva between 16 and 20 June 1816 almost certainly does draw on a scientific dispute, conducted in lectures afterwards published as books, the first of which was the subject of an article in the *Edinburgh Review* the previous year.[2] The novel which grew from this anecdotal beginning introduces a range of scientific *news*, reported as such, particularly in the *Quarterly Review*, in the years 1816–18: topics such as electricity and magnetism, vivisection and Polar

---

† From *Times Literary Supplement*, 4 April 1993. Reprinted with permission of the author.
1. See Lowry Nelson Jr., 'Night Thoughts on the Gothic Novel', *Yale Review* 52 (1963), 236–57; Franco Moretti, *Signs Taken for Wonders* (London: Verso, 1983), 83–108; Anne Mellor, *Mary Shelley: Her Life, Her Fiction, Her Monsters* (London: Routledge, 1988), 40.
2. *Edinburgh Review* 23 (1814), 384–98.

exploration — and the spectre of new radical French work in what became evolutionism.[3]

After a long, costly European war, these were years of recession, social unrest, and much frantic comment, in moods ranging between outrageous and outraged, in media that included popular papers calling themselves black, red and yellow. From early 1817 the pro-government press, including the leading cultural journal, the Anglican and Tory *Quarterly Review*, published articles calling for press censorship, especially of radical materials intended for a popular readership.[4] From 1818 the *Quarterly* several times called for the revival of the long-neglected charge of blasphemy against irreverent writings.[5] In 1819 it for the first time directed this call against a serious book on evolution science — with which, as I shall show, *Frankenstein* itself is directly implicated.[6]

The 1818 *Frankenstein*, which had drawn nourishment, energy, importance from lectures and journals, had lived by the media, and after 1819 might well have died by the media. The public controversy concerning some of the kinds of science represented in *Frankenstein* endangered the book's future, for it read differently after readers became more knowing. It is not so much because of what Mary Shelley thought, but because of what readers thought, that *Frankenstein* became a substantially different and less contentious novel when reissued in popular form in 1831.

However unalike their approaches, modern critics are likely to be looking at the same text of *Frankenstein*. It will be a reprint of this very third edition of 1831, which Mary Shelley not only changed but, in a new Preface, interpreted — as the story of a 'human endeavour to mock the stupendous mechanism of the Creator of the world'.[7] That is not an impression easily left by the novel in its 1818 form. But in 1831 Mary Shelley added long passages in which her main narrator, Frankenstein, expresses religious remorse for making a creature, and it is on such passages of reflection and analysis that the empathetic modern reader is encouraged to dwell. Our current understanding of *Frankenstein* is disproportionately impressed by passages introduced in what

3. See e.g. [John Barrow], 'Capt. Burney, *Memoir . . . on the Question whether Asia and America are Contiguous*', *Quarterly Review* 18 (1818), 457–58 and [G. D'Oyley], review of eight works on the vitalist issue, *Quarterly Review* 22 (1820), 1–34.
4. See especially [R. Southey], *Quarterly Review* 16 (1816), 225–78.
5. E.g. article on John Bellamy's translation of the New Testament, *Quarterly Review* 19 (1818), 250–81.
6. Key evidence for this connection appears in the article on vitalism in the *Quarterly* (1820), for which see n. 3 above. That article is reprinted as Appendix C to my edition, *Frankenstein; Or, The Modern Prometheus: The 1818 Text* (London: William Pickering, 1993); reprinted as a World's Classics paperback (Oxford, 1994), 229–51.
7. Mary Shelley, Preface to 1931 ed., Betty T. Bennett and Charles E. Robinson (eds.), *Mary Shelley Reader* (N.Y.: Oxford University Press, 1990), p. 170.

might be called the composite *Frankenstein*, the product of a decade and a half of religious-scientific controversy.

It is of course standard practice for an editor to select the last version the author revised, on the grounds that no-one has a better right to determine its final form. But, like all rules, this one exists to be challenged. Wordsworth's early versions of 1799 and 1805 of his great poem *The Prelude*, first published posthumously in 1850, are now widely preferred to the much-revised text of 1850. Last year, Simon Gatrell for Oxford's Worlds Classics passed over the standard 1895 text of *The Return of the Native* in favour of the first edition (1878), neatly summarising the historical reasons why the two differed, and the imaginative reasons why the first was to be preferred. The case for *Frankenstein* (1818) resembles these two precedents, since an urgent, unusual, brilliantly-imagined earlier book has been neutered or at best overfreighted with inessential additions. In one respect the case for the early *Frankenstein* is the strongest of the three. The newsworthiness of this novel meant that after publication text and author were subjected to outside pressures which have little to do with aesthetics, and make it hard to say that it was she who changed her mind.

Within the last two decades the 1818 text has become available again. The first scholarly edition by James Rieger (1974, reprinted 1982) remains in print, and since 1990 two new editions based on 1818 have come on the market. The more helpful versions of either text now give some account of the variations between the two. But it requires an external, circumstantial perspective to show how the first *Frankenstein* arose, and why the second is almost a new book.

The single most striking new fact to emerge is the link between *Frankenstein* and the celebrated, publicly-staged debate of 1814–19 between the two professors at London's Royal College of Surgeons on the origins and nature of life, now known as the vitalist debate. The issue was raised in a lecture of 1814 by the senior of the surgeons, John Abernethy, who apparently sought to unite religious and secular opinion with a formula acceptable to both. Materialist science, concentrating on the organisation and function of living bodies, could not, Abernethy acknowledged, adequately explain life itself. A mysterious 'superadded' force was needed, some 'subtle, mobile, invisible substance', analogous on the one hand to soul and on the other to electricity.[8]

Coleridge scholars are aware of Abernethy because Coleridge approved of him, and built on his arguments in an essay, 'The Theory of Life', which remained unpublished in the poet's lifetime. Some modern Shelleyans have recognized that Abernethy's antagonist William Lawrence was Percy Shelley's physician (and in the very years of the

---

8. John Abernethy, *An Enquiry into the Probability and Rationality of Mr Hunter's 'Theory of Life'* (London: Longman, etc., 1814), pp. 48, 52.

vitalist row, 1814–19).[9] But in fact no critic has examined Lawrence's boldly sceptical lectures in relation to the writings of the intellectually close-knit Shelley group, which at this time included Percy and Mary Shelley, Peacock, Hunt and Byron.

Unimpeded by being Abernethy's colleague and former protégé, Lawrence took care to make the materialist position sound like the professional position. A more brilliant, cogent writer than Abernethy, he was also a charismatic lecturer and a formidable adversary. Historians of science make claims, if often cautious ones, for Lawrence's contribution to the long-running evolution controversy. But his major book, *Lectures on Physiology, Zoology and the Natural History of Man* (1819), shows that he can be sceptical and discriminating over new evolutionist positions as over everything else. What seems more certain is that his succinct briefings on current Continental work, the French doctor Bichat's research into the nerves and connecting tissue, or the German J. F. Blumenberg's ethnography, must have opened up the way anatomy and physiology were taught to London medical students in the second decade of the century.

Their friendship with Lawrence probably ensured that both Shelleys wrote more accurately and less speculatively on scientific matters than they otherwise might. But he also had a strong imaginative appeal for their disaffected group: after the defeat of the French Revolution, his style of science offered an alternative way of envisaging progress, free of the old discredited political vocabulary. This was above all *natural history* — the early evolutionists' non-scriptural and for some minds anti-scriptural narrative of the life of animal species. Mankind, the other animals, even plants now appeared capable, in response to their environment, driven by mechanisms of their own, of adaptation or what 1790s progressives had called perfectibility. The writers in turn showed Lawrence an alternative career route: a literary platform from which to address the general public over the heads of cautious colleagues.

It would be possible to treat Lawrence's role in *Frankenstein* as a standard case of influence; some ideas from Erasmus Darwin and Humphry Davy also figure here and there in the novel. But the coincidences between Lawrence's best book and Mary Shelley's are so different in scale that they need following through as, in effect, a single intermeshing story. Both books were associated with aggressive materialism, and this seems to be the main reason why both became *causes célèbres*. It was because each writer took on characteristics of the other's work that Lawrence came to read like a satirist as well as a medical professional, and Mary Shelley could be deemed to have attacked Christianity. In fact it is only when their stories are considered together that we see the extent of the cultural challenge offered by this striking episode in Romantic literary experiment and in the social history of science.

Lawrence was appointed a second Professor at the Royal College of Surgeons in 1815, and in March 1816 gave the two lectures which opened his campaign against Abernethy. The first is a wide-ranging survey of recent Continental work in the physical sciences, while the second, 'On Life', focuses rigorously on the issue raised by Abernethy as physiology and anatomy can properly handle it. For biologists (a word Lawrence allegedly introduced to Britain), life is the 'assemblage of all the functions' a living body can perform. We have done what we can, Lawrence says, to find origins and 'to observe living bodies in the moment of their formation . . . when matter may be supposed to receive the stamp of life. . . . Hitherto, however, we have not been able to catch nature in the fact.' On the contrary, what we can observe of animals is that 'all have participated in the existence of other living beings . . . the motion proper to living bodies, or in one word, life, has its origin in that of their parents.'[1] The materialist thinker sees no means of abstracting the animating power from the animal.

By the time of his 1817 lectures, Lawrence was willing to identify Abernethy as his opponent, and openly to ridicule the argument that electricity, or 'something analogous' to it, could do duty for the soul — 'For subtle matter is still matter; and if this fine stuff can possess vital properties, surely they may reside in a fabric which differs only in being a little coarser.'[2] But even in the more guarded 1816 lectures there was an offensive tone of superiority in the demand that the Life question should be left to the real professionals. In this case that meant excluding chemists, including presumably Davy, whom Abernethy had recruited: 'Organized bodies must be treated differently from . . . inorganic. . . . The reference to gravity, to attraction, to chemical affinity, to electricity and galvanism, can only serve to perpetuate false notes in philosophy.' The great John Hunter, after whom his and Abernethy's lectures were named, would have been on his, Lawrence's, side when it came to method: 'He did not attempt to explain life by . . . a priori speculations, or by the illusory analogies of other sciences; . . . [but] by a patient examination of the fabric, and close observation of the actions of living creatures.'[3]

Mary and Percy Shelley, Lawrence's friends, were living near London in that March of 1816, when Lawrence first put the materialist case against spiritualised vitalism. On June 15 1816, at Geneva, Byron's doctor Polidori recorded in his diary that he and P. B. Shelley had a

1. William Lawrence, An Introduction to Comparative Anatomy, being two introductory lectures delivered at the Royal College of Surgeons (London, 1816), 140–42.
2. Lawrence, Lectures on Physiology, Zoology and the Natural History of Man (London: Callow, 1819), Lecture 3 [1817], p. 84.
3. Ibid., Introduction to Comparative Anatomy (1816), pp. 161–63.

conversation 'about principles — whether man was to be thought merely an instrument'.[4] Fifteen years later Mary Shelley remembered several conversations on subsequent days, with Byron participating, she silently auditing, on 'the nature of the principle of life, and whether there was any probability of its ever being discovered and communicated.' On 16 June, most members of the party agreed to take part in a ghost-story contest.

There surely cannot be much doubt that the group were speaking of the vitalist debate, and presumably of Lawrence's lectures, which were on sale by June 1816 in book form. In fact, Mary's contribution to the ghost-story competition to some degree acts out the debate between Abernethy and Lawrence, in a form close enough for those who knew it to recognise. Frankenstein the blundering experimenter, still working with superseded notions, suggests the position of Abernethy, who proposes that the superadded life-element is analogous to electricity — particularly when he uses a machine, reminiscent of a battery, to impart the spark of life.[5] Frankenstein's other procedures are made unpleasantly anti-life, recalling Lawrence's unfavourable comparison of inorganic with organic methods.[6] The fact is that in 1818 Mary Shelley's portrayal of her hero is harsh, contemptuous, with a touch of Lawrence's sarcastic debating manner. Not so much a mythical Prometheus, more a humble Sorceror's Apprentice, Frankenstein as first devised seems to know too little science rather than too much.

Compared with the professional qualifications of the novel's first two narrators, Frankenstein and Walton, an inventor and an explorer, the Creature has few claims to act as the third. Just as he owes his existence to a unique and unnatural process, he defies all odds, as a parentless being, by learning language at all. Yet the voice in which he narrates the second of the three volumes is impressive, in a strange register appropriate to a witness brought back from the remote past — a phrase the scientific showman Georges Cuvier had recently used to describe the fossils he patiently reconstructed into lifelike animals.[7] He is more eloquent than Frankenstein in the conversations that introduce and end their meeting, and still more persuasive when relating his life-history, an exercise in self-observation, social observation, and retrospective

---

4. (Ed.) W. M. Rossetti, *Diary of J. W. Polidori, 1816* (1911), quoted James Rieger (ed.), 'Introduction', *Frankenstein, or the Modern Prometheus: The 1818 Text* (Chicago: U. of Chicago Press, 1982), p. xvii.
5. See opening sentences, *Frankenstein* (1818), ch. 4.
6. Not only does he rob graves for the flesh of the dead (ch. 3); he performs vivisection ('tortures the living animal'). This, along with other forms of cruelty to animals, was particularly objectionable to humanitarians and principled vegetarians such as the Shelleys.
7. Georges Cuvier (1769–1832) popularised paleontology, in a triumphantly imaginative presentation of the remote past. 'My key, my principle, will enable us to restore the appearance of these long-vanished beasts and relate them to the life of the present' (Cuvier, *Essay on the Theory of the Earth*, Edinburgh, 1815). See also *Edinburgh Review* 20 (1812) 382, and Loren Eiseley, *Darwin's Century*, p. 84.

analysis. By tracking his own maturation, from a solitary to a social animal, the Creature succeeds in the task Frankenstein abandons, that of scientifically following up Frankenstein's technological achievement.

He begins his narration on the night of the experiment, substituting his careful record for Frankenstein's excitable recollection of the same events. Still unable to focus his eyes, the Creature blundered round Frankenstein's lodgings in the big Ingolstadt rooming house, before finding himself, very cold, out in the woods near the town. His visual impressions were still unclear, but he now began to make the distinction between light and dark. He might have died of hunger and exposure had he not found berries he instinctively ate, water to drink, and a cloak to wrap himself in. He responded, pleasurably, to moonlight and birds when still unable to name them, let alone classify 'the little winged animals who had often intercepted the light from my eyes'.

In this chapter Mary Shelley employs language experimentally and imaginatively, in a way that anticipates the scenes in William Golding's novel *The Inheritors* where the Neanderthal narrator describes his first encounters with *homo sapiens*. But there are conventionally-written eighteenth-century precedents, in the literature on Wild Boys and Girls who had supposedly grown up among wild animals, or at any rate isolated from humanity. Already in his *System of Nature* (1735), Linnaeus speaks of *homo ferus* as a distinct human species, 'four-footed, mute and hairy', and lists ten recorded instances from 1544. The most famous case of Mary Shelley's day was the Wild Boy of Aveyron, whose discovery came to light in Paris in 1799. For what it reveals of early human physical and cognitive development, this remains a classic instance, thanks to the devoted teaching and careful reporting of Jean-Marc Gaspard Ikard, the young physician of the Paris institution for deaf-mutes, who cared for the boy and analysed his problems as the loss of nurture by human parents in infancy.[8]

Rousseau and Monboddo enthusiastically contributed to the wider debate, over whether the wild man is a sub-species, and if so how he relates both to advanced man and to the primates. Unlike both, but like J. F. Blumenbach, Lawrence in his *Natural History of Man* (1819) argues against generalising from such cases: the child concerned was likely to have been born an idiot, and had either strayed from home or been cast out. The lack of bodily coordination in a case such as that of Peter of Hamelin, an earlier wild boy brought in the 1720s to England, and the Aveyron boy's difficulty in learning language, had explanations less astonishing than Monboddo's supposition that such children represented a sub-species between mankind and the primates.[9]

8. 'Cast upon this globe without physical strength or innate ideas . . . , it is only in the heart of society that man can attain the preeminent position which is his natural destiny.' Ikard, opening sentence of Preface to *The Wild Boy of Aveyron* [1807], (New York: Appleton-Century-Crofts, 1962), p. xxi.
9. Lawrence, *Lectures on Physiology . . . and Natural History of Man*, pp. 134–40.

A significant aspect of Mary Shelley's treatment of the Creature's rearing in isolation from humanity is its avoidance of idealised, sentimental or scientifically-bold claims. The Creature's life in the woods is neither superior, nor even natural; it raises no question of his belonging to a species other than the human. So firmly is that speculative historical narrative omitted that it seems as if Mary Shelley, like Lawrence, deliberately avoided committing herself to the evolutionist hypothesis both Erasmus Darwin and Lamarck espoused, that all forms of organic life had evolved from single cells. Yet the Creature's life-experience hardly seems scientifically ill-informed, since it bears out the careful physiology of Itard's leading contemporary Bichat, in *Traité sur les membranes* (1800), *Recherches physiologiques sur la vie et sur la mort* (1800), and *Anatomie Générale* (1801), works which explore the functions and connecting tissue of the nerves, senses and organs, and give the most accurate account yet of every creature's sensitive interactions with its environment.

In fact, once it is considered in relation to fiction's established conventions, the Creature's career works on two levels, as a survival-story like Robinson Crusoe's, and as a story which does after all have historical implications, for it can be read as an allegorical account of the progress of mankind over aeons of time. That sidestep into allegory evades, yet for the knowing reader might also bring to mind, the evolutionist's long view of the ascent of the species.

For all the excellence and the intriguing suggestiveness of volume II as a Voltairean fable, most modern readers probably find volume III the most brilliantly imaginative and original part of the book, and this seems as true of its science as of its characterisation. There are signs by now of a rich literary interaction between the Shelleys and Lawrence, one that flows in both directions. In his polemical 1817 lecture on the Life question, Lawrence seems to stray into Mary Shelley's Gothicised rhythms and vocabulary — 'an immaterial and spiritual being could not have been discovered among the blood and filth of the dissecting room.'[1] In turn Mary Shelley seems to draw more in her later scenes on details from different writings by Lawrence, not necessarily contemporaneous. They include entries he contributed to Rees's *Cyclopaedia*, particularly one on Monsters, and an academic paper of 1815 on the case of a boy born without part of his brain, whom Lawrence had cared for in his own home.[2] That piece of fieldwork must surely have helped prompt Mary Shelley's 'hideous phantom',

1. Ibid., p. 7.
2. Lawrence also contributed entries on 'Cranium', 'Generation' and 'Man' for Rees's *Cyclopaedia* (individual volumes undated, edition complete by 1819). The *Quarterly*'s attack on radical science (1820) refers xenophobically in passing to the *Cyclopaedia* articles as borrowings from 'the school of modern French philosophy', naming Cuvier and Bichat, and from unnamed 'freethinking physiologists of Germany.' Percy Shelley had already unwarily drawn attention to the debt of *Frankenstein* to German physiologists, hardly as yet well-known to the English public, in the opening sentences of his anonymous Preface to the 1818 *Frankenstein*.

since *Frankenstein* must from the start have involved a scientist studying
the relations of brain to physical functions, who fosters (or fails to foster)
a monster. Even more clearly, the Lawrence case provided a plot for
Peacock's satire *Melincourt* (1817), in which an intellectual called Forester (full form of the name Foster) adopts an orang-utan and tries to
teach him to speak. Forester fails in his immediate objective, but a
richly corrupt system enables him to secure his protégé a baronetcy and
a seat in Parliament.

Lawrence's *Natural History of Man*, his one fullscale book, takes as
its topic the human species, considered as a variety of animal. Lawrence
states that his text is substantially based on lectures he gave in 1814,
which no doubt explains why so much of it surveys the current state of
knowledge in the appropriate field — ethnography, with inputs from
anatomy and sociology. In his division of racial types into five, and
his emphasis on physical differences between humans and primates,
Lawrence largely repeats Blumenbach, with and without attribution.
But in his freshest, most dynamic passages he works his own witty,
distinctive variations on Blumenbach's memorable observation, 'man is
the most perfect of domesticated animals'.[3] Most domesticated animals
are smaller, weaker, less audacious than their wild-life ancestors. In an
offensive, powerful passage, Lawrence develops a Swiftian put-down to
humanity, by remarking on the tendency of the European upper orders
to 'breed', by sexual selection, for physical beauty and elegance rather
than strength or ability. But to judge by the ugly, stunted London Cock-
ney, examples of degeneracy are plentiful among urban populations.
Lawrence goes on to reflect that inbreeding within the European royal
families has thrown up many recent cases of hereditary weakness and
madness.[4] He need not remind his readers of the obvious example,
England's George III.

Several topics Lawrence considers in his *Natural History* reappear,
in yet more ingenious adaptations, in the third volume of *Frankenstein*.
Mankind as a domesticated animal, pretentious but flawed, could also
be the best way to summarise Mary Shelley's larger theme. Incidentally
she touches on Lawrence's professional issues: heredity, fosterage and
nurturance, sexual selection and the perverse adoption of choices which

3. See entry 'J. F. Blumenbach' (1752–1840), *Dictionary of Scientific Biography*. In a series of
   major articles, Timothy Lenoir has demonstrated that Blumenbach's 'materialist vitalism',
   which was sceptical, cautious and scrupulously environmental, contributed importantly to the
   scientific thought of his Gottingen colleague Kant in the 1780s and 1790s, and in helping
   generate a *philosophy of biology* had a key influence on the early nineteenth-century emergence of the subject (Lenoir, 'Kant, Blumenbach and Vital Materialism in German Biology',
   Isis 71 (1980), 77–108; 'The Development of Transcendental Naturphilosophie', *Studies in
   Historical Biology* 5 (1981), 111–205). As a key English translator and follower of Blumenbach,
   Lawrence's intellectual role takes on enhanced significance; so does *Frankenstein*, once it can
   be seen to convey quite sophisticated biological concepts in a familiar form.
4. *Lectures . . . and Natural History of Man*, pp. 459–60: 'Natural History of Man', Section II,
   ch. VI, subsections on 'Powerful Influence of Attention to Breed' and 'Inattention to This
   Point in the Human Race'.

lead to extinction. She displays them by portraying the aristocratic Frankensteins as unhealthy, even incestuous, in their marriages; in the first edition Frankenstein's bride Elizabeth is his first cousin, who has been brought up like a sister. Frankenstein exhibits a neurotic resistance when asked to fix the date of their wedding. His excuse to himself and us is that he must first make a female Monster for the Creature to mate with, thus helping to underline how much stronger and healthier are the Creature's instincts. Frankenstein indeed seems more aroused when making and dismembering the female Monster than at the prospect of joining Elizabeth on his own wedding night. It is, of course, the Creature who gets there first. This means that Frankenstein has a hand in his bride's death — because he brought the Creature to life, because his neglect of him afterwards indeed made a Monster, and because he neglects Elizabeth too. That hideously terminated marriage kills Frankenstein's father, and raises the prospect that the family will become extinct.

When it comes to parenting, Frankenstein is himself a monster. He will not acknowledge his only child, the Being he chooses to call Monster, Fiend and Demon, though no human father ever played so thorough-going a role in any birth. *Frankenstein* ironically illustrates Lawrence's scholarly observations about parenting — the medical mishaps to which the birth-process is subject; the one sure feature of any birth, which is the involvement of at least one parent of the same species. But, if this parent-child relationship after a fashion obeys the rules, the roles of those involved become perversely displaced. After Frankenstein vows to hunt down his 'progeny', the Creature nurtures Frankenstein to keep him alive, feeding him for example with a dead hare: it's only when killing for Frankenstein that the vegetarian Creature kills for food. He still tries in his way to live by the precept that the child is father to the man — and, anthropologically, primitive man *is* father to sophisticated man. But the Creature has slowly emerged as the dominant partner, though originally he was a dependent, a deformed huge child. Of the two antagonists, he is the stronger and better adapted when the chase ends in the Arctic, where natural conditions are at their most severe. He shares Frankenstein's fate of extinction, but goes to it voluntarily, with a consoling sense that even he now returns to nature.

The sequence of events after publication makes a story on its own, significant and intricate because it involves so many key institutions — the law, commercial publishers, the journals, the Royal College of Surgeons. The three reviews the novel received queried its attitudes,[5] and this is unsurprising since, though anonymous, it was dedicated to the

5. *Quarterly Review* 18 (1818), 378–85; *Edinburgh Magazine and Literary Miscellany* 2 (1818), 249–53; [Scott], *Blackwood's Edinburgh Magazine* 2 (1817–18), 613–26.

1790s radical William Godwin. Even so, Mary had a kindlier, larger press than her husband had in his lifetime — and better reviews than the Shelleys must have feared. But the next year the publication of Lawrence's *Lectures on Physiology, Zoology and the Natural History of Man* provoked the virulent and prominently placed denunciation in the *Quarterly Review* of November 1819. This unusually long opening article surveyed the vitalist controversy over five years, and itself constituted a major event in the public reception of evolution theory. Encouraged by his editor William Gifford, the author George D'Oyley devoted most space to Lawrence, denouncing him for taking the leading role on the materialist side in the vitalist issue. He included Lawrence's other published writings in the indictment, but surprisingly omitted his treatment of heredity and breeding, possibly out of regard for good taste. D'Oyley's tone is exceptionally harsh and personal: after dealing with six other works on either side, he abruptly returns to Lawrence, and calls on the Royal College of Surgeons to discipline him. On pain of dismissal he should be made to withdraw the offending passages, and to undertake not to write again in the same vein.

The Royal College of Surgeons did indeed suspend Lawrence, and, going a little further than asked, would not reinstate him till he withdrew the book entirely. He did so for fear of losing his appointment as Surgeon to some of the London hospitals. The result ironically was that during the next few years several publishers pirated the volume, under cover of a ruling of 1817 by the Lord Chancellor, Lord Eldon, that where a book was blasphemous, seditious or immoral the author should not be protected by the law of copyright.[6] In March 1822, under pressure again from the Royal College, Lawrence tried to claim his copyright, and initially obtained an injunction restraining the firm of J. and C. Smith from selling their edition of his book. The Smiths' lawyers argued that the work was not protected because of passages 'hostile to natural and revealed religion'. After reading both the book and its reviews, Lord Eldon upheld the publishers, even though the book would in consequence remain in circulation, in cheap popular formats. Lord Byron lost similar cases, also tried before Eldon, in February 1822 and in 1823, involving *Cain* and *Don Juan* respectively.

The great notoriety of Lawrence's volume between 1819 and 1822 becomes part of the post-publication history of *Frankenstein*. For the author, her circle, potential publishers, and a significant number of

6. In addition to the first edition by J. Callow (1819), the British Library owns early pirated editions by W. Benbow (1822), Kaygill & Rice (1822) and J. and C. Smith (1823). There was a further edition in 1823 by Richard Carlile, the radical publisher jailed for reissuing Paine's critique of the Bible, *The Age of Reason* (1819). Carlile wrote an *Address to the Men of Science* (1821), singling out Lawrence for praise as a popular radical writer, and dedicated his edition of Lawrence's book ironically to Lord Eldon. See O. Temkin, 'Basic Science, Medicine and the Romantic Era', in *The Double Face of Janus* (Baltimore: Johns Hopkins U.P., 1977), p. 355.

informed readers, whether their sympathies were theological or materialist, the plot of *Frankenstein* was either already associated with Lawrence's style of radical science, or was imminently in danger of
becoming so — until, that is, Mary Shelley removed most of the telltale
signs.

For the 1831 edition Mary Shelley added remorseful passages which
made Frankenstein a more sympathetic as well as a more religious
character; she pared away details of his scientific education and, most
interestingly, changed all those facts about the Frankenstein family's
marriages that in the first edition touch on genetic concerns. Her alterations were acts of damage-limitation rather than a reassertion of
authority. They perhaps seemed advisable when surgeons and their experiments became the objects of public hysteria because of the Burke
and Hare murders in Edinburgh in the late 1820s. What made them
inevitable was that conservatives everywhere now interpreted the plot
of *Frankenstein* as they wished to, and expected most readers to agree.
As a writer in *Fraser's Magazine* (November 1830) remarks in passing,
'A State without religion is like a human body without a soul, or rather
like a human body of the species of the Frankenstein Monster, without
a pure and vivifying principle.'[7] Before Mary Shelley made the novel
fit this description, a journalist confidently claimed it for Abernethy's
rather than Lawrence's side in the vitalist dispute.

LAWRENCE LIPKING

Frankenstein, the True Story;
or, Rousseau Judges Jean-Jacques†

In the past few decades, a period during which Mary Shelley's *Frankenstein* has been received into the canon of English literature — to judge
from the number of editions, books, essays, and course adoptions — a
remarkable critical consensus has grown up around it. Consensus may
seem a peculiar term, as I am aware. For no work has been more hotly
debated. Indeed, the role of *Frankenstein* in the canon is exactly to be
the sort of text one argues about. Like *Hamlet*, *Lycidas*, and *Turn of
the Screw* in previous generations, it furnishes a testing ground for every
conceivable mode of interpretation, in case books or collections of articles where students can be instructed in the infinite varieties of criticism and fledgling critics can cut their teeth on amazing new readings.

7. Quoted Lee Storrenberg, 'Mary Shelley's Monster: Politics and Psyche in *Frankenstein*', in
   (eds.) Levine and Knoepflmacher, *The Endurance of 'Frankenstein'* (Berkeley: U of California
   Press, 1979), p. 166.
† Published (with permission) here for the first time.

Anything goes. One recent text, part of a series of "Case Studies in Contemporary Criticism," amplifies five "perspectives" on *Franken-stein*: Reader-Response Criticism, Psychoanalytic Criticism, Feminist Criticism, Marxist Criticism, and Cultural Criticism. But this merely scratches the surface. Even the Lacanian subgroup of psychoanalytic criticism, for instance, has produced at least half a dozen discrete readings of the novel, focusing on Imaginary and Symbolic mothers, fathers, daughters, and sons as well as the relations, contradictions, and subversions of their Orders; and each of these readings arrives at its destination. Is *Frankenstein* a story of homophobic paranoia? the repression of the proletariat? an abandoned woman? Collectively, the response of modern criticism has been, Why not?

No book seems better suited to this free-for-all. In almost every way *Frankenstein* might have been designed as grist for the contemporary critic's mill. To begin with, everybody misunderstands it; or more accurately, hundreds of millions of people who have never read the book think that they know what it is about, from seeing or hearing about a movie, and most of those people do not have a clue. This universal ignorance invigorates the critic with a rare chance to set things straight. Moreover, the novel represents an ideal of late-twentieth-century literary studies: it bends the traditional canon. Not only is its author a woman, without the pretensions or privileges of a certified male genius like her husband, but also it combines two scorned and outcast, if enduring, genres, gothic and science-fiction. Here is an opportunity to unravel the center of academic literary history and weave some ties to popular culture. Nor should one underestimate another source of popularity: the glamor and notoriety of Mary Wollstonecraft Godwin Shelley's circle. What a set! Even the circumstances in which the book was written deserve a movie (a better one than Ken Russell's). A daring elopement with Shelley at seventeen, the suicide of his wife, wanderings in Europe, passionate reading and writing and other affairs, and finally that hothouse summer of 1816 in Geneva, when Byron called for a ghost story and Mary, not yet nineteen, realized that one of her nightmares might do — what could be more romantic? If *Frankenstein* had never been conceived, the genealogical, psychological, intellectual, political, and sexual complexities of that summer would still provoke plenty of thought.

But one other source of interest is still more important: the mystery of how the novel came to be. According to Mary Shelley's own Introduction, in 1831, people frequently asked her "How I, then a young girl, came to think of, and to dilate upon, so very hideous an idea?" But a more aggressive form of the question might be posed: how did such a young and inexperienced writer, who in the remaining three decades of her life never again showed any phenomenal talent, manage to create a work that still haunts the dreams of much of the human race, a work whose title alone evokes a vision of history that has yet to run its course? *Frankenstein* is more than a book, as everyone knows; it is a myth and a symbol. What is its secret? Not many critics can resist the effort to find out.

The book itself, of course, inspires this fascination with secrets. An undisclosed secret, the principle of life, motivates all the action, and Frankenstein's lonely, obsessive quest spurs a competitive response in many lonely, obsessive readers who pursue, like him, the mystery of creation. Monomania is contagious. Nor does the impossibility of discovering the secret of life, as dark to Mary Shelley as to anyone else, or even of unearthing the ultimate secret of a text, discourage the true cryptographer from digging up every crypt. The pursuit is its own reward. If poststructuralist theory has taught us any lesson, it is that convictions about the indeterminacy and undecidability of all texts do nothing to stem the effort to find unique and compelling readings.

That effort persists when the text itself disappears. A case might be made, for instance, that no text represents the real *Frankenstein*. In an essay on "Choosing a Text of *Frankenstein* to Teach" in the MLA volume, *Approaches to Teaching Shelley's Frankenstein,* Anne K. Mellor makes clear that the text she prefers is the manuscript now in the Bodleian Library, where Mary Shelley's original draft can be separated from Percy Shelley's "corrections"— though since that text is incomplete, its ideal form must be inscribed in a reader's imagination, not on the printed page. Next best would be the 1818 text, which, despite Percy Shelley's stilted, ornate revisions of Mary Shelley's direct and forceful prose, still espouses the values of the original — or at any rate, a "political and moral ideology" that Mellor approves. Last and least is the 1831 edition, fatally compromised (in Mellor's opinion) by a new pessimism in Mary Shelley's philosophical views. Still, 1831 is what almost everyone will teach, unfortunately, since the others have been expensive or unavailable. The conclusion seems inescapable: no stable, authentic text exists or, as Mellor puts it, "*Frankenstein* exemplifies what Julia Kristeva has called 'the questionable subject-in-process.' " Yet Mellor herself does seem quite sure that she knows exactly how that subject-in-process ought to be read; indeed, sure enough to defend the novel against its author's own second thoughts. The dematerializing of the text does not inhibit the quest for its secrets. But it does seem likely to prevent agreement about how to read it. Each reader must learn to make a text for herself.

How then can I speak of a critical consensus? No paradox is involved. For as soon as one examines the current debate about *Frankenstein*, two qualifications become plain. The first is that readings seldom take the trouble to notice, let alone challenge, each other. They simply keep adding one more perspective to the pile. Interpretation of *Frankenstein* is not a zero-sum game, in which each new hypothesis would require eliminating an old one. Nor do critics spend much time trying to falsify any reading, or seeking out any negative evidence to disconfirm a bright idea. The object of this debate is not to prove or refute or win but only to take part, translating the novel into one's own discourse. There is always room for something completely different. Hence most interpretations serenely interpenetrate, threading through one another like an infinite cat's cradle, and seldom if ever touching.

Consider one of the most admired essays on *Frankenstein*, Ellen Moers' "Female Gothic" in *Literary Women*. According to Moers, the crucial scene occurs when Victor Frankenstein first perceives his filthy creation, "the hideous corpse which he had looked upon as the cradle of life." The language describes a stillbirth, and that is the key to its power: Shelley draws on her experience of the death of her own infant children or "the trauma of the afterbirth." Like others, I find this an imaginative and poignant reading. But it does not contradict any other reading, nor could it be tested by evidence from the novel. If one objected that Victor is not a woman, that he does not give birth, that the creature is alive not dead and is not an infant but full-grown, and that the horror arises precisely from the difference between this delivery and all others, Moers might reply that such literalmindedness misses the point. She has diagnosed a psychological effect, not attempted to account for what Mary Shelley consciously thought she was doing. Nor does her reading rival anyone else's. A cultural critic who saw the scene of creation as a miscarriage of technology, or an allegory of the failures of the Industrial Revolution, could cite Moers without discomfort. On this level of insight, contraries can be equally true, and fierce debate need not exclude consensus.

Moreover, contemporary critics do agree, to a surprising extent, on what constitutes the object they are trying to interpret. That is a second, more specific reason to talk about a consensus. However their speculations differ, their practice of describing *Frankenstein* tends to be the same. This distinction might be expressed in many ways, none of them immune to theoretical challenge. One might speak, for instance, of a common understanding of the plot of the novel, as opposed to its theme; but this could be taken to imply that understanding a plot precedes interpretation, rather than being itself an interpretive construction of the text. Similarly, one might speak (like M. H. Abrams) of first-order construing as opposed to second-order "double reading" or deconstruction. I do not propose to engage in this argument. Rather, I will focus on a particular sort of evidence, largely negative. When contemporary critics write about *Frankenstein*, certain scenes and elements of plot hardly ever get mentioned. Still more (or less), though critics do not go out of their way to agree with each other, they do agree in discountenancing a certain naïve or thoughtless reading of the text, a reading they often attribute to most of their students. In this respect, one might identify a strong consensus *against*: a kind of evidential double negative, in which like-mindedness may be inferred by a refusal to discuss something or by a united front against a common enemy.

That front unites critics of very different stripes — for example, all five perspectives in "Case Studies in Contemporary Criticism." To be contemporary, evidently, is to link arms against wrong-headed or *uncontemporary* readings. Late-twentieth-century critics, when they look at Frankenstein's creation, no longer see a Monster, as earlier generations did; they now see a Creature. And other aspects of that creation — for instance, Victor Frankenstein's genius — they do not see at all. During the past few years, I have heard lectures on *Frankenstein* by several of the leading Romanticists of our time, whose approaches could hardly have been further apart. Yet when they referred to the novel, what they did and did not talk about proved to be remarkably similar. Here are a few examples, freely adapted from their general drift as well as that of other critics. Item: Frankenstein is the degenerate offspring of a dysfunctional family; Not Worth Mentioning: every character in the book loves and admires him. Item: Walton and Frankenstein are unreliable narrators; Not Worth Mentioning: the Creature is an unreliable narrator (his narrative appears only within Walton's account of Frankenstein's account). Item: it is impossible to believe Frankenstein's story of how he discovered the secret; Not Worth Mentioning: it is impossible to believe the Creature's story of how he acquired language. Item: the Creature is a natural man; Not Worth Mentioning: the Creature is an unnatural botch of a man. Item: Frankenstein's abandonment of his Creature is an act of unforgivable irresponsibility; Not Worth Mentioning: the Creature murders a small child and frames an innocent woman for the crime. Item: Frankenstein's incredible stupidity, narcissism, and insensitivity to women lead to the death of his bride on their wedding night; Not Worth Mentioning: the Creature kills that bride for no other reason than to get back at Frankenstein. Etc., etc.

My purpose is by no means to make a case for Frankenstein and against the Creature. That would only reverse the situation I have been sketching, a situation of extreme partiality and loaded descriptions. Nor do I intend to question the contempt for Victor that oozes through much recent criticism. But the onesidedness and complacency of contemporary readings, even in summarizing the plot, suggest how firmly a modern consensus has taken hold. To argue against contrary evidence may be a first stage in developing consensus, but a later stage has been crowned with success when critics stop noticing that such evidence exists. We have reached that stage in the '90s.

The strength of this new revised standard critical version of *Frankenstein* is confirmed in an interesting way by some critics who have been forced to notice that other readings are possible. Their students have forced the issue, for these critics follow the method of analyzing readers' responses; and to their credit some of them honestly report what students say. The results are dismaying. Despite the consensus of sophisticated critics, ordinary readers keep looking at the wrong evidence and coming to the wrong conclusions. Even though Mary Lowe-Evans, for instance, has coached her students to read the novel with the eye of an eighteenth-century woman, according to bonds of sympathy that Victor Frankenstein breaks, they still insist on judging the character differently than she does. "My attempts to arouse the students' indignation at Frankenstein's failure to take responsibility for Clerval's death and his reluctance to warn Elizabeth of imminent danger, for example, proved futile." With admirable candor, she admits that "strategies I did not influence and cannot explain" enabled them to exonerate the guilty party. "Only one student saw Victor Frankenstein as a spoiled young man who brought death and destruction to all who loved him, simply to satisfy an intellectual whim." The rest, she supposes, may have been desensitized by preconceptions from films (though films have hardly created sympathy for the mad scientist). At any rate, they go on thinking that Victor is essentially good. Since no one has said that in print for decades, these readers cannot be saved; they stand outside the consensus.

What is at stake in this tug of war between teacher and student comes across strikingly in Anne K. Mellor's account of her very well designed and coercive method of teaching "*Frankenstein* and the Sublime." She begins with three questions: "1. Is the Creature in *Frankenstein* good or evil? 2. Is he innately so? Or does he become good or evil? 3. If he becomes so, what causes this change?" Students divide on these questions, and Mellor suggests that Mary Shelley's own answer is "one of radical skepticism." But the teacher's questioning soon yields to moralizing. The Creature is *not* innately evil, but forced to become so by the characters who deny him access to a human community. By introducing students to the Romantic sublime, expressed by landscape paintings, as well as to Diane Arbus's photographs of freaks, Mellor argues for the need to respond to difference or the unknown with love. "If we read or imagine the Creature as evil, we write ourselves as the authors of evil." Hence Mary Shelley's readers ought to see "all the products of nature — the old, the sick, the handicapped, the freaks — as sacred life-forms to be nurtured with care and compassion." Love thy Creature. And in case students still have doubts, the teacher concludes by warning them that, if they do not draw the moral that she does from the story, they may be responsible for the end of life as we know it. "Only by reading the sublime, the unknowable, as lovable can we prevent the creation of monsters, monsters both psychological and technological, monsters capable of destroying all human civilization." Love thy Creature *or else*. I wonder how many students disagree at this point; or if they do, how many dare to speak up.

Let me be frank: I do not think this represents good teaching. First of all, it begs the question that every reader keeps asking: is the Creature really a product of nature, a sacred life-form, or only a product of man, outside the natural order — a monster, in fact? Next, it begs the question of whether the reader is supposed to excuse the murders of innocent people because the murderer is a victim of prejudice. But most important, it reduces the novel to a late-twentieth-century platitude, giving readers a chance to feel good about their own superior wisdom. Who does not agree that all creatures great and small ought to be nurtured with care and compassion (however badly we may treat one another in practice)? Which of us, in Frankenstein's position, would not invite the Creature home, give him a good hot meal, plug him into Sesame Street, enter him in the Special Olympics, fix him up with a mate, and tell him how much we love him? Surely such treatment would result not only in a better Creature but in a happier ending for everyone — especially the innocent victims. So, at least, runs the liberal consensus, in which I myself deeply believe. But it does not have much to do with the novel that Mary Shelley wrote. For *Frankenstein* does not let its readers feel good. It presents them with genuine, insoluble problems, not with any easy way out. And the modern critical consensus, however symptomatic of the way we think in the '90s, seems to me fundamentally misguided — simplistic and often obtuse.

How then should one read the novel? I do not pretend to have discovered any original reading, let alone the right moral. But I do think that one might take more care to look at all the evidence, not only whatever confirms one's own perspective. Such evidence includes the responses of readers before they have been corrected by right-minded critics. For here too is a consensus — though not the same we have seen. Most readers are pulled in two directions at once. When I ask my students whether the Creature is good or evil, they too are divided, not only as a group but individually; that is, almost everyone can be induced to switch sides. They feel the same ambivalence about Frankenstein, who fills the role of hero or villain with equal flair. In the age of poststructuralism, one might expect sophisticated critics to find more aporias than ordinary readers do. The reverse seems to be the case with this novel. In a good-hearted essay called "Aporia and Radical Empathy: *Frankenstein* (Re)Trains the Reader," Syndy M. Conger argues that students come to feel a radical empathy for the social outcast, so that when Victor, about to bring a mate for the Creature to life, looks through the casement to see the "dæmon," whose "ghastly grin" expresses "the utmost extent of malice and treachery," students are standing "next to the Creature on the outside of the window looking in." Perhaps that is true for her students. It is certainly not true for mine (or those of Lowe-Evans), who almost unanimously vote in support of Victor's decision to destroy his work-in-progress. At best, those sympathetic to the Creature find themselves standing on *both* sides of the window. The critic or teacher may hope to resolve the aporia or blockage of empathy by choosing one favored perspective. Ordinary readers do not. They accept frustration, or keep on changing their minds.

This seems to me very wise. For despite the modern consensus, *Frankenstein* does not admit a resolution. The basic, defining questions it raises in the mind of a reader — is Victor an idealistic hero or a destructive egotist? is the Creature a natural man or an unnatural monster? what moral are we to draw from this strange story? — never receive a satisfactory answer or, rather, receive strong answers that directly contradict one another. This impasse is not the product of any particular critical school. It is the very heart of the novel. Indeed, without it there would be no *Frankenstein* at all. Perhaps a novel that taught students to love the Other would be more instructive, or at least more acceptable to modern tastes. But Mary Shelley's novel teaches something else: that love of the Other and fear of the Other, however logically incompatible, can be equally well motivated; and that idealism can be selfish and destructive as well as altruistic and creative. The troubling thoughts these contradictions raise account for the troubling power of the book itself. Nor is such trouble uninstructive. Whether or not one subscribes to F. Scott Fitzgerald's observation that "the test of a first-rate intelligence is the ability to hold two opposed ideas in the mind at the same time, and still retain the ability to function," some first-rate fiction does offer that test. *Frankenstein* teaches its readers to live with uncertainty, in a world where moral absolutes — even the ones we cling to — may cancel each other out. I do not think that American students should be encouraged to ignore that lesson.

If I am right about *Frankenstein*, however, how have so many intelligent critics happened to be wrong — wrong by consensus? Part of the answer surely has to do with the prevalent critical assumptions of our time, especially our collective identification with victims. This is a complicated subject, and I do not want to trivialize it. But in an age when a surprising number of students feel sorry not for Beowulf but for the dragon that kills him — a monster that was only doing its duty, defending the gold-hoard — it seems far less surprising that an outcast and lonely humanoid Creature should attract so many sympathizers to pity his ill-treatment and excuse his crimes. The popularity of that response accounts, in all probability, for the recent canonization of the novel. Few classic works offer more insight into the psychology of the oppressed and injured. By contrast, heroes like Victor have every advantage and cannot be forgiven. Victor and victim — every decent person knows which to choose.

Yet another reason for oversimplified readings of *Frankenstein* may be some reductive presuppositions about the nature of Romanticism.

Whether in new literary histories or in courses on Romantic literature, Mary Shelley's novel functions as a useful counter-statement, exposing the dangers of individualism and an over-active imagination. Romantic titanism or Prometheanism here takes a fall, tripped up by a writer—often, in this context, the token woman or honorary Other—who perceives the exaltation of desire as a species of masculine arrogance, and recommends instead the "tranquillity" of "domestic affections." There is surely some truth to this view. But what many critics define as an attack on the assumptions of Romanticism might equally be defined as the Romantic mainstream. For the writers of the time were far from single-minded. The modern obsession with finding the essence of Romanticism, its revolutionary difference from everything that went before, has tended to collapse some living arguments into a homogeneous monologue, in which all the major writers jumble ideas together. Yet many of the most interesting thinkers did not agree with anyone, not even with themselves. Indeed, one way of characterizing the age would emphasize its internal divisions or self-contradictions, not only from writer to writer but within individual minds. Hence many Romantic works seem at odds with themselves, admitting opposing morals or even cognitive breakdown. In this respect, the double bind in which *Frankenstein* places its readers might be viewed not as exceptional but as absolutely typical of its period.

My evidence for this proposition will consist of a look at a single source for Mary Shelley's novel. Such reliance on one source entails a risk of the same oversimplification of which I have accused others, as well as an old-fashioned embrace of the principle that one work can be a unique influence on another, rather than part of the endless web of intertextuality. If ever a work was overdetermined—psychologically and historically bombarded with multiple influences—that work is *Frankenstein*. Nevertheless, one source stands out, for its impact on Mary Shelley's sense of the age in which she lived as well as on her writing. My witnesses to its importance include not only Shelley herself but her father, mother, and husband. The work is Rousseau's *Émile*. William Godwin testified that reading it changed his life. Mary Wollstonecraft spent much of *A Vindication of the Rights of Woman* arguing against it, or rather against its views on the education of women, a life-and-death matter for her precisely because she loves Rousseau's spirit and considers him *the* authority on education. Percy Shelley, when he undertook to educate his bright but untutored lover, began by reading *Émile* with her; Rousseau, after all, was the expert not only on education but on the triumph of life. During the composition of *Frankenstein*, the Shelleys read, along with *Émile*, another book about it, and later, when she worked on the Creature's story, Mary went back to *Émile* again. Twenty years on, in the life of Rousseau she wrote for Lardner's *Cyclopedia* (1839), she made clear why she thought the book the greatest of one of the world's great authors: "He shows the true end of education; and he first explained how children ought to be treated like younger men, not as slaves or automata" — or monsters, one might add. Without knowing such truths, a person could hardly be educated. Nor could contemporary readers have missed the influence of Rousseau on Mary Shelley.

Indeed, it is not much of an exaggeration to say that almost everything a reader needs to know about the climate of ideas in *Frankenstein*, as well as its internal tensions, can be found on the first page of *Émile*. Since that page is no longer well known, even among educated people, it had better be quoted in full.

> Everything is good as it leaves the hands of the Author of things; everything degenerates in the hands of man. He forces one soil to nourish the products of another. He mixes and confuses the climates, the elements, the seasons. He mutilates his dog, his horse, his slave. He turns everything upside down; he disfigures everything; he loves deformity, monsters. He wants nothing as nature made it, not even man; for him, man must be trained like a school horse; man must be fashioned in keeping with his fancy like a tree in his garden.
>
> Were he not to do this, however, everything would go even worse, and our species does not admit of being formed halfway. In the present state of things a man abandoned to himself in the midst of other men from birth would be the most disfigured of all. Prejudices, authority, necessity, example, all the social institutions in which we find ourselves submerged would stifle nature in him and put nothing in its place. Nature there would be like a shrub that chance had caused to be born in the middle of a path and that the passers-by soon cause to perish by bumping into it from all sides and bending it in every direction.

In these two paragraphs, Rousseau has gone to the essence both of Victor Frankenstein, the naturally good human being whose compulsion to improve on nature drives him to violate it with a deformed and monstrous rival creation, and of the outcast creature or monster, abandoned to himself at birth and warped like a shrub in the road. *Émile* already adumbrates the two most powerful imaginative feats of Mary Shelley's novel: the hero's crazed longing to surpass his species, and the monster's pathetic account of his frustrated self-education.

At the same time, however, Rousseau has raised a dilemma or contradiction that all his life of writing would not be long enough to solve. If everything nature makes is good, and nature makes man, how does man come to be so unnatural, to love deformity, to make everything bad? The answer, of course, is society, whose institutions stifle nature and disfigure the humanity formed by the Author of things. Nature creates, and civilization deforms. Rousseau has often been accused of stopping his analysis at this point, with a noble savage opposed to a degenerate product of European vice. But in truth he begins there. As a host of modern scholars have insisted, he takes the current, corrupted state of culture as a given, against which the simplicity of a life according to nature is posed not as a nostalgic yearning for a vanished ideal but as a goal whose pursuit would enable people to construct institutions more in harmony with the true interests of human beings. Hence education, exemplified by Émile, must start by understanding what children are, not by dumping loads of learned lumber on their unreceptive heads; and the point of subordinating book knowledge to a fostering of the senses is not to regress to primitivism but to prepare a healthy citizen for the challenges of the modern world. What nature creates, and civilization deforms, a renewed attention to nature can restore.

In this respect, Rousseau's work in general, and *Émile* in particular, ought to be viewed not as philosophy, history, or social science but as a deliberate thought experiment, asking what consequences would follow if society were in fact to be grounded on human nature. A similar thought experiment seems to inspire Mary Shelley's novel. With wrenching literal-mindedness, *Frankenstein* tests each of Rousseau's first principles by fleshing them out and turning them into a story. Mixing and confusing elements, a man makes a monster. Abandoned at birth, a creature is bent out of shape by the prejudices of passers-by. The second page of *Émile* provides another idea to be tested: "If man were born big and strong, his size and strength would be useless to him until he had learned to make use of them. They would be detrimental to him in that they would keep others from thinking of aiding him." Shelley's creature proves the point. Much of the unnaturalness and improbability of the novel responds to the unlikelihood of the hypotheses it checks out: a man fashions a man according to his fancy; a newborn is abandoned in the road; a man is born big and strong. And later in *Émile*, at the point when Rousseau most clearly declares his own faith in the designs of nature, a scornful note looks at another preposterous experiment, the attempt of chemists to hatch life in a test tube. "Would anyone believe, if he did not have the proof, that human foolishness could have been brought to this point? Amatus Lusitanus affirmed that he had seen a little man an inch long, closed up in a bottle, whom Julius Camillus, like another Prometheus, had made by the science of alchemy. Paracelsus, *De natura rerum*, teaches the way to produce these little men and maintains that the pygmies, the fauns, the satyrs, and the nymphs were engendered by chemistry." Here Mary Shelley might have found all the pseudo-science she needed for her experiment in fiction. The new Prometheus, Paracelsus and the alchemists, the manufacture of men: each element would be stirred into the rich stew from which *Frankenstein* is extracted.

Nor does this list begin to exhaust the influence of *Émile*. As more than one critic has noted, the central thought experiment of Mary Shelley's novel tests the principles — Rousseau's principles — of education. Shelley herself was obsessed by the need to repair her own lack of instruction. Though both her parents were famous educational theorists, her mother died after giving birth to Mary Wollstonecraft Godwin, and her father turned away. "The poor children! I am myself totally unfitted to educate them. The skepticism which perhaps sometimes leads me right in matters of speculation, is torment to me when I would attempt to direct the infant mind." He did not direct Mary Godwin's. Shunted away to Scotland, often lonely, she was given the task of educating herself by reading; and certainly she did read. Yet accounts of her romance with Shelley are remarkable for their focus on his training and directing of her mind. A tutor at last! Her journal for those years consists mostly of lists of books, the Shelley family curriculum. And after he died, when she found strength to pick up her journal again, she resolved to stay the course: "above all I must acquire that knowledge & drink at those fountains of wisdom & virtue from which he quenched his thirst. . . . I am beginning seriously to educate myself."

Perhaps Rousseau could help. Each of the three narrators of *Frankenstein* represents a general problem of education as well as a specific aspect of Mary Shelley's background; and in each case the way that the novel frames the problem owes something to Rousseau. Walton's first letter identifies his situation with his creator's: "My education was neglected, yet I was passionately fond of reading." His second letter deplores the "evil to me that I am self-educated," for despite his wide reading (which as Rousseau would have predicted has only made a dreamer) he is "in reality more illiterate than many schoolboys of fifteen," most of all because he lacks a friend — like Émile's tutor or Percy Shelley — who would have "affection enough for me to endeavour to regulate my mind." For good or ill he soon meets such a friend; and Victor Frankenstein's story will complete Walton's education.

Victor's version of his own education is still more complex. To some extent the decisive turn or catastrophe of the novel occurs very early, not in any spectacular hazard of life and death but in the cursory glance that the elder Frankenstein casts at the volume of Cornelius Agrippa his son holds out to him. All misfortunes stem from that moment. If only, Victor says, his father had taken pains to explain the powers and practical uses of modern science, which had exploded Agrippa, he would have thrown the volume aside. "It is even possible, that the train of my ideas would never have received the fatal impulse that led to my ruin." The scene as a whole is almost a parody of several similar moments in *Émile*, when the all-wise tutor finds just the right strategy to avert some threat to his pupil's mental health. But this time the father fails; "It is sad trash!" he tells his son, without taking account of a young man's state of mind. William Godwin could not have been more in-attentive. In the first edition of the novel, Mary Shelley spells out her point, and Rousseau's, with didactic directness: "I cannot help remark-ing here the many opportunities instructors possess of directing the attention of their pupils to useful knowledge, which they utterly ne-glect." The doom of the Frankensteins follows that fault in educational theory. Despite Victor's many gifts and privileges, an arbitrary method of teaching has made him hunger for useless knowledge that poisons his soul.

The Creature, by contrast, does better. Many critics have praised his account of his first inchoate sensations and gradual dawn into con-sciousness as the best thing in the book, and have associated it with Locke's teachings on human understanding as well as on education. Here is the ultimate autodidact, inscribing the most basic marks of humanity on his tabula rasa and acquiring, through the chink that allows him to spy on a poor but noble family, not only language but proper republican sentiments. Shelley designs the passage quite explic-itly as an experiment in learning; she plants a shrub in the road, and watches what happens to it. But Locke would not have comprehended the result. Put simply, the Creature is just too good; put somewhat less simply, he is just too Rousseauesque. As other critics have noticed, he seems an unfallen, innocent creature, who feels love and sympathy as readily as hunger and pain. In his own eyes, at least, he develops as if nature, not man, had formed him, and only rejection by society leaves him deformed. Indeed, nature has also educated him. Everything good in him comes from her, everything evil comes from his secondary ed-ucation in the hostility and prejudice he meets at the hands of men. Rousseau had copyrighted the blueprint.

Yet once again the blueprint seems too simple. For the relatively cut-and-dried didactic formulas of *Frankenstein* do not do justice to the double-mindedness it induces in a reader. Part of the complication stems from the multiple narrators: the reader sees Victor not only through his own eyes but through Walton's and the Creature's, and the Creature's protestations of innocence are reflected through a medium that includes his own creator's repulsion and horror at the murderous fiend he has brought into being. But another source of ambivalence comes from an unresolved enigma in Rousseau's and Mary Shelley's own thought. I have already referred to one familiar way of posing the question: if everything nature makes is good, and nature makes man, why is man bad? But that old riddle is enclosed within the larger ques-tion that Rousseau kept asking, with increasing anguish, about every-thing he saw, whether politics, education, love, or his own relations with other people: *what has gone wrong?* No matter how often he sup-plied an answer, things kept going wrong. When Percy Shelley, in his great last poem [*The Triumph of Life*], perceives a ghastly image at the heart of things and asks " 'And what is this? / Whose shape is that within the car? and why'— / I would have added—'is all here amiss?' " it is no accident that "the grim Feature" who answers "Life" turns out to be Rousseau, nor that after several hundred lines of explanation by that Feature the question "Then, what is Life?" is still no nearer to a resolution. Rousseau may be the expert on "what is Life?" but his final answer usually comes round to a version of "why is all here amiss?" *Frankenstein* ends on the same hanging note. It shows us that everything has gone wrong, and leaves us to search for reasons.

Rousseau's own life embodied that enigma, for himself as well as for most Romantic readers. Through the three major and many minor autobiographical works that consumed his last fifteen years, he kept asking what had gone wrong. Eventually such questions about his life became a shorthand or substitute for his significance as a thinker. Whether negatively, as in Burke's enormously influential portrait of Rousseau as a monster of vanity, or positively, as in Mary Wollstonecraft's, Lord Byron's, and Percy Shelley's sympathetic efforts to define the excess of virtue that had cost Rousseau so dearly, the discussion of what went wrong with his life emerged as a standard Romantic set piece or *topos*. But the full-length masterpiece of the genre remains his second major adventure in autobiography, the *Dialogues*, or *Rousseau juge de Jean-Jacques* (which I prefer to translate *Rousseau Judges Jean-Jacques*). In this extremely overwrought, brilliant, and crazy work, two characters—"Rousseau" and "Le François" (The Frenchman, or Frank)—comb over the infamous author "J.J.," initially condemned without a reading but at last exonerated as the victim of a plot. To begin with, Frank *knows* that J.J. is a monster, whose professions of innocence only compound his crimes. At the end, it is clear that the real monster is society, envisaged as a vast conspiracy against someone whose only fault is being true to nature. Yet the enigma lingers. Rousseau's ability to split himself into three different personalities vouches for the "objectivity" of the argument; he judges his actions from outside. But the same split personality suggests a lack of harmony, or even candor, in the author's own nature. In this respect the diagnosis of what went wrong goes still more wrong, sophisticating the claim of simple truth. The more the author clears his name, the deeper he plunges into the murk, until such questions as what is a name? what is a self? and to whom or what do that name and self belong? take over the script. As some modern admirers have suggested, Rousseau can be seen as a uniquely self-deconstructing author. But that is another way of saying that something always goes wrong.

It would be easy to read *Frankenstein* as an allegory of what went wrong with Rousseau, or more precisely of the Rousseau enigma. Mary Shelley herself avowed that the Genevan setting where and about which she wrote was permeated by reminiscences of the *Confessions* and *La*

Nouvelle Héloïse, and Victor's upbringing, amid "the majestic and wondrous scenes which surrounded our Swiss home," inevitably recalls the
Citizen of Geneva. The sudden light that breaks on him when he
discovers the secret of life, so that "I became dizzy with the immensity
of the prospect," echoes the sudden light that broke over Rousseau on
the road from Vincennes in 1749, projecting his whole life's work from
his insight into the corruption of nature by civilization; and in both
cases the wonder that followed that moment, promising benefits for all
humanity, would lead first to obsessive, claustrophobic work and finally
to bitter disenchantment. Idealism destroys content; both heroes end as
paranoids, in brutal isolation. And another secret haunts them. No act
of Rousseau's life had blackened his character more than his abandonment of his children, who were deposited at the door of the Foundling
Hospital. To his enemies, such refusal to take responsibility proved the
hypocrisy of all his fine professions. When Victor Frankenstein abandons his Creature, therefore, he marks himself as truly Rousseau's disciple if not his accomplice. The appearance of virtue masks a sin passed
down to later generations. Moreover, the well-known theme of the double in *Frankenstein,* in which the Creature seems to represent the dark
or murderous side of his namby-pamby creator, summons up the split
personality we have already marked in Rousseau, who never stops asking how such a virtuous person can be so universally regarded as a
monster. Nor is that reputation all that the Creature and Rousseau have
in common. They also share a sense of themselves as Adam, not only
as innocent but as unique — one of a kind. The boast that opens the
Confessions — "I am made unlike any one I have ever met; I will even
venture to say that I am like no one in the whole world" — applies quite
literally to the Creature. That is his tragedy. And the way that all humanity eventually freezes him out repeats the sublime divorce from
society that Rousseau accepted as his fate, forever defining the Romantic hero.

Yet I do not want to spin out that allegory. What matters is not the
names and history we attach to the story but the tension that lives within
it. Readers who have never read Rousseau, and scarcely know who he
was, nevertheless still recognize the duality of *Frankenstein* and feel the
power of its moral irresolution. Why is all here amiss? is Mary Shelley's
question too. Much as I might like to, I cannot answer that question
and tell you what has gone wrong with life, and neither can the novel.
But the example of Rousseau can help us to examine some assumptions
that are packed into the question. Perhaps what goes wrong in *Frankenstein* has already begun before it starts, in the conditions and terms
that make its conception possible. Perhaps the influence of Rousseau
has penetrated so deeply that it seems identical with what Percy Shelley's Preface to the novel calls "the truth of the elementary principles
of human nature."

In that case, the trouble certainly starts early. One view of what went wrong with Rousseau might be that he never stopped paying for his marvelous opening gestures: "Man is born free, and is everywhere in chains," or "Everything is good as it leaves the hands of the Author of things; everything degenerates in the hands of man." The rhetorical power of such sentences changed the course of history. On the other hand, the self-evident truth that each announces at once — "Man is born free," "Everything is good" — pitches the whole argument on a slippery slope. Who says that man is born free, that everything nature makes is good? Rousseau, while he wears the spectacles of Dr. Pangloss. But as soon as the phrase has slipped out, its absurdity, in relation to what our world is actually like, begins driving him to distraction, or riveting his gaze on the chains and degeneration that bind him. Nor will he give up those phrases; indeed, he would rather sacrifice the world. And so he does. In Jean Starobinski's terms, freedom and natural goodness constitute the pure state of a transparency that inevitably crashes against, if it does not create, an impenetrable obstruction. In deconstructive terms, such words always already inscribe the supplement that will take their place. Just as Rousseau's myth of idyllic childhood ensured that the rest of his life would be one long falling away, so his opening sentences preserve the remnants of an outmoded theology — the doctrine of free will, the argument from design — while sponsoring a universal mourning for their loss. Dozens of later Romantic writers borrowed those earthshaking phrases as well as the aftershock that was bound to follow. To many writers, in fact, the sequence seemed like second nature.

The goodness of nature serves *Frankenstein* in a similar way: as an unchallenged premise that eventually collapses into its opposite. Consider the scenery. Despite the travelogues that Mary Shelley composed during her European journey, the obligatory ecstasies amidst the sublimities of mountains, water, and skies, she does not seem to have been comfortable with the outdoors. Both Shelleys had been disturbed by their recent trip to Mont Blanc, for instance, he because it forced him to consider the possibility that some power outside his own mind existed and might occasionally dump avalanches on even a skeptical head, and she because of the "dreadful desolation." The same desolation presides over much of the novel, chilling not only the arctic descriptions of the beginning and end but the crucial scenes in the "blank and dreary" north of Scotland where Mary Godwin herself had grown up — a better place for romantic fantasies than for living. Against this background, the occasional picturesque raptures of the novel ring hollow. Does Mary Shelley believe that the Author of things has created a world in which human beings are at home? The evidence of *Frankenstein* seems at best ambiguous.

The novelist's most extended descriptive passage, as it happens, supplants the love of nature with an unmistakable irony. As Victor Frankenstein tries to recuperate from the deaths of William and Justine, "the first hapless victims to my unhallowed arts," he travels to Chamounix and walks on the sea of ice, where the "wondrous and stupendous scene" of Mont Blanc almost restores him. "My heart, which was before sorrowful, now swelled with something like joy; I exclaimed — 'Wandering spirits, if indeed ye wander, and do not rest in your narrow beds, allow me this faint happiness, or take me, as your companion, away from the joys of life.' " As he says this, a figure larger than a man's bounds over the ice, "advancing towards me with superhuman speed." Is it a bird? Is it a plane? Oh "sight tremendous and abhorred!" It is, of course, "the wretch whom I had created." But the identification of the Creature with the spirit of the mountain, as well as the Creature's mastery of a landscape where mere human beings cannot survive, underlines the futility of trying to draw comfort or companionship from something as cold and indifferent as nature. The only response to Victor's apostrophe or prayer will be the return of his worst nightmare. Indeed, the scene as a whole might be said to recreate his original mistake: assuming that when he attains the object of his desire he will be able to live with it. The secret hiding place of nature — "Remote, serene, and inaccessible" — has nothing to do with the hopes and needs of people. Perhaps "everything is good" in nature, as an ice field or volcano might be good of its kind; but goodness like theirs is made not for love but for death.

The Creature is also quite good of his kind. In strength, agility, and even brains, in every respect except beauty (which, as we know, is in the eyes of the beholder, or the species) he surpasses humankind, including his creator. Does everything really degenerate, then, in the hands of man? The novel seems of two minds on this question. It plays with fears of the unnatural or supernatural, with evil unleashed through an amoral and irresponsible ambition. Yet it also insists on the human or superhuman sensibility of the Creature, as if Frankenstein's workmanship, on the eighth day of creation, went beyond God's. Even the theme of hubris, therefore, might be subject to challenge. Perhaps the hands of man *can* better nature. In that case, Frankenstein's fault was not his ambition but his failure to look on his work and find it good; Nietzsche deposes Rousseau. The irresolution of the novel on this key issue reaches an almost comic impasse with the moral preached by Frankenstein's last words. "Farewell, Walton! Seek happiness in tranquillity, and avoid ambition, even if it be only the apparently innocent one of distinguishing yourself in science and discoveries. Yet why do I say this? I have myself been blasted in these hopes, yet another may succeed." Right at the point of renouncing his sins, the hero takes it back. To followers of the modern consensus on *Frankenstein*, these last words complete his damnation; *still* he misleads his friend. Yet most readers will grant Mary Shelley the courage of her lack of convictions. Should Walton give up his dreams? Should nature be left alone? Is ambition the source of evil? The novel firmly answers Yes and No.

Indeed, the capacity for arguing both sides of a question, or for providing material to undermine its own first premises, accounts for much of the fascination — as well as the terror — of *Frankenstein*. Moralists may find its doublemindedness weak, but readers find it genuinely chilling. Whom or what can we trust? The novel offers no reassurance. Nature can be the source of death as well as life. Good people do evil, perhaps because of flaws in character but perhaps because of an excess built into their virtues. The sympathy we give to the outcast runs up against his horrible crimes. And readers themselves are everywhere implicated. Precisely to the extent that we identify with Victor's aspirations or with the Creature's belief in his own good will, we learn not to trust ourselves. In the long run everything goes wrong. Faced by so much uncertainty, a reader might well be tempted to accuse Mary Shelley of tergiversation or, more positively, of allowing her instincts as a novelist to triumph over her conscious didactic principles. If this is true, however, it cannot be the whole truth. Too many of her contemporaries shared her ability to see both sides of a question for us to ascribe it to her alone. The age that recast Faust as a lover, the age that idolized Byron and Prometheus and Satan and Heathcliff, was used to entertaining contradictory feelings about its heroes. In this respect also, Romanticism follows the track of Rousseau.

One use of defining the age that way might be to stress the continuities as well as complications in the eighteenth- and nineteenth-century debates about nature, society, and humankind. To put this more particularly: no lasting consensus has ever developed about Rousseau. His place in the canon depends on the passions that form around his contradictions, not on any stable set of beliefs. That seems to me a good basis for canonization. Rousseau does not make us feel good; he passes on his neuroses, and forces his readers, right up to the present, to see that the questions he raises have not been resolved. The endurance of *Frankenstein* draws, I think, on the same open secret, the secret that can never be unscrambled. Fears last longest in the dark. Whether or not my reading has proved persuasive, it ought not to lead to any new consensus, for my moral, like that of the novel, has been that the question of what goes right, as well as what has gone wrong, cannot be explained away. I hope that you will not agree with me too much.

Works Cited

Conger, Syndy M. "Aporia and Radical Empathy: *Frankenstein* (Re)Trains the Reader." *Approaches to Teaching Shelley's* Frankenstein. Ed. Stephen C. Behrendt. New York: Modern Language Association, 1990. 60–66.

Lowe-Evans, Mary. "Reading with a 'Nicer Eye': Responding to *Frankenstein*." *Case Studies In*

Contemporary Criticism: Mary Shelley: Frankenstein. Ed. Johanna M. Smith. Boston: Bedford Books, 1992. 215–29.

Mellor, Anne K. "Choosing a Text of Frankenstein to Teach." Approaches to Teaching Shelley's Frankenstein. 31–37.

———. "Frankenstein and the Sublime." Ibid. 99–104.

Moers, Ellen. "Female Gothic." Literary Women. Garden City: Doubleday, 1976.

Rousseau, Jean-Jacques. Emile, or On Education. Tr. Allan Bloom. New York: Basic Books, 1979.

———. Rousseau, Judge of Jean-Jacques: Dialogues. Ed. Roger D. Masters and Christopher Kelly. Hanover: University Press of New England, 1990.

Shelley, Mary. Frankenstein; or, The Modern Prometheus (the 1818 Text). Ed. James Rieger. Indianapolis: Bobbs-Merrill, 1974.

———. Frankenstein or The Modern Prometheus. Ed. M. K. Joseph. Oxford: Oxford University Press, 1971.

———. The Journals of Mary Shelley. Ed. Paula R. Feldman and Diana Scott-Kilvert. Baltimore: Johns Hopkins University Press, 1987.

Mary Shelley: A Chronology

1797	30 August. Mary Wollstonecraft Godwin [M] born in London. Her mother (Mary Wollstonecraft) dies eleven days later from childbirth complications.
1801	21 December. M's father (William Godwin) remarries (to Mrs. Mary Jane Clairmont). The household in which M grows up now consists of her father, stepmother, a half-sister (Fanny Imlay, the daughter of Mary Wollstonecraft by Gilbert Imlay), and a stepsister and stepbrother (Jane [later called Claire] and Charles Clairmont, children of Mrs. Clairmont by her previous marriage).
1810–11	Percy Bysshe Shelley [P] enrolled at University College, Oxford (matriculated 10 April 1810; expelled 25 March 1811).
1812	3 January. P opens correspondence with William Godwin, whose *Political Justice* he much admires.
	7 June. M goes on long visit to family friends (the Baxters) in Dundee, Scotland. She spends much of her time there until the spring of 1814.
	11 November. M, now fifteen years old, briefly meets P, twenty, and Harriet Westbrook, whom he has just married.
1813	23 June. Ianthe, Harriet and P's first child, born.
1814	Early May. M and P meet again and begin friendship.
	28 July. P (almost twenty-two years old) and M (not quite seventeen) flee to the Continent, accompanied by Claire Clairmont.
	September. They return to England and live in poverty and fear of arrest for debt.
	30 November. Harriet Shelley gives birth to her second child, Charles.
1815	February. M bears, prematurely, her first child, a daughter, who dies within a few days.
1816	January. M bears a son, William.
	May. M and P (again with Claire Claremont) travel to Geneva, where they live near Lord Byron and his physician-companion, Dr. John William Polidori.
	June. M begins to write *Frankenstein*.

July. Expedition to the Mer de Glace at Chamonix.
September. Return to England.
9 October. Fanny Imlay, M's half-sister, commits suicide.
December. Drowned body of Harriet Shelley found in the Serpentine, Hyde Park, London, some weeks after she had committed suicide.
30 December. M and P marry in St. Mildred's Church, Bread Street, London.

1817   27 March. P denied custody, in Chancery Court proceedings, of his two children by Harriet.
May. *Frankenstein* completed.
2 September. Clara, M and P's third child, born.
November. *History of a Six Weeks' Tour* (co-written by M and P) published.

1818   March. *Frankenstein* published.
24 September. Clara, just over a year old, dies.

1819   7 June. William, three years old, dies.
August. M begins writing *Mathilda* (not published until 1959).
12 November. Percy Florence Shelley (M's fourth child) born.

1820   April–May. M writes *Proserpine* and *Midas*, mythological dramas.

1822   16 June. M has miscarriage.
8 July. P drowns in the Gulf of Spezia.

1823   February. M publishes *Valperga*. Second (unrevised) edition of *Frankenstein* published.

1824   Spring. M begins *The Last Man*.
19 April. Byron dies in Greece.
June. M publishes her edition of *Posthumous Poems of Percy Bysshe Shelley* (but later withdraws it on the insistence of P's father, Sir Timothy).

1826   February. *The Last Man* published.

1830   May. M publishes *The Fortunes of Perkin Warbeck*.

1831   November. M publishes revised (3rd) edition of *Frankenstein*.

1835   M publishes *Lodore* (her fifth novel) and also volume 1 of her *Lives of the Most Eminent Literary and Scientific Men of Italy, Spain and Portugal* (volumes 2 and 3 published in 1835 and 1837).

1836   7 April. William Godwin dies.

1837   February. M publishes *Falkner*, her last novel.

1844   July. M publishes *Rambles in Germany and Italy*.

1851   1 February. M dies in London.

Selected Bibliography

Essays and excerpts appearing in this Norton Critical Edition are not listed separately here.

Baldick, Chris. *In* Frankenstein's Shadow: Myth, Monstrosity, and Nineteenth-Century Writing. Oxford: Clarendon Press, 1990.
Bann, Stephen, ed. Frankenstein, *Creation and Monstrosity.* London: Reakton Books, 1994.
Behrendt, Stephen C., ed. *Approaches to Teaching Shelley's* Frankenstein. New York: Modern Language Association, 1990.
Bennett, Betty T., ed. *The Letters of Mary Wollstonecraft Shelley.* Baltimore: Johns Hopkins UP, 1980–83. 3 vols.
Bewell, Alan. "An Issue of Monstrous Desire: Frankenstein and Obstetrics." *The Yale Journal of Criticism* 2.1 (Fall 1988): 105–28.
Bloom, Harold, ed. *Mary Shelley's* Frankenstein New York: Chelsea, 1987.
Botting, Fred. *Making Monstrous*: Frankenstein, *Criticism, Theory.* New York: St. Martin's Press, 1991.
Bowerbank, Sylvia. "The Social Order vs. the Wretch: Mary Shelley's Contradictory-Mindedness in *Frankenstein.*" *ELH* 46.3 (Fall 1979): 418–31.
Branagh, Kenneth. *Mary Shelley's* Frankenstein: *A Classic Tale of Terror Reborn on Film.* New York: Newmarket Press, 1994.
Clifford, Gay. "*Caleb Williams* and *Frankenstein*: First-Person Narratives and 'Things as they are.'" *Genre* 10 (Winter 1977): 601–17.
Cottom, Daniel. "*Frankenstein* and the Monster of Representation." *Sub stance* 28 (1980): 60–71.
Dixon, Wheeler W. "The Films of *Frankenstein.*" *Approaches to Teaching Shelley's* Frankenstein. Ed. Stephen C. Behrendt. New York: Modern Language Association, 1990. 166–79.
Feldman, Paula R., and Diana Scott-Kilvert, eds. *The Journals of Mary Shelley, 1814–44.* Oxford: Clarendon Press, 1987. 2 vols.
Hill-Miller, Katherine C. *"My Hideous Progeny": Mary Shelley, William Godwin, and the Father-Daughter Relationship.* Newark: U of Delaware P, 1995.
Hobbs, Colleen. "Reading the Symptoms: An Exploration of Repression and Hysteria in Mary Shelley's *Frankenstein.*" *Studies in the Novel* 25.2 (Summer 1993): 152–69.
Homans, Margaret. "Bearing Demons: *Frankenstein's* Circumvention of the Maternal." In *Bearing the Word: Language and Female Experience in Nineteenth-Century Women's Writing.* Chicago: U of Chicago P, 1986. 100–119.
Huet, Marie-Hélène. "Unwonted Paternity: The Genesis of *Frankenstein.*" In *Monstrous Imagination.* Cambridge: Harvard UP, 1993. 129–62.
Jacobus, Mary. "Is There a Woman in This Text?" *New Literary History* 14 (1982): 117–41.
Ketterer, David. "Percy Shelley's Contribution to the *Frankenstein* Manuscripts: A Collation." Forthcoming.
Keyishian, Harry. "Vindictiveness and the Search for Glory in Mary Shelley's *Frankenstein.*" *American Journal of Psychoanalysis* 49.3 (September 1989): 201–10.
Kiceluk, Stephanie. "Made in His Image: *Frankenstein's* Daughters." *Michigan Quarterly Review* 30.1 (Winter 1991): 110–26.
Kiely, Robert. *The Romantic Novel in England.* Cambridge: Harvard UP, 1972. 155–73.
Levine, George, and U. C. Knoepflmacher, eds. *The Endurance of* Frankenstein: *Essays on Mary Shelley's Novel.* Berkeley and Los Angeles: U of California P, 1982.
London, Bette. "Mary Shelley, *Frankenstein,* and the Spectacle of Masculinity." *PMLA* 108.2 (March 1993): 253–67.
Lyles, W. H. *Mary Shelley: An Annotated Bibliography.* New York: Garland, 1975.
Marshall, David. *The Surprising Effects of Sympathy: Marivaux, Diderot, Rousseau, and Mary Shelley.* Chicago: U of Chicago P, 1988.
Mellor, Anne K. "*Frankenstein*: A Feminist Critique of Science." In *One Culture: Essays in Science and Literature.* Ed. George Levine. Madison: U of Wisconsin P, 1987. 287–312.

——. *Mary Shelley: Her Life, Her Fiction, Her Monsters*. New York: Routledge, 1988.

Musselwhite, David E.. "*Frankenstein*: The Making of a Monster." In *Partings Welded Together: Politics and Desire in the Nineteenth-Century English Novel*. London: Methuen, 1987. 43–74.

Newman, Beth. "Narratives of Seduction and the Seductions of Narrative: The Frame Structure of *Frankenstein*." *ELH* 53.1 (Spring 1986): 141–63.

Oates, Joyce Carol. "*Frankenstein*'s Fallen Angel." *Critical Inquiry* 10.3 (March 1984): 543–54.

O'Rourke, James. " 'Nothing More Unnatural': Mary Shelley's Revision of Rousseau." *ELH* 56.3 (Fall 1989): 543–69.

Pollin, Burton R. "Philosophical and Literary Sources of *Frankenstein*." *Comparative Literature* 17 (1965): 97–108.

Rieger, James. "Dr. Polidori and the Genesis of *Frankenstein*." *Studies in English Literature* 3 (1963): 461–72.

Roszak, Theodore. *The Memoirs of Elizabeth Frankenstein*. New York: Random House, 1995.

St. Clair, William. *The Godwins and the Shelleys: The Biography of a Family*. London: Faber and Faber, 1989.

Slusser, George. "The *Frankenstein* Barrier." In *Fiction 2000: Cyberpunk and the Future of Narrative*. Ed. George Slusser. Athens: U of Georgia P, 1992. 46–71.

Veeder, William R. *Mary Shelley and* Frankenstein: *The Fate of Androgyny*. Chicago: U of Chicago P, 1986.

Youngquist, Paul. "*Frankenstein*: The Mother, the Daughter, and the Monster." *Philological Quarterly* 70.3 (Summer 1991): 339–59.

Zonana, Joyce. " 'They will prove the truth of my tale': Safie's Letters as the Feminist Core of Mary Shelley's *Frankenstein*." *Journal of Narrative Technique* 21.1 (Spring 1991): 170–84.